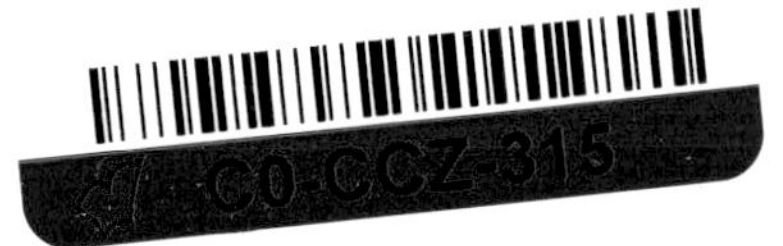

# NATIVE AMERICAN TRANSRACIAL ADOPTEES TELL THEIR STORIES

# NATIVE AMERICAN TRANSRACIAL ADOPTEES TELL THEIR STORIES

RITA J. SIMON
AND
SARAH HERNANDEZ

LEXINGTON BOOKS
A division of
ROWMAN & LITTLEFIELD PUBLISHERS, INC.
Lanham • Boulder • New York • Toronto • Plymouth, UK

LEXINGTON BOOKS

A division of Rowman & Littlefield Publishers, Inc.
A wholly owned subsidiary of The Rowman & Littlefield Publishing Group, Inc.
4501 Forbes Boulevard, Suite 200
Lanham, MD 20706

Estover Road
Plymouth PL6 7PY
United Kingdom



British Library Cataloguing in Publication Information Available

**Library of Congress Cataloging-in-Publication Data**

Native American transracial adoptees tell their stories / [edited by] Rita J. Simon and Sarah Hernandez.
p. cm.
Includes bibliographical references.
ISBN-13: 978-0-7391-2492-5 (cloth : alk. paper)
ISBN-10: 0-7391-2492-7 (cloth : alk. paper)
ISBN-13: 978-0-7391-2493-2 (pbk. : alk. paper)
ISBN-10: 0-7391-2493-5 (pbk. : alk. paper)
1. Indians of North America—Interviews. 2. Adoptees—North America—Interviews. 3. Indian children—North America. 4. Interracial adoption—North America. I. Simon, Rita James. II. Hernandez, Sarah.
E98.I54N38 2008
970.004'97—dc22 2007042426

Printed in the United States of America

∞™ The paper used in this publication meets the minimum requirements of American National Standard for Information Sciences—Permanence of Paper for Printed Library Materials, ANSI/NISO Z39.48-1992.

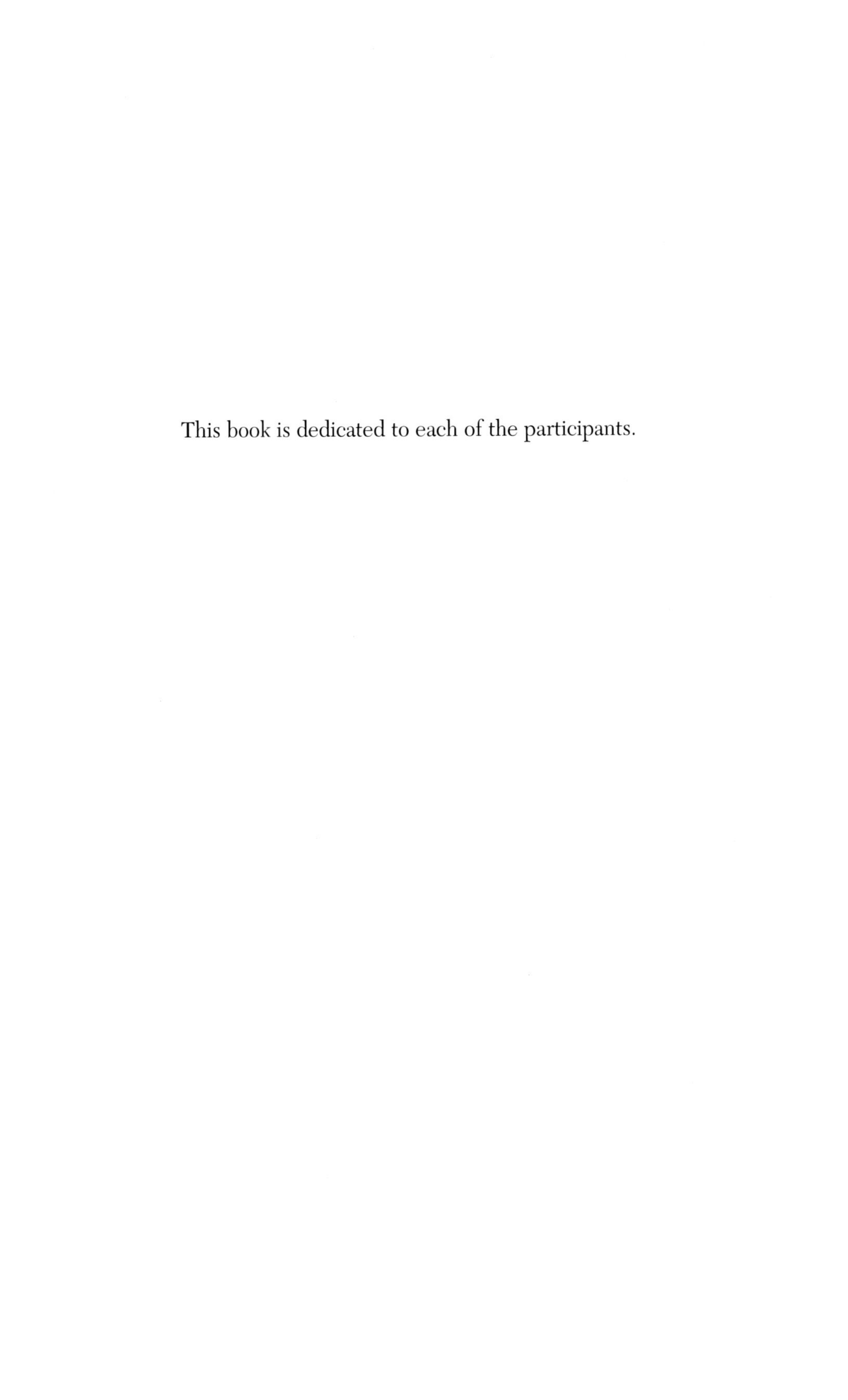

This book is dedicated to each of the participants.

# CONTENTS



* Denotes a pseudonym.

# 1

# HISTORY AND ANALYSIS OF NATIVE AMERICAN ADOPTEES INTO WHITE AND BLACK FAMILIES

Before the passage of the Indian Child Welfare Act of 1978 (PL95-608) which was designed to prevent the decimation of Indian tribes and the breakdown of Indian families by the transracial placement of Native American children, large numbers of Native American children had been adopted. The act was intended to safeguard Native American culture by keeping families and tribes together and within their native environment.

In 1968, Native American minors constituted 7 percent of the population and 70 percent of all adoptions in South Dakota. In Wisconsin, the likelihood of Native American children being removed from their families was 1,600 percent greater than that of non-Native Americans. In Washington State, Native Americas constituted less than 2 percent of the population but 19 percent of the adoptions. Native American families adopted only 19 of the 110 Native American children. The remaining were adopted transracially. In 1969, a sixteen-state report indicated that about 89 percent of all Native American children in foster care were placed transracially.[1]

In 1978, Ann W. Skyne and Anita G. Schroeder reported that Native American child constituted 2 percent of all children legally free for adoption in the United States, or approximately 2,040 children.[2] Overall, the rate at which Native American children were being adopted was twenty times higher than the national rate.[3]

The Indian Child Welfare Act passed in 1978 stated:

Sec. 3
The Congress hereby declares that it is the policy of this nation to protect the best interests of Indian children and to promote the stability and security of Indian tribes and families by the establishment of minimum federal standards for the removal of Indian children from their families and the placement of such children in foster or adoptive homes which will reflect the unique values of Indian culture, and by providing for assistance to Indian tribes in the operation of child and family service programs.

Reductions of transracial placement is supported in Title I, in which all proceedings dealing with Native American child custody are transferred to tribal jurisdiction.

**Title I: Child Custody Proceedings**

Sec. 101

a. An Indian tribe shall have jurisdiction exclusive as to a State over any child custody proceedings involving an Indian child who resides or is domiciled within the reservation of such tribe—Where an Indian child is a ward of a tribal court, the Indian tribe shall retain exclusive jurisdiction notwithstanding the residence or domicile of the child
b. In any state court proceeding for the foster care placement of, or termination of parental right to an Indian child not domiciled or residing within the reservation of the Indian child's tribe, the court in the absence of good cause to the contrary shall transfer such proceeding to the jurisdiction of the tribe—

Sec. 105

a. In any adoptive placement of an Indian child under State law, a preference shall be given in the absence of good cause to the contrary to a placement with (1) member of the child's extended family; (2) other members of the Indian child's tribe, or (3) other Indian families.
b. In any foster care pre-adoptive placement, a preference shall be given, in the absence of good cause to the contrary, to a placement within
    I. A member of the Indian child's extended family;
    II. A foster home licensed, approved or specified of the Indian child's tribe;
    III. An Indian foster home requested or approved by an authorized non-Indian licensing authority; or

IV. An institution for children approved by an Indian tribe or operated by an Indian organization which has a program suitable to meet the Indian child's needs.

### Title II: Indian Child and Family Programs

Sec. 201
The Secretary is authorized to make grants to Indian tribes and organizations in the establishment and operation of Indian child and family service programs on or near reservations and in the preparation and implementation of child welfare codes. The objective of every Indian child and family service program shall be to prevent the breakup of Indian families and, in particular, to ensure that the permanent removal of an Indian child from the custody of his parent or Indian custodian shall be a last resort.

As the figures below indicate from 1996 through 2003 white parents adopted a total of 6,284 Native American children. On a year-to-year basis, the figures look like those in table 1.1.

## COURT DECISIONS INVOLVING CHILDREN WHO WERE MEMBERS OF AN INDIAN TRIBE

In 1975, the Maryland Court of Appeals ruled than the Montana Crow Indian Tribe could regain custody of a seven-year-old child born to a tribal member despite an order issued by the tribal court three years prior granting a white family permanent custody of the child. The court of appeals held that as a state court, it had no jurisdiction in the case: "There can be no greater threat to essential tribal relations, and no greater infringement on the right of the Crow tribe to govern themselves, than to interfere with tribal control over the custody of their children.[4]

In contrast, in 1979, a Texas appeals court upheld a lower-court decision to award permanent custody of a half-Native American child (Sioux) to her non-Indian grandparents,[5] but reversed the lower court's decision to terminate the mother's parental rights. The lower court found that it would be

**Table 1.1**

| *Year* | *1996* | *1997* | *1998* | *1999* | *2000* | *2001* | *2002* | *2003* |
|---|---|---|---|---|---|---|---|---|
| Number of Children | 165 | 212 | 458 | 524 | 877 | 1,149 | 1,149 | 1,328 |

"detrimental" and "unnatural" for the child to be returned to her biological mother on the South Dakota Rosebud Sioux reservation.[6]

In 1989, the U.S. Supreme Court reversed the Supreme Court of Mississippi and held that the adoption petition for a Native American baby was governed by the Indian Child Welfare Act (ICWA) even though the baby had been surrendered voluntarily.[7] The case involved twin Native American babies, known for our purposes as B. B. and G. B., who were born out of wedlock on December 19, 1985, to J. B., the mother, and W. J., their father. Both parents were members of the Mississippi Band of Choctaw Indians (Tribe) and were residents and domicilaries of the Choctow reservation in Neshoba County, Mississippi. J. B. gave birth to the twins in Gulfport, Harrison County, Mississippi, some two hundred hundred miles away from the reservation. On January 10, 1986, J. B. executed a consent to adoption form before the Chancery Court of Harrison County, record 8-10.[8] W. J. signed a similar form.[9] On January 16, appellees Orrey and Vivian Holyfield filed a petition for adoption in the same court, and the Chancellor issued a Final Decree of Adoption on January 28. Despite the court's presumed awareness of the ICWA, the adoption decree contained no reference to it, nor the infant's Indian background.

Two months later, the tribe moved in the chancery court to vacate the adoption decree on the ground that under the ICWA, exclusive jurisdiction over this (and all cases involving Indian babies) was vested in the tribal court.[10] On July 14, 1986, the court overruled the motion, holding that the tribe "never obtained exclusive jurisdiction over the children involved herein. . . ." The court's one-page opinion relied on two facts in reaching its conclusion: first, that the twins' mother "went to some efforts to see that they were born outside the confines of the Choctaw Indian Reservation" and the parents had promptly arranged for the adoption by the Holyfields; and second, "At no time from the birth of these children to the present date have either of them resided on or physically been on the Choctaw reservation."[11]

The court distinguished Mississippi cases that appeared to establish the principle that "the domicile of minor children follows that of the parents." It noted that "the Indian twins. . . . Were voluntarily surrendered and legally abandoned by the natural parents to the adoptive parents, and it is undisputed that the parents went to some efforts to prevent the children from being placed on the reservation as the mother arranged for their birth and adoption in Gulfport Memorial Hospital, Harrison County, Mississippi."[12] Therefore, the court said, the twins' domicile was in Harrison County and the state court properly exercised jurisdiction over the adoption proceedings. The court further concluded that none of the provisions of the ICWA were applicable. Third, the Court rejected the tribe's contention that the trial court had erred in not conforming to the applicable procedural requirements of court: "[T]he judge did conform and strictly adhere to the minimum federal standards governing adoption of Indian children with respect to parental consent, notice, service of process, etc."[13]

The U.S. Supreme Court, in an opinion written by Justice Brennan, reversed the Mississippi Supreme Court and held that the Native American babies were domiciled on the reservation and the trial court was, accordingly, without jurisdiction to enter the adoption decree. The Supreme Court did not find the fact that the children were "voluntarily surrendered" for adoption a relevant consideration in light of the court's stated purpose to address the "finding that the removal of Indian children from their cultural setting seriously impacts on long-term survival and has a damaging social and psychological impact on many individual Indian children."[14]

The Supreme Court's decision in *Mississippi Board of Choctaw Indians v. Holyfield* indicates the degree to which the courts are constricted in their approach to adoption cases involving Native American children. Pursuant to the ICWA and the superior court's determination thereof, courts are required to consider what Congress has identified as the best interest of the particular tribe into which the child was born, as well as the best interest of the child. Moreover, parents seeking to adopt Native American babies are frequently forced to proceed in the Indian tribal courts, with little recourse to challenge the tribal court's rulings in state or federal court.

## RESEARCH ON NATIVE AMERICAN CHILDREN ADOPTED BY WHITE PARENTS

Until the 1960s there was little mention of any major adoption study involving American Indian children.[15] The Indian Adoption Project, a program described in David Fanshel's work *Far from the Reservation* (1972), resulted from a 1957 study that indicated the legal availability of 1,000 American Indian children for adoption, who were living in either foster care or institutions.[16] The project, which lasted from September 1958 to December 1967, was a joint effort sponsored by the Bureau of Indian Affairs and the Child Welfare League of America (CWLA) (neither of which is an adoption agency) initially to promote nationwide conventional and transracial adoptions of between fifty and one hundred American Indian children. At its conclusion in 1968, when most of its activities were subsumed by the Adoption Resource Exchange of North America (ARENA), the project had successfully placed

395 children from 11 states. Ninety-seven of these children were adopted by white families living in 15 different states. *Far from the Reservation* is an examination of the adjustment patterns of these 97 children and their adoptive white parents.

Articles written in the late 1960s, especially those by Arnold Lyslo, Director of the Indian Adoption Project, describe some initial attempts at and success of transracial adoption of American Indian children. These articles examine a series of related adoption programs, many of which were to be incorporated into the Indian Adoption Project.[17]

In 1961, Lyslo stated that 30 Indian children had been adopted, mostly by white couples living in areas geographically distant from the reservations. By 1964, a total of 150 Indian children had been adopted transracially, mostly by families who lived in the eastern states. The degree of tribal acculturation and the availability of social services appeared to be strongly associated with positive feelings toward transracial adoption on the part of tribal representatives. Most of the adoptive parents were described in the reports as being motivated by humanitarian and religious principles and appeared to be making successful adjustments to their children and their community. The children also seemed to be adjusting to their new society.

In 1967, Lyslo reported the results of a survey sent by the CWLA to 102 adoption agencies with significant Indian populations.[18] The results from the adoption agencies indicated that the majority of Indian children were being transracially adopted by white families. Of 1,128 Indian children available for adoption, 66 of the 90 reporting agencies indicated that 696 had been adopted, 584 of whom had been placed with white families. Only 14 were adopted by Indian couples. The remainder had been placed with nonwhite, non-Indian families (for example, black, Mexican, Spanish-American). Several of the adoption agencies implied that were it not for state racial prejudice, more Indian children could have been transracially adopted. Four of the state agencies reported that several tribes, the Hopi, Navajo, Pueblo, and Colorado River, were reluctant to have their children adopted by non-Indian families.[19]

In *Far from the Reservation*, David Fanshel saw grounds for cautious optimism. As shown in table 1.2, he divided his families into seven adjustment levels and distributed them according to the degree to which the parents reported that they believed their adopted child had made the adjustment described at each level.

Only 10 percent of the parents perceived their children's future adjustment as "guarded" (Level 5), and only one child was seen to have a "dim" (Level 6) future. In Fanshel's words,

**Table 1.2. Level of Adjustment Perceived by White Parents of American Indian Children**

| *Number* | *Percent* | *Description of Level* |
|---|---|---|
| 10 | 10 | Level One (Child is making an excellent adjustment in all spheres—the outlook for his future adjustment is excellent.) |
| 41 | 43 | Level Two |
| 24 | 25 | Level Three (Child is making an adequate adjustment—his strengths outweigh the weaknesses he shows—the outlook for this future adjustment is hopeful.) |
| 10 | 10 | Level Four |
| 10 | 10 | Level Five (Child is making a mixed adjustment—generally the problems he faces are serious and the outlook for his future adjustment is guarded.) |
| 1 | 1 | Level Six |
| None | None | Level Seven (Child is making an extremely poor adjustment—the outlook for his future adjustment is unpromising.) |

> More than fifty percent of the children were rated as showing relatively problem-free adjustments (Levels 1 and 2) and another twenty-five percent were rated as showing adequate adjustment with strengths outweighing weaknesses (Level 3). Another ten percent of the children were rated at Level 4—located midway between adjustments regarded as adequate and those viewed as guarded.[20]

Many of the parents acknowledged that difficulties lay ahead and that they expected those difficulties would surface when their children reached adolescence and adulthood. Many felt that the difficulties would be proportional to the "full-bloodedness" of their children and therefore children who appeared less distinctively Indian would have less turbulent experiences. The existence of anxiety or lack of it therefore rested on the degree to which the children were of mixed blood.

In examining which social and demographic factors correlated best with the parents' perceptions of the child's adjustment, Fanshel found the strongest relationship between age and adjustment. The older the child at the time of initial placement, the more difficult the adjustment. Fanshel also discovered an association between age at placement and parental strictness, noting that the older the child, the more strict the adoptive parents tended to be.

The child's sex appeared minimally related to adjustment, boys being defined as slightly more problematic than girls. A family's social position was also related to the child's adjustment.[21] The higher the family's status the more difficulty the child seemed to experience and therefore the more problematic his or her behavior. Fanshel explained this phenomenon by suggesting that parents of higher socioeconomic status set higher standards of behavior for their children and thus had higher expectations of adoption. There was no relationship between parents' religious affiliation or degree of religiousness and a child's adjustment.

It is important to emphasize that all these impressions were based on the parents' responses to their children's adjustment over three different time periods. The professional evaluation of parental impressions (referred to as the Overall Child Adjustment Rating) was the yardstick by which the children's adjustments were viewed, and it served as the basis for predictions for the future. At no time did Fanshel involve the children in attempting to predict future adjustments.

In his conclusion, Fanshel addressed the issue of whether the transracial adoption of American Indian children should be encouraged.[22] He described the costs involved in transracial adoption and concluded that adoption was cheaper than foster care or institutionalization. He established that the children were secure and loved in their adoptive homes. He found that the adoptive parents were happy and satisfied with their children. Nevertheless, in the end, he predicted that the decision as to whether the practice should or should not continue would be made on political grounds and not on the basis of the quality of the adjustment that the parents and children experienced.

Since the publication of *Far from the Reservation* in 1972, practically no additional information has appeared in the professional literature regarding the transracial adoption of American Indian children. Some data may be found in periodic newsletters published by various organizations concerned with both conventional and transracial adoption.[23] These data, however, are usually presented as general categories, and details are, by and large, lacking. For example, in the 1975 annual report of ARENA, one notes that of 238 white, black, Indian, Oriental, and Spanish children who were adopted, 120 were American Indian. One cannot tell, however, whether any of these Indian children were transracially adopted.

It seems reasonable to assume that the limited momentum achieved by the transracial adoption movement as it relates to American Indian children is on the decline. American Indians, like other racial minorities, probably will continue to organize and demonstrate (as in the 1973 "occupation" of Wounded Knee, South Dakota, by members of the American Indian Movement) in order to reawaken both their own and white America's attention to their historic rights. The resurgence of Indian consciousness will undoubtedly lead toward viewing the transracial adoption of their children as yet another form of humiliation—in the explosive jargon of the 1970s, "as a final contemptuous form of robbery."

## OPPOSITION TO ADOPTION OF NATIVE AMERICAN CHILDREN BY NON-NATIVE AMERICANS

According to Carol Locust, Training Director for the Native American Research and Training Center at the University of Arizona College of Medicine, "19 out of 20 Indian adoptees have psychological problems related to their placement in non-Indian homes."[24]

The research on which this conclusion is based is a pilot study conducted by Locust which states:

- Placing American Indian children in foster/adoptive non-Indian homes puts them at great risk for experiencing psychological trauma that leads to the development of long-term emotional and psychological problems in later life
- The cluster of long-term psychological liabilities exhibited by American Indian adults who experienced non-Indian placement as children may be recognized as a syndrome. (Syndrome: a set of symptoms, which occur together. From *Dorland's Medical Dictionary*, 24th edition, 1965.)

Locust goes on to report:

> The Split Feathers themselves have identified the following factors as major contributors to the development of the syndrome, in order of their importance:
>
> 1. the loss of Indian identity
> 2. the loss of family, culture, heritage, language, spiritual beliefs, tribal affiliation and tribal ceremonial experiences
> 3. the experience of growing up being different
> 4. the experience of discrimination from the dominant culture
> 5. a cognitive difference in the way Indian children receive, process, integrate and apply new information—in short, a difference in learning style.

Excerpts from the experiences reported by "Split Feathers" are provided below.

> They gave me everything a child could ever ask for, except my Native American identity. All my years growing up in school I was cut down and made fun

of because I was Indian. I was darker, had dark hair, and I was "different." I grew up resenting who I was, what I was; of course I kept all the shame to myself, therefore building resentment. I am waiting now for enrollment in my tribe and waiting to establish contact with my biological family. I wish I had grown up being proud—like I am proud today.

My foster mother was very abusive. She always said we were dirty because we were dark. She beat us often, made our noses bleed. But the worst thing she did was denying us our Indian heritage. Courts should never let anything like this happen. Indian children need to be with Indian families, not white families that are so different from Indian.

Adoption causes such intense inner pain that you do anything just to get away from it. No one understands you, you are different, and there's no one to talk to. You withdraw into yourself, keep it all inside. That's how I got into trouble with alcohol: it was pain medicine.

I was adopted at age four, started school just before five, grew up in a middle class family that was okay. But I started having dreams about age five about being taken away (from the adoptive home), taken back to my family, by Indians. My family didn't pay much attention to the Indian spirit within me, or to me, either. I communicated more with animals than I did people. In the sixth grade I started having problems with the other kids. Whites, Mexicans and others didn't like me because of being Indian. I got into lots of fights and became a loner.

I am 72 years old. I was adopted into a white family at age one-and-a-half when my mother died. I realized I was different before I ever went to school. When I asked, my foster parents told me I was Indian, and from that day I identified with Indians, because that was what I was. I didn't know who I was, and that heartache and anguish has been with me for nearly 70 years. I hope your study can help me find out who I am before I die. I don't want to die not knowing my true identity. They (the government) sealed my birth certificate so I could never find my identity and never see my blood relatives. The pain of this is never ending.

## NOTES

1. "An Indian Perspective on Adoption," workshop, North American Council on Adoptable Children, Seattle, WA, July 27–29, 1978.

2. Ann W. Shyne and Anita G. Schroeder, *National Study of Social Services to Children and Their Families.* The National Center for Child Advocacy, U.S. De-

partment of Health, Education and Welfare, Office of Human Development Services, Administration for Children, Youth, and Families, Children's Bureau, DHEW Publication no. (OHDS) 78-30150, Washington, DC, 1978.

3. Op. cit. "An Indian Perspective on Adoption."

4. Edward Colton, "Vista Pair Loses Child to Indians," *Baltimore Sun*, November 14, 1974, p. C1.

5. *Brokenleg v. Butts*, 559 S. W. 2d 853 (Tex. Cic. App. 1977).

6. "Indian Custody," *New York Times*, June 19, 1979, p. 12.

7 *Mississippi Board of Choctaw Indians v. Holyfield, et ux*, 490 U.S. 30 (1989).

8. Section 1913(a) of the ICWA requires that any voluntary consent to termination of parental rights be executed in writing or recorded before a judge of a "court of competent jurisdiction," who must certify that the terms and of the consent were fully explained and understood. Section 1913(a) also provides that any consent given prior to the birth or within 10 days thereafter is valid. In this case, the mother's consent was 12 days after the birth.

9. W. J.'s consent to the adoption was signed before a notary public in Neshoba County on January 11, 1986, record 11-12. Only on June 3, 1986, however—well after the decree of adoption had been entered and after the tribe had filed suit to vacate that decree—did the chancellor of the chancery court certify that W. J. had appeared before him in Harrison County to execute the consent to adoption.

10. ICWA specifically confers standing on the Indian child's tribe to participate in child custody adjudications. Section 1914 authorizes the tribe (as well as the child and its parents) to petition the court to invalidate any foster care placement or termination of parental rights under state law "upon showing that such action violated any provision of sections 1911, 1912, and 1913" of the ICWA. See also section 1911(c) (Indian child's tribe may intervene at any point in state-court proceedings for foster care placement or termination of parental rights). "Termination of parental rights" is defined in Section 1903 (1) (ii) as "any action resulting in the termination of the parent-child relationship."

11. Ibid.

12. 511 So. 2nd 918 (Miss. Ct. 1987).

13. Id. At 919.

14. Ibid.

15. Shapiro, *Adoption Agencies*, chapter 7; Grace Gallay, "International Adoptions," *Canadian Welfare* 39, no. 6 (November/December 1963): 248–50; Donald E. Chambers, "Willingness to Adopt Atypical Children," *Child Welfare* 49, no. 5 (May 1970): 275–79; Barbara P. Giffin and Marvin S. Areffa, "Recruiting Adoptive Homes for Minority Children—One Approach," *Child Welfare* 49, no. 2 (February 1970): 105–7.

16. David Fanshel, *Far from the Reservation: The Transracial Adoption of American Indian Children* (Metuchen, NJ: Scarecrow Press, 1972), p. 280.

17. Arnold Lyslo, "Adoptive Placement of Indian Children," *Catholic Charities* 51, no. 2 (February 1967): 23–25.

18. Ibid.
19. Ibid.
20. Fanshel, *Far from the Reservation*, p. 280.
21. Ibid., pp. 326, 328.
22. Ibid., p. 339.
23. For Example, *ARENA News*. Newsletter of the Adoption Resource Exchange of America; *National Adoptalk*, National Council for Adoptive Organizations; *Opportunity Reports*, Opportunity, a Division of the Boys and Girls Aid Society of Oregon.
24. Carol Locust, "Split Feathers . . . Adult American Indians Who Were Placed in Non-Indian Families as Children." *OACAS Journal* 44, no. 3 (October 2000).

# II

# NATIVE AMERICAN ADOPTEES DESCRIBE THEIR EXPERIENCES

## INTRODUCTION

Each of the following twenty interviews lasted between one and three hours. Sixteen of the interviews were conducted over the phone. Two were conducted in person and two were conducted via e-mail. David Houghton's interview was conducted via e-mail because the phone connection did not work, while Nicolas Leech-Crier's interview was conducted via e-mail because he did not have access to a telephone. The names of interviewees that appear in these transcripts were those they wished to be identified by. The names of relatives, places of birth, childhood homes, and names of schools attended are also those interviewees agreed could be identified. In cases where interviewees preferred using a pseudonym, that is so indicated on the transcript.

The twenty participants consisted of thirteen females ranging from twenty-five to fifty-nine years of age and seven males ranging from twenty-eight to fifty-three years of age. Sixteen participants were adopted by white families, one was raised in foster care by three separate white families, one was adopted by a Hispanic family, one was adopted by a black family, and one was raised in foster care by black and Hispanic foster parents. Ten of the thirteen female respondents characterized their relationships with their adoptive families as positive. The other three characterized their relationships as verbally and/or physically abusive and refuse to have any contact with their adoptive families today. Six of the seven male respondents describe their relationship with their adoptive families as positive. One male respondent characterizes his relationship as negative and like the three female respondents, he, too, refuses to have any contact with his adoptive family today.

Eleven of the female adoptees were adopted when they were between three days and three years old. RoSean Kent was placed in foster care when she was six years old and never legally adopted by another family. Diane Ames participated in the Indian Student Placement Program and lived with a Mormon foster family nine out of twelve months of the year. She lived with three different foster families from ages eight to seventeen. Among the female respondents, six are married, six are divorced, and one is in a long-term relationship. One of the female adoptees was born in Canada, one in New York, three in California, and eight in the Midwest. Five of the female respondents are or were married to Native American men. All but one of the women have children. One completed eleventh grade, two completed high school, one has an Associate's Degree, six hold Bachelor's Degrees, one has a Master's Degree, one has a Ph.D., and another has a Law Degree. Two of the women are housewives, one is a student and ten are or have been engaged in positions related to the Native American community.

Five of the female adoptees are enrolled members of their respective tribes. Four have been unable to find their birth families and as a result have been unable to prove that they are of Native American descent. The other four participants have not enrolled for various reasons. Tamara Watchman has been unable to enroll because her birth father, who is Navajo, is not listed on her birth certificate. She has reunited with her birth father and his family; however, she admits that they do not have a close relationship today. RoSean Kent is Cherokee, Dine, and Ute. Her Ute father, however, refuses to claim her as his biological child. She says that she has never considered enrolling with any of her tribes and maintains that she does not need a tribal enrollment number to prove that she is an American Indian. Joyce Gonzales has not enrolled with her tribe because her birth mother has passed away and she has not reunited with her Apache birth father. Shana Greenberg has spent more than ten years trying to enroll with her tribe before eventually giving up. She says that her birth mother's decision not to enroll has prevented her from enrolling with the Mono Indians of California.

All of the male adoptees were adopted when they were between four days and two years old. Two of the male adoptees were born in Canada, one in upper New York State, and four in the Midwest. All seven men indicate that they are enrolled members of their respective tribes. Five of the male respondents are married with children. Two are married to Native American women. One is a high school graduate, two indicated that they briefly attended college, two earned an Associate's Degree, and two earned Bachelor's degrees. All seven of the men indicate that they are or have worked with the Native American community in the past.

We now turn to the transcript of the interviews that were conducted with the twenty men and women described above.

# III

# INTERVIEWS

# 1

# DIANE AMES*

Diane Ames's (Navajo) story differs from many of the other participants interviewed for this project because she was never placed for adoption, but rather participated in the Indian Student Placement Program. The Indian Student Placement Program was established in 1947 by the Mormon Church "in part to fulfill the obligation felt by the Church to help care for Indians in America" (de Hoyos). The program placed Native students in Mormon homes during the academic year in the hope of giving "Indian youth better opportunities for education . . . and to promote greater understanding between Indians and non-Indians (de Hoyos)."

To be eligible to participate in this program, Diane and her siblings all had to be baptized by the Mormon Church. With the permission of their parents, Diane and her siblings were baptized and placed with Mormon foster families nine months out of the year. From ages eight through seventeen, Diane was placed with three separate foster families, whom she describes as "strict, but nice." She notes that the foster homes she lived in differed dramatically from her home on the reservation. On the reservation, she says they "didn't have running water, the bathroom was outside . . . and [you] had to walk forever" as opposed to her foster homes where "everything was inside and it was nice."

---

*Identifying information about this participant has been omitted or changed.

When she enrolled in the program, Diane did not speak English and notes that her foster families taught her the English language. Unfortunately, when she returned home to the reservation in the summer she had forgotten her native language—the Navajo language. As a result, she says that she was "treated different back home . . . they would call [her] names, like [she] was a white person, and didn't belong there [on the reservation]."

Diane believes her parents regretted their decision to enroll her in the Indian Student Placement Program because she ultimately made the decision to live life off the reservation. She did not finish high school, but rather married her high school sweetheart and had children. Her children cannot speak the Navajo language and as a result cannot communicate with their grandparents, which Diane indicates that she deeply regrets. However, she says that she and her husband have raised their children to be proud of their Native background and that she is content with her life off the reservation.

De Hoyos, Genevieve. "Indian Student Placement Services." Retrieved May 30, 2007, from http://www.lightplanet.com/mormons/daily/education/indian_eom.htm.

So your situation differs a little from some of the other interviewees we're speaking to in that you were not adopted, you were placed in foster care, correct?

Yes.

And how old were you when you were first placed in foster care?

Eight years old.

And do you know why you were placed in foster care?

To get an education—go to school, and get an education.

Can you tell me a little bit about your foster parents?

Well, I remember three different foster parents; they were all pretty nice.

Can you tell me a little bit about your first set of foster parents?

I just felt they'd scare you 'til—later on they don't know what's going on. There they speak a different language and you don't know how to speak their language, but you get to learn. They were nice people. I lived with two boys and a little girl there. And they bought me stuff, and I went to school.

AND HOW LONG DID YOU STAY WITH THEM?

For one and a half years, they were down there. Then it was after nine months with them, we would go back home for three months. And then it would start all over again the next fall.

AND THEN THAT'S WHEN YOU MET YOUR SECOND SET OF FOSTER PARENTS?

Yeah, my second foster parents I only lived with them for nine months. They were nice and strict. They're all strict, but they're pretty nice. And I lived with them during the school year, then they sent me home again. So you get to know them and then they send you away, so I don't know.

AND WERE YOUR BIRTH PARENTS—DID THEY APPROVE OF THIS PROGRAM?

My mom and dad, yes, they did. They're the ones that went, you know, they put me on this program so I could get an education and I guess to get away out of the system and stuff that they have down there which a lot of my brothers and sisters were, you know, still down there having problems and they don't live very well.

DID ANY OF YOUR OTHER SISTERS AND BROTHERS PARTICIPATE IN A PROGRAM LIKE THIS?

Only two of my sisters. We all went on programs, but only a couple of us kept doing it over and over. But two of us did it.

AND THEN COULD YOU TELL ME ABOUT YOUR THIRD SET OF FOSTER PARENTS?

My third set of foster parents are nice. I lived with them from seventh grade on until I got married. They were nice. They had six girls. I had six sisters, no boys, and I was about one of the oldest ones. And that was a lot of fun. It was fun to be with them and I still communicate with them these days now. I really respect my foster family now.

AND HOW MANY YEARS WERE YOU WITH THEM?

From seventh grade, until—I lived with them for about five years. Five years, and I would go home in the summer and then they would take me back up after they pray themselves at the church, and get me back to their house.

WAS THE FACT THAT YOU WERE AN AMERICAN INDIAN TALKED ABOUT A LOT WHILE YOU WERE STAYING WITH YOUR FOSTER FAMILIES?

Actually, no. They just treated like you were one of them, except you didn't know the language and they taught you the language, but they, didn't say anything about being different or anything. It was different when you went home. It was, you know, you were treated different, because you forgot your own language, and you knew this other language, English, that they didn't know. You were treated different back home than you were being up here.

IN WHAT LANGUAGE DID YOU SPEAK?

I speak the Navajo language.

AND HOW LONG DID IT TAKE YOU TO LEARN TO SPEAK ENGLISH?

Soon, when you do it everyday, you know, 24/7, you learn it really quick. So probably in about three days or five days you would, you know, pick up the stuff that you needed to learn. Then actually you had to go to school, where you had to learn pretty fast.

So the Indian—you didn't speak the language, was your Navajo language while you were here, so you forgot, you don't have to speak that.

So that made it hard when the end of the school year was done, they put you back on the bus and you make a twelve-hour trip back home and then you get picked up and they start speaking the Navajo language, and you don't know it, you know, and they think you're kind of stupid, or thinking I was dumb, because you forgot your own language and you only know how to speak the English language.

HOW WELL CAN YOU SPEAK NAVAJO TODAY?

I can understand and speak it pretty good. I don't say a lot of the words, you know, like, pronounce them right. But that's okay, at least they know what I'm talking about.

CAN YOU TELL ME A LITTLE ABOUT THE SCHOOLS YOU ATTENDED AND THE PLACES YOU LIVED?

The schools I attended were nice schools, the kids were nice. They didn't treat you like you were different, even though you were the only brown person in that classroom but they all treated you the same.

AND THEN HOW DID YOU LIKE THE SCHOOLS YOU ATTENDED?

It was scary, but people didn't treat you different because you were a different color or anything like that. And the teachers, they were all nice.

SO YOU WERE THE ONLY AMERICAN INDIAN IN THESE SCHOOLS?

Yeah, when they first started and it was scary. You would go to church, and you'd be the only Indian girl there but in all the other places, Indian people, you would see them every once in a while. But they never put brothers and sisters in the same town or, you know, close together, so you didn't know the other people that were in there.

So it was really hard when you're the only Indian person in the church with all these white people and stuff.

AND SO DID YOU ENCOUNTER ANY FORM OF RACISM GROWING UP?

Did I what?

ENCOUNTER ANY FORM OF RACISM GROWING UP?

Actually no, I didn't. I just noticed that I was the only one that was different, but never—they always treated me the same and, you know, they all loved me and things like that—like I was their own daughter. And their kids were like that, too, so I wasn't treated different here.

But when I'm back home, I was different. They treated me different, they would call me names, like I was a white person, and I didn't belong there. And I wasn't their sister no more, and it was different from being with your own Native American family. You were treated different and they called you names and stuff like that. But when you're up here it was a lot different. People loved you for who you are and stuff like that.

WHO TREATED YOU POORLY BACK HOME? WAS IT YOUR FAMILY OR WAS IT PEOPLE OUTSIDE OF YOUR FAMILY?

No, it was my own family, my sisters, especially. They would tell me, I'm white, I'm not really Indian and things like that.

AND WHAT WAS YOUR PARENTS' RESPONSE?

My parents really didn't interfere with us. They would just say, "Oh, she's kind of crazy right now, but she'll be back to normal, you know, before she has to go again." But yes, it takes some months to learn your own language and then you know your language, then you forget the English language again, and you have to come up here and then you start all over.

DO YOU THINK YOUR PARENTS REGRETTED PLACING YOU IN THAT PROGRAM?

I think so. I think they did, because I stayed, you know, after I got married, I stayed up here, and I think that they kind of regret that, because I didn't want to live down there no more, and I wanted to stay up here. Anyway, it's my family. Once my mom said if we never sent you away, you'd probably be down here with us, which, I don't know, might be true, but I like my life up here now.

WHAT TIES DO YOU HAVE TO YOUR TRIBE TODAY?

What kind of what?

WHAT RELATIONSHIP DO YOU HAVE WITH YOUR TRIBE TODAY?

Actually it's pretty good, because we go down there to see my family every once in a while, my uncles and stuff, but my uncles and aunts, they never treated me different. I think they kind of missed me being around and stuff like that, but it was just my sisters that treated me different.

And also because I didn't know the language, or if I had better things and I want better things in my life than what they have. So I don't know if that was just, jealousy or what.

AND DID ANY OF YOUR SISTERS PARTICIPATE IN THAT PROGRAM?

Yeah, actually my mom had sixteen kids. So all of the five boys participated. Some of them only went for one year, and some of them went for two years; and my sisters, I think there was only like four of us that were participants, and two of us stayed in and the other two just went in for like a year or not even that long, and that was it.

SO HOW COME SOME OF YOU STAYED AND SOME OF YOU DIDN'T STAY? WAS THAT YOUR DECISION?

Actually, I think it was, yeah, my mom's decision because, you know, having sixteen kids and then having a lot of us leave all at one time, I think she kind of didn't like it. So she kept some of them out and kept them home and put them in school or a boarding school and sent the other ones up that were older, back up to go to school.

DO YOU REMEMBER WHAT THE PROGRAM WAS CALLED?

No, I don't. It was just a program that the LDS churches did, take some kids. It was a placement program that only the LDS people would take these kids into their home, feed them and whatever they needed for nine months and then send them back.

But it was through the LDS Church. You had to be baptized before you came and stuff like that—placed in these homes and then you had to go to church and stuff like that with them and follow the rules, but it was fine.

So was that life a lot different from the life you had on the reservation?

Oh, yes. That was a lot different from being on the reservation, because eight years old, we didn't have a TV, we didn't have running water, the bathroom was outside, you had to run—walk it seems like forever, and, you know, you had to walk to school. So it was really different. When you came up here, everything was inside and it was nice. You didn't have a lot of the stuff that my foster parents had, we didn't have no toys at home. We made our own toys with mud and stuff like that. And we didn't have nice things, nice shoes, nice clothes, you know, nice coat to keep us warm, and gloves, like that, because my parents—they couldn't afford it. We never were hungry, but we didn't have nice clothes and stuff like that.

So you said you had to be baptized by their church?

Yeah, you have to be baptized. At eight years old, you had to be baptized through the LDS Church, and that got you to get in the program, and then come up here and go to school and live with the LDS family.

So you learned a whole new religion, right?

Yeah, we did. Yeah, we had to learn the religion. Of course, some of my sisters, they already knew, and, you know, my parents weren't really LDS, but they had their own religion, the Native American Church, that's what their religion is.

My grandmother, those guys weren't against the LDS Church, because I think if they were, they wouldn't let us get baptized, come up here, and get an education.

Did you know anything about the Native American Church before you were baptized by the LDS Church?

When I was eight years old, not really. I went to them a couple of times, but I really didn't understand the religion.

And did you have foster siblings?

Foster siblings?

Did your foster parents have children?

Yeah.

And were you close with them?

With the ones I'm with? Yeah, you get close with all the foster sisters and brothers. You know, you live with them for nine months, you get close to them.

Do you still have a relationship with them today?

Yes, I do, with my last foster family. They just treat me like a family, they're just like my family. So we're all pretty close. And their kids are close.

And do you still have friends from the schools you attended?

Yes, I do. I still have my girlfriends that I associate with every once in a while, once a year sometimes, but yes, I still have friends from school.

So what did you do after you graduated from high school?

I got married before I graduated. I married my husband that I knew since seventh grade. We went through junior high, and high school, and then I got pregnant in eleventh grade.

Is your husband, is he white, or is he an American Indian?

He's white.

And do you have any children?

Yeah, I have four boys.

And what is their relationship with your biological family?

They used to see them when they were smaller, because we used to go down there a lot. But now they don't speak our language either, my boys. They can understand some of the words, but they don't speak it. They're close to my family. When they see them, they treat them good.

Is it difficult not speaking your language? Is that something you're criticized for when you're on your reservation?

Yeah, it used to, but now—these days a lot of—even the people that live down there they don't teach their kids the Navajo word and they just learn English. So a lot of the Navajo words are forgotten. And that's what I did with my kids. I didn't teach them my language. They just know the English, but they understand some of the words that my mom and my grandma used to speak to them. So they understand those words, but a lot of it is our fault that we didn't keep that Navajo language going through our kids.

Do you regret that?

Yes, I do, I regret it. It's hard for my mother to speak to my kids, and like, kids can't really understand the language. They have to kind of have, like a translation and that makes it hard to—I blame myself for not teaching them the language so they understand the older generation when they're being spoken to and stuff like that.

How has the fact that you're an American Indian affected your personal and professional life?

Being Native American, it hasn't really bothered me—bothered my life in anyway because I'm different. It hasn't. I don't think it really matters to any of the people up here that I'm Native American.

How often do you return to your reservation?

I used to go at least twice a year, before my dad passed away a couple of years ago. And now it's hard to go down there, so it's just like once a year if I have to go down there.

Do you feel comfortable down there?

With my mom, yeah, I used to just go down there to visit my mom and my uncles and stuff like that, but when you have to make a trip down there, you just go visiting, and then you will have to come back up.

And what do you do for a living?

I work as a processor right now. I've been doing that for almost seven years.

Do you feel secure or insecure about your Indian identity today?

I feel secure about my Indian identity. Well, I like to have my kids know that they're part Native American, and part white, and be proud of who they are. So my husband even tried to learn the language at one time. I even took him down there the first time to meet my grandma. But, you know, when we first got married, they didn't like it. They were, I guess, they were racists, you want to say—on both sides. His parents were the same way and mine were the same way too. I think they were against us getting married, but we did it anyway. We lasted twenty-nine years so far.

Do both of those families still feel that way today?

Well, my mom and my uncles and everybody love my husband more than I think they like me, so—they like my husband more than their own daughter. And his parents, they love me, and both of his parents are gone now, and just his brothers, and we seem to all get along together good, now.

Do you have Indian friends today?

Actually, no, I don't. Just relatives, and that's about it. My kids have Indian friends and stuff like that.

Are your children involved with the tribe today?

No, they're not involved with the tribe. There's this census number or whatever they are that tells them they're part Indian and part white. They have to get enrolled through there, but other than that, that's it. And I tell them, you know, if you ever need help this is open for you in scholarships or schools when they were going to school and stuff like that, but they just kind of do it on their own.

And did your children go to college?

No, they didn't. They graduated and that was about it. And then they worked for my husband.

Do you or your children feel accepted by Indians outside of your family?

I think we are. We really don't go outside of our family too much, so I don't know. We just stay here you know, it's more comfortable and stuff like that, but we haven't really been down home together for a long time, so.

Do you think the white community perceives you as Indian?

I don't think they do. Actually, you know, I've really never thought I was different from them as they are from me so. Just when I was little, but now, we're treated the same and stuff like that. So even with work, the racial stuff is not there. You're not treated different because you're Indian.

Were you glad that you were placed with a white family?

Yes, I am, because I got a good education. And I'm here, and I'm doing a lot, I got things—I don't know how to say it. I have things that a lot of the people on the reservation or down home don't have. You know, I work for what I want, and it seems that they don't understand if they want some, they have to work for it, things like that. So I'm glad that I had the knowledge to realize that I needed to get out of there to do better. Does that make sense?

Yeah. Do you think the non-Indians should be allowed to adopt Indian children?

Not really, because they can do better if they needed to get away and be raised in the different areas.

AND WHAT FACTORS DO YOU THINK SHOULD BE TAKEN INTO CONSIDERATION WHEN PLACING AN INDIAN CHILD IN FOSTER CARE OR PLACING THEM UP FOR ADOPTION?

I don't know. Be sure there is nothing wrong with the family or anything like that. Now, I think they have background checks. In those days we were on placements, and it seems like they did fine with me, so I had no problems. But, in these days they have to do background checks about children being abused, checked for abuse, and stuff like that. So I think they have to be careful. It doesn't matter if they're LDS or non-LDS, they just have to check those backgrounds these days, because a lot of these kids when they come up they don't know the language and it's scary. And I don't think some of the kids would tell if anything ever was happening to them here.

DO YOU THINK A GREATER EFFORT SHOULD BE MADE BY THE ADOPTED FAMILIES OR THE FOSTER FAMILIES TO HELP THOSE CHILDREN MAINTAIN THEIR CULTURAL IDENTITY?

Yes, I think they should. I don't know how they would do it, teach them their own culture, because a lot of these people, the family, they don't know the backgrounds of the kids. So there's not that much information about the kids, send up just like a picture, and say, "Hey, this is," you know, "so-and-so, this is how old she is," and that's it.

They don't send information on how many sisters she has, or her parents, or anything like that. So the foster family doesn't know anything about this kid that they're taking in. Just that she's Indian and that's it. So I don't know how they would try to teach them more about their own culture and stuff like that when they have a different culture.

IS THIS PROGRAM STILL TAKING PLACE TODAY, DO YOU KNOW?

Not that I know of. I think they kind of stopped it a couple of years ago. You don't hear about it no more. I think if it was still going on, a lot of my nephews, their family would send them to boarding school. But now they just stay home and go to school down there.

AND OUT OF ALL YOUR SISTERS AND BROTHERS, WERE YOU THE ONLY ONE WHO—BENEFITED FROM THIS PROGRAM, OR DO YOU THINK THAT THEY BENEFITED FROM THIS PROGRAM, AS WELL?

There's probably about four of us that benefited from the program. The other ones I don't know if they did or not. But there is that four of us out of the sixteen that are doing pretty well.

And do you think that's a direct result of the program?

Yes, it is. I'm sure it is, for being sent away looking at a whole new life away from home, and being up here and looking at all the different things that you can achieve here.

And are you aware of the Indian Child Welfare Act?

I sort of know, because we had to get custody of my grandson. So I kind of know a little bit about it, but not a whole lot.

And what is your opinion of it?

What I know? I really don't know that much about it. I'd like to learn more about it.

Well, basically it says that Indian children should be adopted by Indian families first, before being placed in any other home. Do you think that's accurate? Do you think that Indians should be able to adopt Indian children before anybody else?

If they're going to take care of them, give them education and stuff. I don't know. In a way, yes, it's there, you know, good foster Indian people that get to teach them the stuff they need to learn and things like that.

Do you think race is something that should be taken into consideration when placing children for adoption?

Not really, because, you know, some kids will feel worse being in their own race than they are being placed with another family that's not Indian or white.

Do you have any questions or advice you would like to offer to white families who would like to, or have adopted Native American children?

You know what, I really don't because I've been with my foster families and they taught me what I needed to know, and they loved me. You know, being loved and being taken care of, and things like that I think is what's important; that makes the person what they are these days.

Uh-huh.

Get their love and the support growing up. So I didn't really have my parents. My parents never showed affection or anything like that. So that was different from being up here, being with the white people, you know, because they're all lovable, hugging, and kisses and stuff like that. So that was different.

AND YOU THINK THAT WAS POSITIVE?

With my real family?

WITH YOUR FOSTER FAMILY, HAVING THAT AFFECTION; THAT WAS A POSITIVE EXPERIENCE?

My foster family showed a lot of affection, you know. They would hug you and tell you that you're doing good, and stuff like that. And your sisters were the same way, give you hugs and things like that, so.

OKAY. WELL, I THINK THAT WAS JUST ABOUT THE LAST QUESTION I HAD. WERE THERE ANY OTHER QUESTIONS YOU THINK I SHOULD HAVE ASKED YOU?

I have no idea. But I think that's about it.

OKAY.

2

# ANDREA

Born in Sioux City, Iowa, in 1975, Andrea ——— (Sioux) was adopted by a white couple when she was just two weeks old. She and her adoptive brother grew up in a predominantly white neighborhood in Manning, Iowa, that she admits made her feel uncomfortable. According to Andrea, neither she nor her brother encountered any blatant forms of racism growing up; however, she says that she always felt different because of her "dark skin." In an effort to downplay these differences, Andrea says that her adoptive parents didn't make a "big deal" about her Native American background. Unfortunately, she notes that their indifference made life "difficult . . . because [she] didn't know if [she] should be proud of [being Indian] or if [she] should be embarrassed about it." She says that her uncertainty was further exacerbated by the biased history lessons given in school that vilified Native Americans and glorified European settlers.

As she's gotten older, Andrea says that she has taken it upon herself to learn more about Native American culture. Her attention is currently focused on secondary resources, but she hopes to take a trip to a reservation in South Dakota soon. According to Andrea, she has "no idea what to expect . . . [but] she looks forward to finding out more about [her] heritage." Andrea believes that she is either Rosebud Sioux or Oglala Sioux. Much of her confusion stems from the fact that the adoption agency told her adoptive mother that she is from the Rosebud Indian Reservation and a member of the Oglala Sioux Tribe. The Pine Ridge Indian Reservation (rather than the Rosebud Indian Reservation), however, is home to the Oglala Sioux Tribe. With the support of her adoptive family and new husband, Andrea recently petitioned a judge to unseal her birth records. She hopes that this important first step will help her find her biological family and help her learn more about her cultural background.

WHAT YEAR WERE YOU BORN?

1975.

WHERE WERE YOU BORN?

Sioux City, Iowa.

HOW OLD WERE YOU WHEN YOU WERE ADOPTED?

I was fourteen days old.

ARE YOU AWARE OF THE CIRCUMSTANCES SURROUNDING YOUR ADOPTION?

My birth mother had two other older children and she wanted to go back to school to be a teacher and so she gave me up.

DID YOUR ADOPTIVE PARENTS EVER INDICATE TO YOU WHY THEY DECIDED TO ADOPT?

Yes. My mother was having problems so they decided to go ahead and adopt.

WERE YOUR PARENTS SPECIFICALLY LOOKING TO ADOPT A NATIVE AMERICAN CHILD OR JUST A CHILD IN GENERAL?

I am not really quite sure on that answer. If I remember right, they said they were looking for a Native American but at that point it was probably pretty much open, also.

TELL ME MORE ABOUT YOUR ADOPTIVE PARENTS.

My Mom and Dad both grew up in Iowa, they both farm and are involved in church and in other activities. My father went to Vietnam for a while and then when he came back they met, got married and decided to adopt me and then they adopted my brother also, he's Native American too. They really enjoy camping, fishing, and traveling.

HOW WOULD YOU DESCRIBE YOUR RELATIONSHIP WITH THEM?

It's very good. It was difficult growing up, just because of the fact that I knew I was different. When you grow up in an all-white community and you are the only one with dark skin, that makes it a little bit difficult knowing what exactly you are, and a lot of people thought that I was maybe half-black/half-white, and I still have that once in a while. It was hard, it was different. My mom and I didn't always see eye to eye and I tried to be a lot like her, it's hard to be a lot like your adoptive mother when you don't have the same traits and everything like that. But otherwise we have a really good relationship. I have three children now, and I'm married. And my Mom and Dad are very interested in helping me find my birth parents and helping me find out as much as I can about my Indian heritage for myself and my children. We are all really close.

When did you first realize that you were adopted?

I probably realized very early on. Just because of the fact that I grew up in an all white community and I was the only one with a dark skin, and so I knew I was different all along.

Do you ever remember your parents sitting you down and telling you about it?

Yes. They did, I was nine years old when they sat me down and just explained everything. The best they could for an eight- or nine-year-old. And then as I got older I really wanted to find my birth parents and that has gone to the wayside a little bit, but they've always told me, and were very open and honest about all the information that they could give me and so they have been really informative and helpful on anything that they could tell me that they knew from the home I was adopted from.

What were the advantages of having a brother who was also adopted?

Probably just the fact that I wasn't the only one who was adopted and with dark skin. So whatever I had to go through he had to go through too. I probably took it more to heart growing up, you know people asking questions and people saying things, and remarks about being Indian, and stuff like that. But it made it easier because my brother wasn't like that. He just laughed it off. So he cushioned the front for me once in a while.

Do you and your brother have a close relationship?

Yes. We are very, very close. Although we are not real siblings a lot of people say that we look alike. So it is really funny. That is another thing about my parents. My dad is very dark skinned, but he is not Indian. A lot of people say that I look like him, also. We all just kind of sit back and laugh because we know that I'm adopted and everything. And we are like "oh, yeah, we look alike." Even though we're adopted we are still brother and sister and family and nothing will ever change that!

WAS THE FACT THAT YOU ARE NATIVE AMERICAN TALKED ABOUT A LOT IN YOUR FAMILY?

No. It wasn't. Basically, if I asked any questions, then I was told. I guess when growing up I had a problem going through high school when the fact that it was taught in school that the white people they have the right to boss everyone around so it's like, we (Indians) are the bad ones. I don't know how to explain it. It is just a different scenario when you grow up in an all white community and there's no other Native American. So my parents just really didn't talk about it much and my parents never really ever said anything about my heritage. I think that they didn't want to make a big deal of it. They didn't want us to feel like we were different. I was never taken to a reservation while growing up, I have no idea what to expect if I were to go to an Indian reservation. It would all be foreign to me, I guess. But now that I am older I look forward to going someday and finding out more about my heritage.

DID YOU ENCOUNTER ANY FORM OF RACISM GROWING UP?

Not really. Most everyone knew that I was Indian. So no one really said anything to me. Maybe some jokes once in a while. Now I'm getting more of the Mexican side of it, sometimes people who don't know me think that I am Mexican. It's not really racism toward American Indians. Most people know that I am proud of my heritage. I am very much proud of my heritage, but I don't like it when people say "what ARE you?"

DO YOU THINK YOUR PARENTS PREPARED YOU TO ANSWER THOSE TYPES OF QUESTIONS?

No. I don't think they did because of the fact that it wasn't really talked about. I kind of got my own feeling about how I needed to be proud of my Indian heritage on my own. My parents never really said, you're American Indian and that is something to be very much proud of. They never, ever came out and said that. So I kind of had to go through all that stuff, I guess, on my own. That made it really difficult growing up. Because I didn't know if I should be proud of it or if I should be embarrassed about it. But as time went on and I got older, I am proud of who I am . . . that's what makes me, me.

WHEN DID YOU BEGIN TO LEARN MORE ABOUT YOUR CULTURAL IDENTITY?

Basically just by reading books. Reading books and kind of doing my own research on my heritage, because like I said in school it's not really talked about a lot, like the great battles between the settlers and the Indians, just basically it just talked all about white people and how they did so great. Sitting Bull was bad and Crazy Horse was bad and I think that if there is one thing that I could change it would be for my children growing up that they should be proud of who they are because it is not a bad thing. They should teach more good things about Indians in school.

WHAT EFFECT DO YOU THINK IT HAD ON YOUR CULTURAL IDENTITY GROWING UP, THE FACT THAT IT WASN'T TALKED ABOUT IN SCHOOL, OR THAT WHEN IT WAS TALKED ABOUT IT WAS TALKED ABOUT FROM THE SETTLERS POINT OF VIEW INSTEAD OF THE INDIAN'S POINT OF VIEW?

I guess it probably made me uneasy about being proud of who I was and being proud of my Indian heritage. As I go back . . . I basically grew up white and I have no Indian heritage until I got older and I started doing my own research and reading. So it was very hard. It made me embarrassed or ashamed that Indians are portrayed as terrible people for preventing the settlers from taking over the Indians' land. All the Indians were trying to do was protect their land, hunting grounds, and their families.

WHERE DID YOU GROW UP?

In a town in Western Iowa called Manning.

WHO WERE YOUR CLOSEST FRIENDS GROWING UP?

I hung out with a lot of different people all throughout high school. I was a very social person. Most of my closest girlfriends were all jealous of me because I had such a beautiful tan all year around! That was fun for me to joke with them about while they were all spending money on tanning.

WERE YOU EVER ABLE TO TALK WITH THEM ABOUT BEING NATIVE AMERICAN?

No. It was never talked about. They didn't ask because they didn't know how I felt about it.

DO YOU THINK YOU FELT THAT WAY BECAUSE YOU WERE ADOPTED OR BECAUSE YOU ARE NATIVE AMERICAN, OR BOTH?

I think it was both. A lot of both. My self-esteem growing up was just not where it should be. I was uneasy on where I fit in the grand scheme of things. I wasn't white, so I wasn't like them. I was Native American and I didn't have anybody else to talk to about how I felt about that. And in my family I didn't look like all my cousins and so I didn't fit in there either. I really didn't fit in, but I didn't know who to talk to about it.

YOU TALK A LOT ABOUT YOUR PHYSICAL APPEARANCE. HOW DO YOU THINK YOUR PHYSICAL APPEARANCE AFFECTED THE WAY YOU HAVE BEEN PERCEIVED BY BOTH THE INDIAN COMMUNITY AND THE NON-INDIAN COMMUNITY?

I don't know. I have never been in an Indian community before. I guess my physical appearance didn't bother me that much because I had a tan all year around and nobody else had one, and I didn't have to go tanning. It didn't play too much of a factor in all of that. It was just basically the fact that I was darker than everybody else.

DID YOU GO TO COLLEGE?

Yes. I went to a two-year program but I quit after one year. I have basically just been a stay-at-home mom while my boys were little. But, I would like to go back at some point of time.

TELL ME ABOUT YOUR HUSBAND AND CHILDREN.

My husband is twenty-three years old. He is very, very supportive. I am trying to find my birth parents and he is very supportive of that. He would like to take us on a trip to go to the Indian reservation in South Dakota, and different places so we can teach the boys about their heritage. He is really proud of the fact that I am looking and searching and wanting to know more about it. He is very interested in it also. I have a ten-year-old son, Colton, and I have a seven-year-old son, Keaton, and we have a daughter, Kiara. My first husband (the boys' dad) wasn't very interested in any of this. He wasn't very supportive so it made it kind of difficult. He doesn't really talk about the fact with the boys or support me with the boys about telling them about their Indian heritage, so that makes it a little difficult on me when it comes to the boys. But I know that my husband now will be completely supportive and everything when it comes to Kiara and the boys growing up and knowing more about her Indian heritage.

HOW HAVE YOU PLANNED TO ADDRESS THE ISSUE OF CULTURAL IDENTITY WITH YOUR CHILDREN WHEN THEY GET OLDER?

They both know they are Indian. Some of the questions that they have it is hard to answer because I don't know what tribe I am from. So it is hard to tell much of anything at this point in time. I am working on finding out more information for all of us. When we learn of our heritage we will learn all together. Which will be a good experience for us all to go through. I just tell them to be very proud of who they are. The boys are Native American and German and a little bit of French, and that is something very much to be proud of. The community we live in is an all-German community and so they've got a lot of German heritage festivities and so I tell them that the Indian heritage is just as important as the German heritage.

YOU MENTION THAT YOU ARE INTERESTED IN LOOKING FOR YOUR BIRTH FAMILY. HAS YOUR ADOPTIVE FAMILY BEEN SUPPORTIVE OF THAT DECISION?

Yes. They are very supportive. They know I would like to know for medical reasons and personal reasons. And they are also really supportive just for the simple fact that they know I've always wanted to know and they are concerned on how it is going to go. With an adoption you never know which way it is going to go. They could want to have a lot to do with you and be overabundantly loving or they could just be completely the opposite way, and not want anything to do with you. But I know that with the families that I have, with my husband's family and with my family that the support is there so that whatever I happen to come across in the future with my birth family that I have a great support system that will be backing me up.

WHY DO YOU PERSONALLY FEEL IT IS IMPORTANT TO FIND YOUR BIRTH FAMILY?

I guess because I've always wanted to know where I'm from. Who do I look like? Because right now the only people I look like are my children and I can see my face in them and they look like me, but I wish I knew who I looked like, and where I get some of my little quirks from, and what makes me, me. I'd like to know a little more about my birth mother and I hope that she has done what she wanted to do to better herself and her family situation. I'd also like to know my older siblings and my birth father, but I'd just like to know who they are. Also for medical reasons.

WHAT STEPS HAVE YOU TAKEN IN SEARCHING FOR YOUR BIRTH FAMILY?

I've gotten in contact with the home that I was adopted from. Right now I am in the process of petitioning a judge in Sioux City to open up my birth records and hoping that that will go well. And other than that, I haven't done much else. I've been on the Internet and gone through adoption registries and been in contact with them and put my name on the registry and everything, but that's about it.

Do you know what tribe you are?

Well, I have a difference of opinion on that question. My parents said that the home told them that I was from the Rosebud Sioux Indian Reservation. But I am seven-eighths Ogalala Sioux, and my understanding from the research that I've done is that the Ogalala Sioux are from the Pine Ridge Indian Reservation. So I don't know if I'm from the Pine Ridge Indian Reservation or from the Rosebud Indian Reservation in South Dakota. Knowing just that information would help out a lot.

And so because you are not sure, you haven't been able to enroll in a tribe, correct?

Correct.

And how has that affected your sense of cultural identity, the fact that you haven't been able to enroll in a tribe?

That's one thing that bothers me at this point in time because it goes along with being proud of my heritage and I feel that I want to be enrolled in a tribe so that I can learn more about my heritage through the tribal members and through just doing my own research about the tribe itself.

What relationship do you have with the Native American community today?

None. I've never been to an Indian reservation and I actually, honestly don't know other than my brother anybody who is as much Indian as I am. My brother isn't even as much Indian as I am, he's I think one-half or one-quarter Indian. He looks more Indian . . . he's got the nose and the high cheekbones, which I have too, but he looks a little more Indian than I do. But other than that I can't honestly say that I know anybody more now than when I was growing up.

How has the fact that you are Native American affected both your personal and professional life?

Professionally it has not affected me at all. Other than the fact that when I go to job interviews everybody thinks that I am bilingual, and that I speak Spanish. That bothers me, I guess. But personally it's just the wanting to know the unknown that bothers me more than anything, and I have a lot of questions that I want answered about the tribe that I'm from, about my history, about my family's history. I have a lot of questions. So personally I guess that I've gone through a lot of inner battles on do I leave it alone, or do I find out? As I get older I guess I'm leaning more toward I've got to find out. I am yearning to know more. Personally, it's been rough. It is not easy growing up in an all-white community at all and not being able to be proud of your heritage and tell people about it openly. Then you've always got to wait for the little remarks and stuff like that.

Do you feel secure or insecure about your Indian identity today?

Secure. Very secure. I guess as I got older it was just something that I guess as a teenager my insecurities were high. It was very hard for me to find my place in the world, sounds kind of cliché, but to find my place in the world. It was hard to figure out because everybody else was living with their real parents and everybody else looked like each other and I just didn't fit in anywhere. But as I am growing older I've got my own identity and I've worked through a lot of it. It is just searching for the birth parents and the questions that I have for them when I do find them about my heritage and my background and my family history.

What people or experiences or resources helped you obtain that sense of security?

Probably just through my reading and well, I had a friend who was Cherokee Indian and she helped me out a lot a couple of years ago. She has since moved away, but she helped me out a lot to be proud of who I was and basically I just found my sense of pride in the last few years through friends and family and my husband and myself. I had to do a lot of soul searching I guess. My husband has been my rock and my biggest support of me so far.

You mentioned that you had read a lot of books about your culture. Are there any limitations to relying solely on books for that sort of information?

Yes. A lot of limitations. I don't feel that books in school portray the right circumstances sometimes and so you have to be really picky and choosy. I have felt that the best resources in the past three, four years are on the web. Because of the fact that I can actually get on the Internet and go to the different tribal websites and I can find out more and there's more selection there. Whereas if you go to a library you are kind of limited on what you read and who the authors are.

Do you ever make an effort to contact people from the tribe directly?

Yes, I have. I have spoken to a couple of different people on the Rosebud and the Pine Ridge Indian reservations, and I have probably come across several because I start off by saying that I am adopted and I want to know about . . . and they put me on to another person and they put me off to another person and I probably never get my answers that I'm wanting. So it is difficult for me because I have never really met anybody face to face. I'm always doing phone conversations or via the Internet conversations.

WHAT BARRIERS HAVE PREVENTED YOU FROM FULLY INTEGRATING INTO THE NATIVE COMMUNITY?

Probably the closeness that I have now with my adoptive family and the fact that I have children and I still live in the same town that I grew up in. I'm kind of grounded here with my immediate family and my adoptive family. We live probably eight hours away from the Rosebud Indian Reservation . . . it may even be more . . . so as far as being able to even go there to see it we actually have to take a vacation and stuff like that and it makes it a little difficult with the children being that they're involved in a lot of sports and stuff.

WHAT ARE THE ADVANTAGES AND DISADVANTAGES OF BEING INTERRACIALLY ADOPTED?

I can't really say that I have an answer for the advantages, I guess, because given the fact that I grew up in an all-white community, just growing up was very hard. The disadvantages are the fact that you don't look like anybody you know, you don't know where you're from.

WHAT IS YOUR OPINION OF THE INDIAN CHILD WELFARE ACT?

I wish they would have done it a little sooner, because of the fact of what I went through growing up; 1978 wasn't soon enough. I think that it helped keep the heritage with the Indians. I wish that it would have taken place a little bit sooner just for the simple fact that—I love my family, don't get me wrong, I love them so much because they have always been there for me and we've gone through some ups and some big downs—but I think that growing up probably wouldn't have been so hard if I would have grown up with my own heritage. I can have a sense of pride in who I am but I would not have had to deal with the questions and the jokes and everything else. I think it is a great thing that they did it when they did but I just wish they would have done it a little sooner. From what I read there were children who were adopted out or were put in orphanages or taken away from their heritage whatever way they were taken away from it, growing up and knowing how I had my problems with it, I am sure there were other people out there who had the same problems as I did. So I wish they would have done it sooner but I'm glad that they did it when they did do it. At least then other children wouldn't have to go through what some of us did—the confusion and the not belonging and the not knowing where you fit in and all the questions you grow up with that are unanswered. You don't have anybody that can portray the right answers to you when you are growing up in a biracial family. You don't have anybody that can tell you about your heritage if they don't know themselves that much about it.

In general should non-Indian families be allowed to adopt Indian children?

No. I don't think so. I feel very strongly about that. They can't answer questions for their children as they are growing up, they can't answer them unless they have done extensive research, and maybe possibly if it's an open adoption that might be a little bit different scenario, but when I was adopted there was no such thing as an open adoption and so nobody could teach me about my heritage, nobody could say this and that. But for the most part no. I don't think Indian babies should go out to white people. I don't think so, because it just causes too much confusion for them.

I do think that probably the stigma on it is probably different nowadays than it was then because you're getting more different ethnic groups into communities at this point in time than what you did when I was growing up in the 1980s, but at the same time I think it is very important that the babies that are being adopted out should stay with their heritage . . . the same people that they are so that they can answer questions for them as they are growing up, so then they don't have anything to deal with as far as that confusion and everything else that I said.

Do you have any advice that you would offer to white families who would want to or have adopted Native American children?

Take them to Indian reservations and take them to pow wows and take them to museums and teach them as much as you possibly can because that speaks a million words . . . that alone speaks a million words. It teaches them how to be proud of their heritage, it teaches them about their heritage, it answers their questions for them. Keep them involved because that is something they should be proud of. It is not something they should feel uncomfortable about. Being a Native American, as I learned growing up and as I am an adult now, it is something to be proud of and if I could learn anything I would do it in a heartbeat, so just please keep your children involved in their own heritage.

Is there anything else you think I should have asked you?

I don't think so, I think you covered everything very well.

3

# LESLEE CABALLERO

Unlike many of the other adoptees interviewed for this project, Leslee Caballero (Northern Arapaho/Rosebud Sioux) was not adopted by a white family, but rather was adopted by a Hispanic couple when she was six weeks old. Leslee describes her relationship with her adoptive parents and siblings as "very close." She grew up in a predominantly white neighborhood located in Longmont, Colorado, and admits that both she and her adoptive family encountered subtle forms of racism growing up. However, she notes that her parents chose to live in this neighborhood because they wanted their children to benefit from greater educational opportunities. According to Leslee, her adoptive parents' commitment to higher education led her to the University of Colorado at Boulder where she earned a Bachelor's degree in Psychology and currently works as a counselor in the Center for Multicultural Affairs.

Leslee began the search for her biological parents as a student in college and found them both within five years time. Unfortunately, Leslee discovered that her biological mother passed away in 1977 when she was just seven years old. Fortunately, her mother's family was aware of her existence and were themselves searching for this "lost bird." She was quickly accepted back into the family. According to Leslee, she was a bit more reluctant to contact her biological father because her adoption records indicated that he was not aware of her existence. After several years and with the help of a friend, she made contact with her father and had a close relationship with him until his death last year.

Although Leslee's experience as a transracial adoptee was positive, she is a strong supporter of the Indian Child Welfare Act and believes that American Indian families and communities should be given priority when placing Indian children. According to Leslee, "culture is so important and that's something that [she] miss[es] on a daily basis" and that's something that she's trying to learn with the love and support of both her adoptive and biological families.

WHAT YEAR WERE YOU BORN?

I was born in 1971.

AND WHERE WERE YOU BORN?

In Denver, Colorado.

AND HOW OLD WERE YOU WHEN YOU WERE ADOPTED?

I believe I was six weeks old.

ARE YOU AWARE OF THE CIRCUMSTANCES SURROUNDING YOUR ADOPTION?

Yes.

CAN YOU TELL ME A LITTLE BIT ABOUT THAT?

Yes. My biological mother was in—I believe in Los Angeles, giving some training—I'm not sure what kind of training, job training—but she met my biological father, and he was coming back from the Vietnam War, and he was stationed in San Diego. And so that's where they met. I'm not sure how long they dated or anything like that, but they had a relationship for a few months, and she was pregnant with me, and then she decided that she wasn't going to tell him that she was pregnant. So she moved here to Colorado all by herself and had me all by herself because she didn't want her own family to know about me.

I know that she came here and had me and, she didn't tell her whole family until probably about a year later, maybe. And they were pretty upset with her.

CAN YOU TELL ME A LITTLE BIT ABOUT YOUR ADOPTIVE PARENTS?

Yes. They're here, they're Colorado natives, and they have—I have two older brothers, and they're natural, and they wanted a little girl, and so basically, they had gone to Catholic Charities and you know, being a Hispanic couple in the 1970s, just weren't quite sure of their chances of adoption, but they thought they'd give it a try, and they basically didn't request any race of child. They just said they wanted a girl. And it was really, I guess, unusual, even in those days, to get called probably like six months after their application was completed and say that there was a child. And so that's when they had me, and it just was pretty much a perfect fit for the family.

HOW WOULD YOU DESCRIBE YOUR RELATIONSHIP WITH THEM?

Very close. Very close. You know, I'm thirty-four right now, and just—various times in our lives I've lived with them or they've lived with me, and I usually see them at least six times a year. They live in Las Vegas now, but we're very, very close.

AND WHEN DID YOU FIRST REALIZE THAT YOU WERE ADOPTED?

I don't remember not knowing. They've always told me. I mean, I remember not knowing how to write and knowing that I had another mother out there and trying to write her a letter.

WAS YOUR ADOPTION SOMETHING THAT YOU WERE ALWAYS COMFORTABLE WITH?

Yes. I mean, when I was in high school and I was applying to college, I knew that I was Native American, and I knew that I always ever since I can remember, I wanted to find my family.

But there's certain parts of it, like in high school, that I felt like I would be betraying my parents. They always told me that they would always help me, be supportive of me, finding my family, but it was just the inside voice telling me, oh, you know, this is going to be difficult. It's not going to be easy for any of us. And so I looked for my mother and found her, and then it wasn't until probably about five years after that that I looked for my father and found him.

AND WHAT WAS THAT FIRST MEETING LIKE BETWEEN YOU AND YOUR BIOLOGICAL PARENTS?

Well, when I found my mother, she had died in 1977, so she had died when I was seven years old, so I didn't know her, but when I found her was when I was in college, and actually found a whole new family, and the family had always known about me.

Like I said, she didn't tell her family until she had gotten married probably about a year after I was born and went back up to the reservation, and she had confided in some of her cousins and then, by that time, everybody else knew what she had done, and my grandmother was very, very upset with her.

I can't remember what the question was.

WHAT ABOUT YOUR MEETING WITH YOUR FATHER?

Oh, I was going to say about my biological families. My grandmother knew about me then from the time that I was small. And so, you know, my dad had actually worked for IBM, and so he had been traveling around the country, but there were moments when I was a child when she actually knew where I lived. She had the tribal lawyers looking for me and everything. So I was always in the minds of my mother's biological family, and my grandmother actively looked for me, and so my brothers from that side of the family always knew about me, and my aunts always knew, my uncles always knew, and they always wanted to find me.

When I found them I'd already had things set up for me. I was already enrolled, you know, all the stuff, and it was amazing because they were always talking about how I'd always come back, and I did. And I have a good relationship with my aunts, my cousins, actually, my brothers.

For my dad's side of the family, I had his name, and that was it. So I had called up to the reservation he lived on, and there was only a few people with that name. But I kind of got nervous, because in the adoption records she had mentioned that she had never told him she was pregnant, so I knew it would be very shocking to get a call saying, "Hi, I think I'm your daughter."

And so it wasn't until—it was a complicated connection because I had gotten a job where I had somebody recommend me, and this recommender actually was working on the reservation that he lived on.

And so I gave her his name, and within a half hour, we had him on the phone. And he was skeptical at first, but it was mostly because he had a wife and he had two other kids and of course the wife was like, blood tests and all that stuff, but two days later, he called me and he told me.

He goes, I know you're my daughter. He put two and two together, and I told him about my mother, and he said, yes, he knew. And so he was accepting of me right away, which, you know, as adoptees go, it's highly unlikely for both families to be so accepting, so it's been a really good experience.

AND WHAT TRIBE WAS THAT, THAT BOTH YOUR PARENTS BELONGED TO?

My mother's Northern Arapahoe, and my father is Rosebud Lakota.

AND HAVE YOUR ADOPTIVE PARENTS AND YOUR BIOLOGICAL PARENTS EVER MET?

Yes. When I first met my biological father, my mom took me up there to meet him, and so she met the whole family and within about six months, my father's family had decided to give me a name. And so basically, most of my family had gone up there to meet that side of the family and vice versa. Both my mom and dad on separate occasions and together have gone up to see both families on both reservations.

SO IS IT A GOOD RELATIONSHIP BETWEEN THE TWO FAMILIES?

Oh, yeah. Yeah, definitely.

I WANT TO GO BACK A LITTLE BIT AND TALK ABOUT YOUR CHILDHOOD. YOU MENTIONED THAT YOU HAVE TWO SIBLINGS.

On my own mother's biological side, I have—well, she—I say there's three because I have an older brother—I had an older brother. I never met him. He had committed suicide probably about a year before I found that side of the family. And then I have a younger brother on that side. And then my mother died in childbirth.

AND WERE ANY OF THE OTHER CHILDREN EVER PUT UP FOR ADOPTION OR FOSTER CARE?

No. For my mother, the oldest child, my grandmother took custody of the oldest child, so that was it. And then after she had me, she got married and then she went into the service, and so my younger brother—she also took custody of my younger brother too.

AND YOU HAVE TWO ADOPTIVE BROTHERS OR SISTERS?

Two adoptive older brothers.

AND GROWING UP, WAS THE FACT THAT YOU WERE NATIVE AMERICAN EVER TALKED ABOUT IN THAT FAMILY?

All the time. All the time. It was something that either my parents, they would always tell me, you will find out someday, something that's important to your—to who you are, and you know, they fully supported me in that. Even my extended family knew. Everybody in my family knew that I was adopted, and they also all knew that I was Native American.

And you know, for most of my life, I didn't know what that was, but when I found my family, it was kind of like that missing piece that I've been able to explore.

So you didn't know which tribes you were in until you met your biological family?

Mm-hmm. Yes.

What do you think your parents, your adoptive parents, did to give you a sense of your cultural identity, growing up?

Well, they did what they could. I mean, they'd give me books to read. They talked to me about it and they were pretty honest. We're not sure what tribe you are, but it's something that you need to explore when you're older and if anything came up, they would always try to expose me to whatever culture they could.

Did you talk to your adoptive siblings about that when you were growing up, about being Native American?

Yeah, they always knew. I mean, they would in a joking way, they would sometimes—well, you're the adoptive one. But it was joking. We have a very loving relationship.

Where did you go to school?

I went to school in Longmont, Colorado.

And can you describe the neighborhood a little bit for me?

The neighborhood, we were the only people of color in the neighborhood, so—especially in our high school, too. There was only, like, a handful of Latino families—I knew no Native Americans growing up.

Did you go to college?

Yes.

And where did you go?

UC Boulder.

And what did you major in?

I majored in psychology.

And why did you choose that major?

I had always been interested in it in high school. Just—my interest never strayed from it.

And what kind of work do you do now?

I actually work at a counseling center, and I coordinate American Indian student services.

AND WHAT DREW YOU TO THAT POSITION?

As an undergraduate, I had worked with the American Indian Student Services coordinator there. And just through the experience that I gained from her, I knew that that's exactly what I wanted to do. And it kind of—I always talk about destiny, too, is that it fit because in—when my mother gave me up, in the paperwork that I had, I was able to review it and she gave me up because she wanted me to get a good education.

So, you know, I kind of took that to mean that, yeah, I'm here for a purpose, to get an education, but also—I also wanted to make sure other Native students got an education, too.

AND YOU MENTIONED THAT YOU WERE ABLE TO ENROLL IN YOUR—

In my mother's tribe.

—YOUR MOTHER'S TRIBE. WERE YOU ABLE TO ENROLL IN YOUR FATHER'S, TOO?

Actually, I was able to get hip blood quantum, and my tribe counted some of that toward my membership.

AND HOW DO YOU THINK BEING ABLE TO ENROLL IN THE TRIBE HAS AFFECTED YOUR SENSE OF CULTURAL IDENTITY?

You know, it really gives me a sense of responsibility. It gives me a sense that I need to help my community in any way I can, even if it's down here.

AND YOU MENTIONED THAT GROWING UP, YOU WERE RAISED IN A MOSTLY WHITE NEIGHBORHOOD. DID YOU EVER ENCOUNTER ANY SORT OF RACISM?

Oh, yeah. I mean, definitely growing up, even from close friends. I mean, it wasn't malicious racism, but just a sense of difference that—I knew right away that names and everything were different, and cultural practices and—even growing up in a Mexican-American Latino family, knowing that, yeah, things were different. We didn't quite do the same things the neighbors did.

AND HOW DO YOU THINK YOUR PARENTS PREPARED YOU TO COPE WITH THE RACISM THAT YOU ENCOUNTERED?

I think the reason why we—my parents chose to live in that neighborhood was to give us opportunities and education and to know that it was always my dad's philosophy that I could do anything.

So that was why I think he did that, so that we could go to better schools and know that we had a better education and make our lives better.

How do you think those experiences shaped your sense of identity?

As far as growing up? I just always knew that education was important. I knew that it was important not just for me, but for my family, to create a better life, starting with myself and helping my family.

How has the fact that you're a Native American affected both your personal and professional life?

In the beginning, when I didn't know what tribe I was, it was a part that I wasn't quite sure of and was really uneasy about exploring, just because I was afraid of rejection, as an adoptee, afraid of my own family's rejection, afraid of my community's rejection.

But the woman that I worked with really, really was supportive of me in that and without her, without the center that I work at, it's highly likely that I wouldn't have finished my education.

What ties do you have to the Native American community today?

I do some liaison work with my tribal council, doing various things here in the community, help them out whenever they need me. I go up, and of course, with the family needs, and I'm really close to one of my brothers up in the Wind River Reservation, and then I'm extremely close to my father's family.

It's more of a community kind of a connection, then, I would say, with my dad. And then with my mother's family, it's more kind of like a—I try to be more involved with the tribal politics to know what's going on and how I can help out.

Have you spent a lot of time on the reservation?

I definitely make it a point to go up as much as I can. Possibly, I don't know, twice a year for both reservations.

And what was your initial reaction when you first arrived there?

From my mother's family, it was amazing, the acceptance—and as an adoptee, I totally prepared myself for the rejection, but then when I got there and saw how many people I was related to and how much they wanted to know me and how much I was free to get to know them, it was a relief, and it was a blessing. I felt really lucky. And both from my dad's side of the family, too, you know, having him accept me right away, and having his family accept me was a big thing. It was a blessing.

WHY DO YOU PERSONALLY FEEL THAT IT WAS IMPORTANT TO FIND YOUR BIRTH FAMILY?

Well, I always say that I had a really loving, close family growing up, and there's nothing more that I could have asked for. But there was always that wondering, that kind of ache in your heart that you need to find out.

You know something, but you don't know it, and you need to find out. And for me, I knew somewhere out there, there was a woman who was my mother, and I knew that somewhere out there, there was a man that was my father. Just that need to know them and who they were was really great for me.

HOW DO YOU THINK YOU'VE CHANGED SINCE FINDING YOUR BIRTH FAMILY?

Oh, it makes me stronger, it makes me feel much stronger as a person, as a mother. I just feel so lucky. I feel so lucky. And you know, to the extent it's kind of a detriment that I feel so lucky that things have turned out so good that I feel like I really got to pay something back because it turned out to be such a good thing for me. My families have all accepted me, and I'm doing the work that I really believe in, and I just feel really lucky.

NOW, YOU MENTIONED THAT YOU FEEL LIKE YOU WERE EMBRACED BY YOUR ADOPTIVE FAMILY. DO YOU FEEL LIKE YOU WERE EMBRACED BY THE INDIAN COMMUNITY IN GENERAL?

You know—and that's one thing I always tell people, too, is that when I got to UC Boulder, I kind of had a choice, and back in the late '80s when I went to school, it wasn't that accepted to be multicultural, multiracial, or mixed or anything. A lot of times the communities made you choose, and so when I got to campus, I always had people ask me, what are you?

And it was actually, like I said, the person that I worked for at Native Student Services that helped me. And that community is the one that embraced me. I mean, I can't say that the other community didn't embrace me, it's just that I felt like that community really supported me, and that was kind of my home base when I was there at CU. So that was the community that embraced me.

And, yeah, it wasn't easy because there were some people who were, like, you don't know who you are? So how can you say you're Native? Then, just throughout the years, I've been like, just because I didn't grow up on the reservation it doesn't give me any less of a right to know who I am and who my family is, all of my culture.

So you say that at CU, they made you feel accepted? What sort of things did they do to make you feel that way?

I think it was both the students and it was the staff people on campus, just the staff people always being there was important, always talking to me about what it meant to be Native, what it meant for me to be Native, just because of my circumstances didn't mean I had any less of a right to be there.

And with the Native students, they just accepted me. It was really nice to have people to hang out with and just to be with who you didn't have to explain things to.

Do you feel secure about your Indian identity today?

I do for the most part. I mean, there's moments when—especially in the kind of work that I do—that people will attack you for not growing up on the reservation or not knowing the language or, you know, we're really tough on each other that way. But I just have to remember that it's my personal experiences and my father, from the moment he saw me, he was always telling me tidbits here and there that, it's who you are. Even if you don't know who you are, he goes, you know your blood knows who you are.

He truly believed in genetic memory, and that's why we were able to find each other, and that's how he knew I was his daughter, even though we didn't do a blood test yet. So things like that give me strength. It's the close family connections that I've made that give me that strength.

What does it mean to you to be Indian?

It means taking all of it, not just the good, but trying to deal with everything it means to be Native. I see too many people who will just say they're Native, but yet, like, it's—when it comes to things that are uncomfortable, they'll shy away. When it comes to talking about the politics or spirituality they'll shy away. But for me it means just trying to serve my people and community any way I can, in good and bad.

Well, most importantly, to really pass on to my children. I think that's the future. To listen to what anybody says, my elders, and take it in, not ask too much, not be too prying. I have that right to know and I have a responsibility, actually, to pass it on to my children. I always tell my students, your ancestors fought through so much and survived through so much that we owe it to them to start to try to learn our languages, to at least know something about our people. Whatever you're comfortable with. You don't have to be all-knowing. You've got to carry something on.

HOW MANY CHILDREN DO YOU HAVE?

I have two.

AND HOW HAVE YOU ADDRESSED THE ISSUE OF CULTURAL IDENTITY WITH THEM?

They know what tribes they are. I take them with me all the time to visit their families and I would rather them know firsthand, from the families, being there, talking about it, than just knowing it from a book or knowing just because I said so. I want them to learn from their own experiences, and I'm not going to push it on them so much as just expose them to it.

DO YOU EVER FIND THAT THE WORLD THAT YOU GREW UP IN AND THE WORLD THAT YOU SAW ONCE YOU WENT TO THE RESERVATION—DID THEY EVER CLASH IN ANY WAY?

They did. What I noticed the most was my husband. My husband, he's also biracial—he's Mexican-American and white. And so growing up, he didn't grow up around any minorities or people of color. And so when I first took him up to the reservation, he was highly uncomfortable, didn't quite know what to expect.

I warned him. I said, you know, we're going on the reservation. It's quite a different place in the sense that things happen when they happen. We're not going to go here when you expect, and we're just going to go on the schedule that—we don't have, really, a schedule. And you have to understand the poverty there.

But I don't think he did until he quite saw it. And it made him uncomfortable for a few years until recently. He's really started to come with me and embrace it and know that it's his children, too, that need to know, and he also needs to know about it, too, and develop this relationship with my family, and he has. So I'm really glad that he's come around.

DID YOU HAVE A SIMILAR REACTION TO THE RESERVATION WHEN YOU FIRST SAW IT?

No, not really. I really didn't. It didn't make me uncomfortable, for some reason. I just—I saw the reservation for what it was, and I saw the, yeah, there's a lot of poverty on reservations, but they're also extremely beautiful places, not just landscapewise, but the people, the generosity, the closeness of the communities, the cultural, the spirituality, everything.

WHAT IS YOUR OPINION OF THE INDIAN CHILD WELFARE ACT?

Well, that's what I used first to find my mother. And when I was a student at CU Boulder, the Indian law clinic was a place that Native people could use for legal assistance, and so I used it as a student.

And due to the ignorance of the state system, they didn't quite understand its applications, so we used it to open my records. I took it to understand that it meant this and this and this, and it really didn't apply to me, but we thought we'd give it a try. We did, and we opened my records.

So I think it's actually a good thing. Now people always ask me when I say that, well, would you have rather grown up on the reservation. And I say I cannot change any of my life, and I wouldn't. I was meant to be who I was.

DO YOU THINK, IN GENERAL, NON-INDIANS SHOULD BE ALLOWED TO ADOPT INDIAN CHILDREN?

I definitely think that native families and communities should definitely be given priority.

WHAT ARE THE ADVANTAGES AND DISADVANTAGES OF BEING ADOPTED BY A FAMILY OF A DIFFERENT RACE?

I think unless the family has a real stable base the identity piece can be really conflicted depending on how the parents address it with the child. I can only speak from experience and knowing from an early age that I was Native American was only beneficial to me. That's why I think honesty is the best policy . . . having openness about who children are. I've done a little bit of reading and a little bit of research on this and everything that I read is so negative. It's negative in the sense that Native adoptees have high rates of mental illness or just a lot of long-term problems. I have to say that I feel very blessed. I don't know if it was just destiny or what, but this couldn't have gone any better.

WHAT FACTORS SHOULD BE TAKEN INTO CONSIDERATION WHEN PLACING A NATIVE CHILD?

I think the situation of the family. The family should be given first consideration given their stability and what they can offer the child. If that's not possible, I think the child still needs to go to somebody within that tribal community. If not somebody in that tribal community, maybe somebody in that tribe who is willing to take that child wherever they are. I think culture is just so important and that's something that I miss on a daily basis. It's the cultural aspect that I missed and I'm trying to learn right now.

Do you think that you've been successful in trying to learn?

I've never had any illusions that I would be totally Indian and know everything. I would be setting myself up for failure if I did that because it doesn't give a true appreciation for the family that I grew up with and that culture as well. I truly believe that if you have multiple cultures and multiple identities that it's not a bad thing. I think that being adaptable and having that fluid kind of identity is a good thing. Some people might see it as a bad thing, but it's truly been wonderful for me. I feel like I don't have to choose or partition off myself. It's all part of me and I would not change anything.

Do you have any advice or suggestions for non-Native families that would want to or have adopted Native children?

Definitely be open to that child's culture. Expose them as much as you possibly can. Be open with them. Let them know. I think so many adoptees feel different anyway. There's always that why do I feel different? If you nurture that to say that although it's a different culture, it's not a bad thing and you have the right to know that. And I think that's one thing parents need to know is that they have a right to know. They shouldn't be in opposition of that.

Is there anything else I should have asked you?

One thing I wanted to address is that my mother did die when I was seven and I did know about her my whole life and one thing that has affected me highly is never knowing her. It's a deep sadness that I've always had. It's always been painful as though I knew her when she was alive because she was alive for me. I knew her in my mind and I knew her from family and everything so mourning that loss was pretty painful for me. I don't think people realize that or understand it, but for other adoptees and other people who might be in the same situation you do have that right to grieve as deeply as everybody else does even if you don't know them. I say that because my biological father passed away about a month ago and I'm going through a lot of grieving right now and it's really difficult. Although I only knew him for eight years, he loved me and I loved him and he gave me everything that he could from his heart and I am so thankful for the time that we had. It was so important to me. It doesn't diminish anything that I've had with anybody else in my family. It's just as hard for me as if it were one of my adoptive parents who had gone.

WHAT DID YOUR BIOLOGICAL MOTHER'S FAMILY DO TO GIVE YOU A SENSE OF WHO SHE WAS?

They were very open. They would come and see me and I would go see them. They just shared stories and talked. They treated me like a member of the family. And that's what both families did. They never treated me like an outsider. They treated me like a family member who came back.

4

# VERONICA ROSE DAHMEN

Veronica Rose Dahmen (Chippewa) was born in St. Paul, Minnesota, in 1962 and lived with her biological mother Cathee Dahmen until she was almost a year old. According to Veronica, her grandmother placed her for adoption while her seventeen-year-old mother was at school. She notes that this decision caused a rift between the two that compelled her mother to flee to Rhode Island to live with her uncle, acclaimed Native artist George Morrison. While living with her uncle, Cathee was discovered by an illustrator for the *New York Times* and signed by a modeling agency. She appeared on the cover of several magazines including *Harper's Bazaar* and *Vogue*. Coincidentally, Veronica told a reporter for the *Princeton Union-Eagle* that she grew up reading these magazines and even found copies of some of these issues in her own personal collection.

While her biological mother made a name for herself in New York City and abroad, Veronica was placed in foster care for more than two years until she was adopted by a white couple who raised her and her adopted sister in an upper-middle class neighborhood. Veronica describes her experience as a transracial adoptee as "very, very positive." She notes that her adoptive parents were "very kind, very loving, and very nurturing" and says that they "loved [her] just as if [she] was truly born to them."

With the support of her adoptive family, Veronica began the search for her biological family when she was eighteen years old; however, she failed to make a connection until 2002 when her half-sister, Sarah, responded to a message that Veronica had posted on the Internet. After several phone conversations, the two sisters reunited in Washington, D.C., while Veronica was on a business trip. According to Veronica, she was warmly accepted by both her mother's and her father's families; unfortunately, she never got the chance to meet her mother or her father because both had already passed.

Although Veronica has been embraced by her biological family, she feels that the Minnesota-Chippewa tribal council has "slammed the door in [her] face." According to Veronica, she applied for tribal membership in 2003, shortly after reuniting with her birth family. To her surprise, she was told that she was enrolled in 1992 and entitled to $20,000 in back per-capita payments. When Veronica tried to collect, she was told by the tribal council that her enrollment was "in error." As a result, she was given a new enrollment number and told that her enrollment date had been changed to July 2003, which made her ineligible for the $20,000.

This experience combined with the gratitude she feels toward her adoptive parents has heavily influenced Veronica's opinion of transracial adoption. She says that she is "all for it as long as adoptive parents" allow their adopted children to "nurture" their cultural interests.

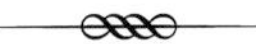

WHAT YEAR WERE YOU BORN IN?

I was born in 1962.

AND WHERE WERE YOU BORN?

In Saint Paul, Minnesota. In Ramsey County, across the river.

AND AT WHAT AGE WERE YOU ADOPTED?

I believe I was almost, you know, a little over three years old. My birth mother kept me for almost a full year and then I was adopted out. By the time I think I was adopted into the new family—to the adopted family, I was about three-and-a-half.

AND WERE YOU WITH FOSTER CARE OR WAS IT WITH YOUR BIOLOGICAL FAMILY FIRST AND THEN YOUR ADOPTED FAMILY?

Birth mother until just before I turned a year old, and then I believe it had to have been foster care and then I was adopted out.

AND DID YOUR ADOPTIVE PARENTS EVER INDICATE WHY THEY ADOPTED YOU?

They did. Both my adopted parents are very strong Catholic and my adopted mother had two miscarriages where she decided that she would adopt two to make up the two that she had lost. And she adopted my older sister, an adopted sister, and then I was the second child.

AND IS YOUR ADOPTED SISTER TRANSRACIALLY ADOPTED AS WELL? IS SHE FROM A DIFFERENT RACE?

No, she's not. She's Irish.

AND DID YOUR PARENTS SPECIFICALLY REQUEST AN AMERICAN-INDIAN CHILD OR DID—OR WERE THEY AWARE OF YOUR BACKGROUND WHEN THEY ADOPTED YOU?

I believe that they were aware of my background. I don't think that that was their intent to pursue a Native American child. I think it is just the way the pieces fell into play.

AND YOU SAID IN AN INTERVIEW THAT YOU MET YOUR BIOLOGICAL FAMILY SEVERAL YEARS AGO. DID THEY REVEAL TO YOU ANYTHING ABOUT YOUR SITUATION BEFORE YOU GOT PLACED FOR ADOPTION?

They did. My situation with my birth mother was that she was the fourth daughter who had had a child out of wedlock in her early teens. By the time the fourth child had given birth, which was my mother—my birth mother—my grandmother was already helping the other sisters, who would be my aunts, and from what I understand, I was told that my grandmother was a *Native American Visionary* and she foresaw great things happen to my birth mother. So after giving birth to me—my birth mother came home with me. This was NOT her intent at first as she had planned on adopting me out. Once I was born she changed her mind and kept me for almost a year, but then it was my grandmother who is actually responsible for adopting me out. My mother went to the school (High School) one day and came home and her mother told my mother that she had adopted me out, and that it was the best thing for her. This was not a decision that my birth mother made. It was the decision that my grandmother made on behalf of my birth mother.

And that angered my mother and she then, in turn, moved out of the state of Minnesota to Rhode Island, which is where she lived with my uncle George (George Morrison) and that's how she became discovered as a huge fashion model. She happened to be in the right place at the right time.

So I guess, yes, I did learn a little bit when I did meet with my biological family. With my mother having passed in 1997, I didn't get the opportunity to be able to go over in detail why things have happened the way that they did, but I was able to get all of my answers, or so I think.

AND HOW DO YOU THINK THAT HAS CHANGED YOU? OR HAS IT?

It has changed me a great deal. I feel more complete, more relaxed on my answers as to why things have happened the way they did. I definitely look in the mirror differently now, because all my life, I—being raised in a white world, I looked in the mirror and saw a white child.

After I was reunited with my first family and got to know my culture, I realized that I am a Native American person and that I should be familiar and get to know what my culture is and that has all kind of come around, and it has been a very easy process of coming around. It is like this falls in place substantially for me.

AND SO WHAT RESOURCES OR EVENTS OR PEOPLE HAVE HELPED YOU ADOPT THAT IDENTITY OR ENHANCE THAT IDENTITY?

Getting to know my first family and listening to them, and watching them and attending the powwow with them. I attended my first powwow on the first year I was reunited—that happened in November of 2002—and attended one this last August in 2005.

And this last one that I attended, I attended it with my husband, and he wasn't familiar too much with the native culture as well, but I think he got a great deal out of being there and experiencing it for the first time and watching me experience it because it is a part of my culture. And then I'm hoping next year in August that my two daughters will join me.

AND WHAT WAS YOUR INITIAL REACTION TO THE POWWOW COMPARED TO LATER ON? WHAT WERE YOUR INITIAL THOUGHTS?

Wow, it was overwhelming. The regalia and the spiritual dancing effects—and I had never attended one. So this was just absolutely incredible to breathe in and experience so many things that I had never seen before, and I think that's why the second time that I attended, it was a lot more comfortable.

I've not danced. I don't know when the time will come that I will, but I—I know that I will in my heart eventually someday get out there. It's just a matter of getting up the nerve and trying on your cultural shoes and going for it. It's hard to explain. I know it will eventually come, but it is just a matter of—I still feel really white, you know—and try to experience it all.

DID YOUR BIOLOGICAL FAMILY ENCOURAGE YOU TO TRY AGAIN IN ATTENDING THE POWWOW?

It was—the first time I attended the powwow, it was really—they kind of—I wouldn't say all circled around me, but I think they were observing how I would react, because there were certainly a lot of family members standing around with me as I was watching for the first time.

And, you know, of course, I had to ask so many questions about what's the difference between the fancy shawl and traditional, and the jingle dresses and—because I've never seen, I didn't know that there were going to be different categories of dancing and all their dancers and how it is lined up with.

The veterans come out and they do an honorary to all of the veterans that are present and past. So I actually needed an interpreter actually for me to explain what was going to happen next so that I wasn't—I guess, I wasn't shocked or—you know, stood back and wondered why this was happening this way.

It was nice to have family around because—and also in a way to—when—because they do this event at noon and then 4:00 and then the following day, they do the same.

After I had seen it at noon and then saw it again at 4:00 and then I believe they do it again at 7:00 with the entire process all over again.

I was a little bit more comfortable with seeing it replayed over and over again where I was able to sit back and ask different family members questions.

I think it hit me one time when I asked one of my cousins if she had ever been out there and participated in it and she had explained to me that her grandmother—or what should be our grandmother, which she is referring to the one that adopted me out—had made her jingle dress costume or fancy shawl or regalia.

And it dawned on me that I didn't get anything like that. It just—you know, when you go through all these emotions that you think—I got the boot, and she got, you know, a nice fancy jingle dress. So I guess it is a time where you stop and think there were so many things that you've lost out on.

WHAT ARE YOUR FEELINGS TOWARD YOUR GRANDMOTHER?

That's hard to say. I know what she was trying to do was more in my best interest. I have a very hard time when I listen to all of the cousins talk about how much they loved her, and she loved them so much and they—and I just feel like this woman was the woman that was responsible for my fate. I have no feelings in my heart when it comes to her.

And in a way, I don't know if it was that she didn't think I was good enough to be in the family, but I don't know.

I just don't really have any warm fuzzies toward her mainly because I think she was the one that was responsible for decision making and the fate of my life.

WELL, LET'S GO AHEAD AND MOVE BACK A LITTLE BIT AND TALK ABOUT YOUR ADOPTED FAMILY. I MEAN, WHAT IS YOUR OPINION OF YOUR ADOPTED FAMILY? DID YOU HAVE A POSITIVE EXPERIENCE OR A NEGATIVE EXPERIENCE GROWING UP?

Very, very positive experience. Very positive, very loving, and very kind. I've participated in a Native American adoption group and have heard the horrible situations that other adoptees went through, and I just have to sit back and close my eyes and think.

It was such a fortunate situation for me to be placed into the adopted family that I was because they were very kind, very loving and very nurturing. And were very attentive and always cared about what was going on in my life and always kept me happy and healthy and loved me just as if I was truly born to them.

So it was a very, very positive experience and one that I do know that was for the better for me.

SO WHEN DID YOU COME TO KNOW THAT YOU WERE ADOPTED?

I think I was about five or six. I saw a birth certificate and I saw the name baby Veronica.

Now, I don't really recall what year it was or exactly how old I was, but I'm thinking it had to have been around first or second grade, between that era.

And I had picked up the birth certificate on the dining room table and asked, "Who is this baby Veronica?" And it made my adopted mother a little uncomfortable, where she managed to, you know, look at me. I gave it back to her and she just kind of—kind of sluffed it off like it wasn't anybody that I would know, but I had a feeling that that was me that was being referred to.

And then I had heard my sister and my mother talking about it. And I came in on the conversation and that's when she had to kind of explain to me that I wasn't really born to her, that I am adopted.

And the way she made it sound is that she didn't make it seem like it was a bad thing. She made it seem like I was picked out of all of the other girls. That she picked me, and other families don't have that choice.

So I guess that kind of—she always tried to make a negative turn out to be such a positive, where she left me with this feeling that I was so special that I was handpicked. That's basically how it came to be that I knew that I was adopted.

AND THE WAY IN WHICH YOUR MOTHER HANDLED THAT SITUATION, IS THAT THE WAY IN WHICH YOU THINK MOST ADOPTED PARENTS SHOULD HANDLE THAT SITUATION WHEN THEY ARE EXPLAINING TO THEIR CHILDREN THAT THEY WERE ADOPTED?

I guess it depends on each situation. Mine, because of this strong background and the love that they gave me—that wasn't an issue. Whereas if I was not given a lot of love and very insecure, you know—I guess it depends on the situation.

I guess I would like to see all adoptees be placed into perfect homes just like I was. However, I know that that's not always the case. But I guess being honest when they do find out and trying to turn the negative into a positive is probably my idea of the best way to handle things.

OKAY. I WANT TO TALK A LITTLE BIT MORE ABOUT YOUR CHILDHOOD. CAN YOU DESCRIBE TO ME THE TYPE OF PLACE THAT YOU LIVED, THE TYPE OF NEIGHBORHOOD YOU GREW UP IN? WAS IT MOSTLY WHITE OR WAS IT MIXED RACE?

It was a very nice upper-middle-class neighborhood in a suburb of South Minneapolis. I lived just a couple of blocks away from Minnehaha Creek, and the main road was Chicago Avenue and on the east side of Chicago Avenue was your upper-middle-class white Caucasian families with integrated, transracial families.

The west side of Chicago Avenue was pretty much the bad side of Minneapolis. Crime rate was pretty high and it was—I would say I wouldn't have any idea what the percentages of people who lived there, but there were very mixed families in that particular area.

And everybody on the west side, you could kind of tell that, you know, upper-middle class is the east side. So there was a very prominent dividing line.

The thing was that they—you had to pass through the west side to get to the east side from my school. So there were a couple of times where I had been picked on, on the way home.

Because I walked home by myself, and I can recall some really uncomfortable circumstances running into kids that would pick on me, and at one time I recall it was pretty familiar, beating me up. But I think that was something that pretty much all neighborhoods go through with certain intercity periods.

NOW, DID THEY PICK ON YOU BECAUSE YOU LOOKED WEIRD OR—

They did—they did. They picked on me because I was a white girl, but you know, not knowing inside I was actually Native American and—

I mean, I've just realized within the last couple of years that, you know, the African Americans refer to themselves as being discriminated against, but percentages of Native Americans are so much greater that the discrimination there is hardly even recognized because it doesn't show up that much as a statistic.

DID YOU ENCOUNTER ANY AMERICAN INDIANS GROWING UP?

I did—I did. It seemed like there were always issues with them though whether or not it happened to be shopping in downtown Minneapolis and you run into them—they'd run around in an alcohol or some kind of a drug-induced stupor. I did not have any Native American friends growing up. All of them were mainly all white Caucasian.

WELL, LET ME GO BACK TO THE SCHOOLS YOU ATTENDED. YOU SAID THAT THEY WERE MOSTLY WHITE, CORRECT?

Right.

AND YOU SAID THAT YOU INTERACTED MOSTLY WITH CAUCASIAN STUDENTS. HOW DO YOU THINK THAT SHAPED YOUR CULTURAL IDENTITY?

That's how I saw myself as being white, is through my friends. Because they were the ideal preppy little white girls. And I felt the same way because I was surrounded by that, when growing up. I guess, I realized I was different because when we'd go on an outing to the lake, they would burn from the sunshine and mine—I could turn into a very dark tan within a couple of days.

And that's, I guess, when I realized that, I mean, I knew it was nice having a very dark brown hair, almost black, that it was—must be a cultural thing. But then again, my sister who is Irish that I was raised with, my adopted sister, Connie, she was also a very dark brunette.

So, we—people actually thought we were sisters. I mean, real sisters, even though we knew inside we weren't biologically related. We did not have a common feature, you know, with each other.

But yeah, my friends were pretty much the ones that influenced my feeling toward myself as I was growing up.

Now, teachers, certain teachers—I had always attended Catholic private schools up until ninth grade. Then I went to a public school. But in the

Catholic private schools that I attended I noticed that the teachers reacted toward me differently than they did to the other students. I was—

DO YOU THINK THAT WAS BECAUSE OF YOUR PHYSICAL APPEARANCE?

I think it was. I really do. And I hate to say that a—you would think that a Catholic nun would react like that. But I can recall certain Catholic nuns that were responsible for, you know, my parochial learning that she reacted differently to different ethnicity in our—in my grade, than the average blond white girl.

DO YOU THINK THAT YOU COULD GIVE AN EXAMPLE?

Being picked last for things, or being given a specific role and whether it be in some sort of a skit or play or musical or anything that has something to do with a coveted-type part. And it just wasn't in the cards for me and I just didn't ever really know why. I hadn't a clue.

But I did see her play favoritism, or I did see a couple of teachers play favoritism toward specific students, and they were the local blond-haired, very good students, that would happen to be a white girl.

SO, HOW WOULD YOU DESCRIBE YOUR CLOSEST FRIENDS, TODAY?

Still pretty close with some of my friends from high school. Lost track of some of the ones that I—you know, that helped me build my mold of who I was.

I have friends, of course, that you've made acquaintances later on in life, and actually have coworkers that are friends, and it's a different feeling being—actually recognizing what your culture is.

Because, it's a process where you don't have to be ashamed of who you are. They accept you for whoever or whatever you are, which is the way I think it should be.

AND HOW INVOLVED WOULD YOU SAY THAT YOU ARE WITH THE NATIVE AMERICAN COMMUNITY NOW?

I wouldn't say I am as involved as I would like to be. There are some issues that I have to work out with my own tribal affiliation which has to do with an enrollment issue.

ARE YOU AN ENROLLED MEMBER OF YOUR TRIBE?

I am enrolled. I have been enrolled—I was found by my sister, by birth, my half-sister, on my birth mother's side in November of 2002. Yeah, it's just been almost three years. Or a little over three years.

However, my tribal affiliation has me registered in 1992, which seemed odd that—I didn't even realize I was enrolled until 2002.

I mean, that is a big difference in years. I mean, it's over ten years. I had no idea I was enrolled, and of course, along with enrollment does come some benefits from being enrolled.

So when I first went to my tribe just to let them know that I would like to gain enrollment, they saw my name and they said, you've been enrolled since 1992.

And they said that there would be some per capita due under that, tribal enrollment number from that date. And then, they had to make some decisions on that and they eventually made a decision that they gave me a new enrollment date of 2002.

And my question was, how has my blood changed between 1992 and 2002? Other than it should be a dollar value thing because they just don't want to pay out what was rightfully due to me.

So, by changing the date from 1992 to 2002, you lost the financial benefits?

Right, right. Which was not a great deal of money, but for me it was a substantial amount. It would have been somewhere in the dollar value of around $20,000, which is a great deal. So I just don't know how other nations can make their own rule like that, when it comes to situations like this.

Because it's for me, I feel like I have tried all my life, you know, once I found out when I was, you know, when I got my background information when I turned eighteen, and realized that I was truly Native American.

I had been trying since the time I turned eighteen to find my birth mother, and I also tried to seek tribal enrollment with the correct tribal affiliate that I was—that I first should have been, you know, affiliated with and because of the closed adoption laws, I never was able to get anywhere.

And then, once I did finally get the keys handed to me, it's like I walked up to the door, knocked on the door of the tribe, and it was slammed in my face.

So, your question about am I very affiliated with the tribe, with my Native American tribal, it has left a sour taste in my mouth of trying to get to know—almost pretty much put up a block because I want to be welcome, but I don't feel welcome. So many Native American adoptees encounter these types of resistances.

And you just do not feel welcomed by your tribe or by Native Americans, in general?

I just don't feel welcomed by my tribal council members. Everyone else, family, Native Americans in general, yeah, I sense a belonging there. But I just don't feel the love with the tribal council, which I think is the common way for tribal council members to behave.

So, how do you think that has affected your sense of Native American identity?

It's almost made me feel ashamed of how they can get away with what they can. Because truly enough—nothing is changed with my bloodline from 1992 to the date that they gave me a *new* date. And the way that they react toward adoptees, that by right should be home, is atrocious.

I just don't understand. But the thing is that I don't need them to help frame up my culture, because I've got a good family background, with my birth family helping me and guiding me, and it's very comfortable and they are always there for me.

Did your birth family encourage you to explore your Native American identity when you were growing up? The Native American culture, did they encourage you to—

My adopted family?

Yes.

No. I had no experience with the Native American culture whatsoever growing up, other than Halloween, where I once was an Indian. And I dressed up like a Native American princess, or a squaw. And went to a Halloween dance party and that was pretty much the extent of my experience of my culture.

Do you know why your adoptive parents never chose to expose you to Native American culture at all?

I think, because the mindset was that I am not. That I am white just like them. And they didn't know anything about the Native American culture, or know anybody who was Native American.

So it was just the best thing to—just be—practice what they knew, I guess.

Do you ever wish that you were exposed to that, at a younger age?

I do. I do. I do know that. And when I went to private Catholic school we did study Native Americans and I did retain a lot of information about that culture, while learning, and to this day I still recall a lot of information that I learned in my eighth grade cultural class.

And knew about wampum and certain bands of Native Americans and where they are located throughout the United States. And I did take a good, you know, a liking to learning about that culture, and it was very helpful and it fills in now because with learning my culture, I still remember back on what I was taught and what I absorbed in my education.

How do you think your opinion of Native Americans has changed since learning that you yourself are a Native American?

My opinion is that they are a culture that is very beautiful and everyone should know something about the Native American culture.

It's hard to explain, but there are so many instances where I just feel like they've just gotten the shaft. And being raised white for forty years and all of a sudden when I look in the mirror, I see myself as a different person.

It angers me to see the way things happened within our own Government. For instance, with this great big, the most notorious case in federal government history, transpiring right as we speak. *Eloise Cobell v. United States.*

She's the one that helped expose the mishandling of the Indian Trust Fund(s), I don't know if you are familiar with that, but, working for the federal government, I had the opportunity to meet Eloise Cobell in the spring of 2004.

And listening to her speak, you just get a sense that the federal government has, in the United States, has just really given the shaft to the Native American people. And it's almost to a point that you just get so angry that in today's society, to think that people can get away with that.

I mean, how these cases drag on and on and on. I'm thinking it's been about six or seven years now that the case has just been playing out, and it's amazing. I am wondering exactly when is it going to get resolved?

Because it seems to me the longer it gets dragged out, the longer we're—the United States just keeps throwing it to the Native American people. I hate to get political—

No, that's fine.

You know, like I said, it is hard because I've been raised white for so long and then now I see a different person in the mirror, and that person cares about how Native American people have been treated.

Whereas, three years ago, yeah, you know, I would have known, yeah, I think I am, I am pretty sure I am. But, since I know nothing about it, it's like I am turning the other cheek—which the whole reunion process has brought me to, you know, to care a great deal about what happens to my people.

DO YOU THINK THAT THE THINGS THAT YOU HAVE LEARNED SINCE YOU DISCOVERED THAT YOU ARE NATIVE AMERICAN IN ANY WAY CLASHES WITH THE THINGS YOU'VE LEARNED ABOUT NATIVE AMERICANS, WHEN YOU WERE GROWING UP?

I don't think so. Not really no, I am—there are some things that I—they absolutely—the way that I've always known the culture to be, that it's very beautiful and they are very caring people.

UH-HUH.

But I guess, with that I know also comes problems with, you know, socioeconomic levels.

That you know that they have poverty, and there's issues with alcoholism and drug use. I mean, it's sad, but I guess I've know that as a white girl, and I see it even more as being Native American.

And we—I see it in different depths of why it is the way that it is. They are very oppressed and—but not every Native American is like that.

I think it's a matter of exposure and if that's all they know, then that's how they're going to be raised and that's how they're going to end up turning out to be.

In my case, I was raised in a very loving home, and I didn't have to resort to or turn to drugs. Not that I didn't. I mean I had my dabblings because people do that in high school. But I had sense enough and more value, self-worth value, to know that that's not what I want to do. There were other things of more importance for me.

It's what some people are doing, but you know, it does not interest me that much. I mean, it was always there, that road was always there if I decided that I wanted to take it. But I didn't, because it's all a matter of how strong you are inside.

AND SO WOULD YOU ATTRIBUTE THAT STRENGTH TO YOUR ADOPTIVE FAMILY?

Definitely would attribute that strength to my adoptive family and their nurturing and the care on how I turned out.

I'D LIKE TO TALK ABOUT YOUR ADOPTIVE SISTER AS WELL. DO YOU THINK THAT HAVING A SISTER WHO WAS ADOPTED HELPED YOU OUT?

Yeah, I do. I do think having an adopted sister helped me out, you know, a great deal.

SO HOW DO YOU THINK HAVING AN ADOPTIVE SISTER HELPED YOU OUT?

She gave me strength, I know, being an older sister. She was my older sister and she gave me the guidance and the experience of what it was like to have a sister would be. Always very positive; she and I are still very close. She, being adopted as well, has seen me through the process of being reunited.

I don't think that she thinks that the reunion process will ever happen for her, although I think she would like it to. It's just a scary situation of what you're going to find. And in my case, I found out a lot.

HOW DID YOUR ADOPTIVE PARENTS FEEL ABOUT YOUR DECISION TO LOOK FOR YOUR BIOLOGICAL FAMILY?

They weren't really involved in it. I, again, started when I was eighteen. I have somewhere in the amount of—I'd say maybe twenty-six letters of attempts, responses from my adoption agency. Each time saying that we'd like to help, but we can't, because of the closed adoption laws.

You know, it was so hard trying to get any answers and I tried, you know, numerous times to try to get information, but always, you know, held back because of the adoption laws.

Not that I didn't try. I did try many times, but wasn't successful until the day and age of the Internet had become available. And then I ended up searching on an adoption search board, which is how my half-sister Sarah found me.

AND SHE CONTACTED YOU?

Yes, she contacted me.

AND WHAT WAS YOUR INITIAL MEETING LIKE?

She called me up on the phone at work and blew me away, because it had been a phone call I'd been waiting to hear forever. And it happened on a Monday before Thanksgiving. I will never forget that call.

DID YOU MAKE ARRANGEMENTS TO MEET YOUR BIOLOGICAL FAMILY RIGHT AWAY, AFTER THAT PHONE CALL?

No, we—I think in that process you kind of feel-out for the first three or four phone calls. "Are you really who I'm looking for?"

But I had a three-page document that was provided to me by the adoption agency when I turned eighteen that gave me some biological background information, which I can certainly fax to you, if you would like to use it or see it.

It names absolutely nobody in particular. It's just says, at the time of your birth, your mother had a sibling who was X-aged, a sister that was this age, another sister that was this age.

So it was very evident that I was with the right family because I actually faxed that information to my half-sister. And when she got it, she realized that this was truly the right person that she was looking for.

We did make plans. I happened to be out on business at Washington, D.C., that particular January. And they live in Manhattan and White Plains, New York, and they drove from New York down to D.C. to visit me for the first time and then—we didn't actually meet until January.

AND DID YOU JUST MEET YOUR SISTER OR DID YOU MEET THE ENTIRE EXTENDED FAMILY, OR—

I met my half-sister who found me and I met my other half-sister. My birth mother had me first and then she had my sister Sarah, who found me and then she had, through another marriage which was her last marriage, she had another daughter and then a son. So I met just the two of the family members. And I didn't actually get to meet the son, my younger brother until that following June, I believe it was. I had gone out to New York to visit and I haven't seen him since then.

IS THERE A REASON THAT YOU HAVEN'T STAYED IN TOUCH OR THEY HAVEN'T STAYED IN TOUCH?

Oh, we stay in touch all the time.

YOU JUST DON'T SEE EACH OTHER FACE TO FACE?

Yeah. It's the distance and busyness in everybody's life. It's bad, because I would love to be able to see them more, but time for my job and my family and trying to get on the airplane and get out and see them, you know, plus the cost of New York is so much.

HAVE YOU MET YOUR FAMILY FROM YOUR BIOLOGICAL FATHER'S SIDE?

I have. I actually met them that following spring. They came up from Kansas City and my aunt came from Oregon, and we met at the White Earth Reservation that my birth father was enrolled in, and I drove up to see them.

AND SO YOU HAVE NEVER MET YOUR BIOLOGICAL FATHER OR YOUR BIOLOGICAL MOTHER? BOTH OF THEM HAVE PASSED?

Yeah.

AND HOW DO YOU FEEL ABOUT THAT?

It's bad. I wish that I had the opportunity to be able to meet them. But I'm—I think that there's a reason why it happened the way that it did.

I think that I would be very angry with a lot of the answers that I would probably have to hear from them and I don't know. They're both gone. And I have heard some stories of their pain they both must have experienced missing out on me being in their life. There's no obstacles in the way, other than the pain and the sense of what you missed out on.

My birth father never told anyone about me other than his older sister, shortly before he died. There are no stories to uncover hearing about how he missed me. Unlike the stories I hear about on my birth mother's side.

I WANT TO FOCUS A LITTLE BIT MORE ON YOUR LIFE AS AN ADULT. WHERE DID YOU ATTEND COLLEGE?

I didn't go to college.

WHEN WE TALKED INITIALLY, YOU MENTIONED THAT YOU WERE MARRIED. CAN YOU TELL ME A LITTLE BIT ABOUT YOUR HUSBAND? FOR EXAMPLE, HIS CULTURAL BACKGROUND AND PROFESSION?

He is of Russian descent, and in the blue-collar work field, or work force. He is an operation foreman for Clear Channel, which is one of the largest entertainment venues worldwide, I believe it is, so he's got a pretty good position there, construction, professional, foreman-type position.

AND HAS HE SUPPORTED YOUR DECISION TO EMBRACE YOUR NATIVE ROOTS?

Yes, he has. At first the search, to find answers to start was really expensive, and we could never afford it, and later on when we could afford it, I had given up hope that anyone was or would be looking for me. I gave up the hope and let it go for many years and out of the blue I got my phone call from my half sister, Sarah. So he has been supportive, but in a way that he would not want me to become hurt from things I discovered. Our lives have changed a great deal since I have come home to my biological family. I am being pulled away down a path I have always wanted to discover and be part of, at times, he is not always on the same path.

AND DO YOU AND YOUR HUSBAND HAVE CHILDREN?

We have two daughters, yeah. They are both graduated from college, and both on their own. They live together, actually. They are both in professional fields that they pursued educationwise and doing very good.

AND ARE THEY ENROLLED MEMBERS OF YOUR TRIBE?

They are not. They should be, but they are not. There have been discrepancies, blood quantum on my dad's side of the family which I think if we could get that corrected they would be able to become enrolled. Unfortunately, it's just too much to fight, and my whole coming home to my tribe was not a very welcoming experience, not at all. I was actually enrolled somehow in 1992. Now keep in mind I was not found by my birth family until the year 2002, but somehow I had been enrolled for eleven years, and I had no idea that I was enrolled.

So you can imagine when I did try to go up to Grand Portage which is Chippewa and my tribal affiliate, I went to them to try to become enrolled and they took one look at my name and they said that I was enrolled. And I had been considered what they call a long lost member. Their intention was that there was money held under that, that enrollment number, since you know, back in 1992. And shortly after they told me that they had made a ruling that they had thought that that was an error, and then they—the good thing was that that they were going to give me a new enrollment number with—which meant all of that money that had been, you know, saved or calculated into that old enrollment number was no longer going to be available to me.

So like I said coming home was not that positive. I mean, I got enrolled, but I just don't see where my blood is any different between now and 1992, and back in, you know, when I was born. It's been a struggle, I have not felt like I've been completely embraced by my tribe. I felt that they have been very suspicious of their own, which I think is a pretty, you know, common trait with tribal leaders. I don't know if you are familiar with that or not. But it seems to be a pretty familiar trait that they don't welcome in band members that should be able to enrolled, and should be entitled to be enrolled.

SO, HAVE THEY BEEN VERY SUSPICIOUS OF YOUR DAUGHTERS AS WELL?

No, I think once I got in they didn't go through the process where I had to prove that they were actually my daughters, but, you know, it's just that feeling like all my life that's what I wanted to do, was be enrolled, and be a tribal member of my tribal affiliates that I should belong to, and it's almost to me if I had to describe it, it would be like going up and knocking on the door of your home, and having the door slammed in your face, because it just was not a very welcoming positive experience whatsoever.

Now, my uncle who is a very famous Native American artist, George Morrison, who was one of the main featured artists—when they opened up the Smithsonian out in Washington, D.C., in December of 2004. I marched with my tribe during that first nation procession when they had that opening back in September. Marched with my band members, and I marched with my immediate family, and I did not get any reception whatsoever from my tribal bandleaders, from Grand Portage. Now you would think that having George being honored in the way that he was, that it would be a very happy time, but I swear when I walked through that march, through that procession, I felt like I was just getting daggers on my back, because I almost felt as if they were thinking, why are you even here? You know what I mean? I just felt like I wasn't welcomed to be there at home.

WHAT WAS YOUR FAMILY'S REACTION TO YOUR TRIBE'S REACTION TO YOU?

I think familywise it was very positive. I think everybody in my birth side of the family was very happy that I was finally enrolled and acknowledged. As for tribal affiliates, like tribal council members, like I said, I had to fight tooth and nail to become enrolled after I had already been enrolled, and felt like fighting it, and, you know, that would entail going through the tribal court process, and I just lost all the energy to try to fight, because it hurt so much to feel like I wasn't welcomed when I knew all along I should have been, you know, back in 1962 when I was born I had every right to be a registered band member then, and it took me until I was little over forty years old to become enrolled, and once I did become enrolled it was a process that I would not wish on anyone.

WAS YOUR BIRTH FAMILY AWARE OF THE MANNER IN WHICH YOU WERE BEING TREATED BY TRIBAL LEADERS?

They were. Yeah, they were, and the sad thing is that some of them live on the reservation and some of them don't. The ones that don't were very understanding and felt really bad at the way things were going and knew that it was a money issue. They (Tribe) did not want to pay that money that they said they were owing to me because, I don't know, maybe just they thought that they would get away with it again like they have before. I don't know. But the ones that lived on the reservation and currently still do felt not like making a lot of noise about it because they still have to live there. Well, it's an injustice that I just think happens on reservations day-in and day-out, and I just don't see how they could rule that way but they did. How do they sleep at night?

Do you want to talk a little bit more about your husband and your children? Did your children want to be enrolled in the tribe? Was that something that they themselves decided?

I think I would like them to be enrolled more than they would. They are not familiar with the culture. They have not attended any of the powwows that I have attended. They have an interest in it, but I think their age that they are at right now, which are twenty and twenty-two, that if they are not still focused on what a great possibility that would be for them, you know, to enrich their lives, I just don't think that they realize it right now. Maybe someday in time they will, but I think right now my wish is that they would be able to be enrolled.

You know, my birth father had the wrong blood quantum written down on his birth certificate. He was a foster child too, and as far as I've been told by his sister that he was—there was an error on his blood quantum which would make an error in my blood quantum, which would make me more than what I am in—on paper, which would also entitle both my daughters to be enrolled. But trying to go through that fight like I've done with the enrollment date, trying to get that resolved with my birth father just seems like it would be banging my head against the wall. It's futile since he is no longer alive.

How have you addressed the issue of cultural identity with your children?

I just think it kind of evolved, you know, I went to the powwow for the first time, and came back and felt more in tune and more enriched by what I saw, and what I had lived up there, and just being able to, you know, be with my birth family and celebrate the powwow with them and see their grand entry for the first time, and coming home and explaining it to them, and then I went back again—not immediately the following year, but, you know, I had a gap in years for attendance, and the second time I went my husband attended with me, and he really enjoyed it. So I think it's a matter of kind of cushioning them and explaining it to them in great detail and talking about it first, and then actually letting them see it, feel it for the first time because they have an idea of what they are going to be expecting, I find myself making comparisons to culture almost daily with what my culture is, and that I am proud to be an American Indian, and it's just—I don't know, like I said it's something I think that just evolves. I am more in tune with it now since I have been found by my birth family than I was five, six years ago when I still looked in the mirror and saw a white girl. Well, it's different now.

The first time I visited my birth mother's grave, located in Grand Marais, I was with my Aunt Barb. She showed me where Cathee was buried, along with other family members; my grandmother and Uncle George. She unwrapped a cigarette so that the tobacco was free, and told me to present an offering of the tobacco by sprinkling it over all the graves. I was shocked at this suggestion, because my mom died of emphysema from smoking. But this was one of the first Native American traditions I was not familiar with. Now I bring tobacco each time I visit the graves.

HAVE YOUR HUSBAND AND CHILDREN MET YOUR BIRTH FAMILY?

They have. They have met members on both sides of my birth mother's side and my birth father's side, and they absolutely adore everybody on both sides of the family. I get calls frequently from both sides, both family members.

HAVE THEY VISITED YOUR RESERVATION?

My husband and I have been there. My two daughters have not yet. I think mainly because the annual weekend which is the rendezvous weekend which is the powwow of the reservation, happens to fall on the same weekend as something that we have done annually for the last twenty-three years. So every weekend—I think it's the second weekend in August, we've always attended the little county fair where my husband's side of the family, and my adoptive parents live up in that little community, so year after year we've always attended the county fair up there, so—since they've done that, you know, for years, it's a tradition for them, so this is quite different to ask them to give that up and come to the reservation because they are not that familiar with what they are going to be getting into over in the reservation, so—and what all the festival and the powwow will entail.

WHAT WAS YOUR AND YOUR HUSBAND'S INITIAL REACTION TO THE RESERVATION?

My initial reaction was that it was absolutely beautiful. It's very well maintained. I have been on some reservations where they're cluttered, you know, very definitely looking like it's poverty-ridden, there's not a lot of money that each family has to maintain their dwelling and keep up their yard and their pets and that. But no, Grand Portage is absolutely beautiful. It does have a National Monument on the reservation, it is a fort that was maintained, I believe, by the Department of Interior, I think. It's absolutely beautiful, and everything is clean, and the housing up there looks very well. There are clinics and daycares and a school system, and it looks like it's a nice little reservation, and it's so far up in God's country. Just breathtaking in certain areas.

When I walk on the reservation, and I am in and around it, whether it be driving around it or four-wheeling around it, or snowmobiling around it, I am very proud to be a Band member, because it's very well maintained. They've done a very good job with keeping it up, up there.

ARE YOU COMFORTABLE IN THAT ENVIRONMENT?

I am. I am comfortable in that environment, but when I walk into the tribal council offices, I want to get out of there. Because, like I said, I just feel like I am not very well perceived, because I tried to fight the system, and I tried to fight band members, or tribal council members—who incidentally one happens to be my birth mother's cousin, which that's very hard to follow, because it's just, you know, they are family, but if they are ruling against you, and I think it's a dictator-type of thing where there they see what's right and what's wrong, but, you know, above them they are being told to rule this way in this fashion because they just, you know, believe that they think that my enrollment was an error, which I just don't see how it could have been an error.

I actually have a copy of the resolution that eleven people voted in favor of my enrollment in 1992, eleven to zero, half my enrollment. Now, how eleven people can come up with that—they think that that can be an error—is beyond me. But it's just like I said, a confounded fact that they don't want to pay out money that they know that I'm entitled to.

DID YOU AND THAT FAMILY MEMBER EVER DISCUSS THIS ISSUE?

No. I didn't. Quite honestly, my meeting with him was very short and curt. I really did not want to have anything to do with the family member. He actually is the Vice Tribal Chair and our first contact was in a phone call and he went into great detail on how much he loved my mother, and how much he respected her, and how much she helped him.

For example, when he went out to New York because she lived out there, she picked him up at the airport and helped him get around.

And I think that a lot of that had to do with my mother, and she was alive at that time in 1992, and it was very possible that she could have had a great deal of, you know, influence in me becoming enrolled. And he basically told me ten minutes after he was telling me how much she helped him. The agent pretty much said, well, we just can't base that on wishes that we wish that maybe she helped you get enrolled. I'm thinking, you're cold.

If somehow I got enrolled, it was right, and I'm entitled to be enrolled. But because somebody is telling you that you think that it's an error, I just don't see how it could be an error, so it was very brief and very curt and I don't plan on speaking with this family member ever again.

GIVEN THE FACT THAT YOUR HUSBAND IS NOT A NATIVE, WAS HE COMFORTABLE ON THE RESERVATION?

He was very comfortable. He actually got along with several people and people he had no idea who they were, whether or not they could be related to me or what. He was very social and hopped right in there and I found him talking and joking with a lot of people and was very happy that he was doing it, and well, quite pleased that he was able to just jump in and get along really great with people. I was hoping that that would be the outcome, but it was much better than I thought. He has not returned to the reservation with me though.

NOW LET'S GO BACK TO YOUR WORK LIFE. WHAT DO YOU DO TODAY PROFESSIONALLY?

I am a purchasing agent for the federal government for the Department of Agriculture.

AND HOW DO YOU THINK THE FACT THAT YOU'RE A NATIVE AMERICAN AFFECTS YOUR PERSONAL LIFE OR YOUR WORK LIFE?

It enhances it a little bit more.

HOW SO?

I'm part of the Native American working group at work. Anything major that happens with agriculture on the reservations, I'm their Native American liaison.

And for example, like, if something were to happen majorly, like, the bird flu, we would be the liaison to go in and explain to the tribes why things are happening and why we would need to perform certain types of quarantines on the reservation.

We haven't had the opportunity to do anything like that in Minnesota but there are certain areas that we have interests in.

SO WERE YOU DRAWN TO THAT POSITION OUT OF A DESIRE TO HELP THE NATIVE AMERICAN COMMUNITY?

Yes, I was.

In what other ways do you see yourself giving back to the Native American community?

Just by learning, and I am part of the Native American Adoptees Group. I think starting there helped a great deal because I am involved with other Native American adoptees, some of whom haven't found their roots yet or haven't been located by their birth family.

So how would you say that you identify yourself today?

I would say that I am now involved more with what goes on in Indian country. I've got concerns on things that happen. I'm more in tune to what seems to happen to the Native American people.

It's hard to say because I'm still really getting used to the culture. So other than just having a big—a strong interest on what happens, probably one of the best things I think was getting to know the culture.

So what do you think has helped you take on that identity?

I think because now I can look in the mirror and be who I really am inside. I—it's just hard to explain that. I know we have used that many times in our conversation, but I had no idea. I had sort of an idea of who I was, but once I was reunited with my birth family and got the answers to all the questions I've had, it closed a circle for me completely.

I now have a good sense of who I am, whereas, for an example, I would always—birthdays are supposed to be such a fun time, you know. You just have a good time on your birthday. But there were always birthdays—every birthday that I can recall having, I cried silently.

Wondering, you know. Wondering, what about me? You know, why? How come? Where are they? How come nobody is trying to find me? That sort of stuff, you know.

Whereas families, you know, God, it's your birthday, you know, we are going to do a birthday cake and presents. And it was almost as if—I just kind of dreaded it inside and now it's not like that any longer. Now, I do have peace.

So now I would like to ask you a little bit more about transracial adoption in general. Are you glad that you were adopted by a non-Native family?

I would say yes.

CAN YOU EXPLAIN A LITTLE BIT MORE?

They, my adoptive family raised me very well. And I had them always looking out for my best interests, making sure that I, you know, was—I had—I was healthy and I was fed and I was loved.

And they let me pursue my interests that I wanted to. And never pushed that I, you know, follow in their footsteps.

And ironically enough, my dad, my adoptive father, is a federal government retiree. And that's kind of the same footsteps I followed in, working with the federal government. So even though I wasn't truly their, you know, birth daughter, I still followed their steps.

And they were very good to me, you know. I just—I am very glad that I was raised in a nontraditional Native American way because some of my cousins that I have seen and that I have met struggle with a lot of issues that were not evident when I was growing up.

And I don't know that if it's because of the way that they were raised or exposed, but I do know that it seems to me that I was in a better-off place, being raised in a, you know, in a traditional white family.

But now I don't think that that's the case for everybody. Like I said, being part of that adoptive Native American Adoptees Group I see and I have heard some of the stories that they've gone through, foster care after foster care after foster care. And having at least two or three of those foster homes be so dysfunctional that it warped them to the point that, you know, they turned to drugs or alcohol or crime.

And in my case that wasn't the way that it was. In fact, I think sitting there in that group of—however many times that I've attended it, I always thought that I was the only one in that group that did not have a so sad story because I wasn't beaten and I wasn't abused and I didn't abuse drugs or alcohol. But I think, like I said, I keep saying that it, I think, attributes to the way I was raised.

SO DO YOU HAVE ANY ADVICE THAT YOU WOULD LIKE TO OFFER NON-NATIVE FAMILIES WHO WOULD WANT TO HAVE OR WHO WOULD WANT TO ADOPT NATIVE AMERICAN CHILDREN?

That's a hard question because of the ICWA law, the Indian Child Welfare Act. I don't know if that's entirely possible nowadays for white families to adopt Native American children, because I think the Indian Child Welfare Act protects them to make sure that they go to Native American families. I don't—maybe you would know if that's possible.

IT IS POSSIBLE BUT IT'S REALLY DIFFICULT.

Yeah.

SO WHAT IS YOUR OPINION OF ICWA?

I can understand where it helps Indian children that were—was it '76 or—

'78.

Yeah, '78. But the ICWA law did nothing for me at that age that I was because I was born in '62. And actually, it should have helped me a little bit more because by the time I turned eighteen, that was when it was in 1979 and when I had been trying to pursue my cultural background. It should have protected me, but it didn't.

Like I said, I have about twenty-six letters that were sent from the adoption agency basically saying, too bad, I can't help you. But, you know, it always wants something.

So I guess it helps people now to protect their identity, to be able to pursue their cultural, you know, their interests, and who they are.

But for me, it just didn't work. It actually did nothing, and I'm not sure how much it would help now or not, but I guess I would rather see success stories like mine. But that's probably not always going to be possible.

SO WHAT'S YOUR OPINION OF TRANSRACIAL ADOPTION IN GENERAL?

I am all for it. As long as the adoptive parents are open to letting the adoptee pursue what their culture is and not holding back. In my case, they didn't hold me back but then the nurturing there or the interest was just never a question. So I'm all for it. I think that it works everyday.

OKAY.

You see everybody in the news like Angelina Jolie talking about going to Cambodia and adopting a child there. And I think that she is very open with letting the child pursue their native roots. And as long as they are okay with that, then I think it's fine.

IS THERE ANYTHING ELSE THAT YOU THINK I SHOULD HAVE ASKED YOU ABOUT YOUR EXPERIENCE?

No. I think we covered a lot.

OKAY. THANK YOU VERY MUCH.

# 5

# DENISE ENGSTROM

In 1966, Denise Engstrom (Tuscarora Nation) was born in Niagara Falls, New York, and placed for adoption three years later when her biological parents realized that they couldn't adequately care for her and her four siblings. Denise was adopted by a white couple who "did a nice job of raising [her]" in Lakewood, Colorado. Although she speaks of her adoptive parents fondly, Denise admits that they could not give her a much-needed sense of cultural identity. In fact, Denise says that her sense of cultural identity did not begin to take shape until she met her birth family at the age of twenty-five. The reunion took place on Thanksgiving Day and was bittersweet because Denise's biological mother had already passed. Her mother's family, however, welcomed her home with open arms. According to Denise, "everything [she] know[s] about being Tuscarora, [she] learned from [her biological family]" who took the time to share their language and traditions with her.

Although Denise was quickly accepted by her biological family, she notes that it took "a good ten years" before she was accepted in the reservation and urban Indian communities. During this time, Denise says that she was considered "an apple . . . white on the inside . . . Indian on the outside." She attributes the origins of this derogatory label to the fact that she initially "followed the white path" more than she "followed the red path" because she was unfamiliar with her tribal language and traditions. She believes that she secured a place in the Indian community by becoming more knowledgeable about and therefore more comfortable with her cultural background. This newfound sense of security led Denise to jobs at the Denver Indian Center and more recently the Denver Indian Family Resource Center where she facilitates the Positive Indian Parenting Workshop.

Denise describes herself as a strong advocate for the Indian Child Welfare Act and believes that transracial adoption should only be considered as a last resort. According to Denise, her experience as a transracial adoptee was not negative; however, she believes that she "missed out" and encourages non-Native families to allow their adopted children to build connections with their tribal and urban Indian communities. She argues that it may be difficult, but non-Native families need to make a conscious effort to ensure that Native adoptees have access to the appropriate people and resources.

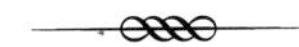

WHAT YEAR WERE YOU BORN?

I was born in 1966.

AND WHERE WERE YOU BORN?

Niagara Falls, New York.

AND HOW OLD WERE YOU WHEN YOU WERE ADOPTED?

I was three.

AND ARE YOU AWARE OF THE CIRCUMSTANCES SURROUNDING YOUR ADOPTION?

Yeah. When I found my biological family, I talked to my father, who's still living, and he told me that when he and my mother found out that she was pregnant and after they had me that—they were both alcoholics and she already had five children, and they felt like they wanted to give me a better life, so they put me up for adoption.

AND WERE ANY OF YOUR OTHER SIBLINGS PUT UP FOR ADOPTION?

My older sister was eventually adopted, and then the other kids were in and out of foster care.

AND WILL YOU TELL ME A LITTLE BIT ABOUT YOUR ADOPTIVE PARENTS?

Both of my parents are white, and my mom, Karen, had worked with people with developmental disabilities, and more recently worked with Jefferson County School Board. And my dad is an engineer or a metallurgist.

And did they indicate to you why they decided to adopt an American Indian child?

They said that they had two of their own children, and they had always wanted to adopt a child. I don't think it was specifically they wanted to adopt an Indian child, but when they went through the process, their social worker said, well, I've got this—wait until you meet this little girl, you're just going to fall in love with her. And that's how they adopted me.

And how would you describe your relationship with them?

You know, we—we're very close now. I think the relationship was strained when I was growing up. It was difficult, but now, as an adult, we have a much better relationship and are very involved with each other. I think before that, it was more difficult.

And when did you first realize that you were adopted?

I've always known I was adopted. They told me from the very beginning that I was adopted.

So whom did you talk to about the fact that you were adopted?

Pretty much everyone. I think that came from the fact that I looked very different than my adoptive family, and so from the very beginning, people always asked questions about how different we looked.

And even my adopted sisters, when we would introduce ourselves to people, and they'd say, this is my little sister Denise, they'd get this puzzled look. And they'd say well, she's adopted. You know, we always had to explain our family. We always had to do that.

So was the fact that you were Indian talked about a lot in your family?

No. We talked a lot about my being adopted. We did not talk a lot about my being Indian, because I don't think they really had the information.

They didn't know about the Tuscarora and Niagara Falls, which is the tribe that I'm from. They didn't know a lot about that. They were not knowledgeable about Indian ways or Indian community or anything. So, no, we didn't talk about it when I was growing up.

Would you say that your parents did anything to give you a sense of your cultural identity?

No. I think part of my cultural identity of, you know, their values and their beliefs, I think they did a really nice job raising me that way. But they weren't familiar with the Tuscarora, with the Indian aspects, and so they did the best that they could, but they didn't really talk about it because they didn't know.

ARE YOU CLOSE WITH YOUR SIBLINGS?

I am. I'm very close with them. That's also been something that's been closer since we've been adults. When we were children, I think like all siblings, we probably fought more, but we've always kept in touch and we're very close now.

AND DID YOU EVER TALK TO THEM ABOUT BEING AN AMERICAN INDIAN?

When I became an adult, we did. Because I made the decision to find my biological family, and they were very supportive of that process. And now, as adults, we talk a lot about my journey and developing my own identity and what that looks like because it's very different than when we were raised.

WHERE DID YOU GROW UP?

I grew up here in Lakewood, Colorado.

AND DID YOU ENCOUNTER ANY FORM OF RACISM GROWING UP?

I did when I was little. When I was in kindergarten—I have a specific experience I remember and that I used to talk to my mom about because I went to schools that mainly had Caucasian or white families that their kids went there. And in kindergarten, the kids used to tease me and they'd say, "God left you in the oven too long." And so I would come home crying from kindergarten. My mom would always, she was always very supportive and loving, but we never really associated that—my darker skin—with being Indian. We didn't really talk about it that much.

HOW DO YOU THINK YOUR PARENTS PREPARED YOU FOR THE CHALLENGES FACING YOU? WAS RACISM SOMETHING YOU ENCOUNTERED A LOT GROWING UP OR JUST PERIODICALLY?

You know, I think it was periodically that I struggled with it, but it was more—I think it was more the confusion of who I was. People would ask, because I'm half Tuscarora and half white, that people were, like, well, if you're Indian, then, you know, they would say, well, are you Greek or are you Italian?

People were always trying to figure out who I was, and so—I don't think I directly, other than when I was really little, experienced any racism. And

I think that as I've talked about this with my sisters, my adopted sisters, before that as I got older, it became more of an advantage that I had dark skin because I would tan like crazy in the summer. And so for me, it became more of an advantage. I never felt discriminated against.

Who were your closest friends growing up?

Mostly kids in the neighborhood. I had mainly white friends that I was close with. And white friends—her name was Katie, and she and I kept in touch all the way through elementary school. She was, like, my first friend, really, and we still keep in touch every once in a while. But most of my friends were white.

Did you interact with any Indians growing up?

No.

Did you go to college?

I did.

Where did you go to school?

I went to UNC—well, actually I started out at Puget Sound in Tacoma, Washington. I went there for my first year, and I was going to go into physical therapy. But then I changed and came to Greeley, Colorado, to UNC, and that's where I got my Bachelor's in Human Rehabilitative Services. And then I went to UCD to get my Master's degree, and I got my degree in Early Childhood Special Education.

And why did you decide to major in those areas?

I think my mom had a lot to do with it because I was raised in a family where supporting, advocating for people with disabilities was an important part of our family. And so it was just a natural progression for me to follow in that field.

So what kind of work do you do today?

Right now, I'm working with the federal government. I work with the Head Start—Early Head Start program, so it's more preschool, early-childhood-oriented. But I also teach positive Indian parenting, which is through Denver Indian Family Resources. I started doing that probably four to five years ago. I started teaching Indian parents about parenting classes and—so I'm involved there.

AND WHAT PROMPTED THAT DECISION?

Well, let's see. You know, I started being more involved in the Indian community probably fifteen years ago when I found my biological family, and that was really where my own cultural identity of being Indian really started developing.

And I started seeking out more connection with the Indian community here in Denver, and one of the things that I did was that I got a job working for the Denver Indian Center in their preschool program. I was their preschool director. And so in that process—that was the Head Start program, and that was probably '99 when I started working there. And we got trained in the Positive Indian Parenting Program for Early Head Start, but then I moved on to another job and didn't use it, but then made the decision that I wanted to get involved with that.

So I can't remember if Denver Indian Families researched and approached me or I approached them, but they were looking to start parenting classes and we just started teaching those.

WHEN DID YOU DECIDE TO SEEK OUT YOUR BIRTH FAMILY? HOW OLD WERE YOU?

I was probably twenty-five. I had talked about it a lot, but it was around the time when I was looking for scholarships for my Master's degree and for any of the Native or, you know, Indian scholarships, you had to have proof of tribal enrollment, which I didn't have. And so I decided at that point that I wanted to seek out my family. But it was initiated mostly by trying to seek out funding. But I think it was more of a deeper level, that I wanted to find my family, too.

WAS IT A DIFFICULT PROCESS, FINDING THEM?

No. After talking to other people who had been adopted and their seeking out their families, it was really very easy for me. It took three phone calls.

I started out, I wrote a letter to the Department of Social Services, asking for access to my identifying information. They said I would have to petition a judge to get that information. And I wrote the judge a letter, and he sent me a very nice letter back.

And what he released was the—I think it was the case worker or the departments of where I was adopted through, the Department of Social Services.

So when I got that information, I contacted the Department of Social Services, and I told them I was trying to make a connection with my tribe to get to my family.

She said, well, I can't give you any information, but I can give you the phone number for the chief of the tribe. And so she gave me that number, and I called the phone number and got an answering machine, and I left a message.

And about three weeks later he hadn't returned my call, so I called back, and he answered the phone. And he said, so, why do you think you're Tuscarora? And I said, well, you know, I have my adoption papers, and I know my mother's name is Marlene, and I have five other brothers and sisters. And he said, I know who you're talking about. And he said, I'll call your aunt. And so from that point on, my Aunt Doreen called me, and I got connected with the family.

And for me, I think I'm very fortunate that it was so easy because they're a very small tribe and so for one chief of the tribe to know who I was talking about—it's because we're so small. I mean, you couldn't do that with other tribes, the Navajo Nation or some of those bigger tribes. It's very difficult to find relatives, but for me, it was very easy.

AND WHAT WAS YOUR BIRTH FAMILY'S REACTION TO YOU?

Oh, it was very emotional because after I found them—my Aunt Doreen just cried on my answering machine when she found out it was me.

And when I went back to meet everyone, people would tell me stories about—that there were people, other people in the tribe, that wanted to adopt me but they couldn't afford to. My aunt, everybody, were very sad that I had to be adopted.

And they told me a story about when, after I was first adopted, my aunts would go to Niagara Falls, and they would sit and they would watch for me. They would see if they could find me, and they didn't realize that I had been moved to Colorado.

And so that was, for me, a very sad story because they had always been looking for me. And they thought—my mother passed away before I found her—and they were all, not excited, but they were all waiting for me at her funeral because they thought for sure that someone would have notified me that she'd passed away.

And so when I finally did find them, those are the kinds of stories that they told, that they always looked for me, they wished they could have adopted me or kept me. And so it was very emotional.

YOU TALKED ABOUT YOUR MOTHER'S FAMILY. WHAT ABOUT YOUR FATHER'S FAMILY?

I met my father at the same time, and initially, he and I did not get along at all. I am his only child. And he's never had children, and so he didn't know how to treat an adult child, and so we had a very strained relationship at the very beginning.

My mother's family and my brothers and sisters, we immediately bonded and had a very good relationship. It was more strained with my father. It took more time for him—and it's still strained.

He lived with his parents at the time, so I met his parents, and I've met his brothers and sisters and his family. He is Hungarian and Polish, and so I haven't really looked into that part of my culture mainly just because I haven't really connected with him and I have had a more strained relationship. But yeah, I've met them. They're nice people.

WHAT WAS YOUR REACTION WHEN YOU WENT TO THE RESERVATION? OR DID YOU GO TO THE RESERVATION?

Yes, I did.

WHAT WAS YOUR REACTION?

When I first went out, it was extremely emotional for me because I had never met anyone that looked like me.

And so when I got off the plane, I saw—it was, like—I went out for Thanksgiving and I got off the plane, and there was all these cameras and all these people and my dad was there and he had, like, a dozen roses, and I was so nervous.

And even coming on the plane I talked to people around me and told them what I was doing, and one of the stewardesses said, oh, take pictures and you know, I'd use the video camera. All these people were offering to help. There were a lot of people from the plane that watched the meeting because it was just so emotional and so exciting that I was meeting them for the first time.

And they—all my brothers and sisters that were living on the reservation—were there at the airport, and so we had like this big meeting. And, my dad had made arrangements for me to stay with someone else so that I didn't feel uncomfortable. So he stayed off the reservation the first time I went out.

And then I went out for Christmas. And my reaction was really more of just being absolutely emotionally overwhelmed because it was—it's kind of like when you feel like there's a part of you that's missing for so long that that was my homecoming, and it was—it felt like coming home.

And from the very time that I met my brothers and sisters and my aunts and uncles and everyone, that there was an immediate connection and immediate bond and immediate love for one another. There was a lot of time that had passed, but they never forgot me.

And so it was really emotional for me, and it was overwhelming because I had never been on a reservation before, I had never met any other Indian people, so I—it was a huge, like—what's the word I'm looking for? That whole cultural piece of it was just overwhelming.

WOULD YOU SAY YOU EXPERIENCED MAYBE A KIND OF CULTURE SHOCK?

Absolutely, yeah. Yeah. I would describe it as that because I was sort of surprised at the poverty on the reservation, the living conditions. It was something that it took me time to get used to and to understand. And the way living on the reservation, I had to get used to that because it wasn't anything that I had ever been exposed to.

DO YOU FEEL LIKE YOU HAVE A GREATER UNDERSTANDING OF LIFE THERE NOW?

Oh, yeah. I would say that. The way that I see myself culturally is I see myself as bicultural now, whereas I didn't see myself as bicultural. I am very comfortable in the white-dominant society, but I'm also very comfortable with my Indian culture and the reservation life and where I come from.

But I can say that that's—it's been sort of a journey of learning because that didn't happen overnight. It's been over the past ten to fifteen years I've developed that comfort level.

AND WHAT PEOPLE OR RESOURCES HAVE AIDED YOU IN BECOMING MORE COMFORTABLE?

When I first found my family, I would say that my aunts and my brothers and sisters were incredibly influential in developing my cultural identity because they talked about being Tuscarora, they talked about our language, they talked about our beadwork, they talked about our traditions.

Everything that I know about being Tuscarora, I learned from them. And I don't think that—I don't feel like there's things that I—I have a lot to learn yet because I wasn't raised on the reservation, but much of what I know about who I am, I learned from them.

But being Tuscarora and being involved in the Indian community, there's also a cultural identity of just being Native American or being Indian.

There's a woman that I'm very close with. And I started—I would say the year after I went home, I started getting involved in the powwow community and started to develop my own regalia or my own outfits.

And I met a woman when I had first started dancing, and she and I developed a friendship, and she was always the one that I sat with at powwows, and she helped me learn about some of the cultural aspects of being in a powwow or just being in the Indian community.

You know, when you greet elders or when you go to an event where there's food, you know, you always—if they're praying, you stand up. You know, if there's food, you always let the elders go first.

You know, some of those cultural things that go across the board for all Native people, those are things she taught me. Those aren't things that my family back home taught me because they're not powwow people necessarily.

So that cultural identity has been blended through being Tuscarora, but also through just being Indian. There's a lot of things I've learned, and she's been—her family has been very influential in helping me learn what that means.

DO YOU FEEL LIKE YOU'VE BEEN ACCEPTED BY INDIANS OUTSIDE YOUR FAMILY, THOSE LIVING ON THE RESERVATION AND THOSE LIVING OFF THE RESERVATION?

Yes. I think initially that was very difficult. It took me, I would say, a good ten years to become accepted, both on the reservation and also in the Indian community in Denver.

When I first got my job at the Denver Indian Center, it was difficult because people didn't know me in the Indian community. And a lot of the Indian people really see me as what they call an apple. You're white on the inside, you're Indian on the outside.

And they don't say that to your face, but they viewed me as that I follow the white path more than I follow the red path. That was initially that she doesn't know about Indian ways, she doesn't know about this—and it was true, I really didn't. I was functioning from a perspective that I knew I was Indian, but I didn't know what that meant yet.

So I was still developing my cultural identity at that time, and the people in the Indian community knew that. I mean, they knew that I was more—I presented myself more white than I did anything else, and that's how I sort of got labeled.

It took me a long time—like, ten years—to get to the point where I became more accepted in the Indian community. And I think I'm very comfortable in the community on the reservation and I am in the community in Denver. I'm very well-accepted.

And I think, for most people, I'm well-respected. They understand my background, but I think in the Indian community they view that as an asset now versus something that's a detriment.

WHY DO YOU THINK THEY FINALLY DECIDED TO ACCEPT YOU?

I think it's a combination of things. I think the Indian community, and I don't want this to sound negative, but they're cliquish. It's, like, who you know and who you're associated with.

And my woman friend was instrumental in helping introduce me to people in the Indian community. And my association with her helped validate who I am.

And also I think developing my own cultural identity, I began to understand more about who I am and where I come from so I could communicate better about being Tuscarora and being adopted and things like that. So that I was developing my own knowledge.

And I was developing more knowledge about what it meant to be Indian and so, between the associations with people and my own cultural developments, I think that's how I became more accepted in the community.

ARE YOU AN ENROLLED MEMBER OF YOUR TRIBE?

I am.

WAS THAT A DIFFICULT PROCESS?

No. You know, in our tribe, your mother has to put you on the roll. And before I was adopted, my mother had put me on the roll, and my oldest sister, Shar, had saved my original birth certificate before I was adopted, so I had my birth certificate—my original birth certificate—so that I would be able to prove that who I am today is the person that my mother put on the roll.

And so—and I think I brought some adoption paperwork with me, and my Aunt Doreen, who's my clan mother, a member of the Beaver Clan.

In our tribe, you follow your clan mother and for, like, Beaver Clan, she would be the person that I would go to for help, and she's the one that we went to the chief and requested to get my Indian ID card. And in order to get that, you have to be an enrolled member, and in fact, I was enrolled.

So for me, it wasn't difficult. We have had more difficulty enrolling children that are a quarter in our tribe because the momentum is that they would like to cut off the enrollment at if you're half. And I'm half Tuscarora, so I'm on the roll, but for example, my daughter, Cheyenne, I've had difficulty getting her on the roll. My sister's daughter, they're having difficulty getting her on the roll.

There are some significant struggles that other people have had, but because my mother had already had me on the roll then, I didn't have any trouble.

What are the advantages of being an enrolled member? Are there any?

Our tribe is probably different than others in that we do not accept federal funding. And so we don't get any money from the tribe.

We don't have any gaming or casinos or anything like that, so there's no specific financial benefit from the tribe.

But we do get, you know, free health and dental and medical through our clinic on the reservation. And I haven't actually signed up for that because I have medical benefits through my job, but that's something I'm going to do because you get free prescriptions, free eyeglasses, free, you know. One of the things that I did take advantage of is, when my daughter was little, and I was out on the reservation, she had a problem with the baby formula, and so we had to have her on hypoallergenic baby formula, which is really, really expensive. Well, when I went out to the reservation, they could get it free.

And on the reservation, they don't do powdered milk because of the water. They do liquid. And so when we went home, my aunt got me a ton of formula—they just ordered, like, a case because they had to special order it, and I got that.

And I came home with my suitcase incredibly heavy because they just loaded it up with that formula, that free formula. So we do get free medical and free dental.

And then, you know, just being an enrolled member of a tribe, I would be eligible for scholarships and things like that. I did not—I had already finished my schooling and didn't pursue that as much, but I would be eligible for that.

I think when you can say you're an enrolled member of a tribe in the Indian community, that's highly valued. If you're not an enrolled member, people tend to, you know, question your affiliation, whether you really are Indian or not.

If you're not enrolled, then it's questionable. People kind of question that. So the fact that I am enrolled makes a big difference in how people view me.

Does it make a difference in how you view yourself at all?

Sure. Yeah. I think it's made a big difference for me personally that I've been able to be enrolled. Because I've seen the struggle that other people have gone through in trying to be accepted in the Indian community when you're not enrolled. And I think that it's very meaningful to me, even though I don't personally benefit from that enrollment, it means a lot to me culturally that I am.

ARE THERE ANY BARRIERS PREVENTING YOU FROM INTEGRATING INTO THE INDIAN COMMUNITY?

I think initially it was really difficult because I was mainly raised in the white community and with a white family. I think initially, it was really difficult because I didn't fit in. I wasn't like them.

There were, I think, some prejudices from people that, you know, I wasn't from the rez, I wasn't full blood, I didn't act like they did, I didn't talk like they did. So I think initially, it was very difficult.

But over the years, I've been able to develop my own experience and my own cultural identity, so I'm very comfortable with who I am, and I think that's made a big difference in my acceptance. I don't think there's any barriers for me right now.

SO HOW HAVE ALL THOSE EXPERIENCES SHAPED YOUR SENSE OF CULTURAL IDENTITY?

I think that if I had not met my biological family, that I would not have the strong sense of being Indian that I do because even being exposed to the Indian community, if you don't have sort of that—and I'm speaking about my own personal experience—if I hadn't had that base of understanding from being Tuscarora, I don't think that I would be as connected with the Indian community. That cultural identity that I have is because I sought out my family.

I was very comfortable with the white community, with my family, with my friends, with all of my associations. It would have been more difficult for me to figure out who I was and I probably would have progressed in this—in a manner where I wasn't involved in the Indian community. I probably would not have been involved if I hadn't found my biological family.

WHAT WAS YOUR ADOPTIVE PARENTS' REACTION TO YOUR DECISION TO LOOK FOR YOUR BIRTH FAMILY?

They initially had the same fears that many adoptive parents do, that, you know maybe I'd love them more or I'd stop my relationship with them. I remember when I went to leave, my mom cried when I left. It was very hard for her when I went back.

I think for the first five to seven years, it was difficult because I would go back to the reservation for holidays, but you know, my parents were used to me being there for holidays, so it was—I think, initially, it was very difficult for them.

But now, there's a real comfort level, and I think that my adoptive family has very much embraced my cultural identity and it's a part of who I am and they very much accept that.

Have your birth family and your adoptive families ever met?

Yes. I was married in 1997, and they had correspondence through mail, but they had never met, and so two of my aunts and my cousin flew out for the wedding, and they got to meet my family, so that was a really important time for me.

And did they get along? What was their interaction like?

You know, at weddings, it's strained to begin with just because it's sort of this artificial event, but they got along fine and, you know, my Aunt Doreen and my mom had a very special relationship just because when I first found my family, my Aunt Doreen sent a gift to my mom thanking her for raising me.

And so that was, like, real emotional. It was like a connection between the two of them. And so while they probably weren't, like, you know, buddies and hung out together, they had a special connection together. And they exchanged Christmas cards every year.

And so they definitely developed a relationship, and they still—my family on the reservation always asks about my adoptive family out here and vice versa. They're very involved through me—on how everyone's doing.

Does your birth family perceive your adoption as a positive thing?

Absolutely, yeah. Yeah.

Do you think your relationship with your adopted family changed as a result of your decision to look for your birth family?

Hmm. Yes. I think that in a sense, it became, like, an additional family, and so instead of like, when you get married, you always have to incorporate the in-laws. Well, for me, it was incorporating my birth family.

And so holidays no longer were just with my adopted family. I had to be shared at that point. And so you change that relationship because I had to then start making decisions about where I was going to go for Thanksgiving and Christmas and those kinds of things.

So it definitely impacted my relationship with my adopted family because instead of saying—like, for example, one of the things that's developed over the years is my concept of home.

When I talk about going home, I'm talking about going to the reservation. But I also see—if I talk about going to my parents' home, that's also home, that was where I grew up.

So that's changed our relationship and how I view things, that when I talk—and I think it's comfortable for them because they understand that when I say, I'm going home, they know I'm going to Niagara Falls. I don't think they take offense to that. I never asked them, but I don't think they take offense to that. They understand what that means.

NOW, YOU MENTIONED THAT YOU WERE MARRIED.

Mm-hmm.

WAS YOUR HUSBAND INDIAN?

No. I initially—when I was growing up and I was dating, I dated strictly white men just because of my upbringing. I had never met any Indian people.

I think initially when I started finding my biological family and I started dancing at powwows, when I started dating Indian men, there was a huge cultural clash. Because for all intents and purposes I was placing my white path on them—my expectations, and it was difficult in relationships with Indian men initially because I didn't have a concept of what that meant, and we were so culturally different because even though I was developing my cultural identity of being Indian, I really followed more of my white path of how I was raised, my work ethic, my interests, the way that I viewed the world. And it was very different, and I had difficulty maintaining relationships with Indian men initially. They would only last, like six months. And so—my longest relationships previously had been with white men because that's—that was what I was comfortable with and that's what—I married a man who was white, and that's our child—you know, we have our child together.

NOW, YOU MENTIONED YOUR DAUGHTER. HOW OLD IS SHE?

She's eight.

AND WHAT HAVE YOU DONE TO GIVE HER A SENSE OF HER CULTURAL IDENTITY AS SHE'S GROWN UP?

I have—ever since she was a baby, I have really enmeshed her in the Indian community. We've always gone to powwows, we've gone to other events in the Indian community, and I've taken her back to the reservation at various times.

But I would say other than her school friends, her best friends are all Indian. And so I've really—I'd say in the last seven to eight years, ever since she was a baby, I've really enmeshed her in everything that I do with the Indian community, and it's actually gone to the extent of I want her to have a really strong cultural identity of being Indian.

And so I've exposed her to the language, I've exposed her to beadwork, I've exposed her to the reservation, I've exposed her to other people in the Indian community, and she's very comfortable. She—for all intents and purposes, she looks like—she's blonde, blue-eyed, her dad is Scandinavian, and she has lots of his coloring. But she'll walk up to you and tell you she's Tuscarora, she's American Indian. She has no problem with her identity. She's very grounded in who she is. Actually, this is a drawing she did.

OH, THAT'S PRETTY. SHE'S REALLY GOOD.

Mm-hmm. She's only eight. Yeah.

THAT'S REALLY GOOD.

Yeah. She's a very good artist, and I think that she embraces that Indian—her Indian identity very much, so—and she's trying to blend that with her dad's—he's Norwegian and Swedish. And so she's also learning some of those things, so she understands that she's bicultural—probably multicultural because she's also, you know, part white with me. But we focus on her Indian identity a lot, and she's very grounded and very proud of that.

BUT YOU MENTIONED THAT YOU'RE HAVING TROUBLE GETTING HER ENROLLED IN YOUR TRIBE?

Yeah, I am. And I think that for me, the fact that she has that cultural identity, and like I said before, when you're associated with people in the Indian community, there is a level of acceptance because of who you're with.

And I have developed enough relationships and friendships and associations in the Indian community that no one questions Cheyenne's involvement in the Indian community. They all know who she is. They all know that her dad is white. They all know that I'm her mom. And so she's been accepted in the Indian community pretty well, I think.

I GUESS RIGHT NOW I WANT TO TALK A LITTLE BIT MORE ABOUT TRANSRACIAL ADOPTION IN GENERAL. WHAT IS YOUR OPINION OF THE INDIAN CHILD WELFARE ACT (ICWA)?

I think it's an important legislation and I've talked with other people about this because in 1966, I don't think ICWA was enacted and so if you think about a lot of the Indian kids that were adopted by white families, their cultural identity, from my opinion, was impacted.

And so I think the ICWA had a huge role in trying to keep Indian children connected with their roots. Giving the tribes opportunities to be involved and making sure that—trying to get Native foster families, if that's the situation.

But I think it's a crucial part of what needs to be in place. And I think that—while I'm not at all so negative about the experience that I had, being adopted, I think my experience would have been different if the ICWA would have been involved because they would have had to contact the tribe. And I think that my circumstances may have been different, so I'm a big advocate for that, for the ICWA.

ARE YOU GLAD THAT YOU WERE ADOPTED BY A WHITE FAMILY?

Yes, I am. I mean, I think that I'm a unique person because I have the ability to, in my opinion, be bicultural, meaning that I was raised in a white family in the dominant white society, that I have some of the values and beliefs that are really beneficial to having a good life. And that being also associated with my own culture of being Indian, that I can blend those two cultures in a way that I feel very fortunate.

DID YOU EVER FIND THAT THOSE TWO CULTURES CLASHED?

Yes.

AND HOW HAVE YOU HANDLED THAT?

I think just trying to be understanding about, you know, the—while I'm a blended cultural person, that I also have to be respectful about the fact that people around me may not necessarily understand that. I talked with my adopted family during some times that they've felt uncomfortable with other Indian people, just because they didn't feel that they related. And I've also had some—I was involved with some Indian men that had difficulty with my white family. And so I've had to negotiate that as far as how much time I spent with each or events we went to and my boyfriend now, Richard, he's really good about understanding who I am and where I come from and is very comfortable in either setting.

We go back to his reservation. He's gone back to my reservation. And we spend lots of time with my adoptive family here. So he has a very strong understanding and support for who I am and where we're at.

But that's not always been the case with other people in my life. I've had to train, negotiate what's kind of been almost like a cultural mediator of sorts, trying to negotiate either one side or the other. And I think that's a real asset for me personally, but it's not always easy.

SO IN GENERAL, DO YOU THINK THAT NON-INDIANS SHOULD BE ALLOWED TO ADOPT INDIAN CHILDREN?

Yes, I do, in general. I mean, if all of the other avenues have been sought out, I don't think it's a negative thing for white families to adopt Indian children because I don't think—I wouldn't label my experience as negative. I think there were some things that I may have missed out on or that could have been done differently, but that doesn't mean that I wasn't raised in a good way. And I think that with ICWA, if you're going to the tribe and you're trying to find other Native families to either be foster parents or to adopt, and you run out of resources, I'd rather see Indian children adopted by a white family than not to be adopted at all.

WHAT FACTORS DO YOU THINK SHOULD BE TAKEN INTO CONSIDERATION WHEN PLACING AN INDIAN CHILD IN AN ADOPTIVE HOME?

I think the adoptive family's openness to helping that child stay connected with their culture, whether that's through their tribe or through the Indian community.

Because, to me, those are two separate things—because your Indian community may not be necessarily your tribe, especially if you're not living in the same area. So if you're looking at a white family who wants to adopt an Indian child, are they receptive to helping develop and build that cultural identity to the best of their ability and staying connected with people who can help do that? Because if they're not open to that, then that child's going to lose out or it's going to be up to their responsibility to do that. And so I think most families would be willing to help their child stay connected, but they need resources and people to help them do that.

To make assumptions that all families know about Indian resources or know about the Indian community or know about the tribes, they have to have resources, families have to have resources in order to help build their child's cultural identity.

AND YOU MENTIONED THAT'S WHY YOU THINK THAT FACT THAT YOU'RE NATIVE AMERICAN WAS NEVER BROUGHT UP IN YOUR ADOPTED FAMILY WAS BECAUSE OF A LACK OF THOSE RESOURCES?

Right. Absolutely. For them, my being Tuscarora, I—I don't think they really thought about that being in the Indian community would be an asset for me.

They thought, well, the Tuscaroras are in New York. We don't live in New York, so we'll live the way that we live. I don't think they really thought about the development of my cultural identity. They're very resourceful individuals. If they had, I'm sure that they could have connected me.

But that's not something that was encouraged or that was—I don't even think back then was even thought of. I think today people are much more in tune with that.

It's interesting. I have a relationship with a woman through e-mail who has adopted two Indian boys, and she often e-mails me and asks for my opinion about things, about how to keep them connected—she's very interested in keeping them connected.

So I've kind of become a resource to her. She'll ask, like, what do you think I should do about this situation, and I'd say, well, if I were there, this is what I would do.

And so I think for families that are adopting Indian children, they need resources and they need support in order to help that child develop their cultural identity because if they're left on their own, they may not be able to find it.

So what advice would you offer to white families who have or would want to adopt Indian children?

I think to stay connected as much as possible with any tribal members, if they know the child's tribe, because I think that knowledge and information from individual members is so much more valuable than book knowledge.

I think it's real easy to do searches on the Internet and find information about Indian tribes and history and things like that. But the individual experiences that tribal members give is so different.

You know, my boyfriend Richard and I have talked a lot about the difference between book knowledge about being Indian and that personal experience about what being Indian is, and that for white families who want to adopt Indian children is to understand that that cultural identity is developed through people.

You can give kids knowledge through the Internet and through books, but it's the people that are really—the elders that are really going to impact them, if they have access to the tribe to see if there's elders that would be willing to provide information and support and resources. But then also to encourage white families that want to adopt Indian children to find out what are the activities in the Indian community where they live. Are there powwows? Is there an Indian center or an Indian family resource center that they could connect with so that that child has an opportunity to stay connected with the Indian community? I think that's really crucial.

COULD WE TALK A LITTLE BIT MORE ABOUT BOOKS WRITTEN ABOUT NATIVE AMERICANS? WHAT LIMITATIONS DO YOU THINK THERE ARE WHEN YOU RELY SOLELY ON BOOKS FOR YOUR INFORMATION?

What's the disadvantage of relying solely on books for your information about your culture? I think that you're missing out on the personal experiences about what being Indian is.

And I can give you an example from my experience of being Tuscarora. Everyone has a different experience of what being Tuscarora means. There are some common threads that people have—like, for example, not everyone in our tribe speaks the language, nor has an interest in that. There are some people that are very passionate about keeping our language going, and then there's other people like, you know, some of my siblings that, ahh, they don't really care about it, it's not important to them.

So that sense of cultural identity and what it means to them to be Indian, I don't think you can capture that necessarily in books because it's very individualized.

Like, for example, I think one of the biggest barriers in writing books is that if you are writing about individual experiences, that's a better avenue than if you're globally saying the Cheyenne do this, or the Tuscaroras do that.

I think it's very difficult to capture in books what the true meaning of being Tuscarora or being, you know, Cheyenne or, Lakota, what that really means because for everyone, that's different.

And I think that's what—if a child or an adult is trying to gain knowledge from books, it may not necessarily be accurate to what's actually happening in the tribe.

SO WHAT DOES IT MEAN TO YOU TO BE TUSCARORA?

For me, being Tuscarora is knowing that I'm from Niagara Falls, New York, and that I'm part of the Six Nations, which is the Cayuga, the Onondaga, the Oneida—there's a group of six tribes.

I'm a part of that, so part of my identity is—I consider myself Haudenosaunee, which is the Six Nations. So that's a part of who I am.

Being Tuscarora is also celebrating, my beadwork that I do. We—Cheyenne and I use the language a little bit, not a lot. But it's that identity of being from the woodland tribes that were somewhat different from the Plains tribes.

And so being Tuscarora to me is also understanding that I'm different from the other tribes and being able to share that with people. They enjoy that.

DO YOU FEEL LIKE YOU HAVE A STRONG UNDERSTANDING OF YOUR CULTURAL IDENTITY TODAY OR DO YOU FEEL LIKE IT'S SOMETHING YOU'RE STILL DEVELOPING?

I have a strong understanding of where I am, and I by no means feel like my cultural identity is complete. There is a lot to learn and to know and to gain.

I'm very comfortable with the fact that I think that your cultural identity is a journey and that it's no different than learning that you learn your entire life. That's my perspective, that you learn your entire life.

I think that there are cultural things that you learn your entire life as well. Because even with meeting people from other tribes, you learn more about yourself and you're able to develop that cultural identity even more.

And I think that that's been something that I've learned over the past few years, is not to make any assumptions about what being Indian is because for everyone it's very different. I'm very comfortable with who I am and where I come from and what my limitations are.

You know, people ask me questions about, dreamcatchers or just some of the typical questions people ask, and I'll—I don't know. I'm, like, I honestly don't know. I can tell you about our beadwork. I can tell you about Tuscarora issues.

I can't tell you about everything that's Indian because that's not where I'm at. And I don't think—if you asked anyone that was really grounded in who they are, that it's a lifelong journey and you learn as you go.

I THINK THAT'S ALL THE QUESTIONS THAT I HAVE. IS THERE ANYTHING ELSE YOU THINK I SHOULD HAVE ASKED YOU?

I don't think so. I mean, I think we covered a lot.

6

# JOYCE GONZALES

Joyce Gonzales (Cherokee/Apache) was born in San Francisco in 1952 and placed with a Caucasian family three days later. According to Joyce, her adoptive parents were deemed "unfit" by several adoption agencies; and as a result, private adoption arrangements were made for the family by a Catholic priest. Joyce notes that her adoptive parents, in particular her adoptive mother, were indeed "unfit" to raise a child. She describes her adoptive mother as "bipolar" and attributes her poor relationship with her to their difference in skin color. According to Joyce, her adoptive mother made it a point to "remind [her] that [she] was different." She also seemed to favor Joyce's brother, who was also adopted, and like both of her adoptive parents, was of German descent. She says that she and her brother were subjected to different forms of treatment and believes that it was "a race thing. That's something you feel in your gut. I actually [resorted to] substance abuse because I had a hard time coping and feeling that I belonged anywhere." Joyce began doing drugs when she was thirteen and continued to do them off and on well into her late twenties.

This lack of belonging compelled Joyce to begin searching for her birth family when she was sixteen years old. With the help of a private investigator, she uncovered the identity of her birth mother; unfortunately, her mother passed away before a reunion could take place. Although she never met her birth mother, she did meet an aunt and formed a relationship with her birth mother's family. According to Joyce, "with [her birth] mother's family there was this whole sense of belonging." She says that this sense of belonging could not even be diminished by the fact that she could not enroll in a tribe. Joyce maintains: "I'm not able to get registered with a tribe, but I'm okay with who I am and nobody can take that away or make it bad or ugly because now I know who I am."

Joyce characterizes herself as a supporter of the Indian Child Welfare Act and argues that "obviously being adopted by a white family is better than being put in an orphanage, but I think that Native people need to adopt Native children. I think the standards need not to be based on white people standards."

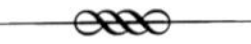

WHAT YEAR WERE YOU BORN?

In 1952.

WHERE WERE YOU BORN?

I was born in San Francisco in a hospital that is not there anymore.

HOW OLD WERE YOU WHEN YOU WERE ADOPTED?

I was adopted at three days old. You know, so it was set up before I was born.

ARE YOU AWARE OF THE CIRCUMSTANCES SURROUNDING YOUR ADOPTION?

Part of them. Yeah.

CAN YOU DESCRIBE THOSE CIRCUMSTANCES FOR ME?

My mother couldn't have children. She had tried, my adoptive mother, she had tried for thirteen years before she adopted a son. I saw, actually, all of the letters recently, and the places wouldn't let her adopt. All of the agencies—which is amazing for 1949–1952. So this priest, she knew this lady who knew this priest, and this priest knew my birth mother was fifteen, had just turned fifteen, and was going to have a baby. She delivered right after she turned fifteen and she couldn't keep it because she was unmarried and the father was in the service. So it was a private adoption. I guess my mom's friend had adopted a child from the priest too.

DID YOUR PARENTS EVER INDICATE THAT THEY WERE SPECIFICALLY LOOKING FOR A NATIVE AMERICAN CHILD TO ADOPT OR WERE THEY SIMPLY LOOKING TO ADOPT A CHILD IN GENERAL?

At that point, they were desperate and seeking a child in general. They were of German descent, my parents, second-generation. Their parents came from Germany. My brother that they adopted eight years prior was of German descent too. So no, I kind of stuck out like a sore thumb, but at that point my mom was just very desperate because no agency would allow her to adopt.

DO YOU KNOW WHY THAT WAS?

Well, the letters said that they found her unfit. Unstable. And she kind of had some problems.

TELL ME A LITTLE BIT MORE ABOUT YOUR ADOPTIVE PARENTS.

My father was a printer and my mom was a bookkeeper. Her work involved secretarial, you know, she did books for these little companies she worked for. Basically, it was just her and the boss and the people who delivered water coolers. I think prior to that she worked for an insurance company or something, but she stayed home when we were preschool. I don't think she went to work until I was like eight years old.

HOW WOULD YOU DESCRIBE YOUR RELATIONSHIP WITH YOUR PARENTS?

Well my father was kind of distant. He wasn't very vocal. He always stayed quiet. Actually, he was the most calm one. My mom was pretty almost bipolar. I mean she would get very excitable. And I was not very close, my mother and I. There was always something missing.

Well, I'm sure it was the color because I remember when I was little she'd be washing me in the bathtub and she was just scrubbing me and hurting me. And she's like, I can't tell what's dirt and what's your skin. There was a lot of stuff like that. Even during my menses, she was always: "Well, you know, you know you're hot-blooded, so you're going to start early." And then her big thing was that I didn't start until thirteen: "Oh I'm so glad, I'm so glad. I was so sure that you were going to start at eight years old." That was constant, constant reminders and weird things that half the time I didn't even get.

The good thing in San Francisco there was specific neighborhoods that people lived in. If you were Irish you lived in one neighborhood, if you were Italian in another and you never really had to go out of your neighborhood because there was a grocery store and everything you needed in that whole area. It's not that way anymore. It kind of changed since the sixties. So I went to a Catholic school in my little neighborhood, which was mainly Irish-American, even my parents were a little different from the rest, but definitely all white. So I even stuck out in the neighborhood and in the school and was picked on quite frequently for being brown. So the difference I think is that I never had anybody in my house that understood that. I was just, I mean there was just nothing to even say to them because they didn't understand that.

WOULD YOU SAY THAT YOU POSSESS STRONG NATIVE AMERICAN PHYSICAL FEATURES?

Yeah.

HOW DID YOUR PHYSICAL APPEARANCE AFFECT THE WAY IN WHICH YOU WERE PERCEIVED BY BOTH THOSE IN THE INDIAN COMMUNITY AND THE NON-INDIAN COMMUNITY?

It's interesting because I'm not registered. You know, I assume my father was a Latino and Indian (Apache—according to his sister), that's what I'm told, and her (my mother's) family lived in Georgia, or her mother was.

I don't have any papers about that. All the records were sealed. Actually, all of my friends are Native and they're very fine with that, but other Native people are very weary and leery of me because of that and where I'm from. For a long time, I didn't fit in and I've been to places where people have been rude to me because of who I am. I've outgrown that now, but it wasn't easy. I moved from the Bay Area up to Chico. When I first moved up to Butte County it was, you know you couldn't even shop in the same store—people of color with white people, so that was very uncomfortable.

HOW DO YOU THINK OTHER PEOPLE'S REACTION TO YOUR PHYSICAL APPEARANCE HAS SHAPED YOUR CULTURAL IDENTITY?

There's a lot of stereotypical—you know I never really thought about it—there's a lot of stereotypical ideas. People just assume things about you, even the assumption: Oh, you only had one brother instead of foster kids in and out of the house we were in. I tell people now there was only one brother, so then they don't pretend like I didn't tell them the whole story about adoption. They're like, "Oh man, you look like you'd have a lot of people in your family." So the stereotypical made me actually feel like I didn't belong anywhere because I wasn't what people thought I should be. Does that make sense?

YEAH. DO YOU FEEL LIKE YOU BELONG SOMEWHERE NOW?

Yeah. But I haven't always felt like that—only in the last twenty years.

WHAT DO YOU THINK HAS HELPED YOU FEEL LIKE THAT?

Because I just, you know, have joined and become a very vital part of the Native American community in this area and watched it grow. I also think there's that whole thing about that purple hat where you're just like this is who I am, take it or leave it, I don't really care. But I also, you know, participated in dance ceremonies. I feel that I belong. At least certainly with my friends more than my family.

I WANT TO GO BACK AND TALK A LITTLE BIT MORE ABOUT YOUR ADOPTIVE FAMILY. YOU SAID THAT YOU STUCK OUT LIKE A SORE THUMB, DID YOU ALWAYS KNOW THAT YOU WERE ADOPTED?

Yeah, it's interesting because I was always told that but I don't ever remember being that. You know it's really interesting. Well, my brother died in 1985 but a friend of his said: "You know your brother told me he was adopted right before he got sick and I was blown away." And I said: "Well, you knew I was adopted." And he's like: "Yeah, but look at you. Everyone knew you were adopted." So I was like, "Oh yeah, I forgot."

Yeah, I was actually very close to my brother. He didn't make me feel different and the differences that we had I even joke about—it was that he was feeling uncomfortable about the differences that I had with my mother. My mother constantly reminded me that I was different.

DID YOUR PARENTS TALK ABOUT YOUR BEING NATIVE AMERICAN AT ALL OR DID THEY JUST MAKE THOSE NEGATIVE COMMENTS?

My dad didn't. My mom did a lot. My dad was actually pretty quiet. But they put me in Irish jig classes. There's Irish on my mom's side. So she actually looked for things that she maybe could identify with I suppose? Although there I was with all these kids that were freckle faced. . . . And yeah, I was out of place there too. It is a joke now though because I can do the Irish jig. People are just blown away by it.

WHAT DO YOU THINK YOUR PARENTS DID TO GIVE YOU A SENSE OF YOUR CULTURAL IDENTITY?

Nothing.

YOU MENTIONED THAT YOU WERE CLOSE TO YOUR BROTHER, DID YOU TALK TO HIM ABOUT BEING NATIVE AMERICAN?

Mainly, we talked about trying to find our parents because he wanted to find his, too. He never did. He did find an aunt right before he died. My mom passed on, everybody's passed on. But that was the main thing because he, too, you know, felt kind of lost.

See times were changing in San Francisco in the sixties too. You know Alcatraz came about. So it was becoming a more powerful feeling for people that were brown. There was red power and all that stuff was going on. So even though I didn't actually belong to any specific group I just couldn't help feel that way and think of myself that way.

DID YOU PARENTS EVER TREAT YOU AND YOUR BROTHER DIFFERENTLY?

Yes, they did.

DO YOU THINK IT WAS BECAUSE OF THE DIFFERENCE IN RACE OR SOMETHING ELSE?

Well, yes, I do. I know that my grandmother didn't like me. My mom's mom didn't like me at all. She would call me gypsy and weird names. She loved my brother. She thought my brother was German. They got along fine—talked for hours. My mom never actually treated me different, she just kind of learned to accept that my grandmother did. But yeah, I was treated differently.

My brother was very smart. He had a photographic memory. He, like at sixteen won a scholarship to go to Russia. He was very smart, so I could never live up to him. I don't think I would have lived up to him even if he wasn't that smart. He got into trouble, but it wasn't even a big thing. He got caught with a joint in his pocket and that wasn't a big thing. I mean my parents were a little upset. I got a DUI and that was a big thing.

Things just changed, expectations about what they thought versus. . . . It was never thought that I should ever go to college and he should and I don't know if that was a boy/girl thing. I think not. I think it was more of a race thing. That's something you feel in your gut. I actually did substance abuse because I had a hard time coping and feeling that I belonged anywhere.

DO YOU THINK YOUR BROTHER WAS AWARE OF THE DIFFERENCES IN THE WAY YOU TWO WERE TREATED?

Yeah, but I also know that he was a protector. He would defend me. I remember one time my parents were gone and he was supposed to watch me. They don't even know that it was me that did it, but I broke this glass thing. We were fooling around in the bedroom and there was this glass vase that my grandmother had brought from Germany. When my parents came home, he took the blame for it because he knew it would have been a lot more had I taken it. For years, I actually kind of believed that he did it because they were so upset and yelling so much at him and that's interesting because it's only in your mind.

YOU MENTIONED THAT YOU AND YOUR BROTHER WERE BOTH VERY INTERESTED IN FINDING YOUR BIRTH FAMILIES, WHAT WAS YOUR ADOPTIVE PARENTS RESPONSE?

They didn't like it. He didn't tell them at all and I didn't tell them until after my aunt found some papers. My mom asked me, "What do you think we are? You think we're just foster kids or parents." I was like, "No, but that doesn't mean that I can't—I shouldn't find where I belong because I definitely belong somewhere else and that doesn't diminish the love or the care or the understanding that I know you did give to me." Personally, for who they were and the times it was I know that she did the best she could for me. I didn't really know it then, but now when I look back at it in retrospect.

She passed away about three years ago and of course everyone's gone—my father's gone, my brother's gone, everybody's gone—it was just me. I ended up taking care of her. Even when she got dementia, she had a room in the hospital, she had contracted a virus that was contagious and so she had to be put in a room by herself; and she could hear people going back and forth in the hallway and she'd be like: "Okay, so that must be your friends out there because they'd be the only ones who'd be that way." You know even in her dementia—not knowing where she was and seeing things that weren't there—still thinking that I was the black sheep. I think I became the black sheep because I was told that so often.

WHAT PROMPTED YOUR DECISION TO SEARCH FOR YOUR BIRTH FAMILY?

Longing. That doesn't mean that there's not love, but there's definitely this huge piece missing and you know you're different. I think different. I'm always upset. That was evident to me and it was evident to them, too. I did not think the same way. We didn't have the same humor. Not only looks and just looking different. I was different.

HOW OLD WERE YOU WHEN YOU DECIDED TO LOOK FOR YOUR BIRTH FAMILY?

Well, I had tried several times and then I would just get frustrated and stop. You know it's interesting, the other thing that might have been something that urged me on too. I don't know. I went to a Catholic school and back then they had pagan babies and for five dollars you could buy a pagan baby. It was for third world countries and I just remember them holding up pictures of little brown babies. So I thought I was a pagan baby, I literally thought that I was one of those kids. So yeah, I always did identify that there were no other kids that were brown. There was actually a girl from El Salvador that came into my class in about the seventh grade and stayed for a little while. There were two black kids that entered that school. They lasted two months because they were teased so much. It was a very weird place to stay and no one to identify with and I think one of the things that stuck with me is that I just think you need to belong and you don't belong when you're living with someone with different values. Even my values are different. That amazes me because you'd think at least through osmosis or something that you would pick up, but no, if they're prejudiced, they're just different and you see things in a different way.

DID YOU TALK TO ANYBODY ABOUT THESE FEELINGS WHEN YOU WERE GROWING UP?

I talked to some of my girlfriends. I cried a lot during that time because there really wasn't too much to do at that time. I felt trapped. I really began to start thinking it was me because you know you got family here. You're not thinking right. We're the ones . . . your parents didn't want you. At one point I remember my mom showing me papers and saying look I paid a lot for you. I didn't find those papers after but I remember that she never did that to my brother. My brother was—they called them the last of the war babies—he was born after World War II. He was through a hospital, but I was private. She gave the church some money. She gave and they paid at the hospital. There's always this—not only are you different and you don't fit— but the circumstances around getting you were different, you were costly, you've always been an inconvenience.

YOU SAID BECAUSE OF ALL OF THIS YOU STARTED GETTING HIGH. HOW OLD WERE YOU WHEN THAT BEGAN?

About thirteen.

HOW LONG DID THAT LAST?

Into my twenties. I'd say, well, I stopped when I had my son at twenty. I started again after my daughter was born when I was twenty-five, so probably twenty-six, twenty-seven, twenty-eight, twenty-nine—I started getting high again.

WHY?

Because I didn't feel like I belonged. I had kids by a white man and my kids, two of them, were towheads. They're not anymore, they were really blond and people were like, "Oh, those aren't your kids." But, umm that uncomfortable feeling about being in my own skin and not belonging was really evident to me all my life.

AND SO WHEN YOU FINALLY STARTED FEELING LIKE YOU BELONGED, IS THAT WHEN YOU STOPPED USING DRUGS?

I started going to ceremonies actually. They had them in Oakland, on 14th Street there was an Indian Center. There were like all-night ceremonies and there were medicine men that came in and performed ceremonies. I thought it's interesting because when I went back to school, I actually went into substance abuse counseling in the Indian community and I'm still working in the Indian community. I started looking at the twelve steps, it was part of my schooling to get certified, they were almost identical to what they were teaching in ceremonies—you know autonomy and who you are. And that is what actually brought me back and then you know we went to the Sun dance in South Dakota. The interesting thing is that at first my mom thought I was crazy when I would tell her where I was going and then she just didn't say anything. It was almost like she accepted that and that was okay. It wasn't like she wanted to talk about it ever, but she didn't talk about it in a derogatory way either. She was a pretty derogatory person.

DID YOU ENCOUNTER ANY FORM OF RACISM IN THE COMMUNITY WHERE YOU GREW UP?

I was called nigger constantly. Yeah, I did. Not in the neighborhood—not with the kids on my block, there were like seventy-two kids on my block and we played kick the can and all that stuff—not in that direct area but in the school I went to I did, most definitely. Like I said, I went to a Catholic School and we had a nun from San Salvador in the fourth grade, Sister Maria Del Rey, she didn't like me at all and I was the only brown kid in that class. I think that was racial because she didn't— I don't know—she did not like me at all. She would tell me don't sing just move your lips. No you're wrong; no, you stay after school; no this, no that. You know she just, she just did not like me, and it was evident, even my friends said she didn't like me.

WERE YOUR PARENTS AWARE OF THIS?

No, no I didn't share a whole lot with them.

HOW DID YOU ADDRESS THE ISSUE OF RACISM?

I didn't, I didn't. I just umm, I don't really know. I cried. I didn't know what to do with it. There certainly wasn't no one else. I remember my adoptive mom said, "Oh you're olive complected." In the second grade, I told my friend that and she said, "You're not, you're brown. I'm olive complected." I had no idea. I was like eight years old.

But no, I didn't. Certainly I did when I was in high school, but things were changing. Things were like that in the fifties—all very cut and dry, and black and white.

GROWING UP, WERE THE MAJORITY OF YOUR FRIENDS WHITE OR WERE THEY OF OTHER RACES?

The majority of them were white because that's the neighborhood I lived in. It wasn't until I was in high school and the county started bringing in students from other schools that it was actually more multicultural—diversity in the classroom. It was also the latter part of the sixties. I graduated in 1970. So there was a lot of diversity throughout San Francisco. There were a lot of people who lived there that were kicking and fighting over it, but I really liked it.

WAS IT IN HIGH SCHOOL THAT YOU FIRST BEGAN DEVELOPING OR UNDERSTANDING YOUR SENSE OF CULTURAL IDENTITY?

Yeah.

DID YOU GO TO COLLEGE?

Not until we moved up here and my kids were in high school. I wanted to move out and I moved out when I was in high school for a year and then moved back home. I moved back home until I finished high school then I got a job and moved back out. I really couldn't wait until I got out. By that time everything that I ever thought—there were some contradictory remarks, derogatory remarks made—there was a lot of arguing going on between my mother and I. Very vicious actually, very uncomfortable.

DID YOU MOVE FAR AWAY FROM YOUR FAMILY?

Well, San Francisco is not a big city. It's only seven by seven miles, but I did move to the other end of town yeah. I moved to the Mission District, which was mainly Hispanic and Indians. I really felt very comfortable there. I liked it there.

WAS THAT WHEN YOU BEGAN GETTING MORE INVOLVED WITH THE NATIVE COMMUNITY?

Yes.

What type of work did you begin doing after you left your parents house?

I worked for the phone company and then I worked at the bank. I stayed there until I had my first son and then I had my second one. I got back to work and then I had my daughter. I think I only worked for a couple of months after I had her and then I didn't work again until she was two or three or something.

How old were you when you got married?

I've been married three times. The first time when I was twenty-one. We separated and divorced when I was pregnant with my daughter. Then I got married again. I got married to an Indian man. He was from the Wind River Reservation, but he kept having affairs so I actually got that annulled though because he never got his first marriage fully—they filed for divorce but they never finalized it—so I just got it annulled. Then I got married to a Navajo-Mexican man. He was clean and sober. He has a machine shop. We were together for nine years but the last three years he had to have surgery on his back and he got strung out first on pain medicine and then we separated. Now I'm married—for the last time to an Ojibwa man.

Was your sense of cultural identity changing or developing throughout the course of these marriages?

Yes.

Tell me a little bit more about your first husband. You said he was white. Do you think you were drawn to him because you were raised in a white family?

I think very much so and I knew him from high school, but I also think you know you stay with what you're familiar with. My adoptive father drank a lot actually. Never during work time though, but when he got home he'd have cocktails and stuff so I think it was really easy for me to slip into this mode. I definitely think he drank because my mom drove him nuts. But yeah that's why I think I married. So my children are probably what you would consider olive skinned more than they're brown. They're not very dark. What's interesting is that they went to high school here in Butte County and my daughter said people are constantly asking her what she was. Compared to me I feel like she is very light skinned but I guess not to her peers.

How have you addressed the issue of cultural identity with your children?

They've been to ceremonies, sweat lodges, and they know all that. They kind of choose not to because they were uncomfortable. Although I see them somewhat coming back. My oldest son and his wife are very into their Christian church. My middle son is actually staying with them because he's got a trial down there. They kind of butt heads a lot over that, but they're still brothers. I mean they've all seemed to have found their place. What's different, I believe, is that we're comfortable—I'm comfortable with who they are. That's way different from how I was brought up. My parents were never comfortable with who I was. My daughter goes back and forth. She certainly has her own spirituality. She identifies herself with Native people. She's quite comfortable with who she is. Her and my older son have green eyes which they get from my mother's side of the family. My mother (actually my birth aunt) had green eyes when I met her before she died. That was really nice. Even those kind of things, it's like okay where did this come from. I have to say it's awful when you go to doctors and they like ask your family history. I know a little bit because my aunt told me now but for years I didn't know.

Can you tell me a little more about your birth family, how you found them and who you found?

Well, I searched—I don't know sometime around sixteen, I think—for my mother's maiden name. The name was actually gone, the name was dead because my grandmother only had daughters. I didn't know that then. I remember wherever I went I would look in phone books for that name so I could find anything. It was interesting, I tried, I went down to San Francisco and I filed some legal papers saying that it was an emotional heartache for me not to know because you could open records for medical reasons so I was trying to see if I could use psychological reasons. The lady down there threw up her arms and said, No, I can't touch this. He won't look at them. Take them away. I was always feeling like I had leprosy or something. I remember I tried to get my original birth certificate. I couldn't get that. I remember writing to the state a few times. I remember I put my name in that thing!

I looked up census for Indian records. I didn't know that they were not enrolled. I just looked them up but nothing. I just felt really lost. I just felt like I just didn't belong. And really, even though I had friends and was participating in the spirituality for instance I still felt—you know, somebody says, What are you? What tribe are you from? And you say, Apache, and its like, What Apache tribe? And all I can say is the Arizona area. You still feel like you're not accepted there either. I don't know. You know those stupid teams that have those mascot names on them? They're called Indians or Braves or whatever. It's almost feeling like that. It's like you know what you are but you don't really fit and you feel fake. It's interesting because at some point not in the last few years but at some point in my life, non-Indians accepted me as an Indian more than Indians would. And that was actually harder than anything because I felt lost. I can't tell them I never found anything about my father.

BUT YOU DID FIND INFORMATION ABOUT YOUR MOTHER?

Yeah. I was at work one day and my friend called me and said, "There's this lady in the paper who helps adoptees. Here's her name and here's her number." She goes, "I don't know, you should just do it." So I did. She was in Sutter County, not too far from here. She told me that her daughter was adopted and that she went with her daughter to the courthouse and they pulled out her file in front of her and said, "Yep, you were adopted, but we can't show you this." I guess she was so insulted by them doing that to her that she started this business. There was $250.00 up front and $250.00 upon completion. I had no money at all, none whatsoever, but I said okay. I'll do it. I got off the phone and I told my coworker and was like, "Wow, I just committed myself to $500.00 I don't have and it's Christmas time." This happened and never happened since, two hours later our board gave everyone at the agency $500.00 for a Christmas bonus. I had a name and that was more than what most people had, but she was the one who found my mom and told me where she was born or buried. When I went there I saw actually that my grandmother was buried next to her, but I didn't know it then but an uncle was buried on the other side. But I remember going down to that cemetery I really wish that there had been a picture on the grave but there wasn't. I wanted to dig it up. I don't know. It was awful. But then that lady called me late and said, I can't leave you like this. Anyway, she did this thing and found out from the site where my mom was buried and stuff and she manipulated the person who owned that graveyard by I don't know how. So she found my aunt. At that time my aunt was living in Santa Fe. So I took a trip to Santa Fe, New Mexico. But before I did that I sent her pictures of me. I didn't want to be rejected. My mom's sister, my adoptive mom's sister never would talk to me, she still won't talk to me. She's ninety years old. She has nothing to do with me. She virtually stopped talking to my mom for years because she had adopted me. So I didn't want any more rejection. I just couldn't deal with any more rejection, so I sent her a picture and then I called her about a week after. Yes, she had gotten the pictures, she was excited. Yes, she would love for me to come down. I had never been welcomed like that from any relative, so that in itself.

So my friend and I, her and I, she was Navajo and her people were on the reservation by Gallup. She wanted to visit family, so we took a road trip down there together. I met my aunt and that was really nice. It was actually like finding some balance. She had the same type of humor I did. She was able to tell me about my mom, tell me about her. She said that they didn't need to know much tribal activity, but a little bit. She talked about her mother. Her mother participated more than they did. They were raised because their father was in the military so they were like in the Philippines and had moved around a lot. She was very nice. She moved to California and then she passed on not too long after that.

WHAT DO YOU THINK YOU GAINED BY FINDING YOUR MOTHER'S FAMILY?

A sense of belonging more than anything because there was no reservation about being me. There was no—"Oh you're brown"—because everybody was the same. It was like when you go to a family dinner and you help them or you cook dinner for them or something like that and you just feel at home, that's how it was.

I actually never felt that way at my [adoptive] mother's house. Everything was: "Don't touch this you'll break it. I know you will. You're awkward." Or: "No you can't do dishes because you'll break them." Or: "No, I don't want you to do the cooking because you'll be sloppy." It was never allowed. It was very weird.

With my [biological] mother's family there was this whole sense of belonging. A sense of pride too. I'm not sure why, but it was there.

HOW HAVE YOU CHANGED SINCE MEETING THEM?

I'm more comfortable in my own skin. My daughter will tell you the same thing. After we visited my family she said: "Mom, I've never felt more comfortable." We had never felt that. I just felt more comfortable with myself and who I am.

I'm not able to get registered with a tribe, but I'm okay with who I am and nobody can take that away or make it bad or ugly because now I know who I am.

You know there is shame when people talk to you in certain ways and make assumptions about you and none of it is good and all that shame is gone. I'm okay.

WHAT DOES IT MEAN TO YOU TO BE INDIAN?

For me, it explains why I feel things the way I do—why I understand what I do. It means belonging to a bigger family than just my immediate family. It means pride. It means that it's okay to actually be verbal about discrimination. Now I can stop it; whereas, before, because I didn't feel like I belonged or didn't feel attached to a family or feel accepted by another family, I didn't do that. Now I have the ability to say something.

It means that the world is bigger than just me and my children. Before it wasn't.

ARE THERE ANY BARRIERS THAT PREVENTED YOU FROM FULLY INTEGRATING INTO THE INDIAN COMMUNITY?

No. Actually, I haven't had any.

HOW WOULD YOU DESCRIBE YOUR INVOLVEMENT WITH THE INDIAN COMMUNITY TODAY?

My friends are all Indians. I worked at the Indian health center. I've dated Indian men. I'm on the board of a nonprofit organization that focuses on Indian education. I feel fully integrated. Yeah.

It's interesting because I don't actually think about that. You're making me think about it and I can't think about a part of my life that isn't involved with Indians. It's who I am. That's how I feel. That's who I am.

WHAT OTHER RESOURCES HAVE HELPED YOU UNDERSTAND INDIAN CULTURE? FOR EXAMPLE, BOOKS.

I read a lot of books when I was younger.

HOW HELPFUL WERE THOSE?

Well, I remember reading about Wounded Knee and I remember being really, really upset about how people treated people. Some of the books made me really sad when they talked about family. When they talked about the family dynamic I felt a huge loss. A really huge loss now that I think about it.

WHEN YOU BEGAN INTERACTING WITH THE INDIAN COMMUNITY, DID YOU FEEL A TYPE OF CULTURE SHOCK?

No. I felt. . . . No. It was kind of like meeting my aunt. It was comfort, pure comfort and I had never really felt that.

ARE YOU GLAD THAT YOU WERE ADOPTED BY A WHITE FAMILY?

Not particularly. No. I really don't want to say anything bad about them because I know they did their best.

In general, do you think non-Indians should be allowed to adopt Indian children?

I think that obviously being adopted by a white family is better than being put in an orphanage, but I think that Native people need to adopt Native children. I think the standards need not to be based on white people standards.

Would you say that you are in favor of the Indian Child Welfare Act?

Yes, definitely and I think that it needs to be enforced better in some places.

What factors should be taken into consideration when placing an Indian child?

Do you mean an Indian child in an Indian home or a non-Indian home or anywhere?

Anywhere.

First of all, the family should be Indian. Second of all, try to help them understand their tribe. I think that's the main thing. Also Native siblings shouldn't be separated and if they are separated they should still be allowed to have contact with each other. It's okay to have families that have multiple children and multiple children in a room.

And maybe, offer help to the family because sometimes kids can be overwhelming. Parents should be able to meet somewhere. For example, there's a group for foster families, but not one for Indians. There's not one for Indians here and there should be.

What advice would you offer white families who would want to or who have adopted Indian children?

Set their kids up with an Indian center in the area. Watch what you say. When my daughter came home from summer school, she said: "Mom, I can do this song in sign language" and it was "One Little, Two Little, Three Little Indians." I wrote this letter to the school board and she's like, "No, Mom. People are going to get mad at me. No, no, no. I don't want to be singled out." I wrote this letter to the school board saying, "you know I don't understand why don't you sing, one little, two little white people. Blah, blah, blah." Anyway, at the end of the year she came home and said, "Mom, our homework is to write our own song and it can't have anything about people. It can only be about animals and that's because of you mom." I was like good. They heard me. You need to be aware of that because that stuff sticks with you.

Make sure that your child's not being singled out. I know that. I went with a mom at the school here because every time Thanksgiving or whatever when they were talking about Indians her son was picked on by the teachers. They'd say can you tell us about that. Obviously, he didn't know about every tribe and they're singling him out and he didn't know all of the answers and that was embarrassing. So you need to be aware of those things and I don't think people in general are. If you're going to have an Indian child in your house, you need to be aware of that.

WHAT ADVICE WOULD YOU OFFER TO INDIAN ADOPTEES? HOW CAN THEY BECOME MORE COMFORTABLE WITH WHO THEY ARE?

I think everybody needs to learn to become comfortable in their own skin. You need to know what tribe you are. Get a hold of your birth certificate, which is easier to do today. Find out about your tribe. Get involved with the Indian community. It's going to be awkward at first.

There's a history too. There's a lot of post-traumatic stress from all of the trauma surrounding the holocaust of American Indian people.

I have a friend who was adopted and she didn't like her birth mother. She had nothing for years good to say about her mom. Anyway she called her bad names. It was odd because she thought her mom gave her away for bad reasons. Now we're planning a trip to go down to her tribe and meet them. Her thoughts have turned around and it's been a lot of work, but she started to realize—well, actually both of her adopted parents died and I think that made it easier for her.

The other thing is that adoptive parents really need to think about—it's not a slap in the face when your child or adopted child wants to find their parents. It's not a slap at all and it's not going to ever take away what you did or didn't do. The child that you adopted—that's going to make them a whole person. I think very often adoptive parents don't want anybody else to interfere. They just want to be the parents.

ARE THERE ANY OTHER QUESTIONS THAT YOU THINK I SHOULD HAVE ASKED YOU OR ANY OTHER ISSUES THAT YOU'D LIKE TO ADDRESS?

No. I hope I didn't ramble on too much.

NO. YOU DID JUST FINE. THANK YOU.

7

# SHANA GREENBURG

Born in Los Angeles, California, in 1966, Shana Greenburg (Mono) was adopted by a Jewish couple who spotted a picture of the toddler on TV in 1967. Shana has a very strong and healthy relationship with her adoptive parents, which she attributes to their candor regarding adoption and race. According to Shana, her adoptive parents were informed by a social worker that she was of American Indian descent and that they should make every effort to put her in touch with the Indian community. As a result, her parents enrolled her in the local Indian Education Program when she was still in elementary school. Shana's involvement with the urban Indian community only increased as she got older.

Unlike many other participants, Shana never seemed to experience a cultural identity crisis despite the fact that she has been unable to enroll with her tribe. She notes that by the time she got to high school and college she "realized that [she] was part of the Indian community, and that's where [she] belonged." As a student at California State University, Shana was an active member of the American Indian student council as well as a member of the American Indian Science and Engineering Society (AISES). She later attended law school at Arizona State University and has been a member of the Native American Bar Association in Washington, D.C., for more than eight years.

At twenty-three years of age, Shana's life came full circle when she reunited with her birth mother on the pilot episode of a short-lived TV show called *Reunion*. According to Shana, they maintained a brief relationship before going their separate ways in 1996 and notes that she has very little contact with any members of her biological family.

Shana says that she is grateful for her adoptive family and the opportunities that they have afforded her, but maintains that she is a "full supporter" of the Indian Child Welfare Act. She believes that every effort should be made to find a "stable Indian family" and argues when that's not possible every effort should be made to keep adopted children in touch with the American Indian community.

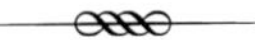

WHAT YEAR WERE YOU BORN?

1966.

AND WHERE YOU BORN?

Los Angeles, California.

DO YOU KNOW HOW OLD YOU WERE WHEN YOU WERE ADOPTED?

I was twelve months old.

ARE YOU AWARE OF THE CIRCUMSTANCES SURROUNDING YOUR ADOPTION?

Yes.

COULD YOU DESCRIBE THEM FOR ME?

Apparently, my biological mother, who was originally from near Fresno, California, had married somebody in the Navy, moved to Alameda, California, had twins, and then when her husband was deployed, she became pregnant with me. And so then she decided to give me up for adoption. And when her husband at the time came back, he took her twin boys, and she moved down to Los Angeles, where her mother and father were living, and put me up for adoption. She stayed in a Catholic—it's like a Catholic home for unwed mothers—I think it was St. Andrews in downtown L.A., until I was born, and then when I was born, she gave me up.

IS YOUR BIOLOGICAL MOTHER NATIVE AMERICAN, OR IS YOUR BIOLOGICAL FATHER?

My mother.

CAN YOU TELL ME A LITTLE BIT ABOUT YOUR ADOPTIVE PARENTS?

My adoptive parents, Linda and David Greenburg, are Jewish, from Kansas City, Missouri. My mom was born and raised there. My dad was born in Youngstown, Ohio, but pretty much raised in Kansas City, Missouri.

My mother's mother, who's my bubbe, is from Russia, and then my other grandparents on my dad's side are from Austria, and they came to this country through the Baltimore port. So I actually have some of my Jewish relatives here in D.C.

So they were married in 1960. They met at IBM, where my mom was a data key entry person and my dad was, like, the maintenance guy. So they met and dated there for a year and got married in Kansas City, and then my dad went to Texas to school.

And they were married eight years before they had their first child, who's my older brother, Greg, and he's about ten months older than me. So they had him when my dad was going to graduate school at MIT in Boston, and then after graduate school, they moved to Los Angeles, where my dad got a job. And while my mom was pregnant with my younger brother, they adopted me. And I'm not sure what else. They're great parents. They've always been very supportive. They've been married now for forty-five years, and they've provided a really good family role model for me.

One of the things I think that was important to me is when they adopted me, they were told by the social worker that I was American Indian and that it would be nice if they could keep me in touch with the community. So they made, you know, efforts to do that. So I was a part of the Indian Education program, growing up in L.A., all through high school.

DID YOUR PARENTS EVER INDICATE TO YOU WHY THEY CHOSE TO ADOPT AN AMERICAN INDIAN CHILD?

No, they just wanted a girl. And at the time, in the 1960s, there were more children put up for adoption that one year than any other year ever, and there were so many children that were placed up for adoption, they were putting us on TV.

So they were watching TV, and they had thought about—you know, they didn't know whether my younger brother was going to be a boy or a girl. But they knew that they wanted a girl for sure—they already had a boy.

So they saw me on TV and then they went right down and said they wanted me, and they didn't know at the time what I was. They didn't really care. They just knew that they wanted a girl.

SO WHEN DID YOU FIRST REALIZE THAT YOU WERE ADOPTED?

I've always known. My parents have always been very, very honest about that, and it's very obvious because my brothers have curly blond hair and blue eyes, and my parents both have curly hair. And so I don't look anything like any of my relatives, so I've just always known. My mom—both my parents have been very open about things as we were growing up.

WAS THERE A MOMENT WHEN THEY SPECIFICALLY SAT YOU DOWN AND TALKED ABOUT IT WITH YOU?

Not that I can remember, just because it was just something that I always knew.

WHO DID YOU TALK TO GROWING UP ABOUT THE FACT THAT YOU WERE ADOPTED OR WAS THAT EVER—

Probably my mom. I mean, my mom was very open and talked about everything. It's kind of like sex. I mean, she—I can't ever remember learning about that because it was just—you know, a part of the conversation, you know, growing up.

So there wasn't one specific time where she sat down and said, okay, we're going to have this talk. It was just, you know, just like growing up—everybody in my family did. It just really wasn't a big deal. I mean, I never felt like—I don't know. I never, like, felt adopted. I mean, I always knew I was adopted, I was different from my brothers, I looked different, but I never felt that it made a difference.

SO DO YOU THINK YOUR PARENTS HANDLED THE REVELATION ABOUT YOUR ADOPTION IN A POSITIVE MANNER?

Yeah. Oh, definitely.

AND DO YOU THINK THAT'S WHAT YOU WOULD RECOMMEND TO OTHER FAMILIES DEALING WITH THIS?

Oh, totally. I mean, I believe that you always have to have open communication with your kids about everything, especially when they look a lot different from other kids.

WHAT DO YOU THINK YOUR PARENTS DID TO GIVE YOU A SENSE OF YOUR CULTURAL IDENTITY?

In the urban areas, you know, they have the Indian Education Program. They have culture night every Tuesday at one of the schools, so we used to go to that.

I got to know all of the other Indian kids in my school, so I kind of grew up knowing them. Because it was in L.A., most of us were mixed with Mexican, so we kind of hung out with the Chicanos, too.

But it just provided me with that community which was different. And—well, because I never felt like I was really Jewish. Even though I grew up in a Jewish family, we didn't grow up near family, really, so my community—the Indian community was my community.

And those other kids growing up in that urban area, that were mixed, that I grew up with, were people that I could relate to.

WERE YOUR CLOSEST FRIENDS GROWING UP INDIANS OR—

Most of them at the time were Chicano—or mixed. I had some friends that were American-Indian. They weren't in L.A.—well, I was in L.A. until I was, like, ten, and then when I moved up to the Bay Area, there weren't as many American Indians so I only had two or three others that I knew about that went to my high school and I hung out with them, again, because we all hung out in the Chicano community.

NOW, YOU MENTIONED YOU HAVE TWO BROTHERS. DID YOU TALK WITH THEM ABOUT BEING AN AMERICAN INDIAN?

Yes. They're aware of all my activities in the community. I can't say they've ever been a big part of the community or understand it or anything.

I mean, it's almost like I've always led this dual life where I have my friends who are, like, all American Indian, and then I have my family, who are, like, all white, Jewish people. And I love them all equally, but they're different. They're very, very different, and I don't feel comfortable mixing them.

HOW DO YOU KEEP THEM SEPARATE OR HOW DO YOU KEEP THOSE TWO DIFFERENT LIVES SEPARATE?

Well, you know, it's almost like anybody. You have your family, and then you have your friends, and even though my family knows all my friends, they don't go to my social events. My family doesn't go to the same social events that I go to.

But I have to say they don't understand a lot of stuff about American Indian culture. My mom tried to take a class one time in college, and it was taught by some crazy white lady, as my mom described her. I was like, yeah, great. And so that was the thing that my mom got as far as community.

And I've taken her to events that I've planned and worked on before—like I made her go volunteer at a powwow one time with me and that kind of stuff. But I could tell it wasn't really something my mom was really interested in.

Were there things that you learned about Native Americans while you were growing up that contradicted what you actually learned once you got involved in the community?

I grew up in an urban area, so I grew up as an urban Indian, and so that's a lot different than being from the reservation. In particular my tribe, once I found out what tribe I was, and I went out there, it was very different than what I expected.

But my former husband was Navajo, so when we got married, we spent a lot of time out on the Navajo Reservation. But since I grew up in an urban area, I grew up with the powwow culture, going to powwows and stuff like that. And by the time I had gone out to the Navajo Reservation, a lot of the powwows had gotten out there, too, so that was part of their culture as well.

But then there were also other things that I didn't know that were different from the urban—I mean, I kind of knew a lot of Indian people in the community who were from reservations, so everything I learned was just kind of from associating with them.

So as far as contradicting, I can't really think of anything right now.

What is your tribal affiliation?

Mono. It's a California tribe over near Fresno.

And did you seek out your birth family?

Yes.

Can you tell me a little bit about that process?

When I was twenty-three I just had an opportunity to—they used to have this TV show in L.A. called *Reunion*, and it was a pilot show. They wanted people to come try out for it, and I sent them a letter saying I wanted to find my biological mother and blah, blah, blah.

And then I went, interviewed, and they picked me, so they paid a private investigator to find her for me. So they found her—turned out she was living, like, eight miles away from me in L.A. And they canceled the show, so I never actually had to film the show, but I got to find her free.

My parents were very supportive of finding her. You know, they didn't feel threatened or anything. They encouraged that. I just never had the resources to look for her.

I don't know who my biological dad is either. I keep thinking I should probably find him—he's probably dead now or something, I don't know. But I don't even—honestly, I don't even know where she is right now. So anyways, I found her. She lived about eight miles away from me at the time. The first time we met, it was at a coffee shop.

She was very, very different from me. She had been married several times, at that time had six kids. I was the only one of those that she had put up for adoption. She was very nice, she's very artistic—I'm not very artistic, but she did teach me how to sew.

We proceeded to meet, like, maybe once a month, just to get to know each other, for a couple years until I moved out of the area. And that was nice, and then I have not seen her since, I think, probably, like, 1996 or 1997. I haven't seen or heard from her. I have no idea where she is.

I've talked to her uncle. One of the things that I was interested in was her family—their family was Mormon and they did not affiliate with the Indian community at all.

So that was really interesting to me because had I not been adopted, I probably would never, ever have been a part of the Indian community at all because they knew nothing. They moved away from Fresno and just never stayed in contact with the tribe or anything and just didn't think that was important.

NOW, YOU MENTIONED THAT YOU HAD SIX BIOLOGICAL SIBLINGS. DO YOU HAVE A RELATIONSHIP WITH THEM?

No. No. Two of them are—the twins that were born before me, I've never met them. I keep thinking, I don't even know if they know about me. I actually had an opportunity to go to a family reunion, a biological family reunion, and that was interesting because nobody knew about me.

WHY DID YOU FEEL THAT IT WAS IMPORTANT TO FIND YOUR BIRTH FAMILY?

Well, the main thing is that I wanted to know what tribe I was. Because, you know, that always came up. Everyone was always, like, "wow, what tribe are you?" And I had to say, "I don't know." No one questioned me or said anything. I just would tell them I was adopted.

And now I tell them I'm Mono, and they look at me like, "well, where's that?" That was my response when she handed me all those papers. I was like, "what? Where's that from?" Then I went up there, and there was nobody up there, and it was weird. It's been weird.

ARE YOU AN ENROLLED MEMBER OF THE TRIBE?

No. No. It's—that's been weird.

Have you been unable to get enrolled or—

The thing is that when I first went up there, it was before gaming, there was no tribal government, there was nothing. So I had to go to the BIA.

And I went to the BIA with my documents and I said, here's my documents, here's my relatives, this and that. And I don't know if you've ever tried to work with the BIA and stuff like that—well, any government entity—it takes forever.

So anyway, eleven years later—and I kid you not—and I had sent in my grandmother's birth certificate, my mother's, then they were like, well, we need your great-grandmother's birth certificate. And I'm just, like, she didn't have one. And so then they were hesitant, but then gaming popped up, and even though at the time my tribe didn't have gaming, they were forming a government, so then the BIA was, like, well, now, they have a government, you've got to deal with the tribe.

So I went over there, these are small tribes. And because my family never affiliated, except for this cousin who I'm trying to track down, they were, like, well, we don't know who your family is.

And even though we have the BIA records, so my family's always been able to get services because of the BIA—the CDIB from the BIA—but I don't know anyone at the tribe. I don't even know what's going on.

I mean, they have their own enrollment process now, and because my mother and all them haven't gone through that process, then they're not going to enroll me or my children.

And now with gaming and all that, I just decided it's just not worth it—I don't need to be enrolled. I'm not going to—right now, it's just—it's like finding my biological father. It doesn't help me define who I am, or whether or not I am Indian.

My kids are enrolled at Navajo, and that's all, so they can't be enrolled two places anyway, and I don't want anybody to start thinking that, well, I only got enrolled for the money. I don't need that.

So how would you say that you identify yourself today?

I identify myself as American Indian.

And when would you say you took on that identity, or was there ever a moment where you just sort of said—

In elementary school.

Was there a specific moment or—

Well, I can remember beating up a girl in kindergarten because she asked me why I wore clothes, so probably then. I remember this girl saying, "well, if you're Indian, you shouldn't be wearing clothes, because Indians don't wear clothes."

So then you beat her up?

I did, and I got kicked out of kindergarten for that.

Did you have a lot of conflict growing up with other students because you had a different cultural background?

Oh, yeah. I don't know if we're going to get to that adolescent cross-cultural adoption thing, but as I reached into junior high, it was very difficult for me because California's very segregated, and either you're white or you were Mexican where I was at, okay?

And I grew up, my brothers are white, my parents are white—you know, I grew up kind of thinking, you know, I was white.

But when I got into junior high and tried to hang out—because, you know, in elementary school, everybody hangs out with everybody, there's no—there's really no racial bonding or whatever—but in junior high, when I got there, I was going to a new school, so it was kind of traumatic for me. I tried sitting by the white kids, and they ignored me, like, literally. I can remember thinking, you know, what's wrong? Whereas the Chicano kids were the ones who were, "hey, come hang with us."

So that was a big issue for me. So there I was in the same school with my brother, who hung out with the white kids, and I was on the other side of the fence, hanging out with the Chicanos. And then it was a huge issue for me and embarrassing that I had white parents. I mean, I never took any of my friends home to meet my parents.

What do you think of that, looking back at it today?

Well, it was just—it was really hard because most of my friends—my dad was a professional and had an education. Most of my friends lived in apartments, and their parents were laborers. I didn't want them knowing that I had more.

And, you know, it's interesting because they knew that my brother was my brother and he had blond hair, blue eyes. They all knew who he was, that he was my brother, because I was always having to stick up for him. Because there was a lot of racial tension there, and at one time, people—my friends would pick on him, so I had to let them know that that was my brother and not to pick on him.

I just think it's an unfortunate circumstance, but I think we all hang out with people that we can identify with. So I think that's probably where I got my start in identifying with minorities.

SO HOW DO YOU THINK ALL THESE EXPERIENCES HAVE HELPED YOU FORM YOUR SENSE OF CULTURAL IDENTITY?

Have helped with my sense of cultural identity? Well, it allowed me to be a part of a community where I feel comfortable.

I don't feel comfortable in the white community, and this is an issue that I face every day here at work because I work with all white people. This is my first job actually working with all white people.

And it's—it enabled me—because when you're adopted, they always have that ongoing conversation about whether it's genetic or socialization, and me and my mom always say that it's a little bit of both.

But culturally, I'm a lot different than my parents—socially and culturally and just the way that I see that things are connected. And I don't know if that's because of people that I've socialized with growing up, but I think also growing up in the urban area and having the urban education—urban Indian education—has really helped me to learn, you know, about the Indian culture.

But the other thing is that when you grow up in an urban area, you kind of learn about everybody else's native culture, not your own, so I didn't really grow up learning anything about Mono people.

Even if I'd known a Mono, I kind of bonded closely with some people from the Plains area, I would go to sweats on Wednesdays, and powwow dancing—and kind of learned it that way.

And it's really—it becomes your social community, and that kind of love and support that I learned through that is I think one of the best things about being a part of the Indian community.

So I don't know if that is related to the question you asked at all—

NO, NO, IT IS. I WANT TO GO BACK A LITTLE BIT AND TALK ABOUT HIGH SCHOOL AND COLLEGE. DID YOU HAVE ANY OF THOSE SORT OF SAME CONFLICTS IN HIGH SCHOOL OR IN COLLEGE THAT YOU HAD IN MIDDLE SCHOOL?

Not really because by the time I was in high school and college, I realized that I was part of the Indian community, and that's where I belonged.

WHERE DID YOU GO TO COLLEGE?

I went to Cal State Long Beach, and they actually had a good Indian population there. And then while I was in college, I worked with the Indian Student Council and AISES and we helped to run an AISES summer camp there for high school students. I also worked with the American Indian Student Council and worked with the Indian Center, and then I also worked in the Indian Education Program through the Long Beach schools, where I was able to even work with other adopted kids. Which was a good opportunity for me.

So did you deliberately choose that school because of the American Indian population?

Yeah, I did, actually.

And what was your major again?

My major was in Psychology with a minor in Anthropology, Cultural Anthropology.

Now, you mentioned that you met several adoptees there. Did you share your experiences with them?

Yes.

Were you able to identify with them well?

I was. I was. For me, it was nice to see that there were other non-Indian parents making an effort to let their Indian kids be affiliated with the community because I think, like I mentioned in my e-mail, I've met tons of American Indian professionals who are adopted.

And for me, it's been a nice little network, and we've shared our experience, sat around the tables. A lot of us are attorneys, actually. So we sat around the table and shared our experiences in meeting our families and this and that. And we all have had very different experiences.

For the most part, would you say that the people you've interacted with have had positive experiences, or would you say they had negative experiences?

I think we all kind of felt the same thing, that it was a positive experience and that we have really great adopted parents.

But it was really different because our lives now, being involved in the Indian community, are so different that what I miss—I think what I miss, had I been adopted by an Indian family, I would have an extended Indian family, and with that comes, like—I always—with my family, if you want to go visit my mom or dad, you go to make an appointment.

With my Indian friends, I tell people all the time—I have three kids—if I became homeless tomorrow, I have probably four or five friends that I could move in with them. I could just call them and say, I'm moving in. And they'd be, like, oh, come on, come on over, you know, sure.

Whereas my mom would be, like, what's wrong, you know or—none of my relatives—none of my white relatives would I ever even approach for that kind of help, you know what I mean?

And I think that's what I miss by being adopted by a white family. I think that's the cultural difference. So that's why I'm grateful to have my community because when I was having problems, they were there for me, and vice versa. When other people have a problem, you're there for them.

DID YOU GO ON FOR MORE SCHOOLING AFTER YOU GRADUATED FROM CAL STATE?

In 1991 I went to Law School at Arizona State University and graduated in 1994.

HOW DO YOU THINK THE FACT THAT YOU'RE AN AMERICAN INDIAN HAS AFFECTED YOUR LIFE BOTH PERSONALLY AND PROFESSIONALLY?

I think professionally it's been really hard here, working for the government, because even though I have the same education as everybody else here, and I even have a nice white, Jewish name, I'm still not, like, a part of the clique or the regular old, Jewish, white attorneys. And I'm not a part of that group.

So I'm still seen by them as an American Indian person, and it's like you're treated almost like you have a bias. My background actually is in Indian law and policy, and when I was first hired here, it was to work on those kind of issues, but I think they felt that I was being too strong of an advocate, so they took me off of that, and I think they thought that because I was adopted that maybe I could just be a token and not be much of an advocate.

So I think it's hurt me in that way because now—it's like, even though I feel like I have the same skills as everyone, I'm still different.

Personally, it's helped me because it's nice to have a good community. I have some great friends that I can rely on. I mean, American Indian people just have that community social sense about them that, oh, your door's open, and you can always find that support there. And I think that's the best part of it.

There can be drawbacks to living in a small community, and I know that, too, but for the most part, I think it's more positive.

So would you say that American Indians are your closest friends today?

I have a diverse friend group but most are American Indian. That and some other Chicano people that I went to high school with whom I stay in touch.

Now, you mentioned that you were heavily involved in a lot of activities in college involving American Indians. What sort of activities are you involved with today?

We recently started an American Indian employees group, the Society of American Indian Government Employees, SAIGE, S-A-I-G-E—saige.org is our website. And I'm the treasurer of that, and we have an annual training conference every year.

What's important about that is that American Indians have always been employed by the federal government, but we've never had a national group representing our interests, and now we have that.

I've been involved with the Native American Bar Association for several years. About five years ago, no, maybe longer—oh, my God, eight years ago, we incorporated the Native American Bar Association here in D.C., so I've been a part of that.

And, well, since I do have four kids, that's about all I can do is be a part. And I'm the treasurer of the National Native American Bar Association right now.

Now, you mentioned you have four kids. How have you addressed the issue of cultural identity with your children?

That's the hard thing about living here in D.C. is that they know that they're Navajo, but at the same time, whenever they talk about themselves and talk about "those Native Americans," it's like they distance themselves.

Which is interesting because they—visually, they look Navajo, and so I try and explain, you're Navajo.

And then another interesting thing is that there's not really a lot of American Indians in Maryland, where I live now, and I do my best to get them out, too. That's where there are other kids their age that are Indian. But there's just not a lot, so most of their friends are not Indian.

I was lucky because in California and L.A. there were a lot of other Indian students there that I could hang out with.

Now, you mentioned that both you and your children have very strong Indian features. How do you think that that's affected the way in which people have reacted to you growing up?

Well, actually, what's interesting is that I have green eyes, and I'm actually pretty light-skinned. But growing up in L.A., everybody was mixed. I mean, I'm sure you—I don't know if you—you live in Denver, right?

YEAH.

Oh, okay, well, Denver, there's probably a lot less mixing, but in L.A., there's a lot of mixing there. So growing up, all the Indian students, they all pretty much looked like me. They were lighter-skinned.

I mean, I used to get a lot of shit because I had green eyes, get teased because of that. But I never realized that I was really that light until I went out to Navajo, and then when I went out to Navajo, people were staring at me. I didn't understand.

And then finally some lady just said, you look white to me. And I was like, what? What are you talking about? And this is when I was twenty-three years old. It didn't dawn on me that I was really that pale, so I wouldn't say I have straight black hair and all that, green eyes, but my skin is pretty light. So I can pretty much pass for almost any culture. I have that multicultural look.

When I lived in Hawaii, a lot of people thought I was Hawaiian. But my kids, because their dad was full-blooded Navajo, have a little stronger features—two of them—and then one of them is lighter-skinned like me. No green eyes, though.

And living where we live in Maryland, I think a lot of people just think they're Asian or Mexican. I don't think they really think of them as being American Indian, I mean, except for, like, in November, when we go to their classes and give the obligatory talk.

SO DO YOU THINK YOUR PHYSICAL APPEARANCE HAS AFFECTED YOUR SENSE OF CULTURAL IDENTITY AT ALL?

It hasn't because it didn't really dawn on me that I was really that light-skinned until I was, like I said, twenty-three, and—I don't know.

Well, you're probably going to laugh, but what's funny is that I've commented on other people—when I was growing up, I would comment on other people. Well, look how white she looks, this and that.

And then finally one of my friends looked at me and she said, "well, you're not that dark. You could pass for a white girl, too." I was like, "what? What are you talking about?"

You know, you have your own perception of yourself growing up and again, because all my friends, we all looked similar and—we're dark, dark brown haired, all that kind of stuff, it just never dawned on me that I didn't really look like them, even though I looked in the mirror every day.

Okay, I just have a few more questions for you. Are you glad that you were adopted by a white family?

They were a great family. I really am lucky. I think one of the benefits of being adopted by a white family is that they taught me a lot of independence and survival skills that I might not have gotten in the Indian community.

So if I could have been adopted by an Indian family that taught me these things, then of course, I would have been happy. But I look at my biological family. None of them went to college, none of my siblings—out of the six of us, none of them finished high school. And definitely none of them went to college.

So I feel like that was a really good influence on me, and I think we need that kind of balance in our community, and then I'll be able to teach my kids that and this is one way that we can empower our community as well.

And like I said, most of the adopted people that I know are professionals that have gone to really good schools—the "good schools" and all. I don't agree with that.

I get really mad when I hear people talk about, well, you know, ooh, they went to Harvard or whatever. And to me, I went to the schools that I went to because of the community support that I was going to receive there and that kind of stuff.

But—so I mean, all things being equal, it would have been nice to be adopted by an Indian family because then I could have probably learned a lot more about the culture.

You know, even though I feel really lucky to know what I know and to be a part of what I've been a part of, a lot of my friends go back home during Christmas to the reservation, they have sweats or they have their ceremonies and stuff like that.

Sometimes I wish I had that. For my kids, they have the Navajo ceremonies that they'll have, but other than that, for me, on my side, there's nothing.

So what is your opinion of the Indian Child Welfare Act?

I agree with it. I'm a full supporter of it. I, of course, was adopted before it was enacted. I think all things being equal, if you can get a stable Indian family, that they should adopt an Indian kid.

Because, like I said, it was hard at times growing up and saying, well, this is my white family, even though they were great parents. And, you know, even today, I'm very close with my parents.

Do you have any advice that you would like to offer white families who would want to adopt or have adopted American Indian children?

Just to keep them involved in the community, make sure they know what tribe they are, let them have contact with their tribe and their community.

Because, you know, to be honest, I think that would have made a ton of difference in my life if I would have been able to, say, go home to the Mono Reservation and have my relatives there and know them, the ones that wanted to be a part of my life, and then also have my parents. I think that probably would have helped a lot.

Because I think a lot of times, when Indian kids are adopted now, they know what tribe they're from, and I think that would be helpful.

I just have one more question. Do you think that there's anything else I should have asked you during the course of this interview that I haven't asked?

Hmm. Not that I can think of. I think you pretty much covered everything.

Okay.

I think the bottom line in adoption, is that it's important that they have the unconditional love of the parents. I think that is the most important thing.

I don't know if you've heard this—I've heard this from my friends that when you meet people and you tell people you're adopted, they're like, so, you don't have any parents. Or, so those aren't your real parents.

And that's just not true. Those are my real parents. That's my real family. My biological mother's not my mom and it's because they've always made me feel like I was a part of their family.

And I think that's the most important thing, and to get that unconditional support—my parents were very good about that, not sending you money when you ask for it, but giving you sympathy because you didn't have it.

Just letting me know, they would just let me know that they were there for me. My mom's always there to talk to me about stuff, and very open and honest about everything. So that made a big difference. I think that's all I have.

8

# ROSALIND HUSSONG

Born in Los Angeles, California, in 1948, Rosalind Hussong (Chickasaw/Cree) was "promised to a missionary in New Mexico" when her adoptive mother, a nurse, heard about her story at the local hospital and petitioned to adopt the newborn. Both of Rosalind's adoptive parents were quite familiar with the adoption process as they had already adopted two other children. According to Rosalind, she had a "really good relationship" with her adoptive parents and says "sometimes I think that I am the only person in the world who didn't grow up in a dysfunctional family." Neither Rosalind nor her adoptive parents were aware of her cultural background. However, she says that she was still subjected to a certain amount of teasing by her classmates who called her "a dirty Indian or Mexican." This teasing along with other negative encounters with Native people adversely affected her perception of Native Americans for a long time.

Rosalind began the search for her birth family when she was twenty-four years old and tried to establish a relationship with her Chickasaw mother and Cree father. She notes, however, that her birth mother never approved of her "lifestyle . . . [and] hated [her] being involved with Native culture." Like her birth mother, Rosalind's birth father did not practice his tribal traditions; however, she has maintained a fairly positive relationship with him over the years. Rosalind attributes their disinterest in Native culture to the negative experiences they themselves faced as Native people. Unlike her birth parents, Rosalind says that she finds it "really positive and stimulating to be part of the Native American culture and to use the experiences and education and the different tools that [she has] to help further things for Indian people."

Rosalind describes herself as a strong advocate for the Indian Child Welfare Act (ICWA) and currently serves as the Director of Behavioral Health Services at the Feather River Tribal Health Organization. She says that she has been called to testify as an expert witness in several cases involving the ICWA. Regarding transracial adoption, Rosalind says: "Do I think transracial adoption is a good thing? No. Do I think it can be a positive experience for children who are involved in it? Yes. I don't think there is a black or white answer."

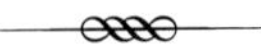

WHAT YEAR WERE YOU BORN?

1948.

WHERE WERE YOU BORN?

Los Angeles.

DO YOU KNOW HOW OLD YOU WERE WHEN YOU WERE ADOPTED?

Twelve days.

ARE YOU AWARE OF THE CIRCUMSTANCES SURROUNDING YOUR ADOPTION?

I am.

CAN YOU TELL ME A LITTLE BIT ABOUT THAT?

I came to find out later that my birth mother was living with my birth father and she had filed for divorce from her first husband. She had a child from her first marriage. It took several years for her divorce to become final in California so her fear was that if anyone knew she was pregnant and living out of wedlock that her first child would be taken away. So she hid her pregnancy and that was the reason she decided to place me for adoption.

IS YOUR MOTHER NATIVE AMERICAN OR IS YOUR FATHER?

Both of them are.

DO YOU KNOW WHICH TRIBES?

My mother was full Chickasaw and my father was half Canadian Cree.

ARE YOU AN ENROLLED MEMBER OF ANY TRIBE?

Yes.

WAS THAT A DIFFICULT PROCESS OR DID YOU FIND IT EASY?

That was a difficult process because apparently during the 1940s it was a common BIA practice to approach Indians who were adults and they would tell them they would give them a cash payout if they would terminate their rights as an Indian, and my birth mother did that. So it was actually through a friend of mine who was with BIA that we were able to establish that that had happened and to get that turned around for me to become enrolled.

HAVE YOU FOUND THAT YOUR ABILITY TO ENROLL IN A TRIBE AFFECTED YOUR SENSE OF CULTURAL IDENTITY IN ANY WAY? HAS IT STRENGTHENED IT?

I am sure it did. At the time I was working for a Native American organization, and everyone thought I was an Indian including me but I wasn't sure and certainly I think just finding out what my heritage actually was became the strongest element in my identity formation; it was stronger than getting back on any kind of roll.

WHEN DID YOU FIRST SEARCH FOR YOUR BIOLOGICAL FAMILY?

I started when I was twenty-four years old.

WHAT PROMPTED THAT SEARCH?

Actually it was an article I read in *Psychology Today* that was written by Reuben Pannor and it really inspired me. I don't know if you've read any of his works. He did a lot of work on adopting Indians, so I went to Los Angeles to meet with him and talk about it and that was really my inspiration and he actually ended up serving on my doctoral committee.

WERE YOUR ADOPTIVE PARENTS SUPPORTIVE OF YOUR DECISION?

At the time I didn't tell them. It was probably about two years after I was reunited that I told them, and then they were supportive.

LET'S TALK A LITTLE BIT ABOUT YOUR ADOPTIVE FAMILY. CAN YOU TELL ME A LITTLE BIT ABOUT YOUR PARENTS?

My parents were both in their early forties when I was adopted and my father was a physician and my mother was a nurse. The reason that they had found me was that I was born in a Seventh-Day Adventist hospital in Los Angeles and both of my adoptive parents were Seventh-Day Adventists and my mother heard about me through some of her nurse friends who saw me there and her friends told her I was already promised to a missionary in New Mexico. Thank God that one didn't work out. And my adoptive parents said, "well, give us a call if the placement doesn't work out." And I also have two brothers and a sister who were adopted.

ARE THEY NATIVE AMERICAN AS WELL?

No.

HOW WOULD YOU DESCRIBE YOUR RELATIONSHIP WITH YOUR PARENTS?

My parents are both deceased, but I had a really good relationship with them. Sometimes I think that I am the only person in the world who didn't grow up in a dysfunctional family.

WHEN DID YOU FIRST REALIZE THAT YOU WERE ADOPTED?

I really don't ever remember a time that I didn't know.

WAS IT BECAUSE YOU LOOKED SO DIFFERENT FROM YOUR PARENTS?

No. I think it was because they told me.

DO YOU REMEMBER WHEN THEY SAT YOU DOWN AND TOLD YOU?

No. I certainly was aware of it by the time I was three. I always knew. Once when I was about two the newspaper came and did a story on our family, about the adoptions and it was just something that . . . my brothers and sister always knew. I don't ever remember a time not knowing.

WAS THE FACT THAT YOU ARE NATIVE AMERICAN TALKED ABOUT A LOT IN YOUR FAMILY?

No.

WHAT DO YOU THINK YOUR PARENTS DID TO GIVE YOU A SENSE OF CULTURAL IDENTITY?

I don't think that my parents knew I was Native American. In fact I am sure they didn't. They had really no information about my birth parents whatsoever. When I asked them what I was they would say, "You're an American." And my birth father's ancestry was French and English, with a dark complexion, so it wasn't like it seemed really strange . . . that I needed to be Native American or something else to fit in there. But they really didn't know anything about my background.

You mentioned that you have siblings who were adopted as well. What advantages were there to having siblings who were adopted when you were growing up?

I think that my siblings were all functional and so there wasn't any stigma placed on being adopted. That was just our family's culture. Looking back on it, I think it would be more difficult being an adopted child in a family where the other children were birth children, because that could probably set you apart in some ways, so I can see that.

Are you close to your siblings?

We all live in separate parts of the country. We see each other, but I wouldn't say that I'm super close to them, but we're still a family.

Now that you are aware of your Native American background do you talk with them about that?

Yes. And they are all very supportive. My adoptive parents were also supportive. I will have to say that when I was growing up, I grew up in Arizona and my parents were extremely open to people, and I was exposed to a lot of different cultures. My dad was the first physician in private practice in Arizona to serve patients from different minority groups. And I know that's hard to believe now. Things are really a lot different now. When he went off to World War II he had a female physician take over his practice so he was really open to other cultures and other ways of seeing things. I can remember we would go up to a Navajo reservation. They also would take in girls to come and help my mother out with stuff and in return they would pay for them to go to college. When I was growing up we had African American and Latino young women living in our house, as part of our family, so it wasn't so strange.

What was your first impression of the Native American community?

I have a very specific memory. I was probably about four years old and I was walking in downtown Phoenix with my dad and I remember seeing a couple of Indian men very drunk. And I remember looking up at my dad and saying "I don't have to be an Indian, do I, dad?" And he said, "You can be whatever you want to be." And that was really my first memories of Indians. But those were most of the Native people that I saw because I grew up in a very sort of affluent family and neighborhood and wasn't exposed to people who were down. Sometimes I saw the kids who were at the Phoenix Indian School.

HOW DO YOU THINK THOSE IMAGES HELPED SHAPE YOUR SENSE OF CULTURAL IDENTITY?

I think that initially they made me really not want to be an Indian. I have many memories of people, and particularly like when I was in grade school and kids taunted me about my coloring, and either calling me a dirty Indian or a Mexican, and that was not a pleasant experience and I really didn't want to be an Indian.

WHY DO YOU THINK THAT CHANGED?

I had a best friend from the time I was eleven, and she is still my best friend, and she really encouraged me and kept saying "Indians are really cool." And I think the thing that really turned it around was I am one of those people who were really involved in the whole 1960s movement and all the civil rights stuff, so at that time it was just when Martin Luther King, Jr., was starting and other things were happening. I just kind of fell into the Indian movement as a subset of the hippie movement.

WHERE DID YOU GO TO COLLEGE?

I went to four different universities. I had my first year at Loma Linda University in Southern California. I got kicked out. My second year was at Arizona State, and then my junior and senior year and work on my Masters Degree was at the University of Florida, and then my Ph.D. at Union Graduate Institute.

WHAT WAS YOUR MAJOR?

Psychology.

WHY DID YOU CHOOSE THAT MAJOR?

I don't know. I was just always really interested in it. I was a pretty prolific reader as a kid and when I was in grade school I read lots of books and it just appealed to me. I am sure it has something to do with being adopted. At least in the beginning, it was time to sort all that out and it seemed like psychology was the way to do that.

IS IT CORRECT THAT YOU WROTE YOUR DISSERTATION ON TRANSRACIAL ADOPTION?

Yes.

WHAT DID YOU WRITE ABOUT AND WHAT DID YOU FIND OUT?

It was a phenomenological study in which I interviewed several adult Native people who had been adopted as infants by Euro-American parents and had been reunited with their birth parents. I was looking at their experience about that, their cultural identity and how that evolved and all that sort of stuff.

WHAT WERE YOUR FINDINGS? DID THE MAJORITY OF THE ADOPTEES HAVE A POSITIVE EXPERIENCE OR A NEGATIVE EXPERIENCE?

The majority had a positive experience. So it is kind of interesting. When I was doing this it was about the same time when ICWA was coming out and there was the attitude that transracial adoption of Indians was a form of cultural genocide. The people in my study had a really strong feeling that it wasn't some kind of cultural genocide but they felt that the adopting parents needed to be doing better in teaching culture to their adopted Indian children. They also felt the whole screening process of choosing adopting parents who were adopting transracially should be better. They felt there should be more of an attempt to leave avenues open so that the person could become connected to their culture and all of them were pretty adamant about their feelings that our adoption records should be opened.

WHAT IS YOUR OPINION OF THE ICWA?

I think it has a lot of loopholes. I have some really strong feelings about some religious and private groups getting around it and I think that some things still need to be addressed. And I think that given the historical background of Indians being adopted by non-Indian families, that ICWA is really a wonderful thing, although it is so complicated. . . . I work now for an Indian health organization and deal with children's services all the time and it is so complicated that even though people may have good intentions they may find it hard to follow ICWA sometimes. I think it needs a lot more work.

HOW DO YOU THINK IT COULD BE IMPROVED?

I think closing the loopholes for one thing.

WHAT DO YOU MEAN BY LOOPHOLES?

I have some pretty strong feelings about the Mormon Church and their practices with Indians and getting around ICWA with what they do, and don't do. Then too they had that whole project where they would bring Indian children into Mormon homes and educate them. It happened even though there might not have been a formal adoption involved and it pretty much had the same effect. And I think when you have a group that has such a strong historical ideology about how Indians play into their religious structure and how it's important to try to convert all the Indians. . . . I can see that as a form of cultural genocide.

Do you have any ties to a Native American tribe today?

To my own tribe, not particularly because it is in Oklahoma and so I don't get back there and I don't know my relatives there. My birth mother, I think I mentioned earlier, had signed away her rights as a Native person. She was absolutely horrified that I identified with the Native Americans and was not open with information about other family members. . . . It was actually my adoptive parents who were much more culturally open than were my birth parents.

Do you still have a relationship with your birth mother today?

No. My birth mother died about two years ago. We had a relationship for about ten years. She was a very fundamental Christian, and was so guilt-ridden with what she had done, she just really didn't know how to deal with it. And she hated my lifestyle, she hated my being involved with Native culture, and she cut off her relationship with me. It was rather like being given up for adoption a second time. I still have a relationship with my birth father, though.

Tell me a little bit more about that relationship.

We talk periodically. It's interesting. I can't say that we have really anything at all in common. I think more than anything, I feel kind of sorry for him. I had three full brothers and a half sister. None of my three brothers, who are younger than I am, graduated from high school. All of them are alcoholics—one is a drug addict. Both of my birth parents were alcoholics. Two brothers committed suicide. They were kind of the poster family for dysfunction. My birth father and remaining birth brother call once in a while, but as far as having a really close relationship, I can't say that we do.

You said that your birth mother sort of abandoned your Chickasaw heritage. Is that true of your birth father as well?

Yes. He was not involved with it at all. He didn't have disdain for it like my mother did, but he just wasn't involved. My birth mother was born in Oklahoma and she and her parents moved to the southwest one year. My grandfather was very involved in the Native American Church. He went around from tribe to tribe trying to get people together to start practicing their culture again. They were then in Parker, Arizona, and he was getting a church organized and one day a bunch of local people from town—non-Native people—came out and told him he needed to get out of town and quit riling up the Indians, and the next day they found him thrown off of a roof. And he was dead. I think there was a lot of fear from my birth mother that if you identified with being Indian a really bad thing was going to happen to you.

HOW HAVE THOSE TWO CONTRADICTORY VIEWS OF NATIVE AMERICAN CULTURE AFFECTED YOU?

I have always, since my early twenties, been working in Native American organizations, without exception, and that's just kind of where I feel comfortable, and I am one of those people that like to take on causes and fights, so I've found it really positive and stimulating to be part of the Native American culture and to use the experiences and education and the different tools that I have to help further things for Indian people.

WHAT OTHER WAYS ARE YOU INVOLVED IN THE NATIVE COMMUNITY?

Besides work, I have a lot of friends who are Native American, I go to ceremonies, I am an avid historian, I get involved in different causes. I teach psychology and Native American studies part-time at a California State University and so I have been really involved with all the artifacts that the University has and trying to get them returned to the local tribes. It is a big part of my life, though I have to say I am kind of a loner and very much of an introvert, so I am not out all the time hanging out with people. I like to live at home and ride my horses and talk to my dogs.

HAVE YOU SPENT TIME ON THE RESERVATION?

You mean living there?

OR VISITING.

I have been back to Oklahoma, I have spent a lot of time on the Hopi and Navajo Reservations when I was heavily involved with AIM. I have spent a lot of time in South Dakota. Here where I live in California we actually have rancherias rather than reservations so I am really involved with three of the rancherias here.

DO YOU FEEL ACCEPTED BY THE NATIVE COMMUNITY?

Yes. I do.

WHAT SORT OF EXPERIENCES HAVE YOU HAD THAT HAVE LED YOU TO BELIEVE THAT?

It is kind of ironic for me because where I work now, and I've worked there for ten years, serves Native people. Probably half of the Native people in our area are from the local rancherias, and then the other half are not from this area or from California. The area is kind of a secondary BIA relocation site. A lot of people that were relocated to the Bay area have moved over here. But what is kind of interesting to me is that lots of times when there are people who want questions answered about cultural things or the correct way to go about doing things in a culturally sensitive way they come talk to me about it. And I think it is quite amazing. I was not raised in an Indian culture and here I am in the situation where people seem to view me as very traditional.

HOW DO YOU ANSWER THOSE QUESTIONS?

Usually I try to help people find the answer within themselves. Sometimes I know the right way to do traditional things. But I do believe that most people have a pretty strong sense of right and wrong and an intuitive sense, and they just sometimes have to look for it.

WHAT DO YOU THINK YOU HAVE GAINED PERSONALLY BY FINDING YOUR BIRTH FAMILY AND LEARNING ABOUT YOUR CULTURAL HERITAGE?

From a larger, generalized perspective the main thing would be just having an understanding of where you come from and what your heritage is. To me and for the other adoptees I've spoken to, that's always been a huge question. Why do I look like I look, why do I do these things. I think it just answers huge questions. I would say in general that is the most important thing. But I am really thankful that my background is Native because I really value the culture and it has become a huge part of my life and my spiritual life. I find a lot of contentment. I wouldn't want to be anything else.

DO YOU HAVE CHILDREN?

No, I don't.

ARE YOU MARRIED?

I am not, but I have a partner of nineteen years.

HOW WOULD YOU SAY YOU IDENTIFY YOURSELF TODAY?

I identify myself as being Native American. There are two things that have really shaped my life. One is my cultural heritage and the other is the experience that I had during the late 1960s and 1970s and I think those two things worked together and complemented each other and that's really stayed with me all my life.

ARE YOU GLAD THAT YOU WERE ADOPTED BY A WHITE FAMILY?

I can't say I was glad I was adopted by a *white* family. I am glad that I was adopted and I'm glad I was adopted by the family I was adopted by. It was particularly helpful to me when I went back and saw what happened to my brothers and how their lives went. There's probably not a day that goes by that I'm not thankful that I wasn't raised with that family. It doesn't have anything to do with them being Indians, but it has to do with all the sickness that was there. I am thankful for the family I grew up with because they really gave me the latitude to be whatever it was I was going to be, and when they found out I was Indian they were thrilled and they were very happy with me that I had had the courage to find that out and act on it. Am I glad I was adopted, yes. But on the other hand I think it is criminal that people adopting can't get the information that they need to find out about their backgrounds and whether they are Indian or whatever. That took me about a year to get the information and I had to lie to people and do all sorts of things to get that information. It was not an easy process. I think that is really wrong.

IN GENERAL DO YOU APPROVE OF TRANSRACIAL ADOPTION?

No, I can't say I do. That's a really hard question. And I struggle with the answer because when I look at where a lot of minority families are who have not had the economic and educational opportunities and have been plagued by things like alcoholism or drug abuse it's not a good place for children to grow up. But sometimes, particularly in the United States culturally, there is a tendency to blame the victim so we blame Indians or African Americans or Latinos or whatever, that they are not good parents or they're not this or that . . . that is a much deeper problem. I am really glad that we have ICWA and that we put a stop to the rampant removal of Indian children from their homes. Because I don't think that most white people have a clue about Native culture. I have done a lot of expert court witness work in ICWA cases and just hearing the comments that social workers make, it just blows you away. When you hear those things, you think these people should never be able to work with or adopt someone of a different culture because they are just oblivious. I was in a court case where the social worker had put this Indian child into a foster place with a Hispanic family and when she was questioned about that her comment was "Well, they're all the same color. I don't see what the difference is." Just unbelievable. Do I think transracial adoption is a good thing? No. Do I think it can be a positive experience for children who are involved in it? Yes. I don't think there is a black or white answer.

WHAT ADVICE WOULD YOU OFFER TO WHITE FAMILIES WHO WANT TO OR HAVE ADOPTED NATIVE AMERICAN CHILDREN?

To do everything they can to help their children to find out information about their birth parents. I think it is unwise for them to not support that. Certainly in the study I did it was really a myth that when adoptees find their birth parents that it somehow limited their feelings for their adoptive parents. Generally what happens is it actually strengthens their feelings for their adoptive parents. I always hear people say "well, I adopted an Indian child and we go to powwows and I buy them Indian books and stuff" and that really doesn't do it and I don't think that a non-Native person or a person who hasn't been raised around Native culture is capable of really teaching their children about that stuff. They can be open to their children finding out but I don't think they can teach it. They need to seek outside help.

HOW WELL WOULD YOU SAY THAT YOU ARE INVOLVED WITH YOUR CULTURE TODAY?

I feel very comfortable with my involvement. I think that when you're transracially adopted that you never become a member of one culture or the other. You are always walking the line and I think the real trick is finding comfort in that.

WHAT RESOURCES OR EXPERIENCES HELPED YOU BECOME COMFORTABLE WITH YOUR CULTURAL BACKGROUND?

Participation, really, and being accepted. I've talked to different adoptees who go back and try to get involved with their tribe and people in the tribe won't accept them. They say "you're just a white person now" or stuff like that. So I think having experiences and feeling accepted is really a big part of that. For me, I worked for the San Diego Indian Center for many years back in the 1970s and 1980s and I just hung out, all my friends were Indian and we were all very much involved in AIM. We did a lot of stuff together and we were involved in projects and we did a lot of protest stuff, and we went all over the country together. I think just feeling like they accepted me as one of them was really all I needed.

IS THERE ANYTHING ELSE YOU THINK I SHOULD HAVE ASKED YOU THAT I HAVEN'T ASKED YOU?

No.

# 9

# JORDAN KENNEDY

Born in 1982, Jordan Kennedy was adopted by an interracial couple when she was eight months old and grew up believing that like her adoptive parents, she too was of Caucasian and African American descent. Jordan says that she always knew that she was adopted, but only recently discovered that her biological mother was Caucasian and her biological father was Native American. Jordan stumbled across this discovery two years ago when she began questioning her adoptive mother about the wording on her adoption papers.

According to Jordan, her adoption papers indicate that her biological father is "tall, strong, and aggressive." She says this description is made even more bizarre by the fact that her biological father is described as "negroid." Confused by this strange description, Jordan pressed her adoptive mother who reluctantly admitted that her biological father was not African American, but rather Native American. Furthermore, she was not the result of a one-night stand, but rather the result of rape. Jordan says she was shocked by this admission, but that she understands that her adoptive parents were only trying to protect her.

At the time of this interview, Jordan had been grappling with this discovery for less than a year. She had decided not to find her biological mother because she "figured that if [her] biological mother was strong enough and good enough to have [her] even though she was raped," she probably didn't "want [this] brought up again." Although Jordan has made an effort to learn about Native American culture, she has not made an effort to interact with the Native community. According to Jordan, she "wouldn't know where to begin" and she'd feel "false going in when [she hadn't] grown up in that culture."

WHEN WERE YOU BORN?

1982.

WHERE WERE YOU BORN?

Edmonton.

HOW OLD WERE YOU WHEN YOU WERE ADOPTED?

Eight months.

ARE YOU AWARE OF THE CIRCUMSTANCES SURROUNDING YOUR ADOPTION?

Yes. I found out that my biological mother had a four-year-old son at the time. She was dating the father of her son and she was raped and got pregnant and gave me up for adoption.

DO YOU KNOW THE ETHNICITY OF YOUR BIOLOGICAL MOTHER AND FATHER?

My mother was Caucasian and my father was Native, first family.

WHAT LED YOU TO BELIEVE THAT YOUR FATHER IS NATIVE?

Myself. I look more Native than negro. I grew up thinking I was negro, but have no characteristics at all. I had a friend a couple of years ago who is half Native and grew up on a reserve and we might have been sisters, the two of us.

HOW COME YOU WERE RAISED BELIEVING YOU WERE BLACK?

I think it was to make things easier. My adoptive father and my brother who was adopted are both black.

TELL ME A LITTLE BIT MORE ABOUT YOUR ADOPTIVE PARENTS. FOR INSTANCE, WHAT THEY DO FOR A LIVING, THAT SORT OF THING?

My adoptive parents, my parents, my mom and dad got divorced when I was six and my mom raised us. And she worked in accounts payable in an oilfield and my dad is in sales.

HOW WOULD YOU DESCRIBE YOUR RELATIONSHIP WITH THEM?

Good. It has been a very open relationship . . . or I thought it was. Then when I brought up everything about my biological parents they came clean and talked to me about it when I asked them.

DID THEY EVER INDICATE TO YOU WHY THEY DECIDED TO ADOPT?

My mom and my dad tried for years to have kids and they never could so that was why they adopted. Back when we were adopted, my brother and I, there didn't have to be a medical reason for the adoption, and the wait lists weren't as long.

DID YOUR PARENTS KNOW THAT YOU WERE INDIAN WHEN THEY ADOPTED YOU?

My mom said that the lady at the adoption agency who had talked to my biological mother told her the whole story but they didn't put it on the adoption papers, so she went along with that. But I think they did know, yes.

AND WERE THEY SPECIFICALLY LOOKING TO ADOPT AN INDIAN CHILD OR WERE THEY JUST LOOKING TO ADOPT A CHILD IN GENERAL?

Just a child in general.

HOW OLD WERE YOU WHEN YOU FIRST REALIZED YOU WERE ADOPTED?

There was no set age. My parents told me right from the beginning. I don't ever remember it being a shock or anything.

YOU SAID YOU HAVE A SIBLING WHO IS ALSO ADOPTED?

Yes.

WHAT RACE IS HE?

My brother is African American.

ARE YOU CLOSE TO YOUR BROTHER?

Yes, very.

WHAT ARE THE ADVANTAGES OR DISADVANTAGES OF GROWING UP WITH A SIBLING WHO IS ALSO ADOPTED?

I don't think it was ever an issue in our household . . . being adopted. It was just the way things go. I could say it was he and I against the world, but everybody we told we were adopted thought it was pretty cool. There was not really a problem.

I know my brother has thought about finding his biological parents and he has talked to me about it, now that we're older we are more of a support system to each other, somebody who knows. . . .

WHAT DID YOUR ADOPTIVE PARENTS DO TO GIVE YOU AND YOUR BROTHER A SENSE OF YOUR CULTURAL IDENTITY?

Nothing at all. My adoptive dad is African American but he's not really close to his roots, and my racial background wasn't really discussed until I brought it up last year.

DO YOU AGREE OR DISAGREE WITH THEIR DECISION TO KEEP YOUR CULTURAL BACKGROUND A SECRET?

I guess I disagree with it just because it was a bit of a shock. You hear one thing all your life and then you hear something else. But it wasn't really life changing or anything. I wish they had told me the truth but I can see why they didn't.

TELL ME ABOUT THE PLACES YOU GREW UP, DESCRIBE THE NEIGHBORHOODS YOU GREW UP IN AND THE SCHOOLS YOU ATTENDED.

Very upper-middle class, white neighborhoods. We moved around when we were younger, but were always in the same sort of neighborhoods because my parents were both well off. We went to the same sort of schools and stuff.

WHO WERE YOUR CLOSEST FRIENDS IN SCHOOL?

Upper-middle class, white. I never had a different race of friends than Caucasian. I just looked dark in coloring. You can't really tell that I am Native . . . always Caucasian friends.

DID YOU OR YOUR BROTHER ENCOUNTER ANY FORMS OF RACISM GROWING UP?

My brother did, very much so. Maybe I did too, a little bit.

HOW DID YOU BOTH ADDRESS THIS ISSUE?

My brother was a fighter so he stuck up for himself, and I kind of just ignored it. It was only in one school for me, but for him it was more because he's black . . . it's a noticeable difference.

DID YOUR PARENTS PREPARE YOU AND YOUR BROTHER TO FACE THIS CHALLENGE IN ANY WAY?

Not really, other than just always making it seem as if there was nothing wrong with us for being a little different. That my brother being black and stuff . . . it was like a nonissue in our house because my dad was black too, so it never really came up until the problems started when my brother was a little bit older.

After high school did you go to college?

Yes. I went to college for two years.

What was your major?

Psychology.

Why did you choose to major in psychology?

I went into nursing to start and I did a couple of psychology classes for the option for the nursing program, and then decided to go into psychology instead.

What kind of work do you do today?

I am at the university now.

So you went back to school?

I got my diploma in psychology and now I'm doing a degree in chemistry.

What do you hope to do with that when you are finished with school?

I'd like to do an environmental chemistry degree and work overseas in developing areas.

Who are your closest friends today, again in terms of race?

My family are my closest friends. My girlfriends are all Caucasian except for my one Native friend that I lived with for years.

Are you married?

Yes, technically I am.

Can you tell me about your husband?

We have been separated for three years. He's white.

Do you have children?

We have one daughter.

HOW OLD IS YOUR DAUGHTER?

She is four.

HOW DO YOU EXPECT TO ADDRESS THE ISSUE OF CULTURAL IDENTITY WITH HER?

I don't know. She doesn't look anything like me. She looks exactly like her father, like white, pale skin. I have darker skin and look tanned . . . so I don't know if I'll ever bring it up at all unless she's a teenager and asks me about my adoption. She knows I was adopted, but I don't know what I'm going to tell her.

HOW DID YOUR LIFE CHANGE AFTER DISCOVERING THAT YOU WERE NATIVE?

I guess I had a chance to really think about Native Americans because my mom remarried when I was twelve, I believe, and he was a wonderful man but somewhat racist toward not blacks so much but Asians and Native Americans too. I guess finding out changed the way I think about things because it's hard growing up, hearing things and then trying to change your perception when it's suddenly relevant to you personally.

DO YOU IDENTIFY YOURSELF AS NATIVE AMERICAN TODAY?

I probably still put Caucasian as I always have on forms and stuff because I don't really look that different. But if people ask I tell them that I am part Native.

DO YOU FEEL THAT YOU POSSESS CERTAIN PRECONCEIVED NOTIONS ABOUT NATIVE AMERICANS THAT YOU HAVE TO OVERCOME TODAY?

Yes, very much so. Probably like I said with my stepdad, more unfavorable ideas about Native Americans and stuff. It is hard growing up hearing things about Native Americans and then trying to change the way you think about them, or myself.

HOW OLD WERE YOU WHEN YOU DISCOVERED THAT YOU WERE NATIVE?

Twenty-three.

HOW OLD ARE YOU TODAY?

Twenty-four.

SINCE LEARNING THAT YOU ARE NATIVE HAVE YOU MADE AN EFFORT TO LEARN MORE ABOUT YOUR CULTURAL IDENTITY?

Absolutely. I am researching things through the university library and on the Internet I found some interesting sites.

HAVE YOU MADE AN EFFORT TO GET INVOLVED WITH THE NATIVE COMMUNITY?

No.

HOW COME?

I wouldn't know where to begin. I think it is still somewhat false going in when I haven't grown up in that culture.

HAVE YOU SOUGHT OUT YOUR BIRTH FAMILY?

No.

HOW COME?

I thought about it when I was pregnant with my daughter to get a more comprehensive medical history. But that faded through the pregnancy and I had her and she's fine and then when I found out the real circumstances with the rape I kind of put the whole idea on the back shelf, because I figured if my biological mother was a strong enough and good enough person to have me even though she was raped, that maybe she wouldn't want that brought up again.

WERE YOUR ADOPTIVE PARENTS SUPPORTIVE OF YOUR DECISION TO SEARCH FOR YOUR BIRTH FAMILY WHEN YOU WANTED TO LOOK FOR THEM?

Absolutely. They have always said that. They would never discourage me I don't think.

WHAT EFFECT HAS THIS DISCOVERY HAD ON YOUR PERSONAL AND PROFESSIONAL LIFE?

None really. I have a good sense of my identity—it doesn't mean that because I'm a different race it affects the way I think about myself.

IS THE FACT THAT YOU ARE NATIVE AMERICAN TALKED ABOUT IN YOUR FAMILY TODAY?

I've talked to my dad about it and I've talked to my brother about it but it is not really a big issue. Nobody has made it a big deal you know.

WHAT IS YOUR OPINION OF THE INDIAN CHILD WELFARE ACT?

I have no idea what that is.

BASICALLY IT IS JUST A LAW SAYING THAT NATIVE AMERICAN CHILDREN SHOULD BE ADOPTED BY NATIVE AMERICANS BEFORE THEY ARE ADOPTED BY ANY OTHER RACE. IN GENERAL WOULD YOU SAY THAT YOU APPROVE OF NON-NATIVE FAMILIES ADOPTING NATIVE CHILDREN?

I have a lot of different thoughts on that one. I suppose it would just depend on the circumstances of the adoptive parents and if they went through the same rigorous testing that all adoptive parents have, then I would agree that the children should stay in their same family backgrounds. I would approve of any adoption circumstances as long as the adoptive parents are able to take care of the children and love them.

WHAT ADVICE WOULD YOU OFFER NON-NATIVE FAMILIES WHO WOULD WANT TO ADOPT OR WHO HAVE ADOPTED NATIVE CHILDREN?

To be honest with their kids and when their kids were older, to find out if they wanted to know about their cultural background and to make sure that they nurtured that in their kids, I would probably say the same about any interracial adoption.

OVERALL WHAT ARE THE ADVANTAGES AND DISADVANTAGES OF BEING TRANSRACIALLY ADOPTED?

I suppose the advantages of being adopted are the more widespread idea of different cultures, I guess as long as you were exposed to your Native culture. And the disadvantage being that you are not connected to your cultural path.

ARE YOU PLANNING TO KEEP LEARNING MORE ABOUT YOUR NATIVE CULTURE?

Absolutely.

WHY DO YOU THINK THAT IS IMPORTANT?

It is kind of important because anybody who is adopted has a question of where they're from. So you can try to find your birth parents or you can learn more about your culture. I think it is a question that remains open, no matter how good of parents your adoptive ones are.

YOU MENTIONED THAT YOU HAVE BEEN READING BOOKS AND LOOKING ONLINE FOR INFORMATION. DO YOU THINK YOU WILL EVER GET TO A POINT WHERE YOU ARE COMFORTABLE TO INTERACT WITH PEOPLE IN THE NATIVE COMMUNITY FACE TO FACE?

I hope so. My friend that I mentioned earlier who is Native, she's involved in the Native association here, in the surrounding area, I would probably go to her and talk to her more about it and then maybe do something with her. I would probably be comfortable.

THAT WAS MY LAST QUESTION. IS THERE ANYTHING ELSE I SHOULD HAVE ASKED YOU OR ANY OTHER ISSUES YOU'D LIKE TO ADDRESS?

I don't think so.

## 10

# ROSEAN KENT

In 1957, shortly before Thanksgiving Day, six-year-old RoSean Kent (Dine/Cherokee/Ute) was removed from her grandparents' home and placed in foster care. RoSean and her two younger brothers were placed with a Hispanic family whom she describes as physically and verbally abusive. They lived with this family for six years until social services intervened and placed them with their biological mother. RoSean and her siblings lived with their biological mother for several months until social services placed them back in foster care because of their mother's excessive drinking. She then lived with a white family for one year before briefly being placed in several other foster homes.

At the age of fourteen, RoSean was placed in a group home. Surprisingly, she looks back on this experience fondly and strongly believes that group homes are a better alternative to foster care. She argues that in the group home she was able to forge a number of positive relationships with girls she could identify with. She was also allowed to practice the tribal traditions passed down to her by her grandparents, which she was discouraged from practicing in foster care. RoSean notes several times that the prayer songs taught to her by her grandfather are "what got [her] through."

At fifteen years of age, RoSean left the group home and was declared an emancipated minor. However, the teenager struggled to make ends meet and soon found herself in need of a home. A classmate took her home and introduced her to his parents who offered her a place to stay. RoSean spent her senior year of high school living with the Lawrence family, a middle-class, black family who asked to adopt her. Although the Lawrence family began adoption proceedings, RoSean left for college before the appropriate paperwork was filed. Even though the adoption was never finalized, RoSean still refers to Larry and Mammie Lawrence as mom and dad. Her dedication to the Lawrence family stems from her appreciation for their love and support. According to RoSean, they encouraged her to embrace her Native American roots and further her education. She notes: "this family was really good to me. They kind of picked up where my grandparents left off."

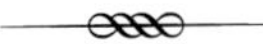

WHAT YEAR WERE YOU BORN?

1956.

WHERE WERE YOU BORN?

In Colorado, southern Colorado.

HOW OLD WERE YOU WHEN YOU WERE ADOPTED?

I was seventeen.

AND WERE YOU AWARE OF THE CIRCUMSTANCES SURROUNDING YOUR ADOPTION?

Yes.

CAN YOU TELL ME A LITTLE BIT ABOUT THOSE?

I had been dealt from foster home to foster home. I went into a group home, and then into another foster home of my own choosing, and they were just a very loving family, and offered to—they asked me, did I want to be adopted? And of course, I was old enough by that time that it didn't matter.

So we started the proceedings and then we didn't quite finish because I was off to college.

CAN YOU TELL ME A LITTLE BIT ABOUT YOUR ADOPTIVE PARENTS?

Sure. They were your normal, average, assimilated black family.

AND WHAT DID THEY DO FOR A LIVING?

My father was an airplane repairman in the Air Force and my mother was at that time a stay-at-home mom, because there were still two little boys in the home with my sisters.

And how long did you live with them in foster care as a foster child?

In this particular foster home, only about a year.

Can you tell me little bit about the foster homes you lived in before you lived with your adopted family?

Let's see. Well, I lived with my grandparents in southern Colorado on a farm. When they were too old to maintain the farm, they moved into the city into Pueblo, Colorado, which was the nearest major city. So—at six years old, I went into a foster home, a family foster home. And there were two other little girls there with me and a younger brother. They were very cruel, mean.

I can tell you more about the ugly stuff in that particular foster home, but to get back to your question, then from there at age twelve, they tried to get us back with our natural biological mother. And so actually there were three kids at that time, and the other one was only two months old when she was taken from my mom. But anyway they put the three of us back with my mother for like a summer.

It didn't work out for them. I went into another foster home a couple of times, a couple of other little quick foster homes that I really don't remember much of. And then those didn't work out or they didn't like me, or I don't know what happened. But anyway, I remember going into a foster home with the people that I call the Wolf, that was their last name. And they were German. I stayed with them for two years.

About that time, I had kind of outgrown the family, or they had outgrown me, and I went into a receiving home called Blinn in Denver. Of course, when they moved us at age twelve, we came together, and I was placed back with my mother. But I was about fourteen—fifteen years old—I was twelve years old when I went with the Wolf and then thirteen, and in and out of the other little miscellaneous foster homes.

And then when I went into Blinn, I was about fourteen. That was a receiving home, and emergency shelter. And so from there, I think, I stayed there for two months, and then this new home called Fanchen. I went into Fanchen, and as one of the first girls to go in there, I kind of was able to set some of the precedents. Being native, I still had some of my prayer ability, still had that core that my grandfather had given me, and some of the girls from Blinn followed.

And that was a really good experience because there were other girls that had been abused and they were very vocal, and me being who I was, and I choose to be a native—and I was very quiet. I didn't say a whole lot and people misunderstood that, but being around them, I learned to talk more. So from there I started a group called Independent Children's Living Program.

And that was through the city, where if you could prove to your social worker that you were independent, you could then get the money that they would normally send to your foster parents or to the group home and you could live on that.

So I would still go on to East High School here in Denver, and some of the other girls that were in the girls' group home tried to do it. They weren't successful proving to the social workers they could be independent. I found out later on that that whole program was taken across the United States.

So, I guess, I'm not sure what you're looking for in terms of, you know, for your research, but I really believe that the first pictures of my life, being with my grandparents gave me what I needed to get through that.

Well, anyway, I left Fanchen and went on an Independent Living Program, and then I got ripped off, taken advantage of, quite a few times, you know, in that year and a half and then I met this family, the Lawrences, who I called my family and the ones who were trying to adopt me. And they were the ones that tried to emphasize, or push me to be, continue to be who I am, my nativeness, being Indian, don't cut your hair, but really pushed for education. So they were instrumental in getting me set up in Boulder, to go to school at CU where I graduated.

AND HOW DID YOU MEET THEM?

I had some friends at school, and one of them was a boy, not really a boyfriend, but a good acquaintance of a group that I was close to, and he took me home one day for lunch. And she couldn't believe, the mother couldn't believe that I was this person living on my own, still in school. She thought it was inappropriate. That was why I was being taken care of—taken advantage of.

And then one day within the same week that I met them, the family, I went home and my roommate, she had moved me out, moved everything I owned out. And rather than to just fall apart, I talked to a couple of my friends, and he said, well, you know, "Come on over for lunch," talk to his mom, you know, and she would fix tuna salad, something—you know, something exotic to me. And so I went over there and she said, "No, you're not leaving. You're going to stay here," and, because I had no place else to go I wasn't going to refuse that and he had a younger sister, she is four years younger than me.

And she kind of took to me, she looked very light-skinned as a black. She was very light-skinned, and had very pretty hair. And she kind of took to me, and wanted to know more about my roots, so that she could learn, you know, more about her roots. And also, I don't think—even at that time, I didn't think that she was—I thought she was adopted. It turns out after they both passed away, her father—our father was not her real father. So that's why she didn't look the same. But that was her real mother.

This family was really good to me. They kind of picked up where my grandparents left off. That big gap that was in the middle was kind of filled, but from that point on, you know, I'm just—I figured, well, I got to get an education, I got to take care of myself. Being a ward of the state, I didn't really have too many options.

Did you want to know more about the foster homes?

YES. I WOULD LIKE TO HEAR A LITTLE BIT MORE ABOUT THE FOSTER HOMES.

Well, when I lived with my grandparents, we were at Fort Garland. I just have to go back a little further. My grandfather taught me a prayer song, he taught me some of the things that I needed like, you know, he used to burn sage and copal. I guess that's what the Hispanic people use, yet I didn't know that there was a difference. I just remember the smell. He taught me that I have to take care of the earth to show others what I know.

And my grandmother was very light-skinned. So she stayed out of the sun. She would always wear gloves, covered up her skin when she went out. But grandpa had really instilled in me, it was, you know, "You are, you know, Indian. Do not deny it. Don't let anybody take that from you." When I was taken from them at Thanksgiving, he started drinking, probably everybody started—my relatives started drinking.

And I was put in that foster home with Hispanic people. They would use their language against me, they would say things in Spanish that were demeaning. After a while, we learned what they were saying. They would say, "Well, she's going to get a beating, because she didn't clean that or she didn't do that." And me being the oldest of four foster children, it was also my job to kind of take care of them, make sure that they weren't—you know, I guess, I had two jobs, one is to take care of the household, but also to make sure that the kids weren't being too abused. Does it make sense?

YEAH. ARE YOU STILL IN TOUCH WITH ANY OF THE FOSTER CHILDREN FROM THAT HOME?

No. I wish I could find them, but I see my brother. And my brother was so abused, and I think part of his problem was because he was put outside, he was alone all the time. At the age of three, he still wasn't potty-trained. He did get him all the way to twelfth grade. I had to come back, but he, he just turned forty-four?—and he just got his first place. So he has been homeless all these years.

And I think part of that is because when I had, when I got custody of him, I had him tested because I knew something was wrong. He couldn't really learn. He had an education of a third grader, when he was in twelfth grade. And I think part of that was just because he had no human contact, you know, he wasn't—he wasn't played with, he wasn't looked at. When I was in that foster home for six years, when we were told not to look at them in the face, that whatever we had in us, that they were able to beat it out of us.

So I think his problem was he stood outside, and I think he had a hard time as an adult to come in. I think that's part of his problem.

I haven't had a lot of problems, but I've always overcome them. I think I still have another big one that I have to conquer and that is my self-esteem. You know, I think that's the reason I just got fired after eighteen years.

But anyway, they would stand me in the corner, on my knees, with my hands up in the air, and, you know, for days that—that's kind of painful, you can't really sit in the corner and not sleep, but when they slept, of course, I would probably sleep for not long periods, but at least they could think I was in the corner. And during the day I would sing my prayer songs that I remembered. Those were the things that would get me through.

AND DID YOU EVENTUALLY LEAVE THAT HOME, BECAUSE THEY WERE ABUSIVE?

I think, out of the six years that I was in there, I saw a social worker maybe three or four times. They were supposed to visit once a year, but I think I only saw them on occasion and never alone. I think there was always somebody from the foster home there.

But I think it was the last one, she knew that something was wrong. She knew immediately that I needed to be pulled out of that home, and she took us to a private place and she said, but you don't have to answer my questions, just shake your head yes or no. And she let me know that she knew that we were being abused and she got us out of there, I think, within a couple of weeks. I wish I knew who she was, but I haven't gone and checked out my records to find out who she was, but anyway she put us back with our biological mother, taking the risk that it's better to be in your own home, or in your own family than to be in a home that's abusing you. You know, we weren't neglected in the foster home in terms of that we were given three meals a day. But now, I know that they weren't meals, they were leftovers and garbage, but I thought they were meals.

So again, we moved from a woman to a family where they are a paycheck drinker once a month and maybe social services had fear that we would get my grandfather's land back. Being urban Indian, you know, that if they took us away, they're thinking that we wouldn't find our way—our way back.

CAN YOU TELL ME A LITTLE BIT MORE ABOUT YOUR EXPERIENCE WITH YOUR BIRTH MOTHER?

She was an alcoholic. Pretty much most of my uncles were. Most of my aunties weren't, but there were times when they went back and forth. And right now, I only have one aunt left alive. She's one of those that goes back and forth, she'll go dry for a year, and then she goes back to drinking.

My biological mother, I don't know what her problem was. She would drink so much, but she didn't know or she doesn't remember, or she's really being honest that she didn't—she thinks she raised us. She has this idea in her head that she raised her kids or maybe she's just floating that around, lately I don't know. But we lived with her so short of a time that I can't imagine that she would think that she did.

I don't know why she would say things like that, but she did other things that were kind of unusual. I don't have much contact with her. Because of that, it is hard for me to accept the things that she had said. You know, I just was never close to her. I was closer to my grandfather.

I was close to my grandmother, but I'm not really close to my aunts and uncles, because of the amount of drinking that they did. Now, I know where my biological mother is. I have her phone number, but she doesn't answer, and I think it's because either she doesn't want to have anything to do with me, or she is not facing reality. And I think she is getting closer to death. You know, she's getting up in years, so maybe she is trying to make amends when she does that. My aunty, because she goes back and forth drinking and nondrinking and because she was in the city, I think she tried to disown me. I can just say that much.

I'm very close to the Indian community, and so she doesn't want me to embarrass her, I guess. So I cannot have much contact with her either. Actually, I don't have any contact with her now. She's even changed her phone number.

WHAT ABOUT YOUR BIOLOGICAL FATHER?

I'm still in the process of trying to locate him. I thought I found him in Ignacio, because the stories that I was told about my father and my mother were that my father was in the rodeo. I think I found the family, and so my father, if this is him, he got married and went to Portland, Oregon, for twenty years. His wife recently passed away, and he moved back to Ignacio where his family is from and he married some young woman to take care of him.

The reason why I believe this is the man is because my aunty, she'd given me some stories, and she said I looked just like my relatives, my aunt—her mother and her sister and her nieces. And because of that look, I was just happy to find anybody on my father's side. So I kind of attached myself to her and she's been very kind and loving to me. That need to find my father has been satisfied, but I really didn't know anyone from my father's side.

And I wondered too if it's not because my grandfather took me away from my mother. Well, I shouldn't say he took me away, but because of the way my mother was, she was going to these rodeos and been around different men that maybe she was offended, and so he raised me this way, you know what I mean. He brought me up in Indian way, but not the rodeo way, not the flagrant way.

Of course, I had uncles that were sheep herders down there too. So I had a certain lifestyle—they had two lifestyles, the farming and the sheep herding. I was the only kid on the farm. So, you know, until age six, I really didn't have much contact with other children. Like, I didn't know that other families had fathers and mothers. I just knew my uncles and grandpa.

NOW, YOU MENTION THAT YOU HAVE TWO DEGREES. HOW WERE YOU ABLE TO KEEP GOING ON WITH YOUR EDUCATION WHEN YOU WERE GOING BACK AND FORTH BETWEEN FOSTER HOMES?

Well, the foster homes I was in was at a younger age. When I came out at age seventeen, and went on to go to Boulder, it got really difficult. You know, being a ward of the state, you don't have any concrete place to call home. And so I went to school at Boulder, and kind of had friends that would take me home. And again, there are the Lawrences. My adopted parents—well, I call them adopted, legally they weren't, but I would go back there. They also had another family of daughters who kind of created friction for me.

And then, you have to deal with that racial thing too, them being black and me being Indian. Their daughters were light-skinned and I became a threat to them, because I looked better as a light-skinned black. And so the girls would make comments that their boyfriends were looking at me, or that I was teasing them. So I stopped being close to my mother and father when they were around. So I couldn't even go back home during the summers or vacation. So I would go with my friends.

And, of course, during this time, my belongings became very scarce. You know, you don't have much to move except books and your clothes. But when it came to the foster homes, I didn't really have any contact. I still have no contact with the white family or the Hispanic or the foster kids that were in the home.

I feel kind of close to a few of the girls from the girls' group home, I call them my sisters. One of them is in Las Vegas. The other one is here, but all the other ones kind of fell by the wayside, because they went off, and did stuff like crime. They were doing drugs, they were prostitutes. I was the only one in the girls' group home that went to school.

The other two that I have contact with were kind of like bordering, you know, between education and their criminal behavior. So even though the two, that we are still very close to, don't do drugs, neither one of them really got their high school diploma. They did eventually go back, in their older years to get their GEDs.

But, I don't really call that family, and it was just this year that I met my aunt on my father's side. The family that I have here in Denver that I call my family are just very close friends. You know, when we kind of say, "You are very close friends or family," and they help me to keep some of the things that my grandfather gave me.

AND YOU SPOKE ABOUT RACISM A LITTLE BIT. DID YOU EXPERIENCE RACISM A LOT GROWING UP?

You know, at the time I didn't know that, but now that I'm a grandmother, so, yeah. Well, certainly, I mean, my degree was called "Adversity of the Truly Disadvantaged." As I made that degree, well, I needed to find words for some of the stuff that I had to go through. I had to witness racism from all groups, and then as I got older, and I was even with Indian people. You know, sometimes it's not what I would call racism, it's more like nationism, you know what I mean.

UH-HUH.

My trying different cures therefore was a mind spinner. Do you know what I'm saying?

YEAH.

It makes sense even among our own people, but in the black community, I was considered light-skinned and they think that you had a little bit more privilege than the darker-skinned ones because you are not the field worker.

When I was with Hispanic people, they were always saying "You are not one of us," and, you know, they think about beating the Indian out of you. It's like, maybe they had their own iniquities, and they thought, "Well, if you're an Indian and you are the first people, then I can take that away from you," and that would elevate them, if you know what I mean.

With white people, there's always that entitlement. I mean, even though these German people were very kind to me, they got religion, and that's why I could not live with them much longer. Because my way of praying was totally different. It was like a belief that was instilled in me from very young, was so different.

And at the time I can remember their daughters thinking that, because I was dark-skinned, I was pretty. And I didn't have to lay out in the sun. But there was still that big difference. And so I didn't see the difference within the family even though they've kind of been good to me. But I did see it when it came to money.

They were very religious and would go to church four to five times a week. My foster father was a preacher, but they also had their own business doing janitorial service. So when we went out to take jobs, their daughters made more money than I did, even though we did the same job or I did more.

So it was like no matter where I went, I've always experienced racism, and even though I've got an associate degree in accounting with a minor in computer science, this stuff was very black and white. You know what I mean?

UH-HUH.

That was just to get me in the door, so that I can complete my degree in the field that I really wanted, that I really needed. So even though I graduated from the University of Colorado at Denver, they didn't have a degree for diversity at the time. The year that I graduated, the following semester, they incorporated diversity. The difference is that I had to have three disciplines in my degree and now they only have two. But I feel like I've lived my life in adversity. I can adapt to different worlds, but I also went to school, to college, and learned, and I continue to learn.

IT SOUNDS LIKE EDUCATION IS VERY IMPORTANT TO YOU. WHAT COMPELS YOU TO KEEP GOING?

The black family was very instrumental in doing that. But I think too, my grandfather would help me make decisions. Life is always learning, you always have to go back, in order to better yourself, you are going to always have to find new things. Whatever is going on right now, you never stop learning.

And some of the things that my grandmother said about being older and—what it's like gaining wisdom. We will always be learning, so part of this means that I have felt that if I was always learning, that that was my core or my basis.

I always felt mature in a school environment because, like a lot of my friends talked about boarding school. Theirs was a harsh experience in that the culture was taken from them. For me, it was a way to ignore what was going on in my real world, and you know, this was like a getaway.

NOW, CAN YOU TELL ME A LITTLE BIT ABOUT YOUR LIFE AFTER COLLEGE?

I got married during college. I got married when I was twenty-four. I had a child at twenty-eight. And then I had another child at thirty-eight. I just recently, five years ago, got divorced. I divorced because he was an alcoholic and I felt that this had ruined my life, which was alcohol. I didn't want to deal with that anymore. And I didn't want my sons who are still at home, to be exposed to that.

In some ways, I kind of feel like I've killed two birds with one stone, because I have taken my sons and my daughter away from that environment. But I've also helped their father realize that, you know, he needs to change it. Supposedly he quit drinking.

I think it saved his life. I think he did good. My aunt maybe, my father's sister, doesn't drink at all. I don't think she drinks either.

WAS YOUR HUSBAND INDIAN TOO?

No, black.

HOW HAVE YOU ADDRESSED THE ISSUE OF CULTURAL IDENTITY WITH YOUR CHILDREN?

You know, my son has a little bit of a problem, probably because he is lighter-skinned, and going back and forth into the black families with his dad and his grandparents. My son has more of a problem with assimilation. And when I say assimilation, I take it a step further and say that a lot of black people have assimilated to Western society, and by that I mean that they are very commercial. Their world is gauged in success by how much money they make, and so my son struggled with that.

My daughter, who is a little bit more dark-skinned, like her father, she is far more like me because I think she grew up when we weren't—I want to say, when we were struggling more. There were times when we would have to go to the thrift stores to get clothes. And even still, you know, I still do that, and I do it on purpose with my son, of course. Now I will have do it more often, because I am unemployed. But, I guess I can adapt to being without funds. I can adapt to being poor. And for the black family it was scorn if you didn't—if you weren't able to financially live in a certain way, that's up to a certain standard. My daughter and my son are exposed to both worlds, because my black family gave me some roots.

In the black community, I'm still considered a light-skinned black person. You know, they accept me. And the Indian community, because of all the work that I do, they have accepted me also. So, my kids, I think, are living with one foot in two worlds. They go to powwows, they go to sweats, they know some of my prayer songs, they know that they have to give back to the community, they have to give back to the people they have to help. They also know that to be black, you don't have to live to a certain standard, but they can adapt, if that makes sense.

CAN YOU TELL ME A LITTLE BIT MORE ABOUT YOUR INVOLVEMENT WITH THE INDIAN COMMUNITY TODAY?

Yeah. Part of my degree was Women's Studies in the Political Science Department of UCD. And I always knew that there were these economic levels, women being kind of at the bottom. So my connection first is to help the women. That way we can help our children and the next generation will be, you know, given some direction. I do a lot of volunteer work. I mean, this weekend, we have a booth at Cinco de Mayo selling T-shirts for AIDS. So, you know, if you have any problems with AIDS, my very close friends will follow up.

They've asked me how can I help? How can I do anything to help our people? I think, they look at me, and they say, "She's doing this, she is an urban Indian, she knows, you know." I call myself the Internet Queen, just to be silly, but a lot of people know what I'm talking about, and that is that I can direct people or make contact to mate this group with that person and, or that person with this group, to make sure that the right or appropriate people are being connected so that we can get the best or the most potential work from our people.

If I had more money, I have a whole lot of other ideas as to how we could make money with money, but right now, our people are struggling to push, push. People like the clinics on the reservation have been in jeopardy. Of course, I just read yesterday that maybe that could be settled. You know, I do a lot of reading. So I try to keep what I read connected to our people in the community in the urban metro area although I still make trips up to South Dakota.

How were you able to maintain your sense of cultural identity?

I think by everything I do. I mean the way I live, sometimes the way I dress, the comments that I have to make to people in general.

What is your opinion of the Indian Child Welfare Act?

I have pros and cons on that, I really do. And the pros, I think, are that we do need to keep our kids or our people—they need to be strongly committed to their families. I think it is better, and, you know I am a fine person to say this, but, and I say that sarcastically, but it's better to me for our kids to have exposure to city life, and what they could achieve, but on the other hand, it doesn't pay to take them away from their relatives. It doesn't pay to take them away from family.

Now if they are being abused, physically abused, you know, I do have a problem with that, because in my case I would have rather have been neglected by my mom one day out of the month—or even a week out of the month—you know, dirty clothes, not fed, whatever—than to be in a home with people that didn't love you or care about you, and abused me the way that they did, and I say again loosely because it was sexual, it was physical, it was—you know, it was a forced world.

On the other hand, I think had the government had their fingers in that child welfare act and what they are doing is trying to detach as many people, tribal people, away from their family so that they can do the same thing that they did to me and my grandparents. If they can detach me from—or any of us from our relatives, if they adopt these kids out, they may not have a way to make their contact back to their roots, and maybe some land would just disappear. You'll have less people complaining about what the government's taking from us. So it's a catch-22.

Uh-huh.

I have pros and cons on that. I do have ideas as to how to fix the problems, and right now there are problems finding Indian homes for Indian children and I don't believe that they should be in foster homes, I don't believe they should be in a family environment. The best thing that worked for me, and I saw it worked with others, is that if they're in a group environment with other kids that are in a same position that they are, the same condition, they are more verbal, they are more assertive, they are more able to help themselves. They are more able to get themselves out of that. They have a little bit more competition among themselves. You know, it's fair—it's a fair competition. If they are put in homes, they are competing in a Western world.

So, if I had a lot of money, I would open up a group home, and I would base it on some of the NIEA schools, the schools that they are building on reservations, but you know, where they have the core, and then they have wings of different age groups. And I would do that in the city. I believe that there are ways to fix some of the problems with the government. Just do it.

You know, one of the big things that's going on—it has been going on, is the government burning the hemp. You know, this is a way to help for people to get away from casinos and other degrading or insulting societal complaints. Why are they doing this? Because they don't want us to be successful. They are not honoring any of the treaties.

DO YOU THINK THAT NON-INDIAN FAMILIES CAN ADOPT INDIAN CHILDREN AND PROVIDE THEM WITH A POSITIVE EXPERIENCE?

That's a loaded question because everything depends. If those families have a true heart, and they honestly want to help Indian people, Indian children to keep their culture, then yes. But for the most part, they really don't have a clue, and they don't learn about Indian ways until after they've adopted a child and at that point, I think it is superficial. I don't think that it is a success. So, maybe adoption is not even an idea, you know what I mean. Maybe, if they grew up being in a group culture, like I was talking about you know, group home, a group environment. And people call them orphanages—it's a really a bad word—but the concept was well intended. If those kids grew up knowing that there are different cultures, that all Indian people are not the same. Maybe there are other Indian families in the city that can come in and pick up those kids and take them and be part of their world on occasion, but yet those kids can still come back to a group environment. I think that would be the ultimate.

That is the epitome of helping our Indian, our children that have no good homes. And that might only apply in the city. I am not sure that it'll really work on the reservations but if it worked here, it will definitely work there.

NOW, YOU SAID THAT THE BLACK FAMILY THAT YOU LIVED WITH, THEY DIDN'T ADOPT YOU?

Legally they didn't. The papers had been processed, gotten started. In 1974, May 20th—I went to school up in Boulder, coming out of East High

School. And because my parents were black, they put me under the Black Education Program instead of the Indian program. I don't think that there were too many Indian students up there at that time anyway. I managed in the BEP program up in Boulder. But, like I said, you know they both really encouraged me to keep going to school, and even in the foster homes and the group homes and my black family, I think I am the only one that ever went to college, continued my education. I think it's because I always felt like I can repair or ignore my condition. You know, I can focus on something else. I could put my mind to something that I thought would benefit me.

And what type of work did you do after you graduated?

From college?

Yeah, from college.

The whole time I have been in college, I was always working full-time or working part-time, then going to school full-time. So it was always both. The last eighteen years, I have been a professional at the Water Board and what has happened to me is pretty devastating because if it can happen to me, it can happen to anybody. But they tried to claim that I was incompetent and if I am incompetent then, you know, there is a serious problem. There are only about four Indians working at the Water Board and I am the only professional, or the only one with, you know, education. I should say higher education.

But the people that are looking at what has happened to me, they are all of all levels. They are professionals, and the majority of them are women, single women with children still at home, a lot of them are women of color, or I should just say people of color and they look and they're saying if this can happen to her, this strong Indian woman, this can happen to any of us. And so, now that I've been out of work for a couple of months and I've been away from the place, I can sit back and I analyzed it, and I think, "Okay, why did this happen to me?" But I don't take it personally now, now that I am away from it, I don't take it personally.

What I've realized is that this was a major move and it's happening across the country. This is a major move and what they are doing is squeezing out as many employees as possible. I don't know if this makes any sense to what you are doing or not, but this whole country is in a mess. They are trying. Corporations, companies, large corporations, are squeezing out as many employees as they can, and eventually they'll open up some windows of retirement and the good old boys—this is the white man's last grasp of holding onto this power. So then they open up the window of retirement and let these guys retire, give them that financial little package and, you know, make their investments or however they are going to spend their time.

But this looks to me like an injustice. So I can't just pretend like what happened to me is just going to go away, but I still have—even though I am not doing my job as an Indian person, I am still doing it as a person of color. So all people—you know, innocent white women with low economic backgrounds. It affects all people of color, and all genders. What's happening to me is going to happen to a lot of people. We are all affected.

In your e-mail, did you say that you are in the process of filing a lawsuit?

Uh-huh. And that's what I mean when I say I have to do something, because by me not doing something, it allows—or it hurts our people. It hurts people of low economic background, it hurts women of color, it hurts Indian people, because we are at the bottom. And so I don't have a choice. I have to fight. I have to fight to become that little teeny person—even though I have two degrees, I was making clerk wages. And I was so burdened everyday with so much stuff that they were throwing at me that I couldn't keep my head up. I couldn't see what was happening. Now, that I have been terminated and I went out on medical leave, I can keep my head up and read, and learn and, you know, educate myself as to what is going on. It's not me personally. But that's what I mean by fighting, I have to fight, just fight, not just for me, for all of us. They can't keep hurting. And those people out there don't know where I come from or what I've been through. You know, I don't go around sharing that. I don't take my own horn and say, well, I did this, I did that. You know, that's not our way.

Well, I think that was my last question. Do you have anything else you think that I should have asked you or any other issues that you would like to address?

No, not that I can think of. I think I pretty much unloaded on you, the cares of a certain childhood, but whatever you do with this information, I hope it falls into the right hands, or people that might need it, and can read it.

# 11

# STAR NAYEA

Singer/songwriter Star Nayea was placed with an abusive, non-Native family when she was two months old. According to Star, her adoptive parents were initially unaware of her cultural background. She believes "if they had any clue that they were adopting a Native child they would have pretty much been appalled." Once her adoptive parents realized that she was not "the Caucasian baby they had dreamed of," she says they began to abuse her physically and emotionally. Star recalls that three days before Christmas, her adoptive mother left her out in the snow. As a result, the six-year old fell into a coma and "almost lost both legs to amputation." Following this incident, Star was placed in foster care for a year, her adoptive mother was institutionalized and her adoptive parents divorced. After the divorce was finalized, Star was once again placed in the care of her adoptive father who continued to abuse her. As an adult, Star severed all ties with her adoptive family.

According to Star, her search for her birth family was hindered by her adoption agency. When she was twenty years old, the agency informed her that she was Irish, German, and Native American. However, she says the agency tried to downplay her Native background because she believes they were operating an illegal adoption ring in the sixties and seventies and they did not want to draw attention to the situation. The lack of information available made it difficult for Star to find her birth family.

Star characterizes her experience as a transracial adoptee as negative, but says that not all experiences have to be negative. She believes that adoptive parents need to be subjected to more thorough background checks and that Native children should be allowed to establish a relationship with their tribe. She argues, "to remove an indigenous person 100 percent from their culture is, in my mind, genocide. It really is. To take something that is so sacred and so precious and so simple and try to remove that human being from what they are completely, in my eyes, is genocide."

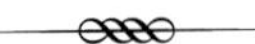

WHAT YEAR WERE YOU BORN?

I really would prefer not to say.

WHERE WERE YOU BORN?

I don't know. I have no clue. I was adopted through the Lutheran Social Services of Detroit, Michigan. And that is the only information I feel comfortable giving. Wherever I was born, they took me away from there and I was brought through the Lutheran Social Services of Detroit and raised up pretty much in different areas of Michigan.

HOW OLD WERE YOU WHEN YOU WERE ADOPTED?

I was two months old.

ARE YOU AWARE OF THE CIRCUMSTANCES SURROUNDING YOUR ADOPTION?

I am aware that it was illegal. All these years later I can say I am aware that it was illegal, but in the very beginning, I had no clue I was even adopted for the majority of my time with that family. And then . . . I think that honestly Jerry Flute was the one who made me aware, because nobody gave me a straight answer. My adoptive father, the Lutheran Social Services, no one ever gave me a straight answer on how I was adopted, why I was adopted. Jerry Flute was the only one that gave me that kind of clear answer as to how it might have gone down. So the circumstances under which I was adopted were definitely illegal, that I know. But that I didn't come to know until I was twenty. I didn't come to realize any of that until I was obviously far removed from it. Then the journey home has been a long and winding search.

DID YOUR ADOPTIVE PARENTS EVER INDICATE TO YOU WHY THEY DECIDED TO ADOPT?

They indicated that they were in the market to get another baby because the second attempt at a child—because they had lost a child. The child had died . . . it was a girl. And after they had had my older brother, they wanted to have another child to make the package complete. I guess my adoptive mother had delivered a child but she came out stillborn, so my guess is that she was probably drinking or something because she was an alcoholic and a diabetic so the girl didn't make it, and so the reason they adopted to begin with was because they wanted to have a girl.

From what I hear, not too soon after she had put in the application, they called her within like a month. There was no background check. At the time she had a real serious mental problem.

WERE YOUR PARENTS SPECIFICALLY LOOKING FOR A NATIVE CHILD OR WERE THEY JUST LOOKING FOR A CHILD IN GENERAL?

A child in general. If they had any clue that they were adopting a Native child they would have pretty much been appalled. As a matter of fact, the first time that my adoptive father realized that I was not Caucasian he definitely flipped out. And I think that the majority of the abuse that I suffered was in lieu of them taking a look at me on the outside and realizing that I was different from the Caucasian baby that they had dreamed of, not to mention my blond haired, blue-eyed brother who was white as snow, and here was me. So the differences were just extreme. I think that in retrospect having me next to him really pushed buttons with all of their racism and all of their prejudiced ways. That's where all the abuse began.

WHEN DID YOU LEARN THAT YOU WERE NATIVE?

Honestly, I finally learned I was Native when I was about twenty. But there was also this tendency and question that would arise throughout my childhood and throughout my youth and in my teenage years. Questions on the way that I looked, questions on why my skin was so dark, questions on . . . I mean it was like that old *Sesame Street* song "One of these things is not like the other." I was brought into a totally Anglo-Saxon home and I was obviously not Anglo.

HOW DID YOU LEARN THAT YOU WERE NATIVE?

It is an extremely long story. The end of the story is in New York, when I met a man, he is from Sisekon Wahpeton, he is Dakota Sioux, he is a spiritual leader of his tribe and I met him in New York state, and I had written my adoption agency five years prior to meeting Jerry Flute and my adoption agency had told me after twenty some odd years that I was Native, however, they tried to downplay that I was Native. They tried to make it look as though I was just barely Native. They said that I was German, Irish, and a little Native from my grandfather's side. On the birth certificate it says Caucasian. When I had written them, I was actually eighteen when I first heard the word "Indian" or "Native" because obviously growing up in white America in rural Michigan or even urban Michigan, it was either black or white. Hispanics were slowly moving in and then you had Lebanese people who were slowly moving in. And even to the Lebanese people I didn't look Anglo. So I would always get questions from them. I would get questions from people who gave me a job in my first bar, when I was eighteen, and I would wait on people and I would be like "Hey, can I take your order?" and then they would look up at me and go "ooooh." I wouldn't get an order, I would get questions about who I was and what nationality I was, because they had never seen anybody who had looked like me. So it was kind of weird. And I was like, "Can I take your order, I'm not here to discuss what I look like." It ended up being time after time after time, people constantly asking me if I was Native, or if I was Hawaiian, or if I was Asian, I would get all of that. After a good long time of this I had finally written my adoption agency and I made the mistake of telling them why I was writing them, rather than just writing them asking for nonidentifying information, I made the mistake of saying, "I keep getting asked if I'm Native, could you please help me out. Because on my birth certificate it says that I'm Caucasian." The Lutheran Social Services was running an illegal baby ring for about fifteen years, the emergency light went off and they thought oh here comes another one, so basically they wrote me a letter back saying, oh you know, after twenty some odd years by the way, not only are you German, Scotch, Irish, but your grandfather was part Native. And then they went ahead and said, "OK, well we're going to search the tri-state area," which would be Michigan, Ohio, and Illinois or whatever it is in that place, and then they came up with no indication, no records, and they finally wrote me a letter back and they said, we searched the tri-state area under your grandfather's "name" and we don't find any records of his birth or his tribal affiliation, yadda, yadda, yadda. I was really frustrated. I went to a friend of mine and showed her the letter and she was studying genealogy and she looked at the letter the agency wrote to me and she read it. The letter said, well, just to get it started, I'm 5'3" or 5'4", and dark hair and dark eyes, obviously native. My "parents" were 5'9" and 5'10", my dad was 5'10", my mom was 5'9", and they were both fair-skinned and one had blue eyes and one had hazel eyes. So my friend who was the genealogist, said you can't come from these two people, the

Lutheran Social Services is b-s-ing you, they are lying to you. I couldn't fathom why they would lie to me. So I had met Jerry Flute and Jerry Flute had asked me a series of questions when he first met me and one of the questions was what tribe are you? And I was constantly asked all the time that question. And I was like, "I don't know, I don't know, I don't know." And Jerry Flute was the first guy to ever say, "why? Why don't you know?" And I said I was adopted, and he said tell me about it. Well, I said, it's a really long story and I sat down and began to tell him. And after that, he began to tell me. He said, "I'll tell you why you don't know where you come from and I have some other bad news for you." He said, "You may never find out where you come from." I was horrified when he said that. He said, "I am with the Association on American Indian Affairs"—he said he had been with them ever since the 1970s and I met him in the 1990s. He said I have been with them for a long, long time, and when I was working with them, I spotted something that was happening, and we reported it to the government, and it had something to do with the BIA and it had something to do with Lutheran Social Service and Catholic churches and they were running a baby ring, basically stealing native babies from reservations from Canada, bringing them down to the states. Nobody could figure out why they brought the babies down into the United States but they did. They brought thousands of babies into the United States and they shuffled them like a deck of cards. They took native babies from the states too, and shuffled them like a deck of cards. So many of them came from Canada, it is just unreal. He began to tell me all of this and I just listened in amazement. And I thought "well, duh, no wonder I am getting such a run around from the adoption agency." When he had revealed all of this to me, I decided to take matters into my own hands and I went to the adoption agency in Detroit, Michigan, and I walked in there and I said I want to see the executive director of the adoption agency, I wanted to see him and speak with him in person, and the lady was very nervous, and I had brought along my little sister for witness, my little adopted sister she has red hair, blue eyes, white skin with freckles. She wasn't my blood sister, she was my adopted sister, and I had brought her along to sort of witness it, and fifteen minutes later the guy came down, and I went in the back with him into one of his offices, and I had with me all the information that they had sent me and all the information that the BIA had sent me, because I had contacted the BIA, too. And I told them who I was and where I was adopted from, et cetera, the whole nine, not realizing the tie between the BIA and Lutheran Social Services, they were in cahoots! So both of them gave me conflicting stories, which is the funny part about it. At any rate, I sat down and I gave him all of this stuff on paper, and he read maybe one paragraph of the first page and then he put it down and he looked at me and he said, "I'm sorry, I think we pulled up the wrong file on you." And I'm quoting him on that. This is the president of Lutheran Social Services of Detroit Adoption. And he said "I think we've pulled up a wrong file on you." And I just looked at him and then Jerry Flute's words never rang more true. I realized that I was in the middle or a product of something that was very serious and very significant and very sordid and very lengthy. I just looked at him, and at that point he said "I'm sorry, we want to help you." And I said there's no need to apologize, but at that point in time I had met Dennis Banks and Russell Means from AIM so I had become this little miniature AIMster at the time. I kind of laugh about it now, but I'm thinking of myself. . . . I was so into AIM at the time and they were so into trying to save us. So the AIM lawyers did investigate, Dennis Banks had the AIM lawyers investigate and he had the lawyers send my adoption agency a letter threatening to sue them if they didn't open up my records and the adoption agency wrote them a letter back saying OK, we'll write a letter to her mother on the reservation and let her mother know she's looking for her. Which is a load of shit because they didn't know who my mother was. We didn't come with a trail of peanuts to find our way back home. There were thousands of babies who came through there. They didn't leave a trail of nuts for us to go "ok, now that baby belonged to such and such on this reservation." It was just a bunch of BS.

SO YOU WERE NEVER ABLE TO FIND MORE INFORMATION OUT?

That was it. That was my last bout with my adoption agency, and I didn't have money to really further the investigation with the lawyers, and regardless of how close I became within it, it's not like these services came for free. And then, you can't get blood out of a stone. If they don't have any information, then they don't have it. They are not going to be able to pull it out of the air and magically make it appear when it doesn't exist. Literally, when I walked in there, they knew exactly why I was there. In fact, to corroborate another part of the story, I had brought my sister along to witness all of this and after we left she said, I'm so glad you brought me along. I said, why? And she said, because you are never going to believe what the secretary said after I had gone back to talk with the president. She said, "Is that girl Native American?" And my sister said yeah. She said, "was she adopted?" And my sister said, "yes, she was adopted from here that's why she's here." And then the secretary went "Oh. . . ." My sister said she got really nervous and she kind of turned around and just shut right up after that. It was an interesting little oral conversation or lack thereof between the two of them. My sister definitely picked up the vibes that the secretary had caught wind of something and she basically knew why I was there. My sister is not involved at all. I just took her along and didn't tell her anything. I said, I want you to do me a favor and I want you to watch their expressions and tell me what happens, that's all I told her. So what she came up with was that they were very suspicious. Whatever Jerry Flute told me was right. He told me a series of things that I didn't want to believe and that was very hurtful. He wasn't meaning to hurt me, but it was the truth. He wanted to spare me the fact that it was an ugly, ugly process and I am sure that the more this gets out there will be people who will corroborate this story. There was actually murder involved. Some of these parents didn't give the babies up willingly . . . they were killed for them. There was bloodshed for these babies. And that was told to me by Jerry Flute as well. We had actually gone on a show, Native American Calling, broadcast in Albuquerque, and we did a show about the subject and the studio lines were lit up the whole show and after the show had ended we had tons of calls from people wanting to call in and talk about the subject. There was never enough time to complete the subject. So it is something that needs to be talked about.

I WANT TO TALK ABOUT YOUR ADOPTIVE FAMILY NOW. CAN YOU TELL ME MORE ABOUT YOUR ADOPTIVE PARENTS, WHAT THEY DID FOR A LIVING, THE NEIGHBORHOOD YOU GREW UP IN, THAT SORT OF THING?

My adoptive family, they were lower-middle class. My dad was a meat cutter, and my mom was a stay-at-home mom, I suppose. My adoptive mom was an alcoholic and she was a diabetic and she . . . there's no other word for it and I'm not being a smart aleck—but she was "Mommy Dearest." I was severely abused by her from the age of infancy 'til I was six years old, so basically the last time I saw my adoptive mom was when I was six. I was in the hospital, I almost lost both of my legs to amputation because she threw me out in the snow three days before Christmas, and I almost lost my legs because of it. And then I ended up in a foster home and all kinds of stuff happened. But my adoptive dad was there the whole time and he claimed he never knew any of this was going on. He claimed he never knew she was abusing me, and all this kind of stuff, he just completely turned a blind eye to the whole situation. So I don't keep in touch with them, I have no clue where they are, although I know that my adoptive mom has passed away.

SO YOU WENT TO A FOSTER HOME WHEN YOU WERE SIX?

I went to a foster home and I was there, probably for about a year while I healed, and the state of Michigan couldn't decide whether to put me back with the father, they didn't really know what to do with me. It dawned on me, didn't they get it? Didn't they get that I was Native? Didn't they get that I wasn't an Anglo-Saxon child? Why didn't somebody say something? Why didn't anybody question any of this? Why didn't somebody say, you know this girl doesn't look Caucasian, what's the deal? But they stuck me in this foster home, and I got fostered by some people and whatnot, and then I got put back with my dad. And it looked for a while like it was going to be a decent start again because I was about eight years old when I got back with my dad and he had got custody of his son, who never got touched by the way, and then he had remarried, and he married my babysitter, and unfortunately he started to abuse me. So I went into an ongoing situation. So this story is not different from thousands out there. There were thousands of us that were abused, physically, sexually, mentally, and spiritually, so I kind of fall into that spectrum of the situation.

Did you live with your adoptive father until you were eighteen?

Oh, God, no. I ran away as much as possible. The first time I tried to run away I was fourteen, and then I came back miserably with my tail between my legs because I couldn't make it on my own out there. It was a very dysfunctional relationship. I know he was trying very hard to be a father but at that point he was a bit jaded with what had happened to me, and his marriage had been broken up, I don't know if he blamed me or what he blamed. All I know is that he was an extremely prejudiced man, too. Because I remember one day I sat down across the table from him and I was about twenty-six and I said to him, "why did you do the things you did, why didn't you let me know I was Native," et cetera, and he said so many messed up things. One of the things I'll never forget was, he said I understand your connection with earth or what you call Mother Earth. I feel that connection every time I mow the lawn, and I said, yeah, and I'm thinking to myself you're crazy. He said, he kind of yelled at me . . . well you weren't black, so you have to be white. And I just looked at him, and I finally got it. He only knew black and white. God forbid I was black because he was so prejudiced. He had told the story to me that one day he had called up the adoption agency because he was scrubbing me and scrubbing me in the bathtub and my brown skin wouldn't come off. And he said he didn't understand why my knees and my skin it was brown, and my knees were black and he couldn't get the dirt off and freaked out, so he called the adoption agency and he asked them why I had brown skin, and they said oh, he told me this, they said "she is a version of what we call black Scotch/Irish." That's what the adoption agency told him. And he said, "what does that mean? Does that mean that she's black?" He freaked out thinking I was African American. And they said, "no, no, that means that she has dark skin and dark hair." Well if anybody has done any research on heritage, black Irish are extremely white with black hair and blue eyes. That's what black Irish are. It is just bullshit. They just kept feeding him bullshit. And so he bought into it. Needless to say he didn't know how to raise a Native baby because god forbid that he had adopted anything but an Anglo baby. So that is one of the things that I dealt with. So needless to say I left home as often as possible. And the police were constantly at our house, because we had disturbances, he was constantly beating the crap out of me and the neighbors were calling the cops.

When did you first realize you were adopted?

After I got out of the foster home, I think it kind of finally came to a head. The first time I ever realized I was adopted was when somebody else told me that and it was a kid. It was a neighbor down the street. They just said, "You know you're adopted." Kids are cruel and you've heard that all throughout the years. But it was true, she said, you know you're adopted. And I'm like, "What?" And I went home and I asked and sure enough she was right. I was like "well, that explains a lot." Duh. I was probably about eight or nine.

So when you asked your parents about being adopted what did they say to you?

Well, psycho mom was already in an institution somewhere, so all I had was my dad and my twenty-year-old babysitter that was now his wife. So her and I really didn't get along too well. So my dad was completely complacent. He didn't want to talk about it. One of the things that I think he was always afraid of was that he was going to get in trouble. I think after a while he started to realize that he had done something wrong, or that somebody had done something wrong. Even ten, fifteen years ago when I sat across the table and I said you know, you could help me try to find my family if you know any information at all. And he was like, I swear, I swear I don't know anything. I swear when I got you they told me you were a white baby, yadda, yadda, yadda. He swears he doesn't know anything. So I'll never get anything out of him.

What was your reaction when he told you that you were adopted?

Oh, God, I don't know. I can't remember. I don't remember much of my childhood. I remember finding out I was adopted, but I certainly don't remember my reaction, other than I'm assuming I was probably making sense of it all. It made a lot of sense to me at the time because I figured that's why my adoptive mom didn't love me and that's probably why I didn't feel love from my adoptive father, either. It was always I was made to please kind of relationship with him. I was constantly trying to win his love and his affection. So there was no father/daughter relationship there. There was like, ok, what can I do for him not to hit me today. Because with him you never knew when it was coming. It wasn't much of a father/daughter relationship, that's for sure.

How many siblings did you have?

I had one older sibling and one younger one who was born after me, when he had been married to the babysitter.

So you were the only one adopted?

I was the only one adopted. I was the middle one. And I was also the only one beaten. I was the only one abused.

Are you close to your siblings?

My brother passed away when I was in my late teens or twenties. When he was twenty-three or twenty-four he died of diabetes and then my sister, the one I took with me to the adoption agency, she and I used to be close, we got our relationship going again because she's nine years younger than me. And the fact of the matter is that our relationship is extremely torn at this point now because she doesn't understand why I don't embrace her attitude at this point. She has a hard time understanding that because she feels like everything that happened to me is not her fault. And it's true, it's not her fault, none of it is. But the fact of the matter is, is that I'm nine years older than her and when that stuff was going down she wasn't even around, and so she doesn't know what happened. She wasn't there. And so we got into some personal arguments lately and heated, and you know what, when you're an adoptee and you learn how to cut ties real quick, so basically that's what I've done. . . . I've cut my ties.

Tell me a little about your life . . . going to school, junior high, and high school. The type of schools, the type of kids you hung out with, that sort of thing?

It was all public schools and honestly, I was an outcast. I was a complete social outcast. I never had any friends. I had landed in a hospital when I was six. I think I was in kindergarten when she threw me out in the snow and so I can't remember. I was in a coma quite a while, and then when I gained consciousness Christmas was over and the new year had come. I had gotten thrown out in the snow and I had missed Christmas and New Years and I woke up in the hospital and everything had passed me by. I had been in a coma. When I came to, that's where the memories kind of start. I spent time in the foster home and spent a year in bandages from my knees down all the time, so my first experiences with school was literally marching into school like a penguin with my legs wrapped, so I was just completely an outcast from the get-go. Even back then I figured out a way to make it an advantage. I made jokes and I tried to get the kids to kick my legs because at that point I couldn't feel anything and I thought that well if nothing else I'll win them over acting freaky. Essentially what really won people over time after time was that I began singing. I began singing and I had taken that little song from the *Wizard of Oz*, "Somewhere over the Rainbow," and that had become my theme song and out on the playground and with me and my bandages on the swing, but before the lunch bell rang there was a crowd of kids sitting around me. So I have to say in all of my awkwardness and just the fact that I didn't look like any of the other kids and plus I had this at the time, this disability, I figured out a way to get good kinds of attention. I was craving good attention so much, so I sang. So it was an on again, off again thing, and I kept trying to sing throughout and I kept trying to see if I could gain acceptance and gain friends and people would stop judging me and stop looking at me and thinking that I looked different from them. I went to an all white school all the way up to high school, and so I was the only colored person in the area and the first time I ever, ever met any other people of different nationalities was when I was in high school, and I had met a girl who was half black and half Hawaiian, and she had become one of my dearest friends at that time because we were the two odd-balls, if you will, and then I had met this other girl who was African American and so it was kind of like the three of us. We were the only colored people in my senior class. But I wasn't very popular. I got stood up all the time and I got made fun of all the time, they had a zillion names for me: chipmunk because I had beady black eyes and big cheeks, which ended up being cheekbones, so that's kind of funny. I had big fat cheeks and when I finally grew up they're like "oooohhh, OK."

DID YOU ENCOUNTER ANY FORM OF RACISM, GROWING UP?

Oh, Yes. It was all over the place. Completely. Nobody knew what I was because I didn't know what I was. All the kids kept saying, well you're not white. And they kept calling me mulatto—they thought I was half black and half white. I was like, no, I'm not, leave me alone. I got made fun of every single day of my life. In my twenties, long after high school had ended, I was still having nightmares. I was still having bad dreams. Back then, I could be your perfect example of teen suicide mixed with the Columbine situation. I was completely ridiculed, I was completely made fun of. I was completely bullied back in the day. That's why today I laugh when I get a high school reunion card. I'm like, "yeah, right. Like I'm going to go back and look at the people I loathe the most in this world."

How did you address the issue of racism growing up, or did you?

I don't think we really know how to address it when we're faced with it. I think that it caused me great concern and great depression. I think how I addressed anything growing up was through my song writing. I had started writing poetry and songs when I was fourteen, so I had taken the love for music and the fact that I loved to sing and then I started disappearing on my own and going into the woods and writing songs about it. It was pretty, emotionally, quite the roller coaster ride, because not only was I getting this sort of treatment at school, but I would get it when I got home.

What did you do after high school?

First of all I joined the Miss Birmingham pageant because I had something to prove to my unaccepting father. So I joined the Miss Birmingham pageant, and I placed first runner-up, which was a blow to my ego, but nonetheless I figured it wasn't meant to be, but I had placed first runner-up. I missed it by that much. I missed it by half a point, which I could care less, trust me. It was just to please papa. It was just to make him look at me differently, like he would finally look at me like a princess maybe. It was all BS.

After that I joined my first rock band, and this is all at the age of seventeen or eighteen. Right after I graduated I got the heck out of there, and joined my first rock band and started playing bars right away in Michigan.

Tell me a little bit more about your music career, getting signed and stuff.

Getting signed has not been easy for me thus far. I have been approached by many labels but thus far none have come to fruition, so I remain an unsigned artist. It is a bit of a blow. Part of the reason I'm unsigned is that it is all Native labels that have approached me. Either I am not Native enough, which I refuse to be, to be quite frank. I didn't grow up Native, I didn't grow up knowing my culture, my language, anything. So far be it for me to sort of push that culture within myself and push it on to other people. I am not going to be something that I'm not. So I remain urban, Native if you will, and I remain completely contemporary. So record labels they don't know what to do with me. They want me to be a Native artist based on the way that I look. I don't know. But when I don't do Native music they get pretty frustrated about that and they won't sign me.

The label that I was dealing with recently, in order to get the record deal with them I had to include some sort of Native influences in my music, and I refused. So the record deal fell through. Either you are going to sign me for me because I am a damned good musician and it just so happens that I'm Native, or you are going to sign me because I am a Native artist which I'm not going to be. So at this point I just remain completely independent. I put out my own music, I write my songs, I find ways to record them, and I find ways to release them. I book myself, I manage myself, for the most part. I have people that help, but for the most part I take care of all of that.

WHAT ARE YOUR LONG-TERM GOALS?

I think bottom line is just to make a difference with my music. I'll give you an example of that. I am not going to name names but there's a man and a woman who I have no idea who they are, but I did meet a woman at a concert that I was giving in Milwaukee. I received an e-mail from her since then who made comments that they really liked one song in particular, the song is called "Come My Way." A lot of people seem to like this song. It was written out of just complete . . . a disheartening experience with my own love life, and my own "soul mate" that I met and who I fell head over heels in love with but then as quickly as he came, he left. And it's a really wonderful, beautiful song that takes the sacredness and the blessing that a human being can bring you in life with their love and their companionship and with their soul connecting with yours. And in this position especially because for me it is the story of another adoptee, and he and I went through these tumultuous life stories on opposite ends of the world but we lived the same exact lives, and then all of a sudden one day out of nowhere we were brought together by a friend, and you can imagine that we had a pretty interesting little meeting. And so this song was written in honor of him, "Come My Way." He knows it, he's heard it. And so this man and his woman who don't know the outcome of my song and how it was written just fell in love with the song. But their marriage was in turmoil. And so I went to Indian Summerfest, this is such a cool story, and I played, and when I got done playing I got down to my table and started signing autographs and selling CDs, and this one woman came up to me and she told me her name and I kind of recognized her name, I thought maybe I'd heard it somewhere. And she looked at me and she said, why didn't you sing "Come My Way"? You know because I was concentrating on all my newer songs, and so I didn't play "Come My Way" and I said, oh, I'm so sorry, and then I started just kind of singing it to her, just a little bit you know, and then she started breaking down, and she broke down into tears. And I was devastated. I reached over and I just held her. And she just wept in my arms and she told me that that song is so meaningful to her and her husband. And long story short basically "Come My Way" saved their marriage because I got an e-mail from her husband much later and he explained that "Come My Way" saved their marriage. What better gift can you give as a musician than bringing music that absolutely reaches into the depths of people and just touch their lives and make a difference? I don't care if I win a Grammy, I don't care if I become Indian country's top selling female artist, like so many people are doing—kind of push you to be this how to explain it. Push me to be everything you can be. If I touch one person's life then I've done my job.

How many albums have you released?

Every single album that I've released, the only one that I've really counted was an independent release. And it was a five-song CD and it has only been a feeble attempt to release these songs that I'm putting out by myself because I have no representation, I have no label, I have no money behind me. So everything that I'm putting out is a half-assed attempt to put out a real product but the only reason I keep putting it out is that I keep getting people saying, "we want your music. We don't care what it is like . . . release your music." So I keep releasing these independent releases which are not necessarily so ready for the big world yet, so I guess that, I guess you might say that the 2001 CD that got released, it was the first one to get released and there are two or three different ones after that. . . . It is all just independent releases of my music, so they're not bonafide CDs unfortunately. They are just different compilations CDs of my music, different versions of everything, because I'll get e-mails from people who say, can I get this song on the CD, can I get this song on the CD. So I'll take the more popular requested songs and I'll throw them all on one CD and then I'll release it as "a compilation" or "the best of" or some stupid thing. I'll just keep trying to release my songs in some sort of a way where people will keep wanting them.

How has your personal life influenced your music?

Music saves me. That's all there is to be said on that. If it wasn't for music, my past would have killed me. I would be dead by now. Either from alcoholism or from self-inflicted . . . just taking myself out. I would have taken myself out years ago.

Do you travel often, touring and that sort of thing?

Yes. As much as I possibly can. And now I am the mother of a nine-year-old boy, the second thing that saved my life is my son. And I take him with me everywhere, this baby is a road baby from the time that he was inside my womb I toured with Dennis Biggs and when I was pregnant with him all the way up to about seven months this baby grew inside of me learning the song, it is quite funny. So he has been everywhere with me, almost every single show I've ever done, even when I was nine months pregnant, just about to deliver, I was playing in Arizona, and I was just about ready to pop him out. He has been there the whole way.

How have addressed the issue of cultural identity with your son?

You know I teach him the things that I was taught. When I met Jerry Flute fifteen years ago back in New York City he had stated to me he was going to take me home. He said, "I'm going to take you home, and I'm going to take you to your first sundance and I'm going to introduce you to my culture and to my family" and he did. He came through with that promise. And he introduced me to Dakota culture and he introduced me to a family out there. This is another story all in itself. I was adopted eleven or twelve years ago by a Dakota family, the Holybones. Rita and Gary Holybone and Rita has since passed of cancer. But Rita and Gary Holybone adopted me on the fourth day of a sundance ceremony and so with that I was taught how to pray, how to speak to my creator in Dakota, in Lakota, so I got taught the basics. Honestly, I'm good at family. They wanted me to move to South Dakota and they wanted me to become a part of their family and live on the reservation but at that point I was so jaded there was no way I could have done that. Family was nothing. I didn't know what that meant, so I couldn't take them up on that offer. But I took what they gave me and what little culture they could possibly give me, I considered a great gift. My son's dad is Navajo and for the longest time he wanted me to become Navajo and I said no, that's not what runs through my veins, and I wasn't comfortable with that at all. I just couldn't be Navajo. I said, there's something else that runs through my veins and I'm just going to hold out for whatever that is. That's why I'm a single mother . . . we just didn't make it. As far as the cultural aspect of what I give to my son, it's Dakota, it's Lakota, I teach him how to speak the little language that I know and how to pray and we burn sage and we go out there with my feathers that were gifted to me every single morning, and I mean it, every single morning we go out and we pray. And it is kind of hard to drag him out there in the mornings, he doesn't want to go and he doesn't understand what it means, but I guess I'm just sort of giving him something that probably would have been given to me if in fact I had that opportunity as a child. I'm sure I would have had somebody teach me how to pray. So that's really all I can do for him right now. Culturally his father is not giving him his culture. His father would probably like to say that I denied him that but the fact of the matter is that he doesn't come around, he doesn't call. And personally speaking, it takes a lot to be a parent. I don't appreciate drop-ins. If you're going to be a parent you're going to be a hands-on parent, it's an everyday occurrence, it's not whenever you feel like it. So I have to limit my contact with his dad because either you're going to do it right or you're not going to do it at all. One day when he's older and he wants to go learn about his—side of him that's fine. But my son really takes after me, and one day I'll find out what side of him that is too. So for now I give him that. . . . I give him the Dakota culture and I teach him how to speak to the creator in a traditional way and I make him say the words, even though he has trouble with it. I make him repeat it and I make him hold the sage and I make him stand alone and I make him have thoughts. When I say make I don't mean to sound like I force him, I just encourage him. I encourage him to search really deep within himself and do all of these things on his own accord because he wants to.

On a daily basis, I am still surrounded with no cultural or spiritual tradition. It is going to have to come from me so my son, sometimes he'll wake up in the morning and he'll see that I am not out. And he'll take a look outside and he'll see, oh she's out there praying. And for me that's important. There's times when I miss my morning prayer and there's times when I am just absolutely adamant about it because to me it is the least that I can do. These small things are the things that I want to pass on to him.

WHEN YOU SPOKE WITH THE ADOPTION AGENCY ABOUT YOUR BACKGROUND THEY DIDN'T TELL YOU SPECIFICALLY WHAT TRIBE YOU WERE FROM?

No. Absolutely not. Identifying information should be revealed and Michigan has a law that says the adoption agency must release identifying information.

SO GIVEN THAT YOU DON'T KNOW YOUR TRIBAL AFFILIATION AND THEREFORE YOU CAN'T ENROLL, HAS THAT HAD ANY SORT OF AFFECT ON YOUR SENSE OF CULTURAL IDENTITY?

No. It hasn't had any affect on my cultural identity. It sickens me that our culture is run by numbers. That I have to verbally or orally dictate a number to prove that I belong. When you cannot . . . when all you have to do is open your eyes and look at me and if you can't tell that I am an indigenous woman you need glasses, that's what I always say. The fact that I would have to in order to get health care, in order to get grants or loans to go to school or to whatever, it is extremely frustrating. And every single adoptee who hasn't found their way home yet will reiterate this point. That it is a sickening fact that when we are standing in front of them and they say, for instance, at the Indian hospital will say do you have your CIB and I'll be like, no, I don't. And they'll say, well you have thirty days to find it and get it back to us. And you just sit there, and you look at them and you say, I've been looking for thirty years for it and now I have thirty days to get it to you, and you just want to tell them to go fly a kite. It is extremely frustrating and it is . . . there is no word to put to it. There is quite the empty feeling that comes over your where you feel as if because of the lack of a number that you absolutely don't belong. If you can't provide a census number or if you can't provide your CIB number, whatever that is, Certificate of Indian Blood, it is just comical. It is absolutely comical. However, I understand the reasons behind it. I understand the political reasons behind it, I understand that this is their way of keeping track of us all just like social security numbers for non-Native people and when we first came on to that sort of thing. However, for indigenous people it would be just a little bit different. And then of course you have a lot of people who are trying to pass themselves off as Native people, which still amazes me. I don't know why people do that. It is quite funny actually, it's hilarious. I meet people so many people, especially when I was touring with Dennis Biggs who were clearly not Native but they looked like Barbie dolls, they came from Mexico or something or China, it was just such a joke. So I understand that there are cases, and it is a case sensitive situation. But Indians who have been through what we have been through will say the exact same thing, that not being able to prove your tribal affiliation doesn't so much affect you culturally, it affects you internally. It affects you mentally. It is just another confirmation that we don't belong anywhere.

How do you answer questions regarding your tribal affiliation?

It's a long story. That's the first thing I say. Then they look at me odd. There's two ways that people . . . when I say that it's a long story, they look at me with interest or they look at me like I'm crazy. If they look at me like I'm crazy I don't bother with them. If they look at me with interest I start explaining it. Because everything that's in this interview is what I have to go through, predominantly. It is a long story, just like this interview is. They don't realize the depths of what's based on this stuff. . . . it is a very long story.

Do you think your inability to get enrolled has affected the way those in the Native community see you?

Oh, 100 percent. I have absolutely no doubt. The only ones who understand us, is us. And when I say us, I'm talking tens of thousands of us. But we are quite outnumbered. We've got tens of thousands of adoptees out there but against a million of native people who are out there who all know where they come from, lucky them. We're completely outnumbered. Some of your natives will understand it. I was adopted into a Dakota family, but I was re-adopted into a Laguna family here in New Mexico. Because they fell in love with my son, and they adopted my son as their grandson because he has no grandparents because my son's father's parents aren't a part of his life at all, so anyway long story short, we got adopted into a Laguna family, and the Laguna family they don't bat an eyelash at it. They know who I am and they know who my son is. They know that we are indigenous and that's all they need to know. There are indigenous people out there who will accept us, but the majority I am telling you when you cannot name your tribe and you can't speak your language and you can't say where your grandfather comes from it's horrifying because the looks that you get from these native, indigenous people and then they just think that it's a big old sob story that you're making up some sort of . . . excuse me, why the hell would I make this up? Where in the living hell am I going to get all of this from? Do you think that this is something that I like to talk about. No. I would give anything in my life if this had never happened to me. But it did. So these people who don't recognize us and won't recognize us because we can't provide tribal affiliation, they need to step back and they need to see what it would be like to walk a day in our shoes, and maybe then there would be a bit more acceptance there.

Do you feel you are secure or insecure about your Native identity today?

I feel completely 100 percent secure that I am an indigenous native woman. I am of mixed blood. I know for a fact that I am not full-blooded, however I am half or better. I am very secure in that. I have met many, many Crees and Ojibaways who could be my family. I don't know if I am them. I look like a lot of people up in Canada. There's no doubt about it. And I've also come across recently some people that I look like, too. I have no doubt that somewhere out there my family is existing. Whether or not they'll find me or whether or not I'll find them that's really up to creator. I have nothing to hide. If I had something to hide I wouldn't be talking about it. That's the thing about it. I would welcome everyone and anyone to stick their nose into this and to start helping me with the hunt. I know for a fact that I'm an indigenous woman. What the other part of me is I can only guess. It's probably Anglo, but I know for a fact that I am a Native, indigenous woman. And that's what I turn to, no offense, but whatever portion of me is non-Native, I grew up that way, and to be quite honest that culture doesn't do anything for me. I was constantly running away from that culture. So I would embrace the fact, but there are some people out there, I'll be honest with you, and it bugs me, that are clearly not Native. They're half white, and then maybe somewhere back in their lineage they have Native blood, but guess what they're going around saying: They're saying they're Native. Or I know a girl who is half Malaysian, and I've met her mom, her mom is full blood Malaysian, and her dad was a white man, and then apparently somewhere in the lineage he has some Native, and she goes around saying that she is Native, Indian. And it just kills me because if I knew an inch of what I was I would be proud of it and I would be supporting it wholeheartedly. All I know this far is that I'm a human being, I'm a single mom, I'm an indigenous woman, but I don't know where I come from and when I do know I'll let everybody else know.

That bothers me, because there's me and thousands like me still out there who can't find our identities, our identities are ties where we come from and there are people playing with this. People play with being Native, and they think that it's fun and they think that it's going to bring them some notoriety and they think that it's going to make them a better human being than they are if they claim that they are Native. Well, that bothers me, that bothers me greatly because it is kind of a slap in the face to me. I am kind of on the fence about whether I say that in the interview. And the more I think about it the more I think I should probably just stick with it because it is not only that, it's that there are some Native artists out there who, I tell you what, maybe I'll get kicked out for this, but I don't care . . . but some Native musicians out there who are all of a sudden Native. But they weren't years ago. They weren't ten years ago, they weren't blah, blah, blah years ago, they weren't Natives. But they're Native today because they want Native American Music Awards, they want Native American casino gigs, and they want Native American festival gigs, and they want the money that comes with it and they want the notoriety that comes with it, and because in the modern world and the mainstream world and the world that's mixed up with Anglos, and Hispanics, and Blacks, and Jews and the melting pot that is America they can't make their way as artists, so they play the Native American card and that bugs the living hell out of me. Because that is the one thing that I don't do. You'll never hear it in my music. And we're talking artists that sincerely wear their culture on their sleeves, even though they have no idea what it means to be Native. They say they know their tribe, they don't go to ceremonies, they don't speak the language, they flaunt being Native, but they aren't Native at all. I think that too many Native American artists out there, indigenous artists out there, musicians there are some who deserve and who have the right to sing those songs because they were brought up that way, they were taught that way properly, they speak their language, they go to their ceremonies, they know who they are. It is their inherited right to be artists. These other artists, and they know exactly who they are, I don't have to name names. These other artists come in and they wear their culture on their sleeves and they make a lot of money doing it, and it just eats me up inside. So that's one thing that I do want to say. And I talk to my son about that. I know him and as a Native artist myself, the only thing I can say is that I'm a Native artist. Do I say it in my music? No. My music is 100 percent mainstream. It is contemporary. I don't play a flute, I don't do any of that kind of stuff. Unfortunately, it gives me a mixed signal in one perspective. The song that was put in the 2006 Grammy Award–winning CD was released, was recorded in 1999 or 2000, I can't remember. The year 2000. It was a song called "Mountain Song." And I had put hints of Native vocables and the producer Tim Wilson put Mike and Primo on there to make up a bunch of stuff that I can't do because I wasn't raised that way. But I'm singing in English, I didn't want to do anything but English. I wanted to sing R&B style English on that song and it is exactly what I did. And in this version to be put in, and they didn't ask my permission to do this, but in this version that they put on the Grammy Award–winning CD, they have me singing vocables, they have me speaking in Indian, which I did do, but in my version that I got none of that was in there, because I told them, you know, no offense but I don't want that in my version. If I add this song on my CD in the future I want to put out, I'm singing in English and it sounds like an R&B song. It sounds really basically what I do. But at that time they tried to make me a little more Native than I was. And so, I think, I want to go backwards, but that is the problem with my music career, is that all these Native labels got on me because my music is not Native enough. My music . . . people look at me and they think oh this is a prime target. We can take this girl and she can sing a bunch of vocables and we'll put some flute music in there and then we'll have another glorious Native artist on our hands. But the second they found out that I don't do that, the second they find out that I'm a rocker or that I sing blues and I sing all in English and that my music sounds like something that you'd hear on the radio today, I completely lose it. So that's what I'm saying. To all these new "Native" artists who have come out using this culture to make money off of, I don't condone it whatsoever. I think it is horrendous and quite frankly I am offended by them. And they know who they are.

I am so secure in myself being Native that I don't have to wear it on my sleeve like the other artists do. Like these other musicians. I don't have to take my culture and put it into my music like these labels want me to. I think it is a shame that we have a Native American category in the Grammy's, I really do. Because every artist that enters into the Grammys under this category has to forfeit or produce some sort of their culture, their heritage to get accepted into that category. I think it is appalling to be quite frank. Because some of our Native artists out there put them on stage with any of these mainstream artists including myself and many other incredible aboriginal artists as well, Native artists who could stand toe-to-toe with the mainstream artists out there, but then we get pigeonholed into this little category that is just ours. But the only problem is with the Native American Grammy category is that it can't be contemporary. It's all got to keep us in the stronghold of just traditional. In the traditional sense—like we're not allowed to experiment, and we're certainly not allowed to catch up to the twenty-first century. They don't allow twenty-first-century Native Americans. I'd be very curious to hear about all the nominees for this year's Grammys, because I know that Jana is one of them, and I'd be very curious because she's a mainstream contemporary, I'd be very curious to see if this record is a record where she's doing traditional stuff in it. Because if it is, it's sad. Because if she should be nominated for a Grammy, then she should be nominated for a Grammy based on her singing in English. The fact that she's Native should just be good enough. So I have a real problem with—it is a double-edged sword. On one side it is an honor and it is a privilege to be an indigenous person, and on the other side it is a curse. Again, we have to put up with so much, we have to put up with so many stereotypes, so many failures, and we have to rise above, and so many journeys that we've been on. We have to figure out a way to change how the world sees us. And so I guess that really my mission is to really teach the ways of the world to Native Americans.

What people, resources, or experiences have helped you obtain that sense of security?

Just meeting other Natives. Just being around primarily the Canadian Natives that I came across because we do resemble each other so extremely. The Natives down here, not so much. I don't look Pueblo and I don't look Navajo and there's just no doubt about it . . . I don't. We're completely two different regions. If you were to take a bunch of Canadian Indians and stick them down here in New Mexico we would definitely stand out. We don't look like them down here and that's all there is to it. When I first went up to Canada it was in 1995, about ten years ago, I remember thinking to myself "I'm home!" I had never seen so many people who looked like me in my life. I was like, "Oh my God." And then I started getting so secure with how I looked and why I looked this way. And I'll never forget I sat in this bar and we were listening to other aboriginal artists perform and what not and I was about to do a performance myself and before I had gotten up I had heard story after story after story of aboriginal artists that stood on that stage and they were all adoptees and they were all taken at birth and they were all put into Anglo homes and I went "oh, my God, I am not alone." It was my first revelation in 1995 that there were so many of me out there and that I was finally not alone. So my security kicked in finally, ten years ago.

How do you think your physical appearance has shaped your cultural identity?

I think it stems from early on when I was a kid and I constantly got teased about the color of my skin and the shape of my face, not so much the color of my eyes because there are a lot of Anglo kids that have brown eyes. It was the look of my eyes. It was the fact that I had Native eyes. And the shape of my face and the fact that I had a different sort of bone structure all together, I think, that got me noticed from the get-go. As I grew, I hated the way I looked. I wanted to be white more than you could imagine. I wanted blond hair and blue eyes. I remember one year I bought a bottle of Sun-In and I used the whole thing on my hair and it turned my hair orange, like an auburn color. Anything to get away from the brown that I was. The only thing that I could not hide was my skin, and I remember being devastated when I was a kid, and I remember thinking to myself that I was a social outcast based on just that alone. I had a friend who was as white as snow and I was as dark as the bark on trees and we called each other ebony and ivory, and we were best friends. She lived up the street from me, and the pictures that I have of us, it is just really. . . . I look at these pictures and I think holy god, and I look at them now and I am comfortable looking at them now because I know that I am looking at a Native woman but back then I wasn't comfortable because I was so different from everybody else.

The way that I looked, and so back then it really affected me. Back then it really affected me. I was really insecure. Compounded with the abuse that I suffered at home and at school and the fact that every time I looked in the mirror I didn't recognize what the hell I was because I didn't look like my family and I didn't look like a single solitary person around me and I didn't know what the heck I looked like. I think it did some detrimental damage back then. Now, I am extremely proud of the way that I look. The fact that I have these features, the fact that my skin is brown, the fact that I have facial structure that would lead one to believe that I am of Native descent. I'm proud of that now. I walk with my head held high, and I wear this armor, this pride, because now I am secure and I know why I look like how I look. I know that there's a reason for it now, but when I was growing up I didn't know and that was the most frustrating part. Especially when you grow up in middle American and you are the only person of color. It is pretty frustrating.

OVERALL HOW HAS THE FACT THAT YOU ARE NATIVE AFFECTED BOTH YOUR PERSONAL AND PROFESSIONAL LIFE?

Maybe my physical appearance is a way to raise the question. Actually, when I think about it now, I thank heaven that I look the way I look like. I am very different looking. I am obviously, like I said in my last statement, I am obviously from mixed blood, which is fine, you know. Aren't we all nowadays? Then predominantly, I am fortunately of Native descent. My guess would be accurate, I am pretty sure it would be French Canadian in me which is probably par for the course. But if it wasn't for the way that I looked when I was a kid, there would have been not one single question raised. I mean that Native people out there who are going around saying that they're Native, and they very well in fact may be Native, but some of them are blond hair, blue eyes, very fair-skinned. Can they get away with being Native? If growing up if I had blond hair and blue eyes and fair skin and I tried to say I was Native, oh my God, people would have laughed their asses off. I mean they do it today still. The fact of the matter is, there are blond haired, blue-eyed Native people out there and that is all there is to it. The fact of the matter that I didn't come out blond-haired and blue-eyed and I'm still Native, it definitely raised eyebrows when I was young. And it carried over. I mean it was always based on the way I looked. Apparently, I don't know how I look, I have no clue how I look, to be quite frank. I look how I look and that's all I can say, but apparently it was enough for people to make comments and to stand up and take notice of me pretty much all of my life, from the day that my white family brought me home up until this very day, when a non-Native person is standing in front of me and they take one look at me and they automatically assume that I am of Native descent or I am of some descent that is indigenous, are you Hawaii, are you Native, are you this, are you that? And then when I am across from another Native person, then the question of the hour is what tribe are you? So I mean, again with the curse thing. I think on one hand it can be a curse, on the other hand it is a blessing. Because I know that if I didn't look the way that I look then I think I would never have questioned my upbringing. I think that for today honestly I would have stayed in touch with my white family. I probably would never have asked questions about me being adopted, if I looked any different. I would have just accepted what the hand of fate dealt me and I was sitting in, and no questions asked. But because of the difference, it was like I said before it was inevitable.

Personally, there is security yes. There is contentment of finally knowing that I am an indigenous woman. But there is a huge hole because I don't know who my people are. I don't know what language I should be speaking. I've survived worse.

ARE YOU GLAD THAT YOU WERE TRANSRACIALLY ADOPTED?

No.

WHAT ARE THE ADVANTAGES AND DISADVANTAGES OF TRANSRACIAL ADOPTION?

Well, nowadays honestly since ICWA was put into place in 1978—all these years later ICWA is not being upheld still. So you have native babies being taken away from the reservation and adopted interracially, and the story, the saga continues. The disadvantages are immense. When I work with the youth, my Native kids all over the United States and Canada I tell them you need to realize how blessed you are that you know where you come from, at least if they are not with their mom and dad at least they are with auntie, uncle, grandma, grandpa, cousins, whatever. At least they know the tribe, their language, and their culture if they want to taste it, it is all right there. They don't know how privileged and how lucky they are because that is the immense effect it had on tens of thousands—all of us without our culture, without our language we are nothing. And we grew up that way. Some adapted. There were success stories like Chris Eyre who was adopted by an Anglo family, and he was loved and he was given all the sustenance to be raised a strong healthy man and all the while they let him know that he was indigenous, and he knew who he was. But then there are those horror stories that I wish a filmmaker like Chris Eyre would pay attention to, and those are our stories, the ones who were ravished, we were wrecked, it still evades me to this day how these non-Native people would adopt these native kids and then beat the living hell out of us. As if we were nothing. And had we stayed with those families . . . that's a double-edge sword. That thought does come into my mind. Had I stayed with my family, whoever they are, would it be with a poor family, what if my family drank, what if there was alcohol or substance abuse there, all of this. Our kids they face it now, but the bottom line is there needs to be more adult mentorship to go in there and tell these kids look, I know it's tough, I know you are dealing with abuse on some levels, but the first and foremost thing you need to realize is, you know who you are, and that is a huge starting point of being able to take off from that advantage. And there are people and help out there for these young babies and these young kids that are getting hurt by their own families. But I tell them time and time again, I don't know what's more painful, and I can't rectify it. I don't know if it would be more painful being beaten by my own blood, or would it be more painful being beaten by people who aren't my blood, regardless I think it is all painful. But what is the most painful of all is not being able to stand up as an indigenous person and not being able to identify yourself because that is the most simple and most powerful and most sacred thing that we have is to be able to identify ourselves.

Do you approve of non-Native families adopting Native children?

With my background initially I would say no. However, it almost can't be helped sometimes because we have so many babies who are abandoned by their families nowadays and there's not enough Native people stepping up to take these babies. And if non-Native people want these babies, there should be a whole, complete agenda of rules in place which would include first of all, making sure that they're fit, a huge background check, which was never done with us, and second of all, constantly making that child aware of who they are if they were to go to a white family that white family would have to keep in touch with that child's tribe, with someone in that family so that they could culturally be brought up as to who they are. Like the white people that adopt Asian babies, or Anglo people that adopt—like Angelina Jolie—perfect example. I adore what she is doing because she is so tied to each culture that each one of her children came from and she is going to make them so aware of their culture, and meanwhile she's giving them a beautiful life which they never would have gotten in any other circumstance. So if it's an Angelina Jolie minus the millions I dig that kind of situation. I think that that's acceptable. But things that were not done thirty, forty, fifty years ago, like the background checks, making sure that these people were fit to take care of babies, and then second of all making sure that these people kept those native babies in touch with their heritage. To try to remove an indigenous person 100 percent from their culture is, in my mind, genocide. It really is. To take something that is so sacred, and so precious and so simple and try to remove that human being from what they are completely, in my eyes is genocide.

Is there any advice you would like to offer non-Native families who would want to or who have adopted Native children?

Just to reiterate what I said. Make sure that they take care of these babies, because all children are sacred, but especially our Native babies are sacred, because we have a long line of ancestors here who are watching everything that has happened thus far and the one thing that our ancestors would tell them is the same thing that I am saying which is to make sure that they know who they are, make sure they never forget who they are.

Is there anything else you think I should have asked or any other issues you'd like to address?

Just the issue of 85 percent of the tens of thousands of children that were adopted out were extremely abused and it is so much more than a removal of a heritage, a displacement of Native babies from their Native ties. It is so much more than that. It is a challenge of survival for these thousands and thousands of kids. It's a challenge not only to culturally survive but to humanly survive for these Native kids and for now these Native adults. Let me tell you something, it doesn't stop there. Half of the work I do today with indigenous kids all over the Turtle Island, is because their parents have screwed up. It's not the kids, it's the parents. Eighty-five percent of it has to do with these parents because they either have a story like mine, or they suffered abuse on the res or whatnot and the parents are not programmed and are not capable of being able to look into their child's own eyes and change the path for their future. It's a big movement that needs to happen, and that's why I agreed to speak out, because not only to speak out on behalf of tens of thousands of me but also to these young Native kids and teens and even to some of these adults letting them know that dysfunction is nothing to be ashamed of and that we are all here for each other, we should be anyway.

Native artists that are out there, especially the ones that are doing well, and making money, I encourage them to give back to their Native communities. Give back to the Native youth that are out there struggling. Some of them are getting the wrong messages from the mainstream music that is out there. And I implore our Native artists to go out there and give them the right message. Unfortunately, and I am going to be blunt here, a lot of our Native artists can't do that because they are not drug- and alcohol-free. Some of them may be alcohol-free but some of them may not be drug-free, and so in my eyes it is not appropriate to go and speak to the kids unless you are completely clean. And it took me a while to get that way. It took me a while to get completely dependent-free of alcohol—everything. And I'm proud, very proud and very thankful to be drug- and alcohol-free and so I encourage and implore anyone who is drug- and alcohol-free to get out there and start mentoring our youth. I'm sure I don't have to say it, I'm sure it is widely known that the Native problems of teen suicide and we have some serious, serious problems with our youth today. We are outnumbered, we are completely outnumbered. The people who come in and help are so outnumbered by the problems that it is not even funny. So, if you are making money, you're touring around, you're performing, if you're in the community I implore you to give a motivational speech or talk to the youth in some way. That's what I do. There is community out there and they know this. When the Native community hires me for a concert out there and they get free advice. It just comes with it. They can utilize me any way they want to. They can take me to their school gym, they can take me to the tribal village, and they get free, free advice from me. If I'm out there singing, I'm out there giving a concert, I'm going to be out there talking for free. And that is obviously separate, and I don't do it professionally, but it's hard because a lot of time the kids don't bring me in for concerts and that's fine. So there is a charge for wellness intervention, and I'm not going to lie to you. I'm a professional, this is what I do. If the community wants to bring me in for wellness and prevention I say OK, what can you afford. They always say what do you charge. I say it's not about what I charge it's about what you can afford, and what you want to give me and that's the bottom line. And I'm not patting myself on the back. But it needs to be said and said out loud. And be proud, if you're going to wear your culture on your sleeve, if you're going to be this indigenous artist, and I can think of a slew of them who are very well off, who are doing great, who are touring. You know, take your head out of your ass. You know what's what and get out there and start talking to our youth, get out there and start giving them a positive message because they look up to you. They buy your CDs, they listen to your music, they go to your MySpace page. Get out there and talk to those kids and let them know they can do it too.

AND YOU BEGAN TALKING TO THESE KIDS BECAUSE YOU YOURSELF EXPERIMENTED WITH DRUGS?

My self-experimenting with drugs was inevitable from my life history. My whole program, Healing Power of Music, is what it's called. It is a wellness intervention program that I put together seven or eight years ago and it initially started because someone said, oh my God, you've been through so much crap, how did you survive? And I seriously turned to the man and said, I don't know. And then I started thinking about it and I thought, my music. I'm like holy crap—anytime I ever thought about how I made it through and how I just didn't decide to take myself out in some way, which trust me, Sarah, many times in my drinking days I tried to drive myself off a highway or tried to. . . . I've tried suicide attempts, I've tried drinking myself to death, I tried it all. I tried it all in my twenties, and that's just the way that it was. Anybody who is in that much pain, you are going to try to hurt yourself anyway you can, and that is exactly what I did. The thing that I have and I don't say this proudly, I just say this as a matter of fact, the thing that I have . . . the weapon that I possess and makes my program successful is that I have lived a life that most of these Native artists haven't. They weren't adopted out. They weren't beaten within inches of their lives on a daily basis so they can't go to these kids and say this is the kind of pain that I survived, the wars that I won. I tried drugs and alcohol to get away from that. The Native artists out there that try drugs and alcohol maybe for an entirely different reason, and they may come up with their own program as to why they stopped or whatever. There are some Native artists out there who are rappers who were in gangs? I can think of a handful of my Native friends who were in gangs who are now recovered from gangs. Kick butt. I'm so glad that they pulled themselves out of that detrimental life experience. Now those artists, those Native rappers could be going out and talking to some of our youth today, and some of them do. Some of them do. Some of the Native rappers go out and tell the youths, look don't make the mistakes I made. For me, I tell the kids, if you're being abused, I've been in the situation that you're in and you need help. Reach out. We're here. I'm here. I'm always going to be here, but nobody was there for me. Everybody knew that I was being beaten, but nobody did a damn thing about it. And that needs to change, because our Native kids today are still being abused. And now it is just starting to change, people are just starting to turn it around, people are just starting to help our kids today. So that's why I put this prevention program together. I spent ten years of my life drinking and druggin'. Ten years of my life *Wasting*, and I say that with a capital "W," *Wast-*

*ing* my life drinking and smoking pot. I was hiding. I had a reason. I had an excuse . . . and that's all it is is an excuse, but I felt it was my right. And once I finally got past that pain it was OK. I didn't need to hide behind that anymore. And now I can stand on my own two feet and I can talk to these kids and in one case, I don't condone people who are going to stand there and tell these kids, hey man you know even though they are adults, they have a right to do what they are going to do, these adults who are talking to these kids, but I'm telling you right now from the kids' point of view they don't want to listen to any adult who is going to stand there and tell them don't drink and then they are going to go out and do it anyway. They don't. If these kids are getting a message from you and then when the program is done you are off into the bar drinking or you're off with your friends smoking, then what kind of a message is that? I've had it brought to me many times by my own kids that I mentor, they say we're really grateful that you talk to us and we're really grateful that you walk the talk.

SO WHEN YOU TURNED TO DRUGS AND ALCOHOL WAS THAT SPECIFICALLY BECAUSE OF THE PAIN YOU EXPERIENCED AT HOME?

Yes. Without a doubt. It started out that way. And then it became just, a plan to it. It started out as being here it is. You know someone who knows you're a teen, and in my high school days I was tempted by beer. You know you went to high school parties and there was beer there, keggers whatever. And I looked at these kids like "Yeah, like I'm going to go home to my house drunk and give my father another excuse to beat the crap out of me." It was a no-brainer for me. So when I was a teenager I didn't touch it. Because if I went home drunk I would get the beating of my life and then some. Like I was even going to give my father a reason to lift a hand on me. I honestly stayed away from it when I was a teenager. But now . . . their parents, and I know this to be true because this has been told to me by some of the kids that I mentor and teach—when their parents will give them twenty bucks and tell them to go away. And their kids will go and buy a fifth or a pack of weed. It is horrifying. That's what kills me most. I could never imagine doing that to my child. Anyway, when I was a teenager I stayed away from it, I had no choice. Our kids don't have that luxury today. Our kids are getting stoned and they're drinking for attention. I didn't need any more bad attention when I was a kid. But then when I was of age, when I turned twenty-one, that was my choice. It was my choice, and I made the wrong choice, and it was my decision and I made the wrong decision for I said ten years, but when I think of it I stopped when I was twenty-eight . . . so it felt like ten years . . . it felt longer. I tell these kids if they could realize I would be a lot further in my music career than I am now, I would be worlds ahead of myself if I had not wasted that much time drinking and drugging. Honestly I wasted so much time drinking and smoking pot, I stopped drinking but I smoked pot for years, and I had my son. And it all stopped right there. As soon as I found out I was pregnant everything came to a screaming halt and my life took a new chapter. And I'm not saying that's the key . . . go out and get pregnant. . . . I am just saying that was the key for my life. My son was the one thing that made me stop . . . for good. There were moments, believe me . . . but it was my mission to never have my son look into my eyes and me be drunk or stoned or anything. There was no way I was going to let my son see that sort of weakness. That's all it is . . . a weakness. We're weak, we've got nothing else to do so we give in to this. And I wasn't going to let my son see me that weak. . . . I wasn't going to give that example to him.

WAS THERE ANYTHING ELSE YOU WANTED TO TALK ABOUT?

No. That's it.

## 12

# TAMARA WATCHMAN

Tamara Watchman (Navajo) never felt the need to contact her biological parents because she knew that they were extremely young when they had her—her biological mother was fourteen years old, while her biological father was seventeen years old. Furthermore, she says that her adoptive parents encouraged her to respect her biological parents for their mature decision. As a result, she says that she always felt grateful to them for placing her for adoption.

In 1995, however, she reunited with her biological family after accidentally bumping into her cousin as a student at Fort Lewis College in Durango, Colorado. After spending some time together, Tamara confided the circumstances surrounding her adoption to her new friend who suspected that the two might be related. Her friend's suspicions were confirmed when Tamara revealed her biological mother's maiden name, which was mistakenly included on her adoption papers. Tamara and her cousin were so excited about their discovery that they headed to Farmington, New Mexico, that night to introduce her to the family. According to Tamara, she was well received and has since developed a positive relationship with her biological mother that she says her adoptive parents fully support.

This reunion helped Tamara "fill in some of the blanks," but didn't drastically change her life because she said by that time she already possessed a strong sense of cultural identity, which she attributes to her adoptive parents and her husband and his traditional Navajo upbringing. As a child,

Tamara's adoptive parents made a conscious effort to involve her in the Native American community. She says that one of the biggest turning points in her life came when she attended camp on the Navajo Reservation. This experience exposed her to ceremonial dances and Navajo creation stories and in effect helped her feel more comfortable in the Native community. She does not oppose transracial adoption, but strongly believes that adopted children need to interact with the Native community.

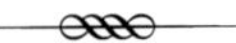

WHAT YEAR WERE YOU BORN?

1971.

AND WHERE WERE YOU BORN?

Albuquerque, New Mexico.

AND DO YOU KNOW HOW OLD YOU WERE WHEN YOU WERE ADOPTED?

I was ten weeks old.

AND ARE YOU AWARE OF THE CIRCUMSTANCES SURROUNDING YOUR ADOPTION?

Yeah.

CAN YOU TELL ME A LITTLE BIT ABOUT THOSE?

Yeah, I accidentally found my biological father in 1995 I think it was, and so I subsequently met both my biological parents. I was already aware of some of this information from the social workers' documentation with my adoption. My dad was Navajo, full-blooded Navajo. And my mom was half German, half Portuguese. They had my sister, Rebecca, the year before I was born. At the time they had Rebecca, my mom had just turned fifteen and my dad, I think he was sixteen or seventeen. So about a year after they had Rebecca, I was born. My mom took me home. So I think my dad's parents were going to raise me, when I was born they wanted to see me first to make sure I was Indian (they thought I may have had another father). So they wanted to see me first before they took me home. And my mom didn't appreciate that.

So she took me home instead, and she kept me for a week I think. Her own mother, my mother's mother, took away the one-year-old—you know, my sister—from her because she couldn't take care of two kids, being barely fifteen. And so about a week later, she (my biological mother) took me to

Social Services and gave me up. I think I was born in April. I don't know what day I was born. I was born either on April 7th or 15th. Neither one of my birth parents remember now. Then they (Social Services) put me in a foster home in Albuquerque.

And my parents who raised me, they picked me up like—oh, on June 24th. I was told that I was born May 11, 1971. I guess the Social Services people changed my birth date by four weeks. My parents picked me up in Albuquerque and took me home to Denver when I was . . . about ten weeks old.

AND COULD YOU TELL ME A LITTLE BIT ABOUT YOUR ADOPTED PARENTS?

Yeah, they are both white and my mom's from Milwaukee, my dad's from Chicago. They are both artists. They were hippies. But not totally hippies. My mom said that they weren't true hippies because they were legally married, they owned life insurance and my dad had a job which few hippies had then. They were really into, you know . . . boycotting and marching and saving stuff and recycling and making their own food and soap and butchering their own goats and milking their own goats. So I was raised with all that in a suburb outside of Denver.

My dad was a professor at Metropolitan State College in Denver. He was an art professor for thirty years. And my mom . . . stayed home and raised us, even though she had an MFA and was licensed to teach art in grades K–12. So I was raised around some of the artists and galleries and the art communities, and that kind of stuff and watched both my parents do their art all the time. It was part of life. And then my mom when, I was about five, became a tutor in English as a second language (ESL). She then continued to work in . . . public schools for about twenty years, teaching kids English. She is not bilingual, but she is an artist and she is a great artist and communicator, she did well with kids, cultural issues, language issues and that kind of stuff, you know, treating their cultures with respect.

DID THEY EVER INDICATE TO YOU WHY THEY DECIDED TO ADOPT AN AMERICAN INDIAN CHILD?

Yeah, one of the things was that they wanted another kid. My mom comes from a long line of people who did not believe in having more than two kids because of the population problem. My parents really enjoyed raising kids but they already had two, so they decided to adopt. I guess they were living in Cleveland. My dad was teaching at the Cleveland Institute of Art. My mom saw an article about interracial adoptions. But she didn't really care about the race of the kid and brought it up to my dad. She just asked "You want another kid"? And he is like, yeah, so they started the adoption papers.

Well, they moved before that came about and they went to Denver, I think in 1969. They started the adoption process here in Denver. In the paperwork there was a list of ethnicities. My parents didn't care what race the baby was so they just marked all the boxes. The first box was labeled American Indian, and that's what they got.

And then my parents waited for—I don't—I've forgotten now—less than a year, and they got a call. They were about to leave for a three-week vacation back up to the Midwest, Milwaukee and Chicago. And my mom was about to close the door and there was a phone call and the social workers said, you know, "we got an Indian kid, in Albuquerque, do you want her?" And they were like, "yeah." So they just made a phone call, instead of going to the Midwest they went to Albuquerque.

It wasn't really the fact that I was any particular ethnicity. It was just that I was a child, and that they knew that interracial children and minority kids were not being adopted at the time, and they were fine with it and I just happened to be an American Indian.

And when did you first realize that you were adopted?

I think I was like two or three. And my mom hadn't talked about it. But one of her friends came to visit. He was like, you know, "have you told her she is adopted?" She was like, "well, you know, she is really young and I think she won't understand." He is like, "you really should." So my mom just went out the front door and I was playing outside. She said, "hey, Tam." I said, "what?" She is like, "you are adopted." Okay, mom.

Whatever information the court gave to my parents, they gave it to me whenever I asked or needed anything. So I have quite a bit of background information about my birth parents, anyway. So that's always out in the open.

And that was accepted—that wasn't weird. They just called my brother and my sister homegrown, and I was store-bought.

How many siblings do you have?

Just two.

And what is your relationship like with them?

It's good. We all live in a same city. And we all have our own families. I see my sister more than my brother just because of where he lives and his career is pretty busy, but we have a really good relationship.

DO YOU TALK WITH THEM ABOUT BEING AN AMERICAN INDIAN?

Yeah, I mean, it's just part of my life.

WHAT DID YOUR ADOPTED PARENTS DO TO GIVE YOU A SENSE OF YOUR CULTURAL IDENTITY?

Well, the best they could do. Pretty much on all the vacations we took, we went to the Southwest. We went to all the different ruins and cultural centers and many kinds of special exhibits and museums. Then when I was in middle school I became more involved in the Indian community. My mom was an English tutor, she dealt with English as a second language. One day a Lakota woman came up to my mom and she is like, listen, we need tutorial services for these American Indian kids because a lot of them speak their native language before English. And my mom was, okay, and she went up to the district and started trying to get Native students in the district to be tested for ESL services. Together, my mom and her friend fought to get the federal funds for Indian education in our district. So through that, my mom became very close with this Lakota lady, and so she pretty much became somewhat like an adopted aunt to me.

And I hung out with her constantly through middle school and high school, with her kids, her family. And then she introduced me to some of her friends and I was offered other chances with other cultural activities, that I was just too embarrassed to take, or too uncertain of myself to take.

My mom got to know a lot of people in the Indian community. And there was a camp that was offered up in Montana through another woman. The camp was open to adopted Indians. Just going up to the camp and learning about different cultural things, but I didn't really take advantage of it because I was like, oh, I'm like half. I don't look Indian enough, you know. They are going to make fun of me, so I wouldn't take those types of opportunities.

One of the most influential experiences that I had occurred in my freshman year. Every year four or five Unitarian Churches got their ninth graders together and visited the Navajo and Hopi reservations for a ten-day trip.

My brother and my sister went and then I went. When I went, I was one of three adopted, biracial kids that went on the trip that year. Two of us were biracial Navajo. And so we went on this trip together, a ten-day trip down to Navajo and Hopi land. To get ready for this trip the church taught us all the Navajo and Hopi creation stories throughout the winter.

We were taught how to be respectful. And when we went down there and we were always expected to be respectful of our hosts, their ceremonies, and all that we saw. On my trip, we went to Rock Point High School and to classes with the students. We slept overnight with the Navajo kids.

We watched the ceremonial dances on Hopi. The trip was always scheduled in the spring to see the dances. And so I did a whole intensive thing, learning the creation stories and going out there and learning about Navajo. So my parents did the best they could.

WHAT IMPACT DO YOU THINK THAT EXPERIENCE HAD ON YOU?

I think it was good. I think that it helped me and exposed me as much as I could be exposed without living in Indian families, and it gave me knowledge, a certain amount of knowledge and then a certain amount of comfortableness with the native community.

NOW, YOU MENTIONED THAT YOU WERE A LITTLE BIT INSECURE ABOUT HOW INDIAN YOU LOOKED. HOW DO YOU THINK YOUR PHYSICAL APPEARANCE AFFECTED THE MANNER IN WHICH YOU PERCEIVED YOURSELF WHEN YOU WERE GROWING UP?

Oh, I think that—that was screwed up. I mean, no matter what the family can do for me, when your sister is blonde with blue eyes, you know, tall, skinny, and you are short, brown, and round and, you know, it's really hard to—it's hard to compare yourself equally with that.

And especially in the community I was raised. I was raised in a really predominantly white community. And I always judged myself based on that, that community and that type of thing, and that was hard.

DID YOU ENCOUNTER ANY FORM OF RACISM GROWING UP?

Yeah, I had teachers that would tell me that I was dirty, that I had hygiene problems. I had a lot of special education issues, especially communication problems, and I remember one teacher in kindergarten, would constantly wipe at my arm, you know. She would say things like "You should take a bath," and stuff like that, and call my mom and say I was having a hygiene problem.

And my mom said . . . she takes a bath every morning, she brushes her hair, she is concerned about her appearance, but she is a little five-year-old who plays. But I remember that teacher made me feel real dirty. You know, I remember in kindergarten little girls telling me I couldn't play with them because only blonde girls could play together and girls with black hair like mine aren't supposed to play with them.

In high school the counselor told me I would not be successful at the school of my choice, and to not even consider CU.

DID YOUR PARENTS PREPARE YOU TO FACE THIS CHALLENGE?

I think in some degree they did just because they were marginalized as well. They did that on purpose, their lifestyle was not mainstream, through their life choices, they marginalized themselves. But that prepared me to a certain degree for not being part of the dominant culture, anyway even with my white parents.

But I think there is something that no matter what—no matter what other people have, but if you haven't gone through it yourself or felt that, half of the racism that is experienced may not be really understood if you didn't live it yourself.

WOULD YOU JUST DESCRIBE IN A LITTLE BIT MORE DETAIL THE PLACES YOU LIVED AND THE SCHOOLS YOU ATTENDED?

Yeah, after I was adopted I moved to one house in Lakewood, Colorado, and my mom still lives there, and I lived there until I went to college. I went to college at Fort Lewis College in Durango, Colorado. I didn't know if I wanted to go to college, but I got that Native tuition assistance and they accepted me and another adopted kid that year. But that was short-lived and I was pregnant by the second year.

So I came back to my parent's home in Lakewood, had my first child and went to school at Metropolitan State College in Denver.

Then I married my husband. We moved into his parent's home in Sheep Springs, New Mexico, on the Navajo Nation. I had my second child and we lived there for about a year and a half. Then we moved back to Fort Lewis in Durango, Colorado, for four more years. During this time I had my third child, worked part-time, and took classes. After I graduated . . . I got a teaching job, and we moved to Tohachi, New Mexico, which was again on the Navajo Nation. I taught and lived there for two years. After my father passed away when I was twenty-eight, I had a strong need to go back to Colorado to be near my family. We went back home here to Lakewood, Colorado, and we bought a house up the street from my mom's house where I was raised.

AND WHAT KIND OF WORK DO YOU DO NOW?

I'm a teacher.

AND IN WHAT GRADE OR WHAT SUBJECTS DO YOU TEACH?

I'm a social studies teacher and currently I'm teaching eighth grade.

DO YOU HAVE ANY TIES TO YOUR TRIBE TODAY?

Through my husband, and hopefully my own family, the Navajo side, and I try to keep in contact. I've met them, both of my biological parents. I've met a few of my other Navajo relatives as well. I met them at my great, great grandmother's funeral. All those years I lived in Durango and Northern New Mexico, my great, great grandmother was living in Farmington, New Mexico, the whole time and I never had a chance to meet her, you know, I met many of my family at the funeral but it wasn't like a great time. So I met them and everybody was aware of me but the contact didn't continue much.

ARE YOU AN ENROLLED MEMBER OF YOUR TRIBE?

No.

HOW COME?

Because when I met my birth parents—the story is my birth mom did not put my birth dad's name on the birth certificate. They (my Navajo family) were suspicious of my genetic makeup. They had to see me before they would accept me. Because of that, when she (my mother) did the paperwork, she did not put my dad's name on that. In Navajo Nation, it is all based on birth certificate. When my second son was born, he was born in New Mexico. I was really wanting to get the kid enrolled with my degree of Indian blood included on his paperwork. I tried to get my records opened. I was born in Albuquerque so I went to Santa Fe, where my birth records were stored, to ask that my birth records be sent directly to Window Rock, Arizona. I was hoping that my sealed paperwork would prove my degree of Indian blood for me and my children.

So they checked it all and Window Rock wrote back to me and said, you know, there is no birth dad on there. All you have is a white lady on your birth certificate. So I think the only way I can get enrolled in my tribe is maybe getting DNA through either of my birth sisters. The first child that my two parents had together, she is an enrolled member. Or through my dad—if he's willing to do it and go to court—go to Navajo court.

SO HOW HAS THIS AFFECTED YOUR SENSE OF CULTURAL IDENTITY?

I think it has affected it because I think there are so many other things that—you know, that get in my way, personally, but I can't fight the fact that a member is just a member, no more or less Indian than anyone else. A lot of people that I know think that the census numbers and tribal enrollment are just a form of controlling and eliminating needed members. I still would feel better with a census number because I don't have anything else to prove what I am except, you know, well, I don't know how to explain it, but anyway, it would make me feel like I'm truly Native.

Do you feel accepted by Indians outside your birth family, even though you don't have your tribal enrollment papers?

Yeah, generally, yes.

And you talked about how your birth family found you accidentally.

Yeah.

Can you tell me a little bit more about that?

Okay. I was in Fort Lewis, like I said, and the first year I was at Fort Lewis . . . I met my first cousin, and I had a conversation with her on the public bus at Durango—but I don't remember that conversation. About two years later, I was up in the Chuska Mountains in the Navajo nation at my husband's family reunion and the woman from the bus in Durango was also there and she recognized me. She reminded me that we had met in Durango and we had the conversation on the bus. My mother-in-law was so surprised.

My mother-in-law was so surprised that I knew someone there, in the middle of nowhere, in the middle of the family reunion, in the middle of the mountains. So my cousin and I had another conversation, still not knowing that we were related. We had both dropped out of Fort Lewis for a while, and we were both planning on going back. I found out that she is related to my husband through marriage.

That was a little bit too close for comfort, you know, the whole I was adopted and wound up getting together with a long lost relative fiasco. Thank God she was related to my husband by marriage, not blood.

Then a couple of years later, we both went back to Fort Lewis. In the administration building, I saw this woman, and I'm like telling my husband, there is your cousin. She saw us as well and asked if I was going back to school too. Well, her boyfriend wound up hiring my husband on the campus foodservice, and so for the four years we lived there, her boyfriend and my husband worked together, and we saw each other occasionally.

And then on my last year, my senior year, I invited her over to my house once—my husband went to Cortez to sell some cattle and I was home with the kids alone for the weekend. So I invited her over. And she looked at some of the pictures that I had on my wall. She said, these pictures—in these pictures, you see, you look just like my uncle Willy, and I was like, well, I was adopted, you know, I'm . . . half Navajo, I was born in Albuquerque, and I gave her the whole story. She just started nodding her head.

She began to tell me that her Uncle Willy had a daughter with a white girl. Her Uncle and the girl were both very young at the time. She told me that one night her mom (later I found out her mom was my father's sister) told her that there had been another, younger daughter that had been adopted out. I had always known that I had a full sibling one year older than me. At that point I found out that that sibling was a sister and her name was Rebecca. My cousin and my sister had spent summers growing up together and they were both a year older than I.

At that point she said, "I think you are her. I think you are my cousin," and so I got out all my paperwork that I had, and I showed it to her and she is like, "yeah, my uncle is a musician, and, yeah, he is from Albuquerque, and yeah and it's an even match." So that night, I packed my kids up with my cousin and we went to my aunt's house. We went to the outskirts of Farmington to the Navajo reservation to a little housing project there.

And we waited for someone to get home, and by this time, I figured okay, if these are my relatives, my sister's name is Rebecca. So the first thing I asked her mom was if my sister's last name was Rease. Someone accidentally left my mother's maiden name in my adoption papers. I had always known my mother's maiden name was Rease. And so I looked at this woman and I said, you know, is Rebecca's last name Rease, because she could be my sister.

And my aunt's jaw dropped, and her eyes got all big and she said, no, her last name is not Reese, but her mother's is. And so we figured out that there are not a lot of German Portuguese Navajos out there. And so I met my Navajo family on the reservation.

Did you ever have the desire to meet your birth family before?

Not too much. Knowing the circumstances of how young they were, I just felt grateful to them. I figured it was probably the best way to deal with me. They adopted me out of love and did it the right away. And so I appreciated them and I respect them, but I have—I didn't have so much insecurity about my life or anything, or I never felt like I was missing anything. I would just think about them, but, you know, I figured they have their lives and I have mine and, you know, they are fine. I'll just say to them, thanks for doing it, and that was it.

Are you comfortable or uncomfortable spending time with them?

I'm comfortable. I've developed a relationship with my mother more than my father, and my father's family was the first that I met, and I was introduced to all of them, but it kind of petered out. It was—again, they had their own issues going on. And I didn't really pursue it that much because it is kind of hard. Meeting, you know, as an adult, all these family members that are people that are strangers. It wasn't like I really pursued relationship building at the time and they didn't either. My mother, on the other hand, found out I was found and she freaked out. She was really sick at the time.

And I guess I brought up a lot of old baggage of hers and so it took her three years before she could contact me, but now that she is physically better and stronger, and she's met me, she is a big part of my family now, not that I see her all the time. But she has been a big influence.

How have you changed since finding them?

Not so much. I mean, I didn't really—I don't think I've changed as much. I think I had to go through a lot of emotions. I also don't think that finding your birth family is a completely magical moment just because the everyday stuff was there.

It was amazing and it is powerful, but, you know, it is still a matter of fact that they got their issues, I got my issues and real life comes into play. It makes me feel good that I know them, and I know who they are and I know their names. I feel like I have brought more people into my family, more love.

So it has filled in some of the blanks, I still don't have much of a connection with my Native family. I would have loved to find my cultural identity through my own Navajo family, but I find more answers from my in-laws than my own Native relatives.

Did your relationship with your adopted family change in any way?

No, not really. It was a hard time. By the time my birth mom was ready to meet me, she was coming down to Denver and my dad—my adopted dad—had just found out that he had esophageal cancer and so my birth mom was uncertain if she should visit at a time when my father was just beginning chemotherapy.

So I called my dad and my dad was like, no, have her come. You know, we want to meet her. And basically, the last conversation I had with my dad was him telling me take it easy with my birth mom, that it was going to be hard, and learn to respect her, and enjoy her, and seven days later he died.

So when I first met my birth mom, it was only two months after my dad died. My grandmother, my dad's mom, had just passed two months before that. I was pretty grief stricken at the time. So I don't remember the visit very much, but my mom still wanted to meet my birth mom, and so they got together, and it was a really cool visit, and it was a long visit. We picked her up in Albuquerque drove her to Denver and hung out in Denver with her and drove her back to Albuquerque, and so we had lots of conversation time. I thank God. You know, I was so busy with grieving over my dad that, you know, I don't remember a lot of the visit, but it was a really good visit. And I mentioned coming to visit me in December or whenever she gets the time. She's come five times now.

HOW OLD WERE YOU THE FIRST TIME YOU WENT TO A RESERVATION?

Well, I don't know. I mean, like I said, my parents were always going through it, for the ruins and stuff, so I was probably four or five. I was little.

DID YOU EVER EXPERIENCE ANY SORT OF CULTURAL SHOCK?

No not shock, it was the fact that my mom remembered me smiling and saying, everybody looks like me, and I didn't feel so fat. I mean—and not that I was fat, I was just, comparing myself to my sister. She was, you know, a bean pole. I was surprised when people thought I lived there. You know, I remember once we were on a trip, and the road had been washed out and so we had to wait and I went off the road to do my business, and when I was coming back—I was coming back toward my parent's car and a man in a truck stopped and asked if I needed a ride back to town. And I was so surprised—and I was like, no I am here with my parents. Then I pointed over to my mom's car, and he was so surprised to see a white couple and he was like, oh, and so he gave my parents directions on how to get where we were going by a different road. It felt good, I felt like a complete stranger yet people thought I belonged there.

And it continued throughout my adult life. I was at a flea market. At that time we would sell hay at the flea market on the weekends. I'd constantly have people that asked me the price of our hay in Navajo, thinking I would understand. I would know enough Navajo to answer back in English the proper way, and then they'd start talking in Navajo and I am like, I don't know Navajo.

Every weekend I'd have to explain to ten to fifteen groups of people how come I don't speak Navajo or, you know, having to go through the hospital stuff. And how come I don't have a census number, so I'd have to explain to every single clerk at IHS hospitals or clinics how come I don't have my census number. They were always surprised that I didn't have one, and they always served me. I guess they could tell I was Indian.

DO YOU FEEL SECURE OR INSECURE ABOUT YOUR INDIAN IDENTITY TODAY?

Living in a city the identity is pretty much what you identify with, and it doesn't really matter as much what you look like.

WHO ARE YOUR CLOSEST FRIENDS TODAY?

Actually, mostly Native women.

DO YOU HAVE ANYBODY HELPING YOU SHAPE YOUR CULTURAL IDENTITY?

I think a lot, when we talk, we talk about issues and stuff. I think what happens is, they accept me without any explanations and they know who I am. Other Native people know what I am. Once I was at the grocery store, in a suburban area. My daughter wouldn't speak to anybody at the time. There was a Native checker, you know, at the grocery store. When she said hi to my daughter, my daughter actually said, hi back, and I was so surprised, I said, she doesn't ever speak to anybody, and the lady said, "oh, she knows an Indian when she sees one."

And I was all surprised, because I never talked to this lady before, yet she knew what we were and, you know, so it still surprised me. So I still have that identity issue. So my friends though, know who I am and I like that, I don't think I have to prove myself to anybody. I may not have ever had to prove myself to anybody but myself my whole life.

TELL ME A LITTLE BIT MORE ABOUT YOUR HUSBAND AND YOUR CHILDREN.

My husband is half Navajo, half Hopi and he was raised very traditionally, by his Navajo grandparents. And one day at twelve his grandfather passed away and he moved up to Denver with his mom and his half brother and stepdad. And I met him in high school when I was about sixteen. Even though he doesn't want to teach our kids the Navajo language—he never taught them Navajo—because he said it hurt his education so much that he didn't want his own kids to have to go through that and have to search for words all the time.

So I am kind of upset about that, because I can't learn Navajo fast enough to teach them.

AND HOW HAVE YOU AND YOUR HUSBAND ADDRESSED THE ISSUE OF CULTURAL IDENTITY WITH YOUR CHILDREN?

I don't think we made any effort about it. They know what they are, right, you know, being on the reservation and they wore their traditional clothes at school performances. It is interesting though that when we moved back to Colorado, the first friends they made were Indian kids. There were at least five different Native families at that school at the time. We became good friends with three of those families right away.

My kids are really comfortable with Native kids. They all identify themselves as Indian. I was involved in the public school Indian education through the parent advisory committee for a few years. My kids participated in our functions, and Indian summer school programs. Both of my sons have attended a summer math and science camp at Fort Lewis for Native kids.

HOW HAS BEING AN INDIAN AFFECTED BOTH YOUR PERSONAL AND PROFESSIONAL LIFE?

My personal life? I think it affected my personal life, because I really had identity issues like I said, growing up with white people. I was constantly trying to figure out where I belonged in the community. I felt comfortable in the Hispanic communities because everyone thought I was Mexican anyway and they accepted me. Then I began to hang out in the black community as well. I felt more accepted and welcomed in these cultures more than the Native community when I was younger. It was probably just my own cultural hang-ups that made me feel so isolated from the Indian community. But yes, personally I had to do a lot of searching and observing. And then my professional life? I think it affected me by guiding my academic, and professional paths. Because I was always interested in culture and identity, I was drawn toward social anthropology.

It began when I was younger, I wanted to belong in these different groups, these different identities, you know, the white community, the Latino community, the black community, whatever, I started really being aware. I think a lot of mixed people are like this. I was always aware of the shared history between anthropology and colonialism, but it was an avenue for me to analyze cultures from the periphery. Anthropology was perfect for me, because I have always perceived myself as an outsider.

So I went to college, and I got into cultural social anthropology and I really enjoyed it. Then at one point in my studies I realized that my husband really felt strongly that he wanted to raise his kids on the Navajo reservation. So there I was with three and a half years of college under my belt, and I am like, well, what am I going to do with anthropology out here (on the reservation)? And so when I went back to college the second time, up to Fort Lewis, I changed my major to education, and decided I would teach.

DO YOU APPROVE OF NON-INDIAN FAMILIES ADOPTING INDIAN CHILDREN?

You know, I approve it, because in my teaching—mainly in my teaching, I've taught at residential and treatment facilities, I've taught at-risk kids, and I have taught lots of kids who did not have families, kids who were in foster homes, kids who were living, you know, locked up, and didn't know where the family was and I figure no matter how much stuff I've had to deal with, you know, maybe an interracial adoption, I still had a great family, and a great life.

And I figured, seeing the kids that don't have that and knowing them and having close contacts with kids that don't have families I don't think I begrudge that on anyone. You know, I think everybody deserves a family. Now, do I think that is the best option? No, I don't. I just don't think so, because I had a family that was really, really trying to help me, culturally. I had a family that showed me how to deal with the dominant culture, being, you know, marginalized.

I saw all that, yet they still didn't understand really a lot of this that I had. And, no matter how much they tried to help me and support me, and did help me and support me, I needed a Native reflection. At some points in my life I needed affirmation from other Natives to make me feel like I belonged. As I get older, I wonder if maybe I would have still isolated myself in a Native family. My cultural identity issues may still have existed no matter what. All I know is I was loved unconditionally and for some reason I still have to learn to love myself with that same unconditional love. And that's what happened.

SO WHAT ADVICE WOULD YOU OFFER TO NON-INDIAN FAMILIES, WHO WOULD WANT TO OR WHO HAVE ADOPTED INDIAN CHILDREN?

I think that museums and ruins don't completely cut it. I think you need to get into the community—I think Native individuals have to be a part of this support system. I don't know. I guess living in or near an Indian community. Finding Native individuals that are willing to form a relationship with the family, to be a model might help.

DO YOU THINK IT WOULD HAVE HELPED YOU?

I think it might have helped me. I think just having friends, Indian kids who became my friends over the years. In retrospect, those kids knew what I was, and because they accepted me, I began to realize I was acceptable to other Natives. These friends came and went because their families would move away, but they were important to me, it is important to have other people to identify with.

I see it as a teacher. Teaching, you know, in Denver, I sometimes teach Native kids. And when I get these native kids, and I don't automatically connect with all of them, there is personality preferences and kids choose who they want as a role model. But I do think that I sometimes become very important to some of them, because it's another Indian person somewhere out here in the middle of the city where you don't see Native people as much. And I think that when they leave the school, a lot of times they're with their family, they're there with their Native family, and it is still important for them to have a relationship with an Indian teacher.

I THINK THAT WAS IT. IS THERE ANYTHING ELSE YOU THINK I SHOULD HAVE ASKED YOU OR ANY OTHER ISSUES THAT YOU WOULD LIKE TO ADDRESS?

No, for the adoption and everything, I would say, it's the language. I think it's really important. I don't think, no matter what, no matter how much cultural stuff you give to kids, if you can't give them their language, I think that the kid is never going to get a full understanding of their Native culture.

And I understand a lot of tribal groups, there's a lot of people that don't know their language, but for me and in my case Navajo is spoken everywhere and when I went back down there it wasn't really the color of my skin, it was the fact that I couldn't speak Navajo. I think having that language would have helped me and I would have understood when I was in ceremonies. I wouldn't have felt like an outsider.

WELL, THAT WAS MY LAST QUESTION. IS THERE ANYTHING ELSE?

No.

OKAY.

## 13

# JEAN WELLS*

The circumstances surrounding Jean Wells's adoption in 1962 are by her own account "mostly unclear." She knows that she spent the first seven months of her life in foster care. She knows, from what the adoption agency told her adoptive parents, that her biological father is Irish and reportedly deceased. She also knows that her biological mother is Ojibwa and suspects that the twenty-one "brush marks" on her arm are the result of a tribal ritual. All in all, Jean knows very little about her cultural background; and as a result, has struggled for many years to come to terms with her sense of cultural identity.

Jean was adopted by a white, upper-middle-class couple who raised her and her adoptive brother in the Midwest. Throughout the course of the interview, she speaks quite highly of her adoptive father, but notes that her relationship with her adoptive mother has always been "strained." According to Jean, her adoptive father talked with her about being Native American, while her mother "ignored that part of her." Jean says that her adoptive mother lacked "cultural sensitivity" and even dressed her in a "cheap Indian costume" for Halloween. Despite her close relationship with her adoptive father, Jean says that she never "felt like [she] belonged" and eventually ran away from home.

*Identifying information about this participant has been omitted or changed.

Jean's adoptive parents responded to this act of rebellion by institutionalizing her in a psychiatric hospital. She says that she was placed in and out of several institutions until she turned eighteen. Although her eighteenth birthday marked the end of this ordeal, it also signaled the beginning of another. According to Jean, she spent the next four or five years homeless, addicted to drugs and alcohol, and working as a prostitute. The turning point in her life came when she found out that she was going to be a mother.

According to Jean, the birth of her son not only compelled her to get off the streets, it also led her to a more traditional lifestyle. She says that she began attending ceremonies and sweat lodges when her son was eight years old to help him overcome a traumatic event in his life. She notes that this experience helped her son heal and helped her develop her own sense of cultural identity. Jean admits, however, that she still feels a certain amount of insecurity in the Native community because she never found her birth family and has been unable to enroll as a tribal member.

Given her negative experience as a transracial adoptee, Jean is a staunch supporter of the Indian Child Welfare Act. She argues: "If I had some type of cultural identity, I wouldn't have lived the horrible life I lived as a teenager." Despite her opposition to transracial adoption, Jean's youngest son was adopted by a white family that she handpicked. She maintains that race wasn't an issue in this situation because she gave her son to a loving family and he, unlike her, is well aware of his cultural background.

---

WHAT YEAR WERE YOU BORN?

1962.

HOW OLD WERE YOU WHEN YOU WERE ADOPTED?

Probably about seven months.

AND ARE YOU AWARE OF THE CIRCUMSTANCES SURROUNDING YOUR ADOPTION?

The circumstances surrounding my adoption are mostly unclear. I know that when my adopted parents took me, I was in an orphanage, but they knew that I was Irish and Ojibwa and I had brush marks on my arm that were done to me as a baby, which is a ritual that some tribes do. I have twenty-one . . . so I was marked before my adoptive parents got me. They said my father died. That was all I was told. And my mother was over eighteen.

CAN YOU TELL ME A LITTLE BIT ABOUT YOUR ADOPTIVE PARENTS?

They were white, upper-middle class, Catholic people. My adopted mother couldn't have children. They were in their thirties when they got me. I was paid for, they got a receipt for me. You know, they made donations to the Catholic organization. But they were good people. My father worked forty years for a large company, and my mother was a stay-at-home mom. She had some issues. I didn't feel very cared for by her. My dad was a different story. My dad would talk about me being Native. He would encourage that. But my mother ignored that, or that part of me. But like with her grandkids, my sons, she's a lot better about that.

How would you describe your relationship with them overall?

My dad was awesome. It was an awesome relationship. My dad died like twenty years ago. The relationship with my mother is still a strained relationship. We hardly talk, she's eighty now. So we hardly talk.

Did they ever indicate to you why they decided to adopt an American Indian child or were they just looking for any child?

I think it was my dad's doing, really. I think my dad wanted to kind of step outside the norm, because we were also friends with a family that had adopted four Native children, so they were friends at the same church, that had adopted four Native girls. But I think my dad wanted to step outside the normalcy of the day. My dad was like that. He was very kind and loving. I was lucky to have him for a father.

When did you first realize that you were adopted?

When I was about, I want to say eight or nine. My brother who was also adopted found the paperwork. My older brother. He found some papers in a closet in my parents' bedroom. So that's how I found out. And then they gave me a book called "The Chosen Baby." . . . I still have that book. It is a book about being adopted.

What was your reaction?

I was really upset and I don't think at eight you really understand it. And I know that from that point on, when my mother would discipline me or get into it I would say "Take me back to my mother." Or "Take me back to the orphanage." Things like that. I didn't look like them and I realized that. And I started using that as a weapon against them and as a child I had some issues anyway, I think. You know when a kid falls down and gets hurt and runs to its mother for comfort, whenever I would get hurt I would never let anyone touch me. I would not allow myself to be held or comforted my whole childhood. So that was something that was unusual about my childhood. I don't know where that came from.

Do you think that your adoptive parents handled information about your adoption in a positive manner?

I think they tried to show me caring. My dad was such a loving man. He tried to love me more. As for my mother, I never ever felt connected to her. She did things that I now find kind of insulting. Like on Halloween, she would dress me up as an Indian, you know what I mean? She'd put my hair in braids, she'd put feathers in my hair, she'd put cheap Indian costumes on me. I would go put that on all year around. On Halloween she would dress me up like that, and at this point I find that insulting. So I don't think she really knew how to deal with my finding out I was adopted. Like I said, she handed me a book, a kid's book, on being adopted.

You mention that your father talked to you about being Native? What did he say?

He just talked about . . . he would tell me about Indian history, what he knew and stuff like that. My dad was a really cultured guy, and it wasn't something to be ashamed of, or whatever. I don't know if . . . he wouldn't talk really about Indian history. He would just tell me Indian stories. I felt like he encouraged that part of me. And cared about that part of me, whereas I felt my mother just cut that off of me. He took me around that family with other Indian girls, so we all knew because we had darker skin, because everyone around us there, because it was a white neighborhood, so I think we all knew we were different. And my dad was okay with that. I don't think I ever really felt different that way with my dad.

What do you think your adoptive parents did to give you a sense of cultural identity?

Nothing. Because I think part of their mission was to turn me into a Catholic and supporting Indian girls. So my dad, I felt, was okay with it. As I got older, that was never discussed, my being Native or anything like that. I felt it got pushed away. So I don't think they did anything, really, except my dad gave me a little information, told me a couple of stories. I wasn't taken to any powwows or to be around Native people, even though at the time there was and is still a Native community that they could have hooked me into and that was never done.

You mentioned that you have one sibling who was adopted. Do you have any other siblings?

No.

Is your brother native as well?

He is white.

Are you close?

No not at all. I don't even allow him to have my phone number. He was very abusive.

Did you talk with him about being Native American?

No. I never liked him. He was very cruel and I wanted nothing to do with him then and he was physically abusive.

You mentioned earlier that you possess strong American Indian physical features. How has your physical appearance affected the way you perceive yourself?

I don't see my features as really strong Native features now that I'm around Native people. But my skin is darker than white people, I have black hair, I have dark eyes, and what happens is I get mistaken for Hispanic a lot. People speak to me in Spanish. But repeat the question because I totally lost myself. . . .

How do you think your physical appearance affected your sense of cultural identity?

I just think it felt different and didn't know why. When you are little you don't really know. I really didn't look like my parents, I really didn't look like my brother. That's a hard one.

How do you think your physical appearance affected the way others saw you, especially those in the Indian community and those not in the Indian community?

Well, outside the Indian community growing up I was mostly mistaken for Hispanic. Native people are confused for Hispanic people. In the Native community, my features are not as strong as others . . . because I am half white, and there is a prejudice in the Native community solely on that. I haven't felt it as much as others, but I think people still look at me—and I'm half white and half native but it's like two worlds I'm involved with and I don't know. It's okay now, more, with the Native community, but I associated with the white community when I was growing up. It's difficult. I think the validation for who I was came when my younger son was born because he is very dark-skinned and black hair and black eyes, and nobody ever questions his identity. I don't know if that makes much sense, but like even in the Indian community you are judged on how dark your skin is, or your hair or your eye color. So I felt like I have fit in neither world my whole life. Because some features are there and some aren't. As I've gotten older, I think my skin is lighter than when I was younger, and my hair got curly after I got pregnant so that was a change.

BESIDES YOUR FATHER, WAS THERE ANYBODY ELSE YOU SPOKE TO ABOUT BEING AMERICAN INDIAN?

There was no one.

CAN YOU TELL ME A LITTLE MORE ABOUT THE NEIGHBORHOODS YOU GREW UP IN AND THE SCHOOLS YOU ATTENDED?

I grew up a block from the Catholic school I attended for eight years. Then I went to a year of Catholic high school, an all girls school. My parents were really into Catholicism. We went to church, I participated in church activities. And then after my first year in high school I ran away. So that was the last time for that.

WHY DID YOU RUN AWAY?

I don't know. I never felt like I fit in that family. I never felt like I belonged. So I left. And I never returned home . . . when they found me they actually institutionalized me. It was an awful thing, I'm sure. But it's hard to describe how you feel . . . but you know, I don't look like these people, I didn't feel any love for my mother, like I said growing up I didn't accept physical affection from my parents. For my dad, I would sit on his lap for a little bit, my mother I never wanted to hug her or be comforted by her. It was a bad situation. Plus my brother was getting so abusive. And so I left.

WHO WERE YOUR CLOSEST FRIENDS IN SCHOOL?

I had one friend at school that I remember saying was my best friend. She was an Italian girl. She had a darker skin color so maybe that's why if I think of it right now. . . . I hadn't really thought about it . . . why I was attracted to being friends with her. And basically she was my only friend. I didn't really make friends.

DID YOU LIKE SCHOOL?

No. I really didn't like school. I didn't fit in any of the cliques that they had going on. I felt like an outcast.

DID YOU ENCOUNTER ANY FORM OF RACISM GROWING UP?

I remember . . . the only thing I can remember is once a man started laughing at me at a gas station and made a motion like he was shooting me, and started talking like he was doing Spanish stuff and then that's all I remember as a young person.

AFTER HIGH SCHOOL, DID YOU GO TO COLLEGE?

After the first year of high school, I was institutionalized by my parents. I didn't attend college until my late twenties, and that was on my own.

HOW LONG WERE YOU INSTITUTIONALIZED?

Until I was almost eighteen. I would run away, be on the streets for a while, they'd find me, put me back in the institution. At first the institutions they put me in were mental hospitals, because they had really no place for teenagers. And I would be with severely mentally ill adults. And then finally they put me in a home and it was a locked facility, and the minute I got a little freedom I ran away from there and so then they finally discharged me because I was almost eighteen.

THEN WHAT DID YOU DO AFTER YOU WERE EIGHTEEN?

I lived on the street until I was about twenty-two years old. And I did everything that I possibly could. I became addicted to drugs, I was an alcoholic, I was a prostitute, I was stealing, I was living a very difficult life, and I was traveling the country. I was looking for something. I didn't know it at the time, but I was looking for something.

WHAT WERE YOU LOOKING FOR?

I think I was looking for identity . . . who I was. Because I had no idea who I was.

WHAT HELPED YOU CHANGE YOUR LIFE?

I ended up getting pregnant and had a kid, and I got sober at twenty-four. I got off the streets, I just started changing my life and finding out about who I was, and then the big changing point for me was when my son was sexually abused and he was put in a hospital and then when he got out and he was on a bunch of medications and I didn't know what to do so I tried to check out people that I had met and he started going to sweat lodges and ceremonies. And that's how I started. Actually, my son started before I did. So that led me back.

During this time, or even earlier, did you seek out your birth family, at all?

You know, when I was young, I remember writing Ann Landers and asking how I would find my family and like right now I've put my name on birth registries, and I know my name and I know my birth name, but it is a really common last name. So I've done things like that but it is not easy because they changed the records. It is amazing to me, like the birth certificate, they changed it to white, the baptismal certificate they put my adoptive parents' name and I wasn't even with them when I was supposedly baptized but they put their names on there, so it's hard to find out. I've written the BIA—they haven't been too helpful. I've tried, I'm still on registries online and every once in a while I'll type in my birth name, but I realize it is a very common last name. My first name is not common, but my last name is. And I hope that somebody finally . . . because of the marks on my arm are significant, I know that . . . so somebody marked me for a reason and I don't think they would mark me and not look for me. But it is very difficult.

Why do you personally feel that it is important to find your birth family?

For me, at this point in my life, it is more important that my kids and grandkids have a sense of identity and the important thing for me is to be on the rolls and to get to know their family. Because in the Indian community family is so important, and they have an adopted family here. I have been adopted into a Native family here, an Ojibwa and I refer to them as brothers and sisters and mom and all that stuff. So I want my kids and grandkids to know their real family, so it is more important for my children and my children's children than it is for me, because I've come to acceptance about it, but I'm always curious. Because when we went up to one of the reservations here and my son saw somebody that looked like me and he was like holy cow mom, that girl looks like you. And to have that sense of identity, to be around people that look like you. Because the buck stops when my kids look like me and my grandkids we all look like each other, that's where it stops. We don't look like anybody else.

Was your adoptive family aware of your desire to find your birth family?

Yes. They knew.

How did that affect your relationship with them?

My dad was okay with it and my mother, like I said, I don't think cared. My brother, he found his birth family. And I was like, why couldn't it be me? His adoption records . . . he didn't look, his daughter did. And his daughter found his mother, but he had no desire to meet her. And to me, that was like I wish that was me, because I'd have met her. It was difficult, because we have adoption papers from the court, we have those, but my brother's mother's name was on the court paper. On mine, my mother's name was omitted, and I don't know why.

YOU MENTIONED THAT YOU WENT TO COLLEGE LATER. WHERE DID YOU GO?

I went to a community college and I got certified as an educational clerk and I worked for the tribe here.

WHY DID YOU DECIDE TO GO INTO THAT TYPE OF WORK?

Prior to that I had worked with juvenile offenders in a school setting in an alternative school setting and I used to talk to them because I'd been in recovery for a while, and I was told you shouldn't talk to these kids, that's what a social worker should do. And then one of my students that I just loved died from a drug overdose and it was really hurtful to me that I wasn't being allowed to talk to the kids. Well I was allowed, but I'd get in trouble for it. So it just made me like, okay, I'll get the letters behind my name and then I can talk to them. That's how it evolved.

HOW HAS THE FACT THAT YOU ARE A NATIVE AMERICAN AFFECTED YOUR PERSONAL AND PROFESSIONAL LIFE?

I started working as a juvenile counselor and I got to meet a lot of Native people and I would talk about it and I would be in staff meetings where if a Native person came through where there was definite racism, like we were getting this Native girl and I asked which tribe she was from, and they said who cares what tribe she's from. It's important to know what tribe somebody is from. I couldn't believe some of the racism there and at one of the places I worked in Illinois people would wear some of those sports logos that I find so very offensive. I got them to stop wearing them while I was there because I complained about it. So a lot of cultural insensitivity. I started thinking about that I want to work with my people, help my people, so I started putting resumes out and like three months later I found out about a job opening up here and I came up here and interviewed and was hired and I took the job. But I left my complete comfort level and moved up here by myself and left everything behind.I've been working here over three years now.

Are there any barriers that have prevented you from fully integrating into the Indian community?

If you are not originally from the reservation there is that barrier. I think that adoptees as a rule are always left out a little bit. We're never completely accepted back in. Plus the tribe I work for is not the same tribe that I am so there is that barrier. But with my clients I work with I feel like they are accepting of who I am and as a Native person and they are maybe more open to me than some of the white counselors. So that is prejudice on both sides. It is a balancing act, but for me personally I have grown so much because I found traditional ways, I've learned a lot, I've been learning the language, I go to sweat lodges, I go to ceremonies, I'm active that way, and that has been passed down to my kids and to my grandkids. That's been helpful. When I started learning traditional ways and the language and everything that helped me inside. It filled a void that I had felt for so long it was unbelievable. It was like coming home. I remember being in a ceremony and saying to one of the elder women there, where have you been, and they said we have been waiting for you. And I could feel that love and acceptance. So I feel more love and acceptance in ceremonies in the traditional world than in the regular Indian community where a lot of Indian people have been assimilated. In the traditional world I feel more loved and accepted.

Do you participate with your tribe in the ceremonies?

I participate in . . . when my son started getting help I found out about an Ojibwa tribe that I could associate myself with and I go there for ceremonies, and I go here for ceremonies, too.

So given that you don't know who your birth parents are, you haven't been able to enroll in the tribe, correct?

Right. I can't enroll.

How has that affected your sense of cultural identity or does it?

It does because part of me knows that that's just a number in BIA but to get services you need an enrollment number, like to go to the clinic or something. People look at that. Part of the way I adjusted to that, because I got tired of the prejudice, is that the family loves me, I am part of that family. It doesn't get me on the rolls, but to me, I have some sisters, I have some brothers, I have a mom now. I may never find my birth mother who was Ojibwa, but I have a new family that loves me like I have been in their family my whole life. And they tell everybody, this is my sister, this is my daughter, and so that helps with me feeling accepted.

HOW DID YOU MEET THAT FAMILY?

There was this gal up there and she was trying to get off drugs, so I sat by her and we responded right away and we got along, and she had just lost a couple of her kids because of drug usage and she was crying and it was very emotional. We were sitting in a lodge. She said nobody understands how it feels to leave a child when it is born, and in the process I have had a child that I have given up for adoption. So I related to her right away on that. And we got close, and then I met her sisters and I met her mother and her brothers and all of them . . . what is really weird, one of the brothers looks exactly like my son. People would say, oh wow, they are related. People even tell me, oh you look like your sister, or you sound like your sister, you all have that crazy hair. People never question that I am not part of that family.

DO YOU FEEL LIKE YOU ARE INSECURE ABOUT YOUR IDENTITY TODAY?

At times I feel real insecure because I don't have the paper. I almost feel like I don't have the proper papers, but then other times I am okay with it. I know what I feel inside, I know what I feel like at ceremonies, I know who I am. But there are still times when people. . . . I don't offer too much information when people start questioning me. . . .

WHAT PEOPLE OR RESOURCES OR EXPERIENCES HAVE HELPED YOU OBTAIN THAT SENSE OF SECURITY?

Traditional values, trusting the things that are told to me, my people. I know a thing that helps was when I read a book written by a Native woman about her flesh offering, like on my arm. How people were marking their kids on the reservation before they were taken, that was a ritual that was performed. I don't know why that helps, but it helps my sense of identity to know that was done to me, that my family loved me and cared about me and other people have seen it and said, yes, that's from your family. That's the Native ritual.

ARE YOU MARRIED?

No.

DO YOU HAVE CHILDREN? HOW MANY DO YOU HAVE?

I have three. One, I gave up for adoption.

WHY DID YOU DECIDE TO GIVE THAT CHILD UP FOR ADOPTION?

I got pregnant when the whole episode with my son being sexually abused was happening. I was living very poorly, not doing really well, and I really still see him and know where he's at. I've worked with the woman who adopted my son, she couldn't have children. That was a growing experience because it made be realize that my birth mother loves me. Because it was so painful to give up that child, but it didn't mean that I didn't love him.

YOU MENTION THAT YOU STILL SEE YOUR SON. IS HE AWARE OF HIS RELATIONSHIP TO YOU?

Yes. He calls me his second mother. And I have taken him and he's done reports on me for school!

THE FAMILY THAT YOU GAVE HIM TO, WHAT RACE ARE THEY?

They are white.

ARE YOU GLAD THAT YOU WERE ADOPTED BY A WHITE FAMILY?

No.

IN GENERAL DO YOU APPROVE OF TRANSRACIAL ADOPTION?

No. But I did it. So I think you look into people's hearts and see if they are culturally sensitive. They let him know that he's Native, and they talk to him about that, and they take him to functions like powwows. I think when people adopt, it's better if Native kids are in Native homes, but back when I was adopted I think they thought that if you were in a white family, your life would be better. Better for Native kids to be with white people. But now I think they just need to know that people need to be culturally sensitive because of their race. They need to look into people's hearts, into who they are as people. I wouldn't trade my father for anything, he was great. I don't think it matters what color you are. But I still think children should still be placed in Native homes. I think if I had had some type of culture identity I wouldn't have lived that horrible life I lived as a teenager.

HOW DO YOU DISCUSS THE ISSUE OF CULTURAL IDENTITY WITH YOUR CHILDREN?

As I said my son was sexually abused. He was going to sweat lodges and things like that. They know who they are. My son understands traditional life. My son when he had difficulties after he got out of the hospital for sexual abuse he went and lived on the reservation with the family that I am part of now, so he went and lived on the reservation with them for a while. My other son, I didn't really know if he was identifying or not but he got his Indian name. He went to the military. My older son went to Iraq, and when he came back from Iraq, I put an Indian name on his pack and I said no one will know what it means. And he said, but mom, I know what it means. So obviously, some part of that identity helped him while he was in war. He had a terrible time but it helped him. He came up here and they did a ceremony for him when he got back from Iraq, gave him an eagle feather. I think they have a greater sense of cultural identity and I know that when they were smaller they were over at my adopted mother's house and she said to them quit running around like a bunch of wild Indians, and they got on her, like Grandma! and she said Oh, I am sorry, I am sorry. Or like when they got their Indian names she wrote them down, she wanted to know what they mean. It seemed like she cared. She cared about what they were learning and what they were doing.

WHAT DO YOU THINK PROMPTED THAT CHANGE IN HER?

Maybe she didn't know how to access culturally sensitive things for me. Maybe she didn't know how to find those things. I knew. I've searched them out and I've found them. And I instilled them in my children. So maybe she knew that was important to them. That maybe she had made a mistake in ignoring that part of me. And with me leaving everything that's comfortable and moving up here she would know how important it would be.

WHAT ADVICE WOULD YOU OFFER TO WHITE FAMILIES WHO WOULD WANT TO OR WHO HAVE ADOPTED NATIVE AMERICAN CHILDREN?

That they meet elders from the child's tribe, that they find Native elders who can work with them to find things that are culturally sensitive to get back that part of them because it does exist and I feel like in my case it was ignored and it caused complete havoc in my life until I found it. I think if they love their child they will want them to find it and not experience that loss and that search . . . that search, it could have killed me many times.

IS THERE ANYTHING ELSE I SHOULD HAVE ASKED YOU OR ANY OTHER ISSUES YOU WOULD LIKE TO ADDRESS?

Through it all I did it, and I am okay.

## 14

# PAUL DEMAIN

Editor of *News from Indian Country*, Paul DeMain (Oneida) was born in Milwaukee, Wisconsin, in 1955 and adopted nearly two years later by a white couple with one adopted son. Unable to conceive, the couple later adopted a little girl as well. Paul describes his adoptive father as hardworking and his adoptive mother as compassionate. He describes his relationship with them as positive, but admits that he was a fairly rebellious teenager. According to Paul, he ran away from home when he was sixteen and briefly experimented with drugs. He emphasizes that "it wasn't necessarily just a rejection of [his] adoption and the question of identity" that compelled him to rebel, but rather attributes much of his behavior to the 1970s, "post-Vietnam era" and notes that by the time he turned twenty-one, he had reestablished a positive relationship with his family.

With the support of his adoptive parents, Paul began searching for his birth family when he was eighteen years old and met his birth mother when he was roughly twenty or twenty-one years old. According to Paul, his birth mother "was joyous and happy and cried" when they reunited and says that he has a "great deal of respect for her." One of the first things she did after they met was give him his birth father's name, number, and address. He says that he and his birth father wrote often, but that they didn't actually meet until 1994 and notes that their relationship isn't as close as the relationship he maintains with his birth mother. He describes his birth father as "nervous about the whole thing" and believes he fears that Paul blames him for the adoption. Paul says "out-of-wedlock children were looked upon very differently in the 1950s" and he doesn't blame either of his parents for his adoption.

According to Paul, "placing a Native child in a Native home . . . would be the preference." He says that "it makes the transition in the Indian community a lot easier when you are not quite as far out of that culture," but also maintains that irregardless of race or culture "a stable home can raise a stable child." In general, Paul says that he does approve of transracial adoption, but encourages non-Native parents to "make a commitment to keep[ing] that child connected to the Native community."

WHAT YEAR WERE YOU BORN?

1955.

WHERE WERE YOU BORN?

I was born in Milwaukee, Wisconsin.

HOW OLD WERE YOU WHEN YOU WERE ADOPTED?

I was about a year-and-a-half or two years old.

ARE YOU AWARE OF THE CIRCUMSTANCES SURROUNDING YOUR ADOPTION?

Yes, I am.

CAN YOU DESCRIBE THEM FOR ME?

I can describe this much. My mother, a member of the Oneida Nation of Wisconsin, was living in Milwaukee and going to school there. She was eighteen or nineteen years old, she was in college, so she had some college education, and my father was leaving for military service, and so their liaison had to do with some kind of a military ball or send off for a whole bunch of people, and they knew each other from school. He came from an Irish Catholic family, very religious, and my mother, a full-blooded Native woman, who I believe was brought up in the Methodist persuasion so I see some family conflicts in all that going on. My father signed my birth certificate so he was there for that particular case of legal work, which is telling in some ways. I know a whole lot of people who had all kinds of problems about the issue of establishing paternity and legal issues around birth. Besides that birth certificate, I believe he signed the authorization for adoption, basically indicating to my mother that because of the issues of race and religion and whatever else was going on he was unable to maintain a relationship.

DURING THAT FIRST YEAR AND A HALF OF YOUR LIFE DID YOU LIVE WITH YOUR BIOLOGICAL MOTHER?

No. I was given up for adoption at birth. It was supposed to be a straightforward giving up for adoption at birth situation. The fact that my mother did have a chance to hold me I think the first evening, or sometime early in the morning when the new nurse came in and I was crying and she brought me into my mother which wasn't supposed to happen was something she was not expecting, but it left a lasting impression on her that a lot of mothers don't have a chance to experience. But my mother had planned on the adoption previous. There was no surprise about the adoption. It was something that was fairly well thought out as an option to get on with life.

TELL ME A LITTLE BIT ABOUT YOUR ADOPTIVE PARENTS.

My mother was originally out of Waukesha, Wisconsin, and father from Indiana, living in Wausau, Wisconsin, which is in the central part of the state. They were of Methodist faith. I think that maybe the adoption agency was trying to pair up certain things like religious affiliation, and the adoption was overseen by the Children's Service Society of Milwaukee, Wisconsin. My adopted mother was unable to conceive, so I grew up with an older adopted brother and a younger adopted sister in the family. We spent a lot of time in and around Milwaukee/Waukesha area, and that is a whole German enclave, German immigrant enclave, and so I've got a lot of fond memories of all the people that I interacted with in terms of Grandma and Great Grandma and some of the other people in my adopted family. I had a hardworking father, I had a mother who didn't work for a living but volunteered her services to hundreds of different organizations—Girl Scouts, Boy Scouts, church work, all that kinds of stuff, so there was a lot of activity in our household. I don't know if that helps to describe them. They were stern disciplinarians, they knew how to spank well in those days when it was still allowed. So there was a lot of organization and structure in the household in terms of child rearing type of background. Alcohol had been sworn off of because of their religious convictions, and so I grew up in a nondrinking environment and most of the close relatives in that family were of a nondrinking status.

OVERALL, HOW WOULD YOU DESCRIBE YOUR RELATIONSHIP WITH THEM?

Now or then?

IN GENERAL. BOTH.

I think there was a certain curve to it, but I think the curve is parallel to what a lot of other curves are for families and children and things like that. I went through a fairly reasonable childhood and upbringing until I turned fifteen and sixteen and very much started rebelling and smoking pot and doing other drugs and trying to exercise a certain amount of freedom. And I did run away when I was sixteen years old. Some of that had to do with the circumstances and the environment of being an adoptee. It is scary around that period, thirteen, fourteen, fifteen—with thinking of what your identity is, and certainly there were a lot of circumstances at the time that also influenced who I was. It was the 1970s, there was a lot of hell-raising going on all over the country. It was post-Vietnam, there was antiwar stuff going on, there was the American Indian Movement involved in the news, and there were a lot of things going on which I gravitated toward. So I ran away when I was sixteen and pretty much from then, that was the severing of the child/parental relationship at one level. So there was a lot of stress during that particular period. But I think just like a lot of other family relationships, if people are able to talk to each other and reach out, the older I got, the more I reached back for different things. Making a stop at the house and getting a really good meal every now and then, once I came back to Wausau from where I had run away to in Florida. To get a really wholesome meal, and there was something about mom's lasagna kind of a thing, and so I went to college, and sometime during college even though I was on my own I needed to borrow some money and I came back to the family again, so I think there was a good four or five years from the time I was probably around fifteen until the time I was twenty-one that the relationship was very strained in terms of all kinds of dynamics. It wasn't necessarily just a rejection of the adoption and the question of identity, but it was also at the same time, when I turned eighteen or nineteen that I enrolled in college, and in order to do that I had to establish my tribal identity for funding and other services. I was at the forefront of some of the rulings of the Indian Child Welfare Act, and I suspect that I was probably one of the first people following some of the Indian Child Welfare Act laws that allowed me to file for my enrollment status at Oneida.

Previously, there were some court decisions which led to the institutionalization of the Indian Child Welfare Act, so there were cases in which adoptees had a right to secure the documentation establishing whether or not they were tribal members. So I was aware of those court cases from reading about them in the news and being interested in those things. I was able to get the affidavits of some kind. I went through a lawyer and through my adoptive parents who cooperated with the retrieval of my original birth certificate to have it compared against the Oneida enrollment office rolls which I or my mother were on. So I did establish enrollment when I was eighteen or nineteen and shortly after that took back my original birth name, which was DeMain on the birth certificate.

Were your adoptive parents supportive of that decision?

I think they were. Yes, they were. If you say, did they support it? Yes, they pretty much supported whatever me or any of my other siblings in that family wanted to pursue over the years. I don't know if they felt happy about it. I don't think that they understood the nature of that request at the time. My whole pursuit of my biological mother and father and so forth. You have to remember though that I am an investigative journalist and so the mindset of inquiring started at a very young age. My family was very open about it, and I was very visibly different than the other two children who were adopted, who were white Caucasians, a younger sister and an older brother. I was sort of the black sheep of the family and during the summer months I stood out very readily. There were always people asking, "who is this?" The dark child you have running around in the neighborhood with all the other freckled, red-headed, dishpan blond kids in the family that existed. So I stood out. It was no secret that we were all adopted in the family, and so at some particular point, probably when I was twelve or thirteen years old, somewhere in that range, beginning to ask questions about the adoption, one of the questions was "What do you know about my mother and father?" My adoptive mother said well, all we know about your mother is that she was an Oneida Indian and that's about it . . . there were no other details . . . but they knew that much from the adoption agency. So I went to the encyclopedia and established the fact that at that time there were 6,000 Oneidas in Wisconsin and 200 in upper state New York and another 2,000 in Southwold, Ontario, Canada, at that Oneida community and thought okay, that's like 8,000 people, and 4,000 of them are males and so that leaves 4,000 women and half of them are under the age of twenty-one, so that leaves 2,000 potential biological mothers in the whole world. That's narrowing the statistics down considerably, which made my potential search much more limited. I had it clear in my mind, and they were aware of that, and so the question is were they supportive? Yes, they were supportive.

I don't think they understood the adoption circle the way it is understood nowadays. In those days, the severance of relationships, the closure of records was so much more firm. You didn't have this circle of people working to provide avenues for adoptees to regain access to the information on their biological parents. I think they understand it real well now because of what I went through, and the experience I forced them through. So my younger sister was just horribly upset with the fact that I would ever do this to mom and dad. They adopted me and gave me the love and upraising and all that stuff. She could not fathom why I would ever search out other family members—my biological family members and mother and father and so forth, only to later have her other sisters who had been adopted out from her biological mother find her and connect and so at that particular point her world view changed quite a bit, but I had already put my parents through this, so the second time around it was a lot easier for people to say, "Come in and sit down, you are Barb's biological sister. Okay fine, come on in, we've already gone through this thing with Paul and it's getting to be an easier thing to deal with." And they did the right thing. They did everything they could to do what they felt was the right thing. And because of it I grew up pretty reasonably well in the world, not that I didn't go through a whole lot of stuff when I was teenager in terms of my drinking and smoking and drug use and hell-raising and defiance of the police and all of the other things, that an awful lot of other people went through at that time. So the answer is yes, they have been generally supportive, more so in the latter years than in the earlier years.

Can you talk a little bit about your adopted sister? How would you describe your relationship with your sister and brother?

I have a great relationship with them. To some extent, as I left the Caucasian community and reentered the Native community the relationship was sort of strange because it was kind of like I didn't know if I'd like that relationship real well. It's like, wait, okay, you've got a white older brother, you've got a white younger sister, you got white parents—that's not exactly establishing your Native identity the way people in the Indian community establish their Indian identity when they go in and say I'm a member of this tribe, I'm a member of this clan, I belong to this family. I didn't have those kinds of credentials so it was fairly awkward in the very beginning. With my adopted brother and sister, maybe it was embarrassing in certain circumstances, but to a great extent during that five- or six-year period where I was headed in several directions at the same time, when I was not quite sure where I was going, I was pretty isolated from the family. When I ran away, my older brother had gone to college and worked somewhere, so I was out of contact with him a great deal. I didn't go to the family reunion stuff that was going on, my younger sister was kind of almost totally mad at me because of everything that had gone on with me running away, and trying to look for my family, and so it was stranger in that period, but I think in the long run, family is family and when you look at the dynamics of the family, if you look back on those things that represent love and caring and sharing and understanding and for me to a great extent teaching because of who I was and how I did all this, teaching them some element that they had never thought they would face and I am well respected and appreciated and loved nowadays. So there was a strained period there for everybody in the family.

What are the advantages and disadvantages of growing up with siblings who are also adopted?

I can't just say that the joint experience is something that is shared. Sure we were all adopted, so we were all adopted, and if this is why we were so different from each other. I really don't think that in family structure that it makes a horrendously lot of difference. A family operates like a family. They can take in a niece or nephew, they can take in an adopted child and merge them into the family and unless people are dysfunctional in some aspect of that, children just simply are merged in and become part of the family. So I think the dynamic of how people are within general families, there are kids that were adopted by dysfunctional families and grew up dysfunctional because the family was dysfunctional. Other people are well adjusted. And I think you can find that in any part of the country, you run into adoptees who are well adjusted, very comfortable with what happened. And especially nowadays you find other people that are still in crisis in part because of the type of environment that they grew up in. There's nothing particular about that environment based on race or ethnicity or religious belief. It's just if you're in a good family, you're in a good family and people allow you to grow as an individual and if you're in an abusive family you grow up to become abusive. So I don't really see any particular advantage or disadvantage to the fact that both my older brother and younger sister were adopted. I think it could have been any combination because all my cousins were not adopted and I have a good relationship with my cousins as well.

Was the fact that you are American Indian talked about a lot in your family?

No, not a whole lot. I don't think it was a center of discussion. I think it was a reason why people purchased some books and went to places. It seems to me that some of the things that stand out in my mind more nowadays probably because I thought about them more during certain periods of my life, even though I can remember bratwurst in Waukesha because on Sunday afternoon so many people had bratwurst. For example, I remember driving through the Menominee Reservation and the impression was that there was this discussion going on about how lucky I was to have a nice home and a nice family because when you looked at some of the houses that were in some areas, because in some areas of the reservation there were very nice, very large houses, but there was a sense of poverty, a sense of a level of distress in other parts of that community. The fact that these houses were up in the woods, and had dirt driveways and all this other stuff was some kind of sign of deprivation. And I was like in the back of my mind, oh man it would be nice to live there and be able to run in the woods all day rather than being in an urban area. So I had this perception. But the family I grew up in was always inquisitive and so there were National Geographics there with things about Indians, there were other books about Indians.

The community I grew up in was Caucasian. Wausau nowadays is dealing with a large influence of Hmong people, but at the time it had very few people of color of any race other than white, and so it is a community where you didn't learn a lot about Native Americans. It only existed in segments where you talked about Indians on Thanksgiving and that was about it. To me, I don't remember special things, but it's like the same impression. Like okay, the pilgrims invited the poor, hungry Indians to the dinner table and fed them. Because Indians are Indians, and the Pilgrims are so advanced they are probably the ones that brought dinner. I think that is the general impression of how people grew up, but probably all over the country as well. Somehow they would be thinking "we have to be superior" to whatever was going on with these poor Indians at the dinner table. Ultimately what it was, was just a lack of instructional material and ability to do things at the time in the school system. It has changed drastically from the 1960s and 1970s when I was growing up because Wisconsin has implemented certain criteria for curriculum in the schools throughout the state so that everyone is beginning to learn about the tribes in Wisconsin and how they are important to politics and government, but that was absent at that time. Like Native instructional material was probably absent across the country during that period.

WHO WERE YOUR CLOSEST FRIENDS IN SCHOOL?

I had lots of different buddies. They were all white guys and white girls when I was young. My first love was a white girl, my closest buddies were people who grew up around me in the neighborhood. In high school, I was not an athletic type person, so I kind of grew up in the crowd that was kind of cool. They weren't the jocks and they weren't the farmers or whatever the different cliques were. . . . I was somewhere in the middle amongst the kind of cool, liberal, open-minded, non-geeky people. Maybe in the whole crew that was fairly average—beer drinkers and people who liked to go out and have a dooby on Friday or Saturday nights once we got to that age where we could go do that. A lot of my old friends still contact me, I still have contact with a lot of people down there, I have a good relationship with them. My Indianness always came up in discussions with them. And certainly I didn't have very good answers. And probably some of those stereotypes of drinking and things like that years ago. I can remember some very awkward types of things and so you get to that age of thirteen or fourteen and you know, you're a goddamn Indian, or you're a squaw or something like that became a derogatory thing that could be directed toward me that could hurt me, so there were some enemies and people that didn't like me that were able to use that to try to get to me.

HOW DID YOU ADDRESS THAT ISSUE?

There are some times I just took care of it physically, which wasn't real well received. Part of what I tried to do over the years was I became a very good kind of verbal fighter. It was words and probably most of the time came back with a verbal harangue that hurt them as bad as they could try to hurt me. You're just a squaw that was adopted. Your parents didn't love you. And I'd come back and say, well, you know, you look like the milkman's son. I centered it on verbal sparring. I think I felt bad. I can remember looking in the mirror and saying geez wouldn't it be nice if I had blond hair and blue eyes and could avoid this crap? I think in the long run, I just discovered it was probably fine being myself. But I think young people go through that process altogether no matter who they are. I think the blond hair, blue-eyed popular kid looks in the mirror and wishes maybe they were some movie star, or something else, so I think there is some wondering about who you would be in your identity search anyway no matter what race, or status. But I often wondered who I could be because I didn't know who my mom and dad was and so I could be anybody I wanted to be. I could be the son or the daughter of anyone out there and so it would have been easy enough to create that kind of scenario where nowadays some young Indian child who is adopted looks in the mirror and says someday I am going to grow up and find my family, and I am sure that one of them is a Pequot and one is a Shakopee and I want to be a Dakota because they make big per capita payments. I think people could envision that, and I think that is what I did a little bit is look around and think of myself as maybe—you're the son of some real big shot person and that's what happened here.

I've worked with a lot of adoptees during my lifetime and I've tried to make sure that those adoptees who we were bringing back home were prepared for the ultimate realization that they were raised in an environment that may have been a lot better than whatever it was that they were given up from. I think people need to have that whole spectrum and they need to know that some of these reunions can be very good.

The circumstances of people in which you can forgive each other and bridge that feeling of hurt and pain and things that go on. Things can turn out very well, but at the same time, a man I helped reunite with his mother, and he met her in a bar and spent about an hour and a half with her in the bar which was where she was eighteen years earlier when she had given him up for adoption, and where she stayed as he came and went, but the second tier to that was that the rest of the family was connected: aunties and uncles and grandmothers and so forth which was a different kind of experience than the real hurt and pain that he suffered meeting his mother at the bar, though I think he was prepared for that possibility. You were given up for adoption, be prepared for the worst. Number one, we may find that your mother or father doesn't exist anymore, which is the case of some adoptees. Number two, we may find that your mother suffered some kind of a horrible situation that prevents her from reconnecting with you—she was raped, the circumstances of her conception with you was a very difficult thing and therefore it is too painful for her to reconnect, and you find her in the bar taking care of her pain and emotions. This is where we happened to find this one mother. But connecting with the other family was what really saved his self-esteem in the long run.

HAVE YOU EVER REUNITED WITH YOUR BIRTH FAMILY?

Yes I have.

HOW OLD WERE YOU WHEN YOU REUNITED?

With my birth mother, I was probably about twenty or twenty-one. It was not too long after I went to college, not too long after I established my enrollment, not too long after that when I got my original birth certificate, it was only a matter of time of going around to other members of the Oneida tribe to establish who my mother was, because her name was on the birth certificate. So I connected with my mother probably telephonically, actually was able to contact my grandmother, and a few hours later got a phone call from my mother, and met her so probably when I was about twenty or twenty-one years old. And one of the first chances that I had to sit down with her and meet with her, she opened up her purse and got out her phone book and wrote the phone number and address for my dad down. And handed it to me, and said, "Here. Here's where he is." And she said, "He was the father of my son." And she kept track of where he was.

Did you meet with him as well?

Yes, I have. He was very nervous. My mother was joyous and happy and cried. He's still nervous about the whole thing, I think more about whether or not I would understand what had happened. The circumstances. I don't think I've ever blamed her or my father for the circumstances of what happened. Out of wedlock children were looked upon very differently in the 1950s and I actually think I commended my father one time for signing my birth certificate. I had written to my father a number of times, and I don't think I met my father. . . . I would have met my mother in like, say 1977, approximately, that coincides pretty well . . . maybe about 1975, when I was twenty years old, 1976, at least telephonically and by letter, had reached her, and talked to her. And probably didn't meet my father until, physically, I think about 1994. Part of that was just because he lives in California, part of it was just that he was living on the other side of the country, whereas my mother lives about five hours from where I now reside and when I lived in Eau Claire she lived about four hours away from where I lived and lived very close to Oneida, Wisconsin. So I was on the rez (Oneida) quite a bit and it was easy enough to look her up.

My father was very nervous about it, but my biological mother was, I think, very happy about some part of reconnecting, knowing her oldest son was just fine, and our relationship has really grown, and now this is 2007, so its been over twenty years.

Maybe about three years ago I had a chance to go to the San Diego area, I had a conference and e-mailed my father and said I'm on my way to San Diego and he came up to meet with me while I was out at the University doing some research there, so I e-mailed my mother and said I'm heading out to California to meet with my dad, Richard . . . just to let you know. Because she always had some interest in it . . . you know, have you talked to your dad lately? What's going on? And so I ended up calling her up. . . . I talk to her about once a week now that she's got a cell phone, so she calls me up and vice versa.

What are you doing, where are you going, how have you been, it's nice and sunny, et cetera. My dad's been married now three times and so I have six or seven other brothers and sisters on that side of the family by him. But my mother said, when you see your dad ask him what's going to happen when you and I show up at his funeral? They are both in their seventies. Number one it assumes that my mother is going to outlive my father, and number two, my mother when she says we're going to show up at his funeral, she means it. I've learned that much about her over the years.

And I have a great deal of respect for her. So there is an interesting dynamic there. And so I asked him, and he was flustered, and so later that day after we were getting ready to head out I said what do you want me to tell my mom about me and her showing up at your funeral. And he turned around and said, when you guys show up they'll be expecting you. And he wrote me an e-mail and said some people may contact you, some of the kids may contact you so where do you want them to write or call you or whatever? So I gave him my address and phone number. There are a lot of interesting things. Can I tell you one little story? My younger adopted sister is named Barb. My mother has a daughter named Barb, so now I had had two sisters named Barb and when I corresponded with my father, he wrote out the names of all of his kids and he has a daughter named Barb, and so I have three sisters named Barb but nobody in the family is named Darrell. Remember that show where three brothers are named Darrell?

Do you have a relationship with your biological siblings?

On my mother's side, but not on my father's side. On my father's side they know about me but it's been a very arm's-length thing. I've never tried to intrude. I don't know what the dynamics are. I've let it be. My father apparently told them that they have a brother, and they can read about me online. I'm fairly well known, I'm a journalist, I'm well published, I'm vocal, I've headed up all kinds of national organizations. They can find out a lot out about me, which is one thing that may have kept them from getting ahold of me, not that they don't want to . . . just that they can find out a lot about me without having to call me up directly. On my mother's side, I had a brother and four sisters. I have a younger brother that passed away before I got to know him. My closest sister in age is kind of indifferent about me personalitywise, whatever. I had one sister, Patty, who called me up within days of finding out about me, and her birthday is one day before or after mine, and she says that my emergence into the family explains some dynamics that had occurred during one of her birthday parties, where my mom apparently at some point in the whole thing disappeared and was in her bedroom crying and my sister never understood that only to realize when I emerged that her birthday party set that internal emotion off about where was I and was I okay. I think a mother internally always thinks about that. That's the reason some mothers give their children up for adoption and if they don't have a way to deal with it they get into drinking and other things. But my mother felt it around my sister's birthday, so it explained a few things. I have another sister a little bit younger, once she started calling, we'd go out to dinner, we'd do this, we'd do that, and there was a lot of excitement about it, and then I have one sister who is very close to my younger brother whose dynamic is very unique and I think it is just differences in family and children and people. She's kind of like motorcycle babe in the family and she had a real difficult time trying to reconcile all kinds of things about me. In fact she was the first person that I approached in the family when I forced the issue of meeting the family. I had contacted my mother much earlier and at some particular point around the time when my half-brother was killed in a car accident, it was before that, that who I call my stepfather now (my biological mother's husband) had called me up and asked me a lot of questions. Well why are you trying to come into this family? You were put up for adoption, those records were sealed. Well, the girls are all in high school. They can't know that their mother had a child out of wedlock, it would be devastating to the moral and physical image they have of their mother, and all this other stuff.

This is the dynamics of what occurred in my adoption. My mother became pregnant and it became obvious that my father had abandoned or would not maintain a relationship, so my mother's to-be husband spent a lot of time with her during that pregnancy and it is a situation where he may have said, look, I'll marry you, but I don't think considering all the factors that we need to start our family with this child. So after he's born he will be given up for adoption. They got married something like a month or so after I was birthed, they became married, and I think it was within nine or ten months after that my first closest sister was born. So that was part of the dynamics, but it was very much hidden in the agenda of things to his family. His family never knew anything about me. And so at some particular point when I found out that my brother had been killed because I went down to Manitowac, Wiscoinsin, to where brother and sisters were going to school and got pictures out of the yearbook of all of my sisters and there was a tribute to my brother Larry who had been killed in a car accident. There was this gut-wrenching feeling that I had never got to meet him. Because Lynn's proposal was that until the girls are all grown up and out of high school I don't think you should come around and meet them. And I said fine, whatever.

After I found out that Larry was killed I went to the bowling alley and bar in the apartment building complex that they owned, it was called the Stueber House in Manitowac, Wisconsin, and when I walked in my sister was bartending on the other side of the bar, and I had a beer or two, and I asked where her mother was, and she said it was none of my business. This is the motorcycle babe in our family. And I said, well I was a friend of the family. And she said, "I don't know who the hell you are. How can you be a friend of the family? I don't know who you are." And she was off to serve some more customers. And I said, well okay, I don't like the way this feels. And I just said, look, I need to let you know that I'm your brother. And she said, I only had one brother and he's dead. So you might as well get out of here. I don't know who you are or what you want. I've got a lot of customers to serve here. Something like that. So I did leave. And that was in the late afternoon/evening. The next morning I get a phone call from my sister, one of my other sisters, and she said, Oh my God, we were all called together for a family meeting. My mom was in Chicago and she said we're having a family meeting in Manitowac tonight and everyone's got to be there, and so everyone went up there to find out what it was. This is what it was. My youngest sister had basically called mom up and said, "look, there was this guy sitting on the other side of bar that said . . . " that's the way it went. It was not a real happy situation for my mother. I am sure it was kind of an initial crisis, and she had to say, look this is what happened and she probably had to tell them, look I've been in contact with him for a couple of years already, I know where he lives, lots of questions about circumstances, but I think that that was the hump that the family needed to get over in their life, because now it seems the relationships have grown stronger with everyone including Sharon, I call her the Harley babe all the time because of the language she uses, and how she comes across. She doesn't like to deal with me very well, but it is just part of her personality.

How have you changed since finding your birth family?

I think I have always been a person that has just grown and grown and grown. It's like the older you get the more you realize you don't know anything and you have experienced only a touch of what is available in the whole world. It's growth, it's intellectual growth, its relationship growth, its understanding growth, you learn how to forgive, you learn how to proceed. What's her problem, whatever it is it's probably hers and I can still be nice to her. I don't reject anyone for any particular reason. I think the dynamics of the relationship is something that is well known to Indian country in terms of adoptions and reconciliations in families and stuff like that.

I think adoptions and the such are better hidden in the Caucasian community, because there isn't the issue of enrollment or ethnicity in a tribe. There's a lot of interest in people to establish who their tribe is because it is kind of cool or neat to be an Indian nowadays, and there might be money there if you are a member of a certain tribe, so there is kind of a drawing card for Indian adoptees to search out their history. And I do believe that in the Indian community because of the number of children put in institutions and adopted homes historically, the experience is much more acceptable, much more common. Still a lot of healing needs to go on over it. But I don't think that anything that has happened in this relationship would not allow me to grow as a person who would understand and not deal with people from, like I say, there are some segments of society like the Christian Right who bury stuff way deep down in life and rhetoric and years later you find out that some number one evangelical Christian moral ethic person is having an affair while he's accusing Bill Clinton of having an affair and that's all evil.

I just think that those are human dynamics that go on and there is denial in other communities and there lies a significant difference, that because of what happened in the Indian community, it is a much more open subject and if we didn't have a lot of the other dysfunctional things going on in our community with broken families, alcohol, and drugs that it would be a situation that would be dealt with even more openness than it is. And now you got the situation of disenrollments, tribes actually trying to limit the inclusion of members of the family because of blood quantum, money, and other issues. So there is a lot of scrutiny, and that whole return to the community is not an easy one for some people who have to make that trail back, and they never feel real comfortable in the Indian community having been raised in the non-Indian community and they don't necessarily feel comfortable being a person of color in a white community.

ARE THERE ANY BARRIERS THAT HAVE PREVENTED YOU FROM FULLY INTEGRATING INTO THE INDIAN COMMUNITY?

No, I don't think so. I'm the kind of guy that just doesn't let a lot of those things affect me. I just find them and move around them, move under them, move over them. That's the way I've been all my life. I wanted to come back and I did, and there are people who can make hay of who I am but they can't deny the credentials that I now carry in the Native community where I am someone that people seek out to speak for ceremonies or for other reasons. I have positions within some of the religious societies that are not earned easily. In the community here, I am among some people known by my Native name and play that role of a messenger, and there are probably not a lot of people in the community who were even born and raised here that are able to fulfill that role. People don't know my history. People wouldn't know. I've been in service to the governor's office from 1982 to 1986, and had people from other reservations come in and start telling me how it was to be this or to be that, and I was always, even though I was just twenty-four or twenty-five, spending a lot of time with elders in ceremonies and everything and in some cases they just kind of grabbed me and folded me into what was going on.

That is always an interesting dynamic, when you get people talking to you about who they think you are and who they are proposing they are, telling you about the ceremonies and everything and you've been to all the ceremonies they are talking about but you haven't seen them there. So a lot of people, unless I talk about it, wouldn't know that I was adopted, was in the governor's office, and very pro-supportive of the Indian community on treaties and fishing rights and other things.

I would have white people come there and say "If you only understood how white people think" . . . and I would say in the back of my mind, okay I'll get to hear this story, because I was raised in a home where people hunted and fished and had the sports ethic rather than a sustenance ethic or whatever it might be. I was raised around a lot of white people so I had a pretty good observation of what was going on, which really gave me the skills of doing the same thing the Metis community did during the 1700s and 1800s . . . a hundred-year period where half-breed and mixed-blood people played an integral role between the tribes and non-Indian community. I am related to the Morrison Clan of the Great Lakes, the Morrisons were Scottish immigrants from the island of Lewis who married—came to the Great Lakes area, married several Ojibway women, had many, many children, and that was the first rule of their children, they were highly educated, and they weren't treated like white people because they weren't white, but they weren't treated like Ojibway people because they didn't see themselves as Ojibway people. They were half-breeds and mixed bloods, halfway in between. They became the translators in treaties, they told their family members what was going on in the treaties to be able to secure certain things in a better way and understanding them. So they were really middle people in a community for a hundred years and I think that is the role that many adoptees play nowadays. They can walk into the community and they can walk into the medicine lodge. I can translate what an Ojibway elder is saying to the people in the Ojibway language or I can walk into an office building in a suitcoat and tie very easily and feel somewhat comfortable. I don't prefer suitcoats and tie. I wore them in the governor's office for four years and that's the only time I ever wore them. It's just a preference.

But I can do that if I need to. I can go to Washington, D.C., and deal with presidents and presidential candidates and political races and all the things that I've done. I already helped run a vice presidential campaign for the Green Party with Winona LaDuke. She called me up as an Ojibway person from the White Earth Reservation, and said Paul, "I need someone who can understand all of this political stuff and this structural management stuff and how to relate to non-Native people, but I also need someone who understands me." So I very much became an in-between person in terms of trying to run a vice presidential campaign and relating to what needed to be done for Native people and relating to what needed to be done to the political structure on the outside of it. So it has made me very adept at times.

I'd like to go back a little bit and talk about your education. You said you went to college. Where did you go?

I went to the University of Wisconsin, Eau Claire.

And what did you take at school?

I went into journalism and pre-Law.

What did you do after you graduated?

I didn't get a four-year degree. I did about two-and-a-half to three years. I ended up getting an associate's degree in mass communications, but I never graduated with a BA. I ended up coming up here to Lac Courte Oreilles during the summer, I was kind of getting burned out with college. It didn't feel like I was doing enough on the ground. And so I was invited by Dr. Rick Germaine who at the time, I think, was twenty-four or twenty-five, was probably the youngest tribal chairman in the United States at that time in 1978 or 1979. Very articulate, very progressive, very much into education, and he asked me to come up and do the tribe's newspaper here and I ended up getting snagged up. The rest of the story is history and I have seven children and seven grandchildren, and two more on the way.

I started my family up here and I never did go back full-time to school. I have other credits. But I'm about eight to eleven credits short of getting a BA and I want to finish it one of these days. So I never did finish my career there. I had been planning to try to graduate from UW-Eau Claire and going to the University of New Mexico if I remember right with Sam Deloria's pre-law program. It was attractive, but I got kind of bored in college for awhile. It was like 1975 or 1976, a couple years after Wounded Knee, Jumping Bull Compound shoot-out, American Indian Movement stuff, and there was all kinds of things swirling around me, and lots of opportunities as tribes kind of blossomed during that period, and so I had an opportunity to get away for a summertime and that was in 1978 or 1979 and so it has been thirty years.

WHAT MADE YOU WANT TO BECOME A JOURNALIST?

I think that my high school teacher saw that as probably my best "avenue." I go back and look at material that I collected, stuff when I was in high school that I had written. It is certainly interesting, exciting stuff, very shortsighted. I started writing mainly about justice and law: how it was against the law for a school administrator to search your locker looking for marijuana. What was your right as a student to be represented by counselor or parents if you were found to be truant? What kind of appeal you had from a suspension. How an adult on his own, say he was sixteen years old and he ran away and convinced his mom and dad to give him a release paper saying this guy is on his own, because if he came back home, he would say "I'm going to run away again, anyway, why don't you just release your parental rights to me and if I get thrown in jail I get thrown in jail."

I had a job, I'm going to school, and so I can be late going to school in the morning and sign my own excuse for being late. You have to excuse Paul because he was late today because he couldn't make it here in time . . . Signed, Paul. . . . And the school officials would have to accept it because I was my own parental person. I was not the ordinary person growing up, probably not the ordinary person today, either. But the teachers that I had really, really tried to focus me in high school on writing, and I became a co-editor of the high school newspaper, and that became my ticket to go to college. I really think that that last year in high school when I came back from Florida and was graduating I began to see that I wanted to start writing about Native people. When I ran away to Florida I met several Native people. When I came back to Wausau there were several Native people in my high school who were at a local home, some kind of an institution for kids who had been in trouble at home—a group home. So I started dating and dialoguing with different Native people, probably from about the time I was sixteen, seventeen, eighteen. I drew a little bit of strength from some of those relationships and I was beginning to develop an identity from some of the Native people that I had met in Florida who were Seminole, and when I came back basically I was allowed in to enter UW-Eau because I was a Native person. So at that particular point, that became my ticket and I entered

Eau Clair, and I got exposed to Native people on-res, off-res, the Native American club, fried bread sales, trying to help put the powwow together, traveling to other powwows, you know there are always powwows in the spring at all these colleges and you go to the powwow and then you get together with all the students later for a meal and then you go on to the local Native pub, so it became that kind of a little circular thing. So I see that evolution of me beginning to writing a lot more about Native American things. We need a voice of our own. We are not reading enough about our own perspective. There isn't enough out there. So there was a whole evolution in me saying someday I wanted to own my own newspaper. And I do now. I came and worked at the *LCO Journal American* for a while, then started *News from Indian Country* sometime later.

GROWING UP, WHAT EFFECT DO YOU THINK THE MEDIA HAD ON YOUR PERCEPTION OF YOURSELF?

In my family there was always a morning newspaper at the doorstep. So my adoptive father read newspapers, watched the evening news, and I read newspapers and watched the evening news. To a great extent, it's funny, I can see that a lot of people don't do that. There's no newspaper, there's no six o'clock evening meal or five o'clock evening meal with the news on in the background, which in our house was the way it was. Nowdays you may go to the Internet and find the news, if you're looking for Native news or anything else as far as that matters. My perception at the time was simply that there was not enough Native people who were being written about. Whether it was a curriculum, whether it was media. There was not a lot of focused newspapers, like there's *Oklahoma Indian Times*, *Native Peoples*, *Navajo Times*, whatever it might be. There was just a lack of anything being produced out of the Indian community when I got here. The *LCO* (Lac Courte Oreilles) tribal news was a mediocre, four-page kind of sheet about local news and then there was *Akwesasne Notes*, and *Wassaja* around that time. But really what there was was just a total lack of news generally speaking, just like there was a lack of music or film or other voices from the Native community. I remember like maybe there were two eight tracks with Indian music on them, there was maybe like a forty-five and an LP with music from the Smithsonian Institute. Nowadays there's a new release every week out of Indian country, and powwow CDs with all kinds of specialty music. So things have changed dramatically in terms of access to media for Native people. Nowdays young Native people growing up in high school, if they have a problem with their identity they can go online or select a book, or listen to all the music you need, or whatever it is you need to tell you who you are supposed to be, because there is a lot of stuff out there. So it was a lack of all kinds of things, a lack of proper representation that focused me on that career. Remember in the 1970s you had the dynamic of the American Indian Movement which brought Native news into people's homes, and to some extent I was attached to that, as someone who believed in the potential of the movement, I had the friends and relatives who were involved in it. As I came into college I tried to stay away from being affiliated as a "member" of any of that, because I was trying to be impartial as a journalist, even though you still have—I tended to move in that direction a great deal, because I thought it was at that time something that was a positive. Part of the problem is that there weren't a whole lot of other positives being shown to people, so even that movement toward the American Indian Movement and the excitement of what that represented was kind of a cloak and dagger type of symbol. It turns out that there were drug dealers and they murdered people within the movement and they did all kinds of other things that hurt our people as well, and so the leadership may still go to jail for those murders that were committed twenty or thirty years ago, and it might be very hard for me to convince you of that argument, other than the fact I'm an investigative journalist and have talked to people who know the truth, but I was drawn to that because that tended to be the media focus at the time.

And then in the last dozen years or so you have this dynamic called the poor Indians at Pine Ridge or Navajo country living in hogans, at Pine Ridge they're in their cars, or the rich Indians, the Pequot or Shakopee Mdewakanton Sioux. And again there's a gap in coverage. Where are the ballerinas? Where are the astronauts? Where are the Olympians? Where are the stargazers, and intellectuals and geophysical people? When you have been in the newspaper business as long as I have—give me a subject and I will find you a Native person who has taught it and who has taught it real well. Jim Pepper led the world in teaching people how to play the saxophone to the outer edges of everybody's capability, his industry recognized him for that, a Kaw Indian. What do you want me to talk about, because I will find you a Native person or a tribe or someone who has accomplished that and maybe did it better than anyone else. So I think it is really good nowadays that we have Native people who are doing Native publishing, acting, productions. We have Native people who are doing movies. Chris Eyre, who is an adoptee, is a film producer. There are all kinds of people doing great things and the number of adoptees doing them is rather astonishing, except for that common denominator, people who have their feet in both ethnic canoes.

You mentioned that you were married and have children. Can you tell me a little bit about your family? Tell me about your wife, her ethnic background, her profession.

She is a member of the Lac Courte Oreilles Ojibwe Tribe here, she is an accountant.

How many children do you have?

I have seven children.

How have you addressed the issue of cultural identity with your children?

We are all involved. . . . I am involved with ceremonies, my wife is involved with ceremonies, my youngest son who is now five years old is in an immersion school. He has been in school since he was two and a half. My oldest son who is now twenty-eight years old is involved in Drum Dance ceremonies. It's the whole spectrum. They have gone to tribal schools, been involved here on the reservation since they were very young. We are on a reservation and we're involved in the tribal community in lots of different ways. Active in powwows, active in ceremonies, active in politics, active in harvesting. Just going through all the regular things that any family on the reservation would be involved with. Athletics, music, school teacher conferences, feasts, powwows, skating. We're a pretty typical family, busy all the time.

I would like to talk about transracial adoption in general. What do you think are the advantages and disadvantages of being transracially adopted?

Well, I think that there are a lot of benefits of placing a Native child in a Native home. I think that would be the preference. I don't see it always as the ultimate decision necessary, especially with some of the adoptions I see nowadays, where people are required to keep in touch with tribal culture and the tribe's politics and make sure the children are enrolled and those kinds of things. I think a stable home can raise a stable child. Years ago I did some kind of a film production here in Wisconsin for adoptions to try to get some more Native families open to adopt Native children. And I was used as the kind of a guy was raised without a culture and everything and I think that it was a stalemate, because a Native child at some point has to learn everything about culture protocol from a Native community and still deal with everything they have to learn outside of that culture. But I think everyone to some extent has got to do that. I think a Native person living in a Native home nowadays pretty much has to understand off reservation culture and norms and so forth to be able to excel. There is a certain benefit in tribes trying to keep their children within their own tribal culture, the second tier being to keep them within the Native culture, you know a Chippewa being adopted by a Cherokee family or an Oneida being adopted by a Menomenee. I think there is a certain comfort zone there that's helpful. I think that it tends to be a preference in my mind, that I prefer to keep a child within an extended Native family whenever possible. For example, my daughter had twins and she gave birth to another daughter shortly after that and went through a breakup in the family, and as a single parent in that particular point was having a difficult time taking care of three children and so the youngest daughter spent a lot of time at her aunties house. Her auntie ended up adopting her and so my granddaughter has basically what she calls two mothers. She has her biological mother but she knows that her aunty is her mother also. She's aware of the relationship situation . . . there are no family secrets, but the child is being raised within the family. She gets to see her natural mother, her grandfather whenever, in passing, during family events.

Just like I say sometimes, I have the benefit of having two mothers, two fathers, and all the grandparents that went with them plus stepfathers and all kinds of extra relatives. And lots of siblings that want to interact with me. I have a larger family than most people do, and I can draw on some of the strengths of family members within that. I think that is a preference that's a good goal. I think it makes the transition in the Indian community a lot easier when you are not quite as far out of that culture, or out of your own extended family, but I don't think it is an absolute.

DO YOU APPROVE OF NON-NATIVE FAMILIES ADOPTING NATIVE CHILDREN?

Yes. I do approve of it. I think if you find a family that is dedicated to raising the children, that is the first goal. Some of these children need to get into a stable household. But I also think that in terms of judging people capable of adopting children, they need to be able to show a fairly open and general understanding of what is available out there in the Native community and make a commitment to keep that child connected to the Native community, so there is less of a shock factor as that child is probably going to come back home at some point.

IS THERE ANY OTHER ADVICE THAT YOU'D LIKE TO OFFER NON-NATIVE FAMILIES WHO HAVE ADOPTED NATIVE CHILDREN?

I think they need to subscribe to *News from Indian Country* because that is one reason we produce it, but they need to subscribe too, and listen to

Native programming, Native music, whatever it is they need to come of a better understanding what this child represents. I think it is helpful to keep in touch with the Native community. When a child is being adopted into a non-Native family I think that that family should make a commitment to keep in touch with things that are going on in that community. And to offer that child the ability to form relationships in the tribal community. I don't think it is necessarily healthy to put a Navajo child into a Caucasian home halfway across the country in New Jersey. I think that can still succeed, but I really think that the preference, there are levels of preference, that say if you are going to reach out to the Native community to adopt it is not just because you are going to adopt a cute, dark little child . . . oh, he's so cute, black eyes and dark complexion . . . we need one of those. I don't think that that should be the intent. The intent should be to provide nurturing but within an environment that is open to opportunities to experience their own culture as much as possible and within reach of that child to experience an atmosphere that is close to the environment they came from.

Is there anything else I should have asked you?

No, I think you asked all the relevant questions. Good luck on your project.

15

# DAVID HOUGHTON

Adopted by a psychologist and a schoolteacher in 1967 when he was one week old, David Houghton (Da'naxda'xw First Nation) describes his adoptive parents as "honest, hard-working people." In 1970, David's adoptive parents moved him and his sister from Vancouver, British Columbia to England where they spent their "formative schooling years." According to David, racism was not a problem for him growing up because he was "a typical white kid." He says, "I always thought of myself as Anglo. I always was and still am an Englishman."

David reunited with his birth family in his early thirties and is now an enrolled member of the Da'naxda'xw tribe. He notes, however, that he finds it hard to believe that he is "in fact an Indian" and says that this knowledge "[hasn't] registered in [his] head properly." Clearly, David is in many ways still grappling with his sense of cultural identity. He says, "I now know something of my culture. I am part of it," but is quick to admit that he is "in constant culture shock."

According to David, the greatest disadvantage of transracial adoption is a "lack of [cultural] connection. Although he is currently struggling to re-establish this connection, David notes that he is not completely opposed to transracial adoption. He reasons "there are good and bad people in all walks of life. Whether a Native or non-Native family is best suited to the care of a child is a purely bureaucratic decision."

WHAT YEAR WERE YOU BORN?

1967.

WHERE WERE YOU BORN?

Vancouver, BC.

HOW OLD WERE YOU WHEN YOU WERE ADOPTED?

One week.

ARE YOU AWARE OF THE CIRCUMSTANCES SURROUNDING YOUR ADOPTION? PLEASE DESCRIBE.

Yes, but only found out the details in the last two years. My mother was twenty, and attending UBC. She was trying to complete her nursing degree.

TELL ME ABOUT YOUR ADOPTIVE PARENTS.

My adoptive parents were professional educators. My father and mother lived and worked in Vancouver in the midsixties. My father has a Ph.D. in psychology, and my mother was a schoolteacher.

HOW WOULD YOU DESCRIBE YOUR RELATIONSHIP WITH THEM?

Very good. They are honest hard-working people.

DID THEY EVER INDICATE TO YOU WHY THEY DECIDED TO ADOPT AN AMERICAN INDIAN CHILD?

No they did not. I have no idea why they would do that.

WHEN DID YOU FIRST REALIZE THAT YOU WERE ADOPTED? WHAT WAS YOUR REACTION? DESCRIBE THE CIRCUMSTANCES.

I think I would have been six or seven. I thought it to be quite an exciting thing. I can't remember the circumstances. There was never a secret about it. I was told I was adopted, and I was told I was native.

DO YOU THINK THAT YOUR ADOPTIVE PARENTS HANDLED THIS REVELATION IN A POSITIVE MANNER?

I think they did. I must admit I was highly skeptical about the Native part of it, but they assured me that was the case.

WAS THE FACT THAT YOU ARE AN AMERICAN INDIAN TALKED ABOUT A LOT IN YOUR FAMILY? DESCRIBE.

It was occasionally. They didn't really know very much, apart from the fact I was from the Northwest coast. There were some books that they had bought back with them from Canada. I would read the stories and look at the artwork of the region.

WHAT DID YOUR ADOPTIVE PARENTS DO TO GIVE YOU A SENSE OF YOUR CULTURAL IDENTITY?

Not very much, they knew very little of the culture. It was always going to be my choice. I am sure if it became a must do thing for me when I was younger they would have supported me in any way they could.

DO YOU HAVE SIBLINGS—BIRTH OR ADOPTED?

One sister in England. I of course have many more now that I have discovered my birth mother.

ARE YOU CLOSE TO YOUR SIBLINGS?

I suppose so.

DO YOU TALK WITH THEM ABOUT BEING AN AMERICAN INDIAN?

It was never a hot topic of conversation in the past. It was acknowledged, but never really explored. I now definitely talk about it a lot more. It is something I am becoming aware of as I am now part of my culture.

DO YOU FEEL OR HAVE YOU BEEN TOLD THAT YOU POSSESS STRONG AMERICAN INDIAN PHYSICAL FEATURES? HOW HAS YOUR PHYSICAL APPEARANCE AFFECTED THE WAY IN WHICH YOU HAVE BEEN PERCEIVED BY BOTH THOSE IN THE INDIAN AND NON-INDIAN COMMUNITIES? HOW HAS YOUR PHYSICAL APPEARANCE SHAPED YOUR CULTURAL IDENTITY?

No I don't. It has never affected other people's perceptions of me in the past. Now of course I am an Englishman. Living in England shaped my cultural identity. My appearance and skin color meant I was an Englishman to everyone I met, unless I told them I was adopted and had native roots.

HOW DO YOU THINK YOUR PHYSICAL APPEARANCE AFFECTED THE MANNER IN WHICH YOU PERCEIVED YOURSELF AS A CHILD, AS A TEENAGER, AND AS AN ADULT?

I always thought myself as a typical Anglo. I was always and still am an Englishman. The difference now is I am part of my culture. I am discovering what it means to be part of an extended family and how that is a central part of our culture. As a teenager I became curious about my heritage. It was never a big thing for me; I just accepted the fact and just carried on with my integrated life in England. As time wore on I would tell people I was from the Pacific Northwest coast, but you know somewhere within me I could not quite believe it.

To whom did you talk to about the fact that you were an American Indian? What people or resources aided you in this process? Have you read a lot of books about your tribe? Do you feel that they offer an accurate portrait of your culture? Are there limitations to relying solely on books for this information? What effect did the media have on your perception of yourself?

I would be told I was Indian by my mother and father, but they never pushed it on me and said you have to go and find out about it. I read some books and looked at the wonderful art of this region. The stories always seemed to make sense to me. I had no idea of what tribe I was affiliated with. So I never knew where I came from.

I understood that there is a lot of distinct variation within the tribal groups of this region. Not knowing where your roots are confuses the process. You read lots of different things about the different peoples of the region. I gave myself an overview of the cultures of the Northwest coast. Reading these things did in fact give me a fairly accurate description of the strata of the cultures. There are great limitations within the constraints of the books available on culture. They are of course written by and for Western consumption. I have developed my own ideas about media over the years, and this had no effect on my perception of myself.

Where did you grow up?

I grew up in England for the most part.

Describe the places you lived and the schools you attended. Did you encounter any form of racism growing up? How did you address this issue? Did your parents prepare you for this challenge?

I left Canada in 1970, lived in various parts of England until I was twelve. At this time my mother took my sister and me to London. I spent all my formative schooling years here. Racism was never a problem for me. I was a typical white kid.

Do you remember learning about Native Americans in school? What did you learn? Would you say that the information you learned about Native Americans in school differs dramatically from the in-

FORMATION YOU LEARNED ONCE YOU BEGAN INTERACTING PERSONALLY WITH THOSE IN THE NATIVE COMMUNITY?

No. Nothing. Native Americans are not something that was part of any curriculum I encountered in England.

WHO WERE YOUR CLOSEST FRIENDS IN SCHOOL?

My closest friends were your typical childhood friends. There was ethnic diversity within our little group. Indians, Pakistanis, and West Indians.

DID YOU GO TO COLLEGE? WHERE? WHY THAT SCHOOL? WHAT WAS YOUR MAJOR?

Not when I was supposed to. As soon as it was possible, I took the option to leave education behind me. I went back to college when I was thirty. I went to the closest college to where I was living. I was interested in music, and took a music technology course.

WHAT KIND OF WORK DO YOU DO NOW?

I work within the health profession.

WHO ARE YOUR CLOSEST FRIENDS TODAY?

My closest friends today are members of my family.

DO YOU HAVE ANY TIES TO AN AMERICAN INDIAN TRIBE? EXPLAIN.

Not that I know of. I have not found my birth father. There is a possibility that I could have connections through that side of my birth family, due to the geographical location I think he came from.

WHAT TRIBE ARE YOU?

Da'Naxda'Xw. This is a tribe within the Kwakiutl region. They live on an island at the mouth of Knights' Inlet, on the Johnston Straight. This is part of the Kwakwaka'wakw-speaking peoples. I live in Kingcome Inlet, who are the Tsawataineuk.

ARE YOU AN ENROLLED MEMBER OF A TRIBE? WHY OR WHY NOT? HOW HAS THIS AFFECTED YOUR SENSE OF CULTURAL IDENTITY OR DOES IT?

Yes, I am a status card holder. It says Da'Naxda'Xw. I applied for status when I arrived in Canada, and got it. I don't think this affected my cultural identity in any way. It just now meant I was a statistic, it was now official.

How has the fact that you are Native American affected both your personal and professional life?

It has never affected my professional life in the past. Now it has a bearing as I am part of a First Nations community.

Are you married? If, yes to whom?

No, I have never been married.

Do you have children?

Yes I have two boys, who live with their mother in England.

How have you addressed the issue of cultural identity with your children? Why do you think this is such an important issue?

I have told them that they now have a heritage and roots in Canada. They can if they so wish in the future embrace this side of themselves and find out about their extended family. It is an important issue. I think that being told you have these connections with a far and distant culture is not enough. Somehow you have to make that connection, and I am afraid that it is really a physical connection. To the land and the area you come from. Until you take this step and experience the place of your ancestors, I don't think you are going to get it.

How do you identify yourself today?

I am an English Indian. There will always be a part of me that is English. I spent a long time living in that culture. It is something that will never leave me.

When did you take on that identity? How?

It has to be my identity. I live on a remote reserve. My mother lives here as did her mother. It is where I come from. I now know something of my culture. I am part of it. I participate in the traditional gatherings in the big house. Potlatch and feasting are things I have now experienced. I now have a place in our traditional society.

Have you sought out your birth family? Why or why not? How old were you when you decided to look for them? What prompted this decision? Are you comfortable or uncomfortable with spending time with your birth family?

Yes. I left it till I was in my midthirties. It was always something I knew I would do. It was an inevitable thing that was always going to happen. The decision was made, when I realized that after living out of London for a number of years, I was ready to move back to London after going to college. When I sat and thought about it, did it really make any difference if I went to London or Vancouver? I decided that I could take that chance and move to Canada. I am comfortable spending time with my family. It was a little hard to begin with. We all had to go through the process of familiarity. We all had to learn about each other.

WHY DO YOU PERSONALLY FEEL THAT IT IS IMPORTANT TO FIND YOUR BIRTH FAMILY? HOW HAVE YOU CHANGED SINCE FINDING YOUR BIRTH FAMILY?

I thought it was something I would do at some time in my life. It was never something that was on top of a list or anything like that. It just was it was going to happen. People in England say I have changed. I personally can't see it, but I must have. I have changed in the perspective I may have had about family. It is now such a different thing. I have a massive extended family, and this is only half of it. I still have to make my way east, and look for my father.

DID YOUR ADOPTIVE PARENTS SUPPORT YOUR DECISION TO SEARCH FOR YOUR BIRTH FAMILY? DID YOUR RELATIONSHIP WITH YOUR ADOPTIVE FAMILY CHANGE AS A RESULT OF THIS DECISION? HOW?

They did support my decision. Once done my mother asked me why I had not done it years ago. It did change my relationship with my adoptive family. I am now a long way off. I am on the other side of the world.

DID YOU RETURN TO YOUR RESERVATION? DID YOU EXPERIENCE ANY TYPE OF "CULTURE SHOCK" UPON RETURNING TO THE RESERVATION? DID THESE TWO WORLDS CLASH IN ANYWAY? IF SO, HOW?

Yes I did. I am in constant culture shock. It was an overwhelming thing to meet a lot of my family. Now I am on a steep learning curve. The reservation has a lot of things to deal with. There is of course the charming legacy of colonialization. I have been part of the culture that was responsible for suppressing the culture of my people. I lived all my life in a world that is totally ignorant of the things that have been done by it in the past.

ARE THERE ANY BARRIERS THAT HAVE PREVENTED YOU FROM FULLY INTEGRATING INTO THE INDIAN COMMUNITY?

No.

DO YOU FEEL SECURE OR INSECURE ABOUT YOUR INDIAN IDENTITY TODAY?

I am secure in the knowledge of my ancestry. I do however find it hard to believe that I am in fact an Indian. As I did in the past it doesn't seem to have registered in my head properly.

Do you feel accepted by Indians outside your birth family? Describe.

I am accepted. I am part of their lives now. I have been given an Indian name, I take part in cultural activities, albeit in a small way.

What are the advantages and disadvantages of being transracially adopted?

The advantage would have to be the fact you have the opportunity to succeed in a different environment, even though I personally did not take my education seriously until I was much older. That would be the only thing that springs to mind. The disadvantages are in the fact of your lack of connection, whether you knew about it or not.

What is your opinion of the Indian Child Welfare Act? Do you approve of non-Native families adopting Native American children? Explain.

I do not like the motivation behind the initial move to approve non-Native families to take on these children. It can only be considered as a racist act. I have no problem with adoption. It is something that happens. It is however a game of Russian roulette. I think you must take a pragmatic view on this, there are good and bad people in all walks of life. Whether a Native family or non-Native family is best suited to the care of a child is a purely bureaucratic decision. This is a system that is just not satisfactory.

Do you have any advice that you would like to offer non-Native families who would want to or have adopted Native American children?

Make sure that a connection is made with the society and culture that the child belongs to. To acknowledge this is something I really believe.

Is there anything else I should have asked you or any other issues that you'd like to address?

No.

16

# DENNIS JONES*

Born in Milwaukee, Wisconsin, in 1972 and adopted one year later by a white couple, Dennis Jones (Menominee) agreed to participate in this interview, but was not particularly forthcoming with his responses and wished to remain anonymous. He describes his adoptive parents as "interesting people . . . with a lot of problems" and notes that they are estranged, but does not care to elaborate on their relationship. He mentions that his adoptive parents adopted two other Native American children and raised all three of them in a predominantly white neighborhood. Growing up, he says that he had few friends and was subjected to racism—primarily from his adoptive family.

Dennis reunited with his birth family shortly after applying for membership with the Menominee Indian Tribe of Wisconsin. He says that he has met his birth mother and that they occasionally speak on the phone, but he does not describe his relationship with her as close. When describing his birth mother, he says that she had "a relationship with a man and I was the product of that . . . she claims that she couldn't take care of me so she talked to some people and that took care of that issue." Dennis is not only opposed to transracial adoption, but to adoption in general. He argues that "adoption is not the solution for anything."

---

*Identifying information about this participant has been omitted or changed.

WHAT YEAR WERE YOU BORN?

I was born in 1972.

WHERE WERE YOU BORN?

In Milwaukee, Wisconsin.

HOW OLD WERE YOU WHEN YOU WERE ADOPTED?

I was about a year old.

ARE YOU AWARE OF THE CIRCUMSTANCES SURROUNDING YOUR ADOPTION?

My birth mother had had a relationship with a man and I was a product of that. And she claims that she couldn't take care of me so she talked to some people and that took care of that issue.

CAN YOU TELL ME A LITTLE BIT ABOUT YOUR ADOPTIVE PARENTS?

They are interesting people. They've got a lot of problems though, they've got a lot of problems, I'll just leave it at that.

HOW WOULD YOU DESCRIBE YOUR RELATIONSHIP WITH THEM?

I don't have one . . . estranged is the word.

WHY DID THEY DECIDE TO ADOPT.

I don't know.

WERE YOU THE ONLY CHILD THEY ADOPTED?

No.

HOW MANY SIBLINGS DID YOU HAVE?

There were two other children who were not their birth children.

AND WHAT RACES WERE THEY?

Native American.

DO YOU HAVE A RELATIONSHIP WITH THEM?

I talk to them every once in a while.

SO ALL THREE OF YOUR ADOPTIVE PARENTS' CHILDREN WERE NATIVE AMERICAN?

That's right.

DID THEY EVER INDICATE TO YOU WHY THEY DECIDED TO ADOPT CHILDREN?

No.

WHEN DID YOU FIRST REALIZE THAT YOU WERE ADOPTED?

When I was growing up.

DID YOUR PARENTS SIT YOU DOWN AND TALK TO YOU ABOUT IT SPECIFICALLY?

Not really.

WAS THE FACT THAT YOU AND YOUR SIBLINGS WERE NATIVE AMERICAN TALKED ABOUT A LOT IN YOUR FAMILY?

No.

WHAT DID YOUR ADOPTIVE PARENTS DO TO GIVE YOU A SENSE OF YOUR CULTURAL IDENTITY?

Nothing.

CAN YOU TELL ME A LITTLE BIT ABOUT WHERE YOU LIVED AND THE SCHOOLS YOU ATTENDED?

Many. When I was growing up.

WERE THE SCHOOLS YOU ATTENDED PREDOMINANTLY WHITE?

They were predominantly white.

DID YOU ENCOUNTER ANY FORM OF RACISM GROWING UP?

Yes.

FROM OTHER STUDENTS?

From my own family.

HOW DID YOU ADDRESS THIS ISSUE?

Just dealt with it. Lapped it up.

DO YOU FEEL OR HAVE YOU BEEN TOLD THAT YOU POSSESS STRONG NATIVE AMERICAN PHYSICAL FEATURES?

No, no one's said that.

DO YOU THINK THAT YOUR PHYSICAL APPEARANCE AFFECTED THE WAY IN WHICH YOU WERE PERCEIVED BY OTHERS IN THE COMMUNITY?

Yes.

HOW SO?

They called me "chief" . . . there was the physical representation so they know who I am. I even had a Native American name.

HOW DO YOU THINK YOUR PHYSICAL IDENTITY HAS AFFECTED THE WAY IN WHICH YOU PERCEIVED YOURSELF?

That's a pretty tough question. I don't know.

DO YOU REMEMBER LEARNING ABOUT NATIVE AMERICANS AT YOUR SCHOOL?

A little bit.

WOULD YOU SAY THAT THE INFORMATION YOU LEARNED IN SCHOOL DIFFERED DRAMATICALLY FROM THE INFORMATION YOU LEARNED ONCE YOU BEGAN INTERACTING PERSONALLY WITH THOSE IN THE NATIVE COMMUNITY?

Yes.

WHO WERE YOUR CLOSEST FRIENDS IN SCHOOL?

I didn't really have friends.

GROWING UP, WHOM DID YOU TALK TO ABOUT THE FACT THAT YOU WERE NATIVE AMERICAN?

No one.

AFTER HIGH SCHOOL, DID YOU GO TO COLLEGE?

No.

HAVE YOU FOUND YOUR BIRTH FAMILY?

I have.

CAN YOU TELL ME A LITTLE BIT ABOUT THEM?

My birth father is unknown. And my birth mother lives in Green Bay, Wisconsin.

AND WHAT TRIBE IS SHE?

Menomonee.

DO YOU HAVE ANY OTHER SIBLINGS FROM YOUR MOTHER?

No.

WHAT PROMPTED YOU TO SEARCH FOR YOUR BIRTH FAMILY?

I don't know.

HOW OLD WERE YOU WHEN YOU DECIDED TO LOOK FOR THEM?

I think I was about twenty-nine.

CAN YOU TELL ME A LITTLE BIT ABOUT THE SEARCH?

I went to Wisconsin and applied to have my enrollment, my birth certificate. Upon approval from the birth mother, they contacted her, and they gave me her name after she said it was okay.

HOW HAVE YOU CHANGED SINCE FINDING YOUR MOTHER?

Grown wiser.

HOW WOULD YOU DESCRIBE YOUR RELATIONSHIP WITH YOUR BIRTH MOTHER TODAY?

I don't know. We talk sometimes.

CAN YOU DESCRIBE THE FIRST TIME YOU MET?

I talked to my mother on the phone.

HAVE YOU MET HER IN PERSON?

Yes. I met her in person.

DID YOUR ADOPTIVE PARENTS SUPPORT YOUR DECISION TO SEARCH FOR YOUR BIRTH FAMILY?

No.

DID THEY EVER EXPLAIN TO YOU WHY NOT?

I don't talk to them.

WHEN DID YOU STOP TALKING WITH YOUR FAMILY?

About four years ago, five years ago.

DID YOUR RELATIONSHIP WITH THEM DETERIORATE WHEN YOU DECIDED TO LOOK FOR YOUR BIRTH MOTHER?

No.

ARE YOU AN ENROLLED MEMBER OF YOUR TRIBE?

Yes.

CAN YOU TELL ME A LITTLE BIT ABOUT THE ENROLLMENT PROCESS?

When I was about nineteen or twenty years old someone told me that I could apply for enrollment for a tribe and they sent me the application. In Wisconsin again, they allowed people who were descendants to apply and be looked at for enrollment, and I enrolled myself after identifying family information like who your birth parents are. So I went through that process.

HOW HAS YOUR ABILITY TO GET ENROLLED IN YOUR TRIBE AFFECTED YOUR SENSE OF CULTURAL IDENTITY, OR DOES IT?

It doesn't, but it's helpful.

HOW SO?

Well I live on the reservation and there are benefits I receive.

HOW HAS THE FACT THAT YOU ARE NATIVE AMERICAN AFFECTED BOTH YOUR PERSONAL AND PROFESSIONAL LIFE?

Tremendously.

CAN YOU GIVE ANY SPECIFIC EXAMPLES?

The fact that I work primarily with Native Americans. My profession is pretty much surrounded by my work within the community.

WHAT DO YOU DO FOR A LIVING?

I work in a lot of things, but currently I am setting up a Bureau of Indian Affairs Detention Center. It is just one of the things I've done within the Indian community.

WHERE DO YOU LIVE TODAY?

My home residence is in Wisconsin, but I am temporarily assigned in Texas.

ARE THERE ANY BARRIERS THAT HAVE PREVENTED YOU FROM FULLY INTEGRATING INTO THE NATIVE COMMUNITY?

No.

Do you feel secure or are you secure about your Native American identity today?

Yes.

What people or resources aided in obtaining this sense of security?

My wife.

Is your wife Native as well?

No.

Do you have children?

I do.

How many?

One.

How have you addressed the issue of cultural identity with your child?

The last name. She knows who she is.

Has transracial adoption been a positive experience for you?

No and yes.

Can you explain?

By adversity we learn a lot of things that we might not have learned at all. So although it's been very adverse no one changes for the worse.

Do you approve of non-Native families adopting Native American children?

No.

Why not?

I don't think adoption is the solution for anything.

What advice would you offer non-Native families who have adopted Native American children?

Get rid of your own personal problems before you adopt or even think about it.

THAT WAS MY LAST QUESTION. IS THERE ANYTHING ELSE YOU THINK I SHOULD HAVE ASKED YOU OR ANY OTHER ISSUES YOU THINK I SHOULD HAVE ADDRESSED?

Yes. I got another one for you. There's a book written by a man, an autobiography. His name is Olaudah Equiano. He was kidnapped in the seventeenth century, taken from his family, and put on a ship and sent to America first, but somehow he became adopted I guess you would say (he didn't call it adopted in his autobiography) but separated from his family and under the guardianship of a British foreign officer. Now the man wrote his book at the end of his life when he was converted to Christianity and it is a very inspiring story of some of the adversity that people have although they may not realize it when they are separated from their family and some of the grief and trauma that accompany that separation. I guess there are more books too written by people who talk about some of the adversity that they faced during the time and how they respond to it and grow. I guess that's what I want to communicate to the reader about adversity, and about how it functions in the psychology of the adopted person, or someone separated. I would recommend the guy's book because it is a classic story of what we think of as adoption, and he never called it that, he called it other things. But it is a good picture of the psychology of a person who is separated from his family and was never reunited again, but still learned from his experiences, and educated the public about life and challenges. There are other books on slavery that talk about modern-day adoption, but back then they called it slavery. I think it would be an excellent presentation because his story was very valuable and has taught me a lot about who I am because it is about how he learned about himself and teaches us who he is, and I can learn about who I am.

WHAT DO YOU THINK YOU LEARNED ABOUT YOURSELF FROM READING HIS BOOK?

I learned that there are positive things that can come from adversity and that if they only see negative aspects, you are not going to make any progress, but when you realize that obviously some people have it a little bit worse than you, I think it helps you put it into perspective. Because I really wasn't kidnapped and beat up by people who really seriously hated me . . . not as bad as he was, let's put it that way. So it puts it in perspective.

17

# PAUL LAROCHE

Born in 1955, Paul LaRoche (Lower Brule Sioux) always knew that he and his brother, Mark, were adopted, but they did not know that they were of Native American descent. This discovery was made by Paul's wife after his adoptive parents passed away in the late eighties. According to Paul, his wife stumbled across a letter that indicated that his parents had adopted "a child from Indian Country." Wrought with grief over the death of his adoptive parents, Paul asked his wife to "pursue it." Five years later, she found his birth family and put him in touch with his biological brother, whom Paul says he was reluctant to meet. Growing up, he said, "it bothered [him] when [he] thought about [his birth family]. It bothered [him] because [he] thought that it would just absolutely hurt [his adoptive] parents" whom he describes as "wonderful people." Aside from these feelings of guilt, Paul also admits that "a fear of rejection haunted [him]" and discouraged him from pursuing a relationship with his birth family. Fortunately, Paul's fears proved to be unfounded as he was warmly welcomed backed into the family and into the tribe.

Shortly after reuniting with his birth family, Paul, his wife and their two children moved to the Lower Brule Sioux Reservation in South Dakota. According to Paul, their first year was difficult because living conditions on the reservation were substantially different than those in the suburbs. However, he notes that this difficult transition was meliorated by the love and support of his birth family and tribal community. During this time period, he notes that his birth family and several elders taught him Lakota culture, language, and music and encouraged him to pursue his musical career. Eventually, Paul and his two children "began a little musical group called Brule" and have since released ten albums, which Paul describes as the "world of rock and roll fused into the world of Native America." Although he incorporates elements of traditional Native American music into his own work, Paul says that he is careful "not to exploit certain things" and "seeks the approval of community elders" before releasing any albums. The musical group, Brule, has won several music awards, including two Native American Music Awards last year.

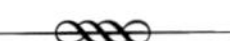

WHAT YEAR WERE YOU BORN?

1955.

WHERE WERE YOU BORN?

I was born in Pierre, South Dakota.

DO YOU KNOW HOW OLD YOU WERE WHEN YOU WERE PUT UP FOR ADOPTION?

The records indicate that I would have been about ten to twelve weeks old.

ARE YOU AWARE OF THE CIRCUMSTANCES SURROUNDING YOUR ADOPTION?

Yes, I am.

WOULD YOU MIND SHARING THOSE WITH ME?

Not at all. I can begin by telling you that my biological parents resided on the Lower Brule Sioux Reservation, which is in central South Dakota. As we go on through the questions I can probably touch on some of the other parts of this. My adoption was a little bit unique, in fact they all are. I have had the opportunity to talk to hundreds and thousands of people over the last ten years about adoption stories, but ours is such that there's still a little mystery to it. It sounds like my mother was going through some hard times, actually . . . my mother and father. I never met them in the course of all these years. This is information I've gotten from other family members and things of this sort. She made a decision to adopt me out. The year was 1955. They were living on the reservation. Pierre is just to the north of our reservation boundaries by about 25 miles. I was one of four children in our family. The rest of the children remained with the family and on the reservation. And the circumstances that led to my adoption while others stayed on the reservation are still and probably always will remain a bit of a mystery. We were never able to complete that. She never shared with even her closest or most intimate friends or family the reason for the adoption. But I can share with you, over the course of this interview, she did leave a trail of information. So there would be a trail for me to answer certain questions.

A little bit about the adoption itself: I was born June 23, 1955. And just one other thing about that particular year, and we think it contributed to the adoption, but we don't really know for sure. We only found this out recently. The years 1954 and 1955 were certainly, I know, difficult times on the reservation, our family particularly was going through some difficult times in terms of poverty, oppression, living quarters were such that there wasn't much in terms of where they lived, and to complicate things those happened to be the years when the Army Corps of Engineers came through and down the Missouri River and built a series of dams, all the way from North Dakota and down into Nebraska, and of course the dams which are now structures that we see on the Missouri River were built for hydroelectric power. It caused a lot of chaos in the reservation. The river cuts right through the heart of the Lower Brule Sioux Reservation. Although that was land, people who had dwellings along the river had to relocate, and had to move elsewhere, so I believe that my parents were part of a people who had to go through a major relocation at that same time . . . the same year I was being born. So there were a lot of things happening on the reservation during that year, 1955, that might have contributed to the adoption.

TELL ME A LITTLE BIT ABOUT YOUR ADOPTIVE PARENTS.

I always refer to them, to this day, as my parents. To me they were and always will be my mother and father. They were wonderful parents. I know now that I was very fortunate to have been placed in a home with two wonderful, loving parents. Their names were Irma and Clarence Summers. And we lived in Worthington, Minnesota, which is not too far from the South Dakota reservation where I was born. I would say geographically we are only speaking about a three-and-a-half-hour difference. But I have come to realize that it may have been a different country as well, because of the vast differences in southwest Minnesota, where the small town of Worthington is situated, and the reservation here in South Dakota . . . they are like two different worlds. But I was lucky to have been placed in a warm, loving home, wonderful parents. I look back on this today and what I believe is the main ingredient in an adoption is an abundance of love. I think if you can give the child a loving home that there will be a contentedness. I certainly have the best of memories as a young boy and I owe it all to my two wonderful parents. My adoptive parents, Irma and Clarence . . . wonderful people.

Did they ever indicate to you why they decided to adopt?

As I recall, I probably was about six or seven when I was able to grasp the fact that I was adopted. And it didn't mean too much to me at the time. I loved my parents and they obviously loved me and so the adopted part never really meant too much to me in terms of the whole logistics of it. They were unable to have children. I believe it was my mother. My mother and all her sisters all suffered from the same problem of not being able to have their own children. So there were a lot of adopted children in our family at the time . . . not only my mother but her sisters, my aunts, adopted all of their children. So there were a lot of adopted children there.

Were your parents specifically looking to adopt an Indian child, or were they just looking to adopt a child in general?

I believe they were just looking to adopt a child in general. And the reason they ended up with a Native American child I believe is this: I have a cousin on my adopted family's side. She is about ten years older than I and she is a Catholic nun. At the time of my birth she was working in the hospital in Pierre as an x-ray technician, and I have talked to her since, she's still living. She has led me to believe that they had resources up there at Pierre hospital to help to situate Native American children off the reservation. I didn't ever pursue it that far, and whether it was all legitimate or not, I don't know that either, but I do know that there were probably a lot of children that came through St. Mary's Hospital in Pierre and I was one of them and having had a family member who worked there I think that was probably the connection that my parents came across when they were searching for a child.

You mentioned that a number of your other family members are adopted. Are any of them Native American?

Yes. My adopted brother, the two of us grew up as brothers, he is also Native American. We are five years apart, I was the older of the two of us. And he came kind of by the same process as I did. He was placed out of Pierre hospital and I came from the Lower Brule Sioux Reservation and we now know that my brother Mark came from the Cheyenne River Reservation.

Do you have any other siblings?

I have two living biological siblings on the reservation. A brother and a sister. My brother, Fritz, is one year younger than I am, he actually remained on the reservation, and a sister who is older than I am by about five years and she is living in Pierre and on my adoptive family side it was just Mark and I, the two of us are in our family.

What were the advantages of having a brother who was also adopted and who was also Native American?

Well, you know I didn't realize it at the time, I don't think either of us did, as we grew up. I can probably answer this by telling you that I think our heritage had little to do with the fact that we got along well. I think the fact that we were both adopted was of comfort and certainly may have helped us to bond a little bit in a way that may not have been if one of us had been biological and the other adopted. But as I recall to the best of my memory, I don't recall ever over the course of the years Mark or myself dwelling on the fact that we were two adopted children. I'll emphasize many times during the course of our interview, we felt like we were two brothers, part of the same family, and with that we had two loving parents.

Did you two ever dwell on your cultural backgrounds?

Let me share this with you. There is another twist in our story and the twist goes like this. We were never told of our heritage. Back in those days what my parents told me when it came to my heritage was that I was redskin Indian and yes, I was different than the rest of the kids. Darker complexion, dark hair, but French Canadian trail always seemed to satisfy anyone who would ask ever if I was . . . "what nationality are you, Paul?" French Canadian. My parents were not inaccurate. I have now realized that I am part French Canadian, but my bloodline runs like this. Essentially I am three-quarter Lakota and one-quarter French Canadian. And there is a lot of French Canadian influence in certainly the Lower Brule Sioux Tribe but also in most of the Sioux tribes the French Canadian influence runs pretty deeply. You could see it in the names if you examine the enrollment rosters for any of our tribes you see a lot of French names in there. I never questioned that and the question may arise "Why did they do that?" and I can address that right now. I never had the chance to ask them before they both passed on. It doesn't seem to be important. But I believe, and this is a guess on my part, that it was a protective device. I think that back in the 1950s and on into the early 1960s these would have been the years when I would have been given the information, I think it was just unpopular to have Native American heritage in your families, and certainly we know now that many families have buried that information back in earlier decades. And of course it is popular today. Everyone now searches for a little bit of Cherokee, or whatever they may have on their family tree, and they seek that out with every resource. But back then I can tell you that I don't think it was popular, and I think they just kept that secret as a protective device. The small town of Worthington, Minnesota, where I grew up was not very culturally diverse back in those days and I would have been the only Native American person in Worthington, and probably would have suffered at the hands of different comments and racism. I think that probably as I look back on it, it wasn't totally inappropriate to have kept that secret.

So when you were younger it never crossed your mind that you might be Native or you were never told by other people that you looked Native?

Never once. And that's an honest to God fact. I've talked to relatives and friends now in later years and I think people may have thought that, but it was never spoken and I don't think I have a friend or acquaintance or family member who ever once said "Hey, Paul, are you sure you're not Indian or something?" That never happened. So honestly there was enough of a buffer there for whatever reason that it just never came up.

Can you describe in a little more detail the places you lived and the schools you attended growing up.

The small town of Worthington is a town of 10,000 people, the population hasn't changed too much over the years. It is a small midwestern farming community for the most part. I was raised in a Catholic household so I attended the St. Mary's Catholic grade school in Worthington. So I was raised with a pretty strong religious background by my adoptive parents. It was not a bad school to attend. I was immersed into that. I was an altar boy in my younger years, I was the church organist for a period of seven years. Grade school ran up to grade seven in those days, and then junior high and high school were two public schools that I attended. And relatively good schools. I was able to do pretty good in the school systems. I was not very highly academic but I took advantage of sports programs and really when I talk to a lot of my former classmates years later, a lot of us say that we would never want to go back to our school years again. I wouldn't say that. I would go back at the drop of a hat. I had a good time coming up through the school system and I have good memories and those were good days. I enjoyed every year. And I never had a bad year, it was all good.

How old were you when you learned that you were Native American?

I was thirty-eight. Both of my adoptive parents died within one year's period of time. And it was between 1986 and 1987. My mother was the second to pass on after my father died. He had a heart attack and my mother had cancer . . . so she tended to the household in that certain period of time after my dad was gone, and she kept track of all the important information over the years. She was kind of the bookkeeper for the family, so right after she died we were given the task of going through the house and started to collect the heirlooms and belongings and papers of our parents for all those years and it was my wife, Kathy, who stumbled across an envelope that had been basically hidden for years. It wasn't sealed in a safe, but it was tucked away in a place where I would never find it. It was a single envelope. I never found any other information. One envelope that contained a little information on my adoption and she stumbled across it during this process one afternoon of going through drawers and dressers, and you know her heart almost stopped when she opened it up and there were two names on there, there was my name Paul Edward Summers, the name I grew up with, and there was another name on there, Arlen Fay LaRoche, which we now know to be my biological name. And there were innuendoes in the letter that this may be dealing with a child from Indian country. So that was the first hint that we had, and she didn't even share that with me until a little bit later on. At that time, I think she realized what the situation was.

And what was your reaction after learning that?

At that point in time, there you are. You are trying to absorb the loss of not one, but two parents within a year. And you are here and you are deep within the grieving process. It was more information than I could process at that time and I asked my wife if she could deal with it, pursue it, not to take it the wrong way, but when the time was right I think she knew that I could come back and reexamine the whole thing but at that moment I was too deeply in the grieving process and in fact she allowed me five years after the loss of my mom to get to a point where we were ready to deal with that.

And after that five-year period, did you begin looking for your birth family?

During that five-year period, unbeknownst to me, she had started the process with just the information that she had in that single letter. And with the help of this cousin of mine that I talked to you about earlier, the cousin of mine on the adoptive family side who was the Catholic nun, they were able to go back and to actually retrace most of the steps. And I think out of courtesy and I had voiced that I didn't want to deal with it because it dealt with a different culture, and I needed to find a place in my heart where I was comfortable with the loss of both parents and as an adopted child I was one of the adopted children who never liked to think about another family, another set of parents, another . . . it bothered me when I thought about it. It bothered me because I thought that it would just absolutely hurt my parents to even talk about it, and I never had a curiosity about it or about a different family, different world, different way of life. So I grew up with my own story. Even after both parents were gone I had a certain amount of guilt that I carried about the delay starting to get information for the new family. During that five-year period after the loss of both parents, Kathy moved things along and by the year 1993, which is five years after the loss of my mom in 1987, she had actually had it arranged to where I received a phone call from a gentlemen we didn't know apparently but we believed he was my biological brother. And that happened two weeks before Thanksgiving in 1993. That first phone call.

DID YOU SPEAK WITH HIM?

I did. Unwillingly. First I had asked my wife to be onhand to ask the questions, and obviously my cousin, Yvonne, the Catholic nun I keep referring to, she was the first liaison. She was the one who started to put the calls in around the reservation to check this LaRoche name out and she had traced it back to a family and she passed that on to us. And that was my wife Kathy, who was going to take over the job as liaison. And so the first phone call came in and I had asked her to kindly just talk and find information and pretend as though I wasn't there. I was terribly nervous. The one emotion that ran through me continually through the process and it took quite a while to get past that, but it was the fear of rejection that haunted me during that early part of the process of getting to know them, the other family. But the phone conversation took place and lo and behold, Kathy put me on the phone kind of against my wishes, but . . . I am glad that she did. We went on to speak for several hours and we still didn't have the paper trail and physical evidence that we needed but it seemed as though it was quite likely that we were brothers, biological brothers, and we went on to speak at great length about our various lives and backgrounds and it occurred to me yet in that first phone call that we had led two drastically different lives. Drastically different lives . . . but we came from the same place. He was only a year younger than I am . . . he stayed on the reservation. I was a year older, I was taken off. And the contrast in our lives was overwhelming.

DID YOU GET THE REST OF THE FAMILY LATER?

I mentioned that this was two weeks before Thanksgiving in 1993 and at the end of the phone conversation my brother's closing words were to come on home. And we didn't know quite what he meant by that other than the fact of "come on out" . . . but we did. We did come home for our first reunion . . . our first reunion was on Thanksgiving Day in 1993. So my wife and my son and daughter who at the time were still high school age, the four of us packed up our car and as you can imagine the families in Worthington were apprehensive, not so much on my side but on my wife's side. My mother and father were both gone but her family, she still had a living mother, brothers, and sisters. To say there was some apprehension would be an understatement but we went with our heart and we packed everything I thought we needed and we took off for the reservation for the very first time ever. We had a wonderful reunion, a wonderful, joyous reunion and the first weekend itself, it was so overwhelming that we speak of it to this day. What a loss of being able to encapsulate emotions, you can't get to words. I mentioned earlier I had a fear of rejection. I think most adoptive children probably do. I can understand that completely. They have every reason to tend to suspect that they might be failing to pursue, or would rather not see you resurface. In my case, I think we maybe were lucky again in the fact that both biological parents were deceased at the time that I came home, so if there had been a bigger reason for the adoption it was all buried and we would never find out and my mother and father were both gone so when we returned it was to living siblings . . . my brother and sister were still living. It was my brother who first brought us in and that first weekend we met all the other family members that we could get to and we're still meeting family members to this day—thirteen years later that we've never met before. But we met a lot of family members on that weekend, mostly aunts and uncles, nieces and nephews that resided there on the reservation. We had a very joyous reunion. The thing I talk about with them always is the fact that it still overwhelms me to this day that we were accepted back in so quickly not only into our family but into the community and back into the tribe as well. The tribe itself seemed to be very open to bringing back into it a lost child, a lost family member.

How would you describe your relationship with your birth family today?

I would describe it as very healthy, very good, very positive. I haven't noticed anything in the line of resentment or jealousy. I know these are negative things I hear when I talk to so many people. We came back into a very healthy family. You know, reservation homes and families suffer greatly from many different types of dysfunctions, and are amplified from mainstream America. And so that certainly is the case on our reservation as well as all the rest of the Lakota reservations, whether it is Pine Ridge, or Rosebud, or anywhere else. So when you think about resituating yourself from a comfortable suburb, affluent suburb of Minneapolis, out onto an Indian reservation I think the number of dysfunctional homes is not small. I think we ended up in one of the few families that seem to have it all together. They are successful entrepreneurs or ranchers and relatively intact in terms of the other dysfunctions that plague the reservation life, so we ended up in a good home with good people.

How have you changed since finding your birth family?

How can I say it? I would say, I read a book here a while back before this all happened. I did a lot of motivation reading because I was frustrated out there in the regular workforce. I am an artist and a musician and that has plagued me my whole life in terms of work and occupational things to do. So I read a lot to try to understand this whole thing. I read a great book a while back, it's very popular. By Stephen Covey and it's the *Seven Habits of Highly Effective People*. And in that book he uses paradigm shifts, and that's the best term I can use to describe what I've gone through. The paradigm shift that Stephen Covey used in the book he shows you a sketch and tells you that the sketch is of the side of a building or the side of a mountain, and he asks you to look at it and see what you come up with. You go through this chapter and he shows you this sketch again and this time he says this is a picture of an elderly woman in profile. And you see it is. And he says that the paradigm shift that you've gone through is that you perceive the same set of lines but now you see them from a totally different perspective and they take on a new look and a new meaning. So life for me at that moment, totally shifted gears. I went through a paradigm shift. I would say that with the knowledge of becoming Native American and with the acceptance of the tribal family that I have taken a 180 degree shift from what I used to be and from how I lived and how I looked at the world and how I looked at other people. I have gone through a complete transformation in terms of my value system, in terms of how I function and I think the biggest shift has been spiritually.

DID YOUR RELATIONSHIP WITH YOUR ADOPTED FAMILY CHANGE IN ANY WAY AFTER MEETING YOUR BIRTH FAMILY?

I think at first I might have sensed a little bit of resentment in my brother in the fact that we had gone to search this out and it wasn't long after our first visit that this became the topic of almost every conversation almost for years in our family. My brother's a great guy but I might have sensed just a little bit of resentment in him. He never voiced it, nor did he ever take it to a point where it was noticeable, but I think I sensed it a little bit. But for the most part they were very happy for us, they were excited, they shared in the excitement that we had gone through. And so I would say that the biggest impact it had on our adopted family was probably two things: I think that it became a wonderful part of our life for all of our family members, I think they all shared in the joy we had gone through, the apprehension disappeared. It took some time, especially when we made the decision to move back on the reservation. That was a tough move in terms of acceptance from our adopted family, but in terms of my brother, the closest member of my family, I think it encouraged him to seek out his own background, too. Actually, seven years later from our reunion, he went through his search and was able to find his biological family as well. He may have not done that had we not done it first.

DID YOUR PARENTS EVER DISCOURAGE YOU OR YOUR BROTHER FROM TRYING TO FIND YOUR BIRTH FAMILY?

When they were living my adoptive parents, I guess I'll be honest with you, I don't think my brother or I ever had the slightest inkling or desire or burning passion to seek out our other families or even to inquire about it, as I recall. Mark or I never broached the subject. Out of respect for our parents. We never talked much about it. Mark and I never talked about it. He and I never sat down and talked about Hey you know, we're both adopted, what's the deal here? It never came up. It leads me to believe that in a best-case scenario that we were in such a comfortable and loving home that you maybe don't think too much about it. It could be that . . . others I've talked to . . . you know others who want to seek out their other families early in life even in their late teens or early twenties while their adopted families are still living, I've heard of all kinds of situations, I've heard of open adoptions where the children knew about it right off the bat, the families kind of shared the children between the two families and I think that that's fine. In our case, it was just that different. And it was my wife, Kathy, she and I got married when we were quite young. We got married when we were nineteen and twenty years old, and I think that Kathy carried a greater curiosity about my background than I ever did and it never came up between the two of us when we were dating or when we got married. I always just said that the time may come, it's certainly not now. And she was respectful of that, and she allowed me to keep that in its right place for many years. Of course I was thirty-eight before we ever really put the pieces together so almost for a twenty-year stretch she was able to keep that in its place that I had requested.

AFTER HIGH SCHOOL, DID YOU GO TO COLLEGE?

I went on to two years of trade school. I just don't think that I was academically college material. But I did pursue two years of tech school up in Minneapolis. Minneapolis was kind of the place to go if you came from southern Minnesota, so I attended technical school to learn architectural and civil engineering, drafting, and design, I studied those two respective fields, and ended up branching off into the technical parts of those in terms of drafting. I always was kind of artistic in my younger days, I like to draw, so I ended up getting into the drafting field and it has served our family well over the years. It was a trade that was good. There was plenty of work out there in various engineering fields for draftsmen, so it wasn't very fulfilling in terms of the artistic or the creative side, but that helped to pay the bills when the times were lean so it was good that I got through two years of school after high school.

TELL ME A LITTLE BIT MORE ABOUT YOUR WIFE AND YOUR TWO CHILDREN.

I met my wife when we were in high school and we began to date in my junior and her sophomore year, we were one year apart in terms of grades, a half-year apart in terms of age. And it was kind of like a storybook meeting, the two of us fell in love right away, early on, and were married young. You don't see that much anymore these days, but I wanted to complete those two years of school after high school, and we married immediately after those two years of school. A wonderful, wonderful woman, my wife. Great family that she came from, very stable and well respected in Worthington. Two wonderful children. The son is the elder of the two. They are twenty-eight and twenty-six, respectively. And I think that the one thing that I talk about these days about the children and about Kathy I think over the years they watched my plight closer than another family may have watched their father kind of go through trials and tribulations. Most of my life before the reunion was a series of cycles of struggle of trying to get into the world of music and then being rejected and having to get out and going back into the regular workforce and having to leave music sit there and take care of bills and then jump back into music when things were built up a little bit. Have a crash and then back into the workforce. And you can imagine this caused a bit of turmoil within our family in terms of a stable home environment. The consistent home environment my parents provided for me I was not able to duplicate inherently for our children but they were healthy and I think that they were intact and they always pulled for me. I speak about the fact that my wife has sacrificed many things over the years so that I could pursue my love for music. Now and certainly with this reunion, and this story goes on from there and we have gone on to be part of a wonderful career in the world of music but it's only because of the patience they had returning to the reservation. Many different little things have happened. So you know, I have a great family, a very understanding family. They stood by my side the whole way.

How did you and your family's life change after you found out you were Native American?

It changed drastically. I think that I'll try to encapsulate it for you. All of us except for my wife, Kathy, took on different identities. You can't help it. You become a different person. How do you become part of a different culture instantly. You think about somebody telling you in one phone conversation that I don't think I told you that it wasn't until my brother called me on that phone conversation two weeks before Thanksgiving 1993 what the deal was . . . but my brother's first words were, hey, bro, you're Lakota. You're skinned. Once that started to sink in, I had to absorb that, when you now take on a different identity and one that you've read about and seen in the movies that has carried with it a lot of stigma. Can you imagine today someone who thought they were part Native American and part French Canadian, think about this if someone said to you today, you don't know this but you are part Iraqi or Iranian, whoever told you. Because of the turmoil you've seen and heard about now part of you is on the other side of the fence. My perception of Native American was one paradigm when I grew up and now, in an instant, I am that paradigm that I imagined, so I have to reevaluate the whole process. How you think about it, have there been any negative thoughts (I don't think I had any negative thoughts) if I had any negative thoughts I would have realized that I focused those negative thoughts on myself not on somebody else. Standing on the other side of the fence, so you kind of have to go through a shift and it's an amazing thing. I think it really causes you to bare right now to the part of our human existence that I call the spiritual element. I never examined it closely when I was young and certainly nowadays I don't but I certainly realized I was Native American and with relatively high blood content so I wasn't one of those people who say that they have Native American way back in their family tree, in their great, great, great grandmother was part Cherokee, I'm three-quarter of Lakota. So you are right in the middle of the culture all of a sudden, definitely. And so my children are too. My children are too. They are still in the bloodline and are able to enroll in the tribe, and so now this whole world we are seeing in the part of the reservation it is our home, our world, the exploration of who we are and who my children are is still going on today. It's very heavy stuff.

YOU DECIDED TO MOVE BACK TO THE RESERVATION. WHAT LED YOU TO MAKE THIS DECISION?

Through a lot of encouragement. You can imagine. At the time all this was happening, this reunion back in 1993, I should tell you that we had moved from Worthington up to Minneapolis to make our home up there, and we did for many years. Our children grew up in the school system in Minneapolis and we actually settled in the suburb of Golden Prairie, one of the most expensive suburbs you could end up in. We were trying to provide the best for our children and our son was very involved in the sports program so we heard it had some of the best programs in the state so we situated ourselves up there but we were way out of our league always in terms of could we afford to be there. When you talk about a transition from Golden Prairie, Minnesota, to Lower Brule, South Dakota, you may as well pack up your bags and head out on a missionary trip to Africa or South America or something. That difference in the environments are just two totally different worlds. But we had visited there, we had gone back for the reunion, we had seen this world, we had seen this reservation. It just so happened that at that point we had come up to a low point. In terms of our struggle to try to stay in this expensive suburb of Minneapolis, we had kind of reached a point where it had almost imploded on itself. We were struggling financially. I had been out of music, I almost had given up on music, so in terms of where I was inside was at a low point, in terms of my self-esteem and I had started to slip into some bad habits myself and the family had noticed that. I would say that our family reached a low point. And it was our family out in South Dakota that said well, come on home . . . come on home. And even then, our family kind of looked at each other and said, "what, come back to the reservation?" Even at first it felt so foreign to us. It was impractical, it could never be. And we thought maybe this comment to come home would maybe be years later, Kathy and I would after retirement go to the reservation. But we started to realize that if you believe in these sorts of things where you are shown a direction to follow and you could try to follow that, and we thought we were shown a direction and we just had to take a leap of faith. And we did. We packed up and we basically took our belongings . . . we didn't have much back in those days, and we moved in one day in the summer of 1995. We packed up and we headed back and we moved onto the reservation, and there we were. Totally new world.

WAS IT A DIFFICULT TRANSITION?

It wasn't terribly difficult. The first summer was the toughest I would say. A couple of things that are important to mention in this story. One is that it is one thing for myself and our children to come to the reservation. We are now tribal members. The story was out, the word was out, so we were congratulated. There were handshakes and everyone was happy to see us come back. As you might know, it is kind of common in the Native American communities there is a stronger sense of family, and greater family unit so to speak. And so closer attention is paid to family members. So having a family member come back after many years of departure is a joyous thing. But my wife, now, Kathy . . . here's Kathy . . . a blue-eyed, blond Scandinavian coming on the reservation. She could have easily been given a hard time, but I would say that she was accepted back into this community just as openly as the rest of us were. I think she would tell you too she has never once faced criticism or racism or reverse racism or anything of that sort. She was made to feel totally comfortable. But the first summer was the most difficult. My brother, my biological brother, had found us this little house right on the little reservation housing community. You can't compare it to the town I grew up in. Where I grew up there was towns and towns had a business district and neighborhoods and reservation towns are different. Many of them don't have business districts, they have little housing areas that are designated here and there that are just kind of scattered around the reservation. So there wasn't really a town. We ended up in this little housing area. And it was a very rough start. The house was very dilapidated, we had some problems when we first moved in that we had to overcome, and life in the little reservation town was not really good, too good in terms of activity and things of that sort. We did stick it out for three months. But by the fall we had found a beautiful little house up in the country that we moved into and it has been our retreat, and our little dwelling, our little paradise, speaking to you from there right now. We are seven miles out of town, on top of a bluff that overlooks the Missouri River. And that became a very peaceful place for us. It has kept us connected with the community, and our brother's place is only seven miles away from here. So once we got that squared away, once we got into the right place, everything started to fall into place as well.

YOU SAID YOUR WIFE WAS VERY SUPPORTIVE. WHAT WAS YOUR CHILDREN'S REACTION?

It was a good move for them. I don't know if our children are just different. It's a combination of things with our children. I think I mentioned to you earlier my children always supported Kathy and I, first of all. I think they always felt that their parents were trying hard to do something a lot of parents don't do, like my pursuit of the arts was such over the years that instead of my children being resentful or angry at me in pursuit of this they have always been very encouraging. So they instantly realized too that this new life that we were embarking on was an exciting world to them. I think they looked at this more as a great adventure, much like imagining young kids taking off for an excursion to South America or Central America or some exotic place that we had never seen before. To them, coming to this reservation from Minneapolis was like, wow, this is wild, this is awesome. So they kind of had that excitement about it. Of course they were welcomed back into the community and they made friends. I think for the two of our children it was a healthy process as well. I guess I will say this now, I've said it before, they think that we are very, very lucky in this whole process. We are one of the stories that had a happy ending. Everything seemed to click pretty much just right. But we were lucky all the way around.

HOW HAVE YOU ADDRESSED THE ISSUE OF CULTURAL IDENTITY WITH YOUR CHILDREN?

We went through a process of what I have referred to as reverse assimilation. What I mean by that is while many of our people, Native American people it seems to be the most popular movement right now is for the people and the children on the reservations to want to assimilate off and want to be off the reservation and out into mainstream. The flow if given the right opportunities given the path of least resistance is to go into the mainstream. You don't find very often someone coming from mainstream back into the culture. And it is quite rare. So we were one of the families that went through this reverse assimilation process. Now we wanted to absorb, we wanted to learn, we have read extensively, we've had the wonderful opportunity to learn firsthand from our elders and tribal family members, and we have been able to attend ceremonies and social events and powwows and naming ceremonies. While many people in the world would be fascinated with a visit to the reservation we have been able to jump into the heart of it for more than a decade. So for us it has been just totally fascinating and wonderful all at the same time. We're still going through it. Speaking for myself and I'll be going through this reverse assimilation process for the balance of my life. I'm fifty-one years old today and I started when I was thirty-eight and I missed out on the early years so I'll be spending the rest of my life trying to learn and educate myself and understand not only the social aspects of our people, but the spiritual and the religious and the political and all these things, we work on them daily and weekly and it adds up to years. You can never replace having not grown up on the reservation. All you can do is try to absorb it as best you can.

Are there any barriers that have prevented you from fully integrating into the Native American community?

No. No barriers whatsoever. In fact we have been given totally free rein to go as deep into the culture as we feel comfortable with and by that I mean I have been allowed and encouraged, just on an individual basis, and I have been given opportunities to go so far back in the culture that I have attended some of the most sacred and spiritual of the ceremonies and I will continue to do that. Because it is the decision that I made. When I came back to the reservation I realized one of the things I noticed is that not everybody is of traditional thinking. I think most reservations are probably the same. There is a division there in terms of folks who are more contemporary and those who are more traditional. My family that I was reunited with follows more the contemporary side, to be honest with you. But I suppose because of my artistic streak all these years, I certainly lean toward the traditional side. I don't know if I'd grown up on the reservation if I'd want to carry that to want to be traditional or not, I don't know. But that's certainly how it has worked out. I don't feel there have been any barriers on the reservation. Certainly if I wanted to attend a Sundance ceremony or go on a vision quest I think that I would be supported and I would be given plenty of support in our community once you come back into this world you are part of the greater tribe as well. So I have friends from Rosebud, friends from Pine Ridge and Cheyenne River, all the various Lakota reservations. There is somewhat of a support system among the traditional thinking people so I haven't found a single barrier. One that I kind of anticipated and expected to be there really hasn't shown itself. That is the one you would carry from being one of the children who was sent out and has come back. I was ready for a little bit of resentment from some of the people, maybe jealousy or something. But I've never seen it. I've never come across an individual or a group of people who have shown anger toward me for coming back or any slighter version of that. It hasn't happened. I don't know. It's been support and acceptance along the way. It comes not only from people in my generation, it is in the elders above me, and the young children. So I'm going to continue to explore that and work on assimilating back into my culture.

YOU MENTIONED THAT YOU AND YOUR CHILDREN ARE ENROLLED IN THE TRIBE. CAN YOU TELL ME A LITTLE BIT MORE ABOUT THE ENROLLMENT PROCESS.

I run into a lot of people on my travels and one of the most common things I hear is that Oh, we've got a little Native American blood in our family tree too. My great, great, great grandmother was part Cherokee and of course but they always stop and the story ends that nobody kept the records, we can't find it, and nobody can prove it. That's the most common story.

And another kind of story is that I'm part Native American but my family buried information when I was a kid and so we're on a search right now, can you help us. I hear that story quite a bit. And in our case it happened like this. Because of that one envelope I told you about—without that envelope we might not be having this conversation—that envelope was a legal document that had my biological name on there, and it had my adopted name on there, all on the same piece of paper in reference to this adoption that took place in Pierre, South Dakota. So when we came back, part of our process of coming back here was to sort out the paperwork. In other words I never really felt like I assumed my true identity until the day that we walked out of the court with the actual papers. Here's what happened: we took the envelope that we had along with the information that my cousin had, the nun, and we went to the court in Pierre and were able to get a release of information document from the judge there. And that allowed us to go into the Pierre hospital and to go back into their records. The release was such that and my cousin still had enough contacts in the hospital that we went back into their archives and went back into their old files and lo and behold we were able to find my original birth certificate that had remained in the file in the Pierre hospital. On my original birth certificate was the same name that appeared on the envelope that we had from my house that was on my birth certificate and my birth certificate listed my mother and father . . . it listed both of their bloodlines. It was an easy process for us once we had that document approved, we put it all together and we had adequate information not only showing that we were who we were but that in fact showed our actual blood quantum along with everything else. So because of that there are certain various tribes have got certain points of where your blood quantum is enough for enrollment and where it is not. It's relatively high, I think it's a quarter or something like that in most of the Lakota tribes and so we were well above that, and it was enough to where myself and my children were certainly qualified to get our enrollments and again we pursued that. I am not in search of and of course with the stories out these days many people think that you're in search of hidden fortunes from casinos and things of those sorts. There is no such thing on our reservation or throughout the Lakotas . . . our reason for wanting to become tribal members was certainly a matter of the heart, and a matter of pride and kind of reclaiming our lost heritage, and so we did.

YOU MENTIONED THAT YOU ARE A MUSICIAN. CAN YOU TELL ME A LITTLE MORE ABOUT YOUR CAREER?

I struggled in the early years and it was my adoptive parents who encouraged me to get into music because they realized that as a young boy I suppose every child shows their certain talents and demonstrated love for music so they allowed me to get into music and I was an old rock and roller. I got into the world of rock and roll and was in my first band when I was fourteen years old and have then been into a lot of music ever since, and over the years I learned not only to perform but to produce music and to write music and to record music and to do all these things. But struggling to the point where I gave up on it, basically, just gave up on the whole thing at about the age of thirty-five. It had caused enough turmoil for our family. As you can imagine, part of our homecoming weekend was to share life stories so we began to tell our new family all we had been through in the world of music and there came a point when they stopped me and said, we should tell you something here. They took me to a wall full of pictures and there was a photograph of a beautiful elderly Lakota woman dressed up in her regalia sitting at an old upright piano. The piano was outside sitting in prairie grass about two feet tall, and she's playing it, and here it was my great, great grandmother. Mary Lou Alban, she was the only one in the community at the time who played the piano and she played by ear the same way I do and she really was important to the community because of her musical connections, so the story goes out. And my new family says, really you must not give up on your music because now you can go back into the world of music but you are to represent our people and our culture and our stories. So the thing that I lacked during the early years of music was I lacked the heart, I lacked the spirit, I lacked the story, I lacked the substance, the stuff every artist really has to have to make their stuff shine, and so here it was set right on the platter right in front of me. Even then I was a little apprehensive because I didn't want to have it appear that I was trying to use the culture and exploit it in some way. So I really took my time, but the family encouraged us to get back into music and tell the story of our people and to tell the stories I had been given. Bring them out to the world, use music as a format, so that's what we did. And it totally went past our wildest expectations. We began a little musical group called Brule, to get name recognition for our little tribal community and I don't know what to tell you. It's gone past our wildest expectations. We're eleven years into it and we still have our family group, my son and my daughter, myself, my wife is our manager, so we have a family group. We travel now and we've now recorded and released ten CDs. We've gone all over the world and we've been called to go over to Europe to go to the peace conferences to be music ambassadors for our culture and we have received numerous awards over the years for our efforts in music, and it just goes on and on. Very lucky. It was an infusion of the culture into the music. All I really did was combine the music I had grown up with as a young kid in the world of rock and roll and fused it to the world of Native America and it became something totally new.

DID YOU MAKE AN EFFORT TO LEARN MORE ABOUT NATIVE AMERICAN MUSIC?

Oh yeah. I've studied. It's part of the assimilation process I mentioned earlier. I'll be working on that the rest of my life. I have worked extensively on learning as many of the old traditional songs as I possibly can. We've always had several other members in the band, along with our family members, and even today we have a very prominent individual in our group who is from Pine Ridge. He is totally unique and he is so important to not only our family but to our people. He grew up as a young spiritual leader so we live together, we travel together, we work together and every day we can he encourages me to learn my language, teaching me to brush up on my Lakota, teaching me to study the old songs and to can the old stories, and of course I think there is one key word that I should throw into this thing when I talk to you about fusing these two different musical styles together to come up with a totally new art form. The key word that I found is respect. Because you don't want to take spiritual elements, you don't want to exploit certain things, but there are certain social aspects of our music that you can safely fuse into other musical styles. And that is how we have done this.

Again, we are very careful with how we do it. We always do it with the approval of our community of elders, we always ask before we release them and we are careful about it. I was taught that right at the very beginning and it has been a good lesson. There are people out there in the world who have done this differently and they have this new musical frontier and they do it in kind of an exploitive way and so I think that you can't do that. You've got to be very careful.

I work every week of every year I work a little bit on my traditional stuff.

Do you feel secure about your Native American identity today?

I do. I do feel very secure about it. I feel very proud about it, I'm comfortable on the reservation, I'm comfortable with my identity, while I will always remain a product of two worlds I have never moved so far that I have lost my identity from the first half of my life and I think that even if I reach 100 percent where I think I need to go into the culture I'll still be at the 50 percent point part World One and 50 percent part World Two and finding that common ground between these two worlds has now presented something totally different and we never expected that when this all began either and what that really is is that I found that being a product of two worlds and someone who's lived in both and understands both pretty well that you can then start to work as a diplomat or liaison for the two and so I've turned this whole thing into really kind of a life mission and what I've done is turn to music in my life and to use it. I want to be somebody who works on kind of healing, being the process between two cultures and to open up the doorway between these two worlds and to facilitate this process of bringing the two values and the two worlds a little closer together. I've found great joy in fulfilling that mission.

What people, resources or experiences have aided you in obtaining that sense of security?

I would say first and foremost it is our two families. I think that the acceptance by my biological family probably demonstrated to the community that this was going to be a warm and open reunion and once the family accepted this and proudly presented this to the community, I think the community took pride in having us back, and the tribe took pride in having us back. Once the tribe took pride in having us back I think that whole culture began to show signs that they were proud we were back and we're doing something good out there. And it's been that way on both sides as things happen to our families over on the other side of the fence. Once they saw what was going on they took great pride in knowing that we had done this and made this move and that our communities took pride in that back in Worthington, and then it went from pride in our community to being a product of Native America and recognized our efforts so it went all the way down the ladder on both sides and is very encouraging.

HAS INTERRACIAL ADOPTION BEEN A POSITIVE EXPERIENCE FOR YOU?

Absolutely. In our case, I would say that I think I could safely say that I've talked to thousands of adoptees. I'm very public, I perform in front of thousands of people every month and we have published a book about this whole thing. I would say that we have certainly landed on the high end, the positive side of the story like this. I can tell you that we have had probably the most positive of experiences that I've ever come across so has it been a positive experience? Absolutely. Of the highest kind.

WHAT HAVE BEEN THE ADVANTAGES AND DISADVANTAGES OF BEING TRANSRACIALLY ADOPTED?

The advantages were probably this: This is a very personal perspective. By having been removed from this culture, taken out into mainstream America, placed in a warm loving home, given an equal opportunity to become what I was supposed to be, in other words parents that encouraged me and loved me to develop as a child and then having had the opportunity to take back what the American education system of mainstream America has to offer and to bring that back into Native America at a point in life where I could still do something with it has been a totally overwhelming wonderful ticket in life. It depends what you want to do with it from that point on. In my case, I've elected to do something positive with it, when we are in possession between two things and you understand them both you can work for great positive wonderful things if you want to, so that's what I've done with that.

On the negative side, what are the disadvantages of this? Maybe one disadvantage is that sometimes I think it would have been nice to grow up on the reservation for better or worse. I think I could have done okay, but that was certainly not in the cards in our case, so I had no choice over that. Was there a disadvantage to growing up adopted in mainstream America over the reservation? No, not really. For some reason we were protected too from the vicious racism and discouragement that would have happened along the way. So the disadvantages I would have to say are very few. The advantages in our case are numerous. So we fall heavily on the being able to report back on the advantages of being a cross-cultural.

In general, do you approve of non-Indians adopting Indian children?

Yes, I do, although I tell you what. In my studies I have found now that it does not happen as much as it used to. I read up on this thing that we would know as the Indian Child Welfare Act, and so once again back at the point in history where I was being adopted out it was still common and I know now in today's world it is more complicated to adopt a Native American child. The process is difficult. The bureaucracy is such that it has to go through the tribal families before anything can happen and because of the deep family bond in our culture there will always be a willing family that will take a child in. Unfortunately the child may end up in a dysfunctional home but that's the way it operates now. The child is more apt to get put in a dysfunctional home on the reservation instead of being placed out into a warmer type of home off the reservation. I'm not quite sure about that whole thing. I have to examine it closer. I can certainly see why they were careful . . . about why the act was passed, but there was continually large scale adoption of children off the reservations. I believe at one point it was another step in the elimination of the numbers of people in our culture, there was a big flow of children off the reservation at one point, children being removed and taken out. I think that has been halted and reexamined. I think now more children stay on the reservation, so the adoption process of Native American children is probably a lot less than it was in 1945 or 1955 when I was born. I have no problem you know. You've listened to my story. I have no problem with a Native American child being raised by a non-Native family, but it would certainly depend on how that child's life is treated. Are they given a chance to come back to their culture. I have a few mixed emotions about it. But because my life is an example of what can happen I'll always stand for that process happening. I think it can happen and work out and have wonderful results.

What advice would you offer non-Indian families who would want to or who have adopted Indian children?

Quite simply put, the main ingredient in that child's life is going to be love. That child has to be given a warm loving environment so that the child can develop and grow properly. The imparting of information about the culture may or may not be important until that child is much older. I do think it is important now at this point that that child be allowed at some point in their life to come back and explore what their culture means to them, and I don't think that should be kept secret. I don't hold that against my parents,

I think the common practice in those days was to keep that information secret, it was a protective device and it wasn't intended to be harmful, or malicious, but times have changed and I think that information should be given to that child, and let the child be on his own when he is ready to go back into the other culture or to explore other family members, but certainly it is a beautiful culture, and the world is such now that the world is eager, it is so strange. There is such a fascination with Native American Culture and I truly believe that our culture has a lot to bring out to the world at this point in history. I think we are an important group of people spiritually at a point in history where American will be my example, but we are starting to implode in terms of our values and our integrity in terms of spiritual beings. That can come back to us, it can come back to our country, it can come back to our world from the edges. In terms of getting that child a properly functioning household and a warm, loving environment to grow up into certainly I think that it can be done by non-Native parents.

THAT WAS MY LAST QUESTION. IS THERE ANYTHING ELSE I SHOULD HAVE ASKED YOU OR ANY OTHER ISSUES YOU WOULD LIKE TO ADDRESS?

You've gone through all of your things. I'm pleased to hear that somebody is doing a study on this. I've had so many people ask me, I mean I never expected that one day there would be so many people with such a fascination for one individual who has had a chance to go back and forth between two different cultures. And so I am thankful that you considered us for your collection of stories and I hope I can bring a certain element to your collection of stories. I can tell you that I know that we will be on the high side in terms of the positive outcome, because I can relate to you incidences that are on the exact opposite end of the scale. I have run across many of them. I know that there are very sad stories in this process as well but we've been really fortunate and I don't know how unique we really are. I hope there are more that have had this opportunity like us, but we've been selected for some reason to be in this collection, so I never expected to have a sense of purpose quite so great and so bright in my life and have a mission at the end. I am very, very fortunate. I hope that helps you to put a balance in this collection of stories.

# 18

# NICOLAS LEECH-CRIER

Nicolas Leech-Crier (Saddle Lake Cree) was born in Edmonton, Alberta, in 1978 and placed in foster care for nearly eighteen months until he was adopted by a white couple in 1979. Nicolas describes his adoptive parents as "the most decent, responsible people [he] ever encountered" and notes that they had a close relationship until his adoptive mother passed away in 1989. After his adoptive mother died of cancer, Nicolas says that he became a "behavioral nightmare" for his adoptive father who returned him to foster care when he was twelve years old. According to Nicolas, he was placed with a Native family for one year and immediately began to experience "culture shock." After a year, he was placed in a Native group home where he began experimenting with drugs and alcohol.

Nicolas does not seem to harbor any ill will toward his adoptive father, but notes that their relationship is "distant at best." He says that he is unable to get close to anyone because of his "own personal issues." According to Nicolas, these personal issues include alcoholism, prison, and homelessness. He says that he has struggled with his addiction to alcohol off and on since he was a teenager. During those times that he was sober, he says that he attended classes and worked as a writer and research assistant. When his addiction got the best of him, he says that he was homeless and forced to perform "temporary, grunt manual labor." At the time of this interview, Nicolas had just gotten back on his feet. He did not have access to a phone and had to e-mail his answers to us, but he had secured a new job in landscaping and was hoping to return to school in the fall.

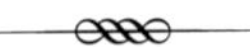

WHAT YEAR WERE YOU BORN?

Sunday, January 29, 1978, Aquarius, Year of the Horse.

WHERE WERE YOU BORN?

The Royal Alexandra Hospital in Edmonton, Alberta, Canada.

HOW OLD WERE YOU WHEN YOU WERE ADOPTED?

Eighteen months.

ARE YOU AWARE OF THE CIRCUMSTANCES SURROUNDING YOUR ADOPTION? (THAT IS, WHAT DO YOU KNOW ABOUT YOUR BIRTH FAMILY?)

I really do not know much about the pre-adoption period of my life. I was apparently in foster care until I was matched with my adoptive parents in 1979. They said I was healthy when we met, so they assume my care must have been adequate.

TELL ME ABOUT YOUR ADOPTIVE PARENTS. WHAT DO THEY DO FOR A LIVING?

My adoptive parents were/are the most decent, responsible people I have ever encountered. My father, David, of Irish/Scottish descent, immigrated to Canada from California in 1972 and worked in a wide variety of occupations, including stints as a prize-winning photojournalist and a forest ranger, before returning to school and becoming a petroleum engineer. Today he runs a well-test analysis company. My mother, Shirley, was born in England and moved to Canada while still a young girl. When her and my father met, she was attending college in Calgary, but then quit to get married and have children. All was well and good until I was ten years old and she developed a malignant brain tumor. She was hospitalized for a long time. Then she died. Since, my father has remarried to an amazing lady, Lizzy, and seems pretty happy. She works with him as a business manager.

HOW WOULD YOU DESCRIBE YOUR RELATIONSHIP WITH THEM?

I would describe my relationship with them as distant, at best, and yet unusually strong for my particular generation and cultural and social circumstances. The distance mainly has to do with my own personal issues (addictions, street involvement, prison, etc.), and the discomfort they cause me in facing these people who have shown nothing but compassion and love for me and who have made great efforts to instill in me a healthy value system and for whom I have caused immeasurable grief and heartache. Were things different, that is, were I to be actually living a healthy and stable life, I have no doubt our connection would be much stronger.

Why did they decide to adopt? Did they ever indicate to you why they decided to adopt an American Indian child?

According to my father, my mother was in a hurry to have kids. She'd already suffered an ectopic pregnancy that destroyed half of her system and apparently the doctors felt chances were good that it would happen again. As for any sort of cultural inclination: "Kids were kids," they thought. Peculiar how my mother's sense of urgency was foreboding of her early passing.

When did you first realize that you were adopted? What was your reaction? Describe the circumstances.

I have pretty much always known I was adopted. At least, my parents were always open and honest about it. I probably did not actually fully understand the concept until I was into grade school and began to feel my way around the reality of it all. Before this, I do not really recall it making much of a difference in my life. I was basically just another happy suburbanite kid, oblivious to things like race or even social class, I suppose. Once I understood though, for a long time it made me feel special, like I was somehow privileged to have been specially selected. Until, of course, racism reared its ugly head. Then I began to have questions, wonder what it was that made me different and why I couldn't have been raised by my birth family, whoever they might be. I recall much confusion throughout this period. Much fascination, as well. Simply, the notion that parents could actually give up their children and someone else would come along and take care of them, was intriguing to me. As was the fact that I was the only person I'd even known (aside from my siblings) who was adopted.

Do you think that your adoptive parents handled this revelation in a positive manner?

Yes. Obviously, they understood that questions regarding my adoption were inevitable. They knew that the best way to handle this was to be honest and forthcoming right from the beginning and that this in turn would make the learning process easier for me, which indeed it did. I cannot recall exactly what I may have asked, but it was probably the basic sorts of questions: Why did my parents give me up? What happened to them? Will I ever see them again? All of these were answered as sincerely and honestly as possible, considering what little information they'd actually had concerning my origins, et cetera.

WAS THE FACT THAT YOU ARE AN AMERICAN INDIAN TALKED ABOUT A LOT IN YOUR FAMILY? DESCRIBE.

Maybe not "talked" about, per se, but certainly acknowledged. I was always told "you're Native." I believe they may have even been able to give me a tribe: Cree. Again, honesty was their policy, although their knowledge of the history or culture of aboriginal peoples was limited and much of my understanding of these issues came later on, through various other life experiences.

WHAT DID YOUR ADOPTIVE PARENTS DO TO GIVE YOU A SENSE OF YOUR CULTURAL IDENTITY?

I remember my Pop spending weeks of evenings making this giant yellow thing from nylon, with a big rainbow on it. We took a trip out to the mountains to cut down a bunch of pine trees and skinned the bark from them in our backyard. When it was finally done, he called my brother and sister and I together and asked us if we would like to learn how to set up a "tipi." I remember thinking "Cool." We set it up in the backyard and there you had it: white parents with three Native kids, who now had their own family tipi to go camping with (we were big into camping). It was waterproofed, had a floor and best of all, it made us stand out wherever we camped. We were all so proud of that tipi, despite our youthful ignorance of its cultural significance, simply because our Pop had made it himself and it was just plain cooler than those ugly trainers and tents everyone else camped in. All in all, I believe they did their best to encourage a sense of identity, pride, and understanding concerning my heritage: taking us out to the Indian Village at the Calgary Stampede each year, local powwows, et cetera. I was really only seeing half the picture here (the positive half, I guess), but half a picture is better than no picture at all.

DO YOU HAVE SIBLINGS—BIRTH OR ADOPTED?

In my adoptive family there are three of us, all aboriginal. I am the oldest, then my brother, Colin, then our younger sister, Kelsey. I also have birth siblings. An older sister, Joanne, and a younger sister, Nicole.

ARE YOU CLOSE TO YOUR SIBLINGS?

No. Again, I deal with personal confidence issues that keep me at a distance.

DO YOU TALK WITH THEM ABOUT BEING AN AMERICAN INDIAN?

I have. I have even spent time on my brother's reserve (he never has). It seems to me that I am basically the only one who has shown any real zeal toward my cultural experience. But that's okay. They'll come around.

DO YOU FEEL OR HAVE YOU BEEN TOLD THAT YOU POSSESS STRONG AMERICAN INDIAN PHYSICAL FEATURES? HOW HAS YOUR PHYSICAL APPEARANCE AFFECTED THE WAY IN WHICH YOU HAVE BEEN PERCEIVED BY BOTH THOSE IN THE INDIAN AND NON-INDIAN COMMUNITIES? HOW HAS YOUR PHYSICAL APPEARANCE SHAPED YOUR CULTURAL IDENTITY?

Oddly enough, Native American is usually the last thing people guess. I have been told I look Greek, Spanish, Black . . . heck, even been guessed white once or twice. I do in fact look Cree, if you know how good the Cree tend to look (Ahhhh, jokes!). As for how it has affected my cultural identity, it's like this: Calgary is smack dab in the middle of Blackfoot country and the Blackfoot have their own distinct sort of beauty, which of course, mainstream society assumes is how we all must look, because there's really no difference, right? So, basically I find people tend to presume that because I don't look "Indian," (i.e., long-haired, buckskinned, stoic and savage demeanor) I must not be.

HOW DO YOU THINK YOUR PHYSICAL APPEARANCE AFFECTED THE MANNER IN WHICH YOU PERCEIVED YOURSELF AS A CHILD, AS A TEENAGER, AND AS AN ADULT?

I would say that it has at times caused me huge amounts of personal inner turmoil and at other times I've wondered why I never took up modeling. I never really took to the "braids and feathers" type thing (mainly because my hair is far too kinky, I end up with a massive "fro") and never having actually *been* a rich kid, my style has always been "thrifty," to put it mildly. I survived. However, I prefer to believe that I am beyond aesthetics now, mainly thanks to a decade of street life that taught me: This ain't no fashion show babe, this is Life.

TO WHOM DID YOU TALK ABOUT THE FACT THAT YOU WERE AN AMERICAN INDIAN? WHAT PEOPLE OR RESOURCES AIDED YOU IN THIS PROCESS? HAVE

YOU READ A LOT OF BOOKS ABOUT YOUR TRIBE? DO YOU FEEL THAT THEY OFFER AN ACCURATE PORTRAIT OF YOUR CULTURE? ARE THERE LIMITATIONS TO RELYING SOLELY ON BOOKS FOR THIS INFORMATION? WHAT EFFECT DID THE MEDIA HAVE ON YOUR PERCEPTION OF YOURSELF?

I never really spoke to anyone about it. I just sort of went along with my life and when it would come up, which was rarely, I would basically just reference the images I'd seen my whole life in conventional medium: TV, movies, etc., that portrayed us a "noble savages." When someone asked me if I could hunt buffalo, I would reply, with a straight face "Duh, of course I can, but I left my bow and arrow at home." As for books and media, it is a well-known fact that mainstream school curriculum, in North America anyway, tend to bias in favor of Eurocentric interpretations of history and the media can rarely be counted on for anything other than selective, technical accuracy, which really makes it only more likely to perpetuate racist misconceptions already entrenched within the majority of society's collective awareness. The effect this had was that I eventually became, as cliché as it may sound, lost, "adrift between two worlds."

WHERE DID YOU GROW UP?

After my adoptive mother passed on, I became a behavioral nightmare for my father and eventually I was returned to foster care at twelve. I was placed with a native family and immediately began to experience culture shock. These Indians were what would probably be deemed as, socioeconomically speaking, poor. Not destitute or anything, but they lived in a townhouse, with seven people under one roof. Not exactly what I had been used to, growing up in the rich white suburbs. As well, they were the first Native people I had ever gotten to know and for the first little while I didn't like them at all. They spoke with what I perceived, at the time, as a crude and embarrassing accent. This, obviously, was due to the fact that English was not their first language—Blackfoot was. I lived there for about a year then moved to a Native group home in Calgary, called Nekinan ("Our Home" in Cree), and spent six years crossing the threshold between fundamental ignorance to total reception of my cultural reality. I learned a lot about the history and the truth. I also learned a lot about why we are in many of the situations we are today. But mostly, I was still just young and wanting to fit in. Nekinan helped me do this. Us six or seven kids were family and we were very close, both with each other and the staff, who worked in rotating twelve-hour shifts. Of course, this is where all the addiction issues began as well, but all in all I remember mostly good things about my time there.

Describe the places you lived and the schools you attended. Did you encounter any form of racism growing up? How did you address this issue? Did your parents prepare you for this challenge?

For years, I was the only native kid in school, so I was still not interacting with any sort of contemporary peer group, which hindered my learning and acceptance a great deal. As for racism, I know it existed, but the type of people I usually hung with, social outcasts, nerds and the like were, as far as I was concerned, beyond this type of mindset. It simply did not concern us. We were unpopular plenty as it was, why bother? As I mentioned, my folds were very open-minded people. My father, in particular, had experienced prejudice and discrimination firsthand as a youth growing up with long hair in the 1960s. Obviously not quite the same thing but, as he always taught, the principle still stands: fight back with your mind, your spirit, and your heart, not your fists.

Do you remember learning about native Americans in school? What did you learn? Would you say that the information you learned about Native Americans in school differs dramatically from the information you learned once you began interacting personally with those in the Native community?

I do not really remember much about what we were taught in school regarding Native people (it was most likely obsolete and slanted anyway), but I do remember my spirit swelling with pride whenever Indians were brought up, which was of course, seldom. I also recall my spirit nearly crumbling with shame, confusion, and hurt since I've begun my "real life" education—from those first derogatory slugs, sniggers, and laughter by young and carelessly naïve minds out in the school yard (indeed, made in my very presence—I don't "look" Native, remember), to the most recent years of drinking in a dingy alley with a seventy-five-year-old aboriginal World War II veteran, a true Canadian hero, who to this day has still never received any sort of recognition or compensation from the government that sent him out there. The same government, in fact, who upon his homecoming told him he still did not have the right to vote and advised him to return to the reserve and pick up his welfare cheque. They never taught these things in school. It was all bannock and beads and the blood-spattered Sundance, and Hey Yah Yah, Hey Yah Yah.

No wonder ignorance is so rampant.

Who were your closest friends in school?

Close? Never close. There were other misfits that I hung with, but only within the guarded chambers of school itself. Outside the classroom, I lived pretty much in my own little world. I'm probably still living there today. The ones I did connect with though, as I mentioned, were always the outsiders, the ones who knew that I was Native and didn't care because their parents had fortunately taught them that the true value of humanity stems from acceptance. Or maybe they just knew no one else would hang out with me and took pity. Either way, I never really bonded with my peers until around high school, when fitting in with the badass "Nichi" bros became my all-consuming endeavor.

DID YOU GO TO COLLEGE? WHERE? WHY THAT SCHOOL? WHAT WAS YOUR MAJOR?

In the fall of 1999 I completed a six-month "Pre-Employment to the Arts" initiative, funded by the federal government. Through this project, I somehow began to realize that I was somehow a writer. I applied to attend some high school upgrading courses at the local community college and upon seeing my ability the faculty placed me in Grade 12 English and some computer courses. I did well at these, earning Honors standing. I was not eligible to apply for postsecondary. I applied to the Southern Alberta Institute of Technology and was accepted into the Journalism Arts two-year diploma program. With help from my band (tribe, nation), I paid for my laptop and a few thousand dollars worth of photography equipment and I began attending classes full-time in fall of 2000. I lasted about a month. I dropped out when I realized that my life was just still too chaotic, too unmanageable to allow such a major commitment. I still kick myself for that decision today. In fact, I would say that this has been the defining characteristic of these last few years of total depravity: lament.

WHAT KIND OF WORK DO YOU DO NOW?

During my upgrading I was offered a position as a writer/research assistant with a national monthly called *Aboriginal Times*. I took the job and wrote for them for two years. Loved it. Livin' the dream, straight up. I even was able to conduct an interview with Buffy Sainte-Marie. Due to some management issues, I chose to leave in 2001 and basically went back to the type of work all the other drunken homeless people were doing? Temporary, grunt manual labor. Stuck with this off and on, until today. See, last summer I managed to stay sober long enough to complete a course in which I received a few minor industry tickets (Forklift Operation, First Aid, etc.) but all told, I have just been trying my best to live tucked safe underneath this dreadful rock of isolation (which has apparently taken me years to design for myself, somehow without my ever realizing I was doing it). Then, three weeks ago I moved to Vancouver, BC, and just today, in fact, have found work as a landscaper, and do plan to return to school in the fall, for real this time. I still write on occasion and have been trying to put more effort toward art lately, but the great novel is still to come. So, things are never as bad as they seem, or so it seems.

WHO ARE YOUR CLOSEST FRIENDS TODAY?

Drunks, drug addicts, homeless vagrants, criminals, prostitutes, and of course good-hearted shelter staff. Like I said, just today I landed what will be my first full-time job in a while. So, solvency will take a while and knowing my sensibilities, socialization of any other kind will take longer.

DO YOU HAVE ANY TIES TO AN AMERICAN INDIAN TRIBE? EXPLAIN.

Not American (unless you agree with me that we are all One), but yes, I belong to Saddle Lake First Nation, which falls into treaty #6, signed in 1876 by about fifteen chiefs from the northern Alberta/Saskatchewan region. We are Cree.

ARE YOU AN ENROLLED MEMBER OF A TRIBE? WHY OR WHY NOT? HOW HAS THIS AFFECTED YOUR SENSE OF CULTURAL IDENTITY OR DOES IT?

Being part of a tribe helped me to realize the importance of knowing one's historical heritage, but as most Natives will tell you, a "status" card is just a card. Obviously, being Indian means more than a number in a government ledger. It is a way of life, a moral philosophy, and a sense of place and cultural identity that we can only realize for ourselves through our life experience, and by listening to the words of our elders, who know truth from having gone before.

HOW HAS THE FACT THAT YOU ARE NATIVE AMERICAN AFFECTED BOTH YOUR PERSONAL AND PROFESSIONAL LIFE?

In some ways it has caused frustration and strife: ignorant fools always bemoaning the "Indian Problem" (i.e., I didn't steal your land, why should I pay? How come you Indians get everything for free? Why are so many Indians on welfare? Yadda, yadda, yadda). In some ways it has been amazingly convenient (i.e., schools swoon over talented Native writers, no one on the street dares fuck around with Natives—we're tough. Oh yeah, chicks dig it).

ARE YOU MARRIED? IF YES, TO WHOM?

Nope. As one ex put it so poetically: I'm not "marrying material" Huh.

Do you have children?

None. Yet. One day, hopefully.

How do you identify yourself today?

I am a human being, Nehiyaw (Cree), an artist, a lover, a believer, and a basically not-ugly young male Canadian.

When did you take on that identity? How?

I took on this identity when Creator and my mother both decided to gift me with it at birth. It is the only identity I could or will ever have, so why not shout it out, loud and proud?

Have you sought out your birth family? Why or why not? How old were you when you decided to look for them? What prompted this decision? Are you comfortable or uncomfortable with spending time with your birth family?

I discovered my birth family through a total fluke. I was covering an aboriginal youth conference outside of Calgary and talking with a friend of mine (I knew I was from Saddle Lake at this point) who was also from Saddle Lake and he introduced me to his dad. We got to talking and he mentioned that he thought he might know who my family are. That night I got a call from my aunt Margaret, my mother's sister. I was amazed to the point of total speechlessness. My biological mother, Helen, had passed on from cirrhosis a few years earlier, so I never had the privilege of meeting who I have been told was an incredibly strong and gracious woman. But I met my sisters, Joanne and Nicole. That was the summer of 2000. I have not seen them since. Again, mostly due to my own insecurities. I hope to remedy that soon.

Why do you personally feel that it is important to find your birth family? How have you changed since finding your birth family?

I have not changed, unless you count regression. I felt it was extremely important to find my family; they are, after all, my family. But when I did find them, I don't think I was quite ready. I was in fact doing really well at the time, as were they, yet I somehow managed to find my way back to that ol' slippery slope we call addiction, and poof! Any trace of self-respect that might have been there was now gone, like so much sacred smoke carrying tragic prayers of woe off to a distant and unknown hope. But there is one very important thing I've learned about change: you can always change again.

Did your adoptive parents support your decision to search for your birth family? Did your relationship with your adoptive family change as a result of this decision? How?

Yes. As always, they support me no matter what. I think my stepmother might have said something like "don't you forget about your Pop now," but of course, that was never a consideration for me. I love my Pop. Like I said, I'm still distant, but he knows I love him and all the rest of my family. Both families, actually.

Did you return to your reservation? Did you experience any type of "culture shock" upon returning to the reservation? Did these two worlds clash in any way? If so, how?

I returned to Saddle Lake once. To meet my sisters and attend the annual powwow. No culture shock. I had already been around my people for years (even done some grass dancing and drumming myself, too), so it actually felt great to go to my first "home" powwow. I fit in easily with my family and even met some new friends. I had basically already been desensitized toward the poverty thing, from trips to the Blood reserve with my foster family, but these were *my* people. Man, seeing my uncle Marvin dance in the men's grass competition and, being traditional, not compete, that was about the coolest damn thing ever.

Are there any barriers that have prevented you from fully integrating into the Indian community?

My alcoholism. Their alcoholism. My reckless sensitivity to a past I know, yet do not know. The government that still claims to care, while simultaneously enforcing assimilative measures against my people. The society that allows this to continue. Fear. Shame. Anger. I could go on.

Do you feel secure or insecure about your Indian identity today?

Secure? Identity theft is probably the industrialized world's biggest threat at the moment. But who's gonna steal an Indian identity? Nah, I'm fine. Like I said, being Nehiyaw is more about walking the walk and less about talking the talk.

Do you feel accepted by Indians outside your birth family? Describe.

You'd have to ask them. Like anywhere, you have your good and you have your bad. I have mixed with both and sometimes not mixed with any. Take me or leave me, that's what I say.

ARE YOU GLAD THAT YOU WERE ADOPTED BY A WHITE FAMILY?

I'm glad I was adopted and didn't have to grow up in a poverty stricken, alcoholic environment. Odd that I ended up there anyway, eh?

WHAT IS YOUR OPINION OF THE INDIAN CHILD WELFARE ACT? DO YOU APPROVE OF WHITE FAMILIES ADOPTING NATIVE AMERICAN CHILDREN? EXPLAIN.

Wow, I've spent years dealing with child welfare and I have never once been asked these questions. Naturally, I have some issues. My opinion of Child Welfare is one of bitter resentment mixed with even more bitter resentment. For years, all through the foster home and group home phases, I watched social workers sideline children and youth and go about making major decisions for people they knew nothing about and whose opinions they never seemed to even want to hear, let alone acknowledge. Especially, in the Native Child Welfare system, where if the social worker wasn't white, it was an Indian trying to be white, I would constantly perceive an attitude of condescendence and superiority, always being told that I was incapable of knowing what I wanted because I was "too young" and since I obviously had behavioral issues, why should they listen anyway. Never once was I asked what I wanted. Anyway, I'm glad that's over with now. I personally think it did more harm than good. As for whites adopting Natives, I can't really say.

Obviously, each situation is different. I was blessed with a loving set of adoptive parents, who never abused or neglected me and who always encouraged me to seek out my own identity in the world with passion and honor. Not everyone will be so fortunate. In general, if the parents are proven to be strong and healthy and good, then it should not matter what race they are. Race is a basically illusory and counterproductive notion anyway. It is not what's underneath that matters either. It is what we do that defines us.

DO YOU HAVE ANY QUESTIONS OR ADVICE YOU WOULD LIKE TO OFFER WHITE FAMILIES WHO WOULD WANT TO OR HAVE ADOPTED NATIVE AMERICAN CHILDREN?

Let us learn from our mistakes and use this knowledge to create a better world for future generations. Teach children to be proud of their heritage. Teach them the value of education and respect for the environment. Let them be whatever they want to be and help them find their way on this journey by asking them questions about it. Lead by example. Trust. Never forget that all people have a right to an identity of their own and that this identity can only be discovered by them. If these values are nurtured in earnest, the fruits of your labors will bloom tenfold. As the elders teach, we did not inherit this land from our ancestors, we borrowed it from our children.

IS THERE ANYTHING ELSE I SHOULD HAVE ASKED YOU OR ANY OTHER ISSUES THAT YOU'D LIKE TO ADDRESS?

Not really, I am just thankful for such an amazing opportunity to speak on these topics. It has been enlightening, to say the least. Thanks to Sarah for introducing me to this incredible project and thanks to my family for giving me a great story to tell and thanks to my elders for teaching me what it means to be myself.

Migwetch (Thank You).

## 19

# JONATHAN OLD HORSE

Born in 1969, Jonathan Old Horse (Oglala Lakota) was taken from his twelve-year-old mother two hours after his birth. According to Jon, his mother was an orphan living at Oglala Community School in Pine Ridge, South Dakota, when she became pregnant with him. He said he was taken from his mother's care without her consent and placed with a middle-to-upper-class white family.

Jon and his two siblings, one of whom is also an American Indian adoptee, grew up in suburban neighborhoods located in Iowa, California, and Colorado. He describes his relationship with his adoptive family as "very good" and mentions that they took him and his brother, Andrew (Standing Rock Sioux), to powwows and tried to involve them in the urban Indian community. Jon notes, however, that despite his parents' best efforts to help him develop a sense of cultural identity, he often tried to "hide" the fact that he was Indian. He says, "I really had a hard time. I didn't like to explain myself to people."

According to Jon, his attitude changed after he was discharged from the Army National Guard. In the army, Jon says, "they are happy to have an Indian within their ranks because they know the history of the Lakota people." After being discharged, Jon also reunited with his birth family who took the time to answer his "questions about anything and everything" and taught him the Lakota language. Since reuniting with his birth family, Jon has become a sundancer and regularly attends powwows in the Pine Ridge area.

Jon believes that there are advantages and disadvantages to transracial adoption. He says that he is grateful to his adoptive parents for instilling within him a strong work ethic and for ensuring that he received a good education. The disadvantage is that he had to struggle to learn his tribal traditions and form a healthy sense of cultural identity. He says that he is not opposed to white families adopting Native American children, but encourages adoptive parents to respect their children's culture because "sooner or later . . . it's going to be calling them back to be Indian again."

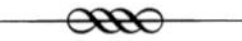

WHAT YEAR WERE YOU BORN?

1969.

WHERE WERE YOU BORN?

Sioux City, Iowa.

HOW OLD WERE YOU WHEN YOU WERE ADOPTED?

Six weeks.

AND ARE YOU AWARE OF THE CIRCUMSTANCES SURROUNDING YOUR ADOPTION?

Yes, I am.

CAN YOU TELL ME A LITTLE BIT ABOUT THAT?

My mother was an orphan. My grandma and grandpa passed away when she was nine, and—my uncle and my aunt—they had her go to the OCS, which was the primary boarding school. And when she was pregnant with me, she was twelve years old. And the policy back then in the late 1960s was to take all the young pregnant girls to the Florence Crittenton Home in Sioux City, Iowa, by bus.

And they kept them there 'til the baby was born. And she said that, you know, there was nobody there to say that this wasn't right, this wasn't a good thing to do, because they were orphans—there were no older people to take care of her. And she never signed away any papers to give me to anybody. They just kind of took me, because that was the policy back then. And she got to hold me for two hours, and they took me away. And then on the 27th of March, they put her on a bus and took her back to Pine Ridge Indian Reservation.

AND WHAT DO YOU KNOW ABOUT YOUR BIRTH FATHER?

My birth father—his name is Joseph Charging Crow. He is from the Eagle Nest district of Pine Ridge Indian Reservation. He's a Vietnam veteran.

AND CAN YOU TELL ME A LITTLE BIT ABOUT YOUR ADOPTED PARENTS?

My adopted parents, their names are Dean and Sharon. They're now divorced. My father has a Ph.D. in sociology, and my mother has a masters in education. And their first choice—my dad's first choice was to adopt Portuguese children. But at the time, they had an overabundance of Indian children. They were having a hard time trying to find Portuguese children. They asked if they were willing to adopt an Indian baby. And they have one birth child which was my sister—that's their biological daughter.

SO HOW DO YOU DESCRIBE YOUR RELATIONSHIP WITH THEM?

It's very good. We had a hard time kind of dealing with their divorce, because we were little kids. They've really—my family, my Lakota family, they've told them how many times that they are thankful that they took us, and you know, raised us to be strong good men.

AND WHEN DID YOU FIRST REALIZE THAT YOU WERE ADOPTED?

We've known our whole lives.

HAVE YOUR PARENTS EVER SAT YOU DOWN AND TALKED TO YOU ABOUT IT?

Yes.

AND THEY'VE HANDLED THE REVELATION ABOUT YOUR ADOPTION IN A POSITIVE MANNER?

I think so. They did their best, as we were in an urban environment, to always let us know that we were Indian. Took us to powwows and read books and all those kinds of things. They did the best they could for me in an urban community, not knowing any Indians personally in their community. When we then lived in Ames, Iowa, they knew a lot of people that were Muskwaki they were always trying to let us know that we were Indian.

HOW MANY SIBLINGS DO YOU HAVE?

I have two.

WHO ARE ADOPTED?

Yeah, all together. On my adopted family, I have a brother and a sister. And then my biological family, I have five brothers and six sisters.

AND YOUR ADOPTED BROTHER IS INDIAN TOO?

Yes.

AND IS HE FROM THE SAME TRIBE OR IS HE FROM A DIFFERENT TRIBE?

He's from Bull Head community, Standing Rock Reservation.

AND DID IT MAKE IT EASIER FOR THE BOTH OF YOU TO HAVE ANOTHER SIBLING WHO WAS ADOPTED AND WHO WAS INDIAN WHEN YOU WERE GROWING UP?

I don't really think it made any difference. Me and my brother have always been close to each other. I think that's why they ended up adopting another Indian boy.

SO ARE YOU BOTH CLOSE TO YOUR SISTER?

Not really. I mean, we talk and all that, but we're not—I don't talk to her as often as I would my brother. She has a rather different lifestyle and a different view on things.

CAN YOU DESCRIBE THE PLACES YOU LIVED IN AND THE SCHOOLS YOU ATTENDED?

We lived in Iowa, lived in Denver, Colorado, we lived in Fresno, California. And then we moved back into the suburbs of Denver, and then I lived in Alaska for some years.

DID YOU ENCOUNTER ANY FORM OF RACISM GROWING UP?

When we lived in California, we were mistaken for being Mexican. But growing up in the communities that we did it was almost a sickly outpouring of showing off their Indian children in their schools to the different people.

DO YOU FEEL OR HAVE YOU BEEN TOLD THAT YOU POSSESS YOUR OWN AMERICAN INDIAN PHYSICAL FEATURES?

Yes.

AND HOW DO YOU THINK YOUR PHYSICAL APPEARANCE HAS AFFECTED THE WAY IN WHICH YOU'VE BEEN PERCEIVED BY BOTH THOSE IN THE INDIAN COMMUNITY AND THOSE IN THE NON-INDIAN COMMUNITY?

Well, in Denver, the Denver community there's all kinds of different tribes there. And they have a strong bond with each other. And then there's another kind of Indian who's always got a strong animosity. Especially those different kinds of Indians have five, six different types of Indian blood that run through them and when they—when they're around the full-blooded Lakota people, they're kind of snobby—snotty to you.

AND HOW DO YOU THINK THIS REACTION AFFECTED YOUR OWN SENSE OF SELF?

I don't think it really bothered me. And I felt more bad for them, because they had to explain why they have five or six different tribes and that claim just to make themselves more Indian.

TO WHOM DID YOU TALK TO ABOUT THE FACT THAT YOU WERE AN AMERICAN INDIAN?

Apparently nobody. Actually, when I grew up, I really—I had a hard time with it, being Indian, you know. I don't know what the deal was as I started getting older. I was finding myself being the same Indian, actually and was trying to hide it. It wasn't until—I guess I've always known who we were—being Indians. I really didn't start to want to be Indian 'til after I'd gotten out of the army.

YOU DIDN'T KNOW ANYTHING THROUGH THIS?

Growing up, I really had a hard time. I didn't like to explain myself to people. Like, how come you don't look like your mom or your dad? Do you know if those are your parents? You don't look like them. I was around a lot of Mexicans, there's quite a few Mexicans in the area that we're at—not their culture, just them.

WHO WERE YOUR CLOSEST FRIENDS IN SCHOOL GROWING UP?

Race-wise?

YES.

My closest friends growing up—I had a white friend and we were friends with the only black family in the whole school district where we went to school.

DO YOU REMEMBER LEARNING ABOUT INDIANS IN SCHOOL?

Yes.

AND WOULD YOU SAY THAT THE INFORMATION YOU'VE LEARNED ABOUT INDIANS IN SCHOOL DIFFERS DRAMATICALLY FROM THE INFORMATION YOU

LEARNED ONCE YOU BEGAN INTERACTING PERSONALLY WITH THOSE IN THE INDIAN COMMUNITY?

They were too stereotypical of Indians when they did their instructions in my school days, and I learned a lot more by being around Indian people.

DID YOU GO TO COLLEGE?

Yes.

WHERE DID YOU GO?

I went to the Oglala Lakota College, and then I went to Aurora Community College in Colorado.

AND WHAT WAS YOUR MAJOR?

History.

AND WHY WERE YOU INTERESTED IN THAT SUBJECT?

I've always liked history, and maybe being able to go back into those times right now and to look into things from a different perspective and to see how—what happened in the past, kind of, and it molded how we live now and how it's going to be later on in our lives.

WHAT KIND OF WORK DO YOU DO NOW?

I'm a chef, and I'm in the Army National Guard, but I'm in the process of going back on active duty, army status.

WHO ARE YOUR CLOSEST FRIENDS TODAY?

My closest friends today?

UH-HUH.

Their names are Howard and Jason. They're both soldiers that I served with in the army.

DO YOU HAVE ANY TIES TO THE INDIAN TRIBE TODAY?

Yes, I do.

AND ARE YOU AN ENROLLED MEMBER OF YOUR TRIBE?

Yes.

AND WAS THAT AN EASY PROCESS OR WAS THAT SOMETHING THAT WAS DONE FOR YOU?

Once I met my family—the day after our first meeting, we went to the Enrollment Office, and held out the packet and deed that my mother and father were landowners. All you had to do was just wait for the next enrollment meeting and you would already be a member.

HOW HAS THIS AFFECTED YOUR SENSE OF CULTURAL IDENTITY OR DOES IT?

Being enrolled?

YES.

I don't know. At first, I thought it was a big deal to be enrolled, but you know, I've been around Oglala Pine Ridge Indians now for about ten years, and that really doesn't mean anything, that enrollment number, to me right now.

I WANT TO TALK A LITTLE BIT MORE ABOUT YOUR BIRTH FAMILY. DID YOU DECIDE TO SEEK THEM OUT OR DID THEY SEEK YOU OUT?

It was both. They had tried for years and years to try to find me, but they, like, couldn't get anywhere. After I was sixteen or seventeen, I started kind of looking, but then I left for the army and put all that on hold.

HOW OLD WERE YOU WHEN YOU FIRST FOUND THEM?

I was twenty-six.

AND WHAT PROMPTED YOUR DECISION TO LOOK FOR THEM IN THE FIRST PLACE?

I'm not sure. I think it was just to have a little something that was empty inside me. I had had a dream, and the dream led me to my father-in-law. He's my father-in-law now. He is a spiritual leader in the Denver community that failed to search me out. And he helped me find my family because it was drawing on me. They kept calling on me to try to come back to be an Indian. And I think that's what I needed to even out my life, was to come back to what I really belong to, and not be an outsider in the white community.

HOW HAVE YOU CHANGED SINCE FINDING YOUR BIRTH FAMILY?

Since finding my birth family, I've been a sundancer for almost ten years now, tenth year this summer. I'm a helper at the Sundance. I dance with powwow traditional dancers, powwow singers, on the Pine Ridge Indian Reservation and around the city areas. I have a wife, and I have two children, and we just adopted an Indian boy last year. And those are children that I needed to really take myself home, I think.

HOW WOULD YOU DESCRIBE YOUR RELATIONSHIP WITH YOUR BIRTH FAMILY?

Close.

AND DID YOUR ADOPTED PARENTS SUPPORT YOUR DECISION TO SEARCH FOR THEM?

Yeah, they did. I thought my dad was going to have a hard time with it, because he doesn't have any sons to pass on his last name.

DID YOUR RELATIONSHIPS WITH YOUR ADOPTED FAMILY CHANGE IN ANY WAY AS A RESULT OF YOUR DECISION?

No.

ARE THERE ANY BARRIERS THAT HAVE PREVENTED YOU FROM FULLY INTEGRATING INTO THE INDIAN COMMUNITY?

No, not really. When I first came back, no one knew who I was, and you know, I had to work really hard to get to know people, and I didn't know, being adopted, how it would ever work out. It didn't even matter to them anymore. And to them, I've always been here. Whatever happened before then, when I was little, it doesn't matter to them anymore. They're happy that I'm back.

DO YOU FEEL SECURE OR INSECURE ABOUT YOUR INDIAN IDENTITY TODAY?

Very secure.

AND WHAT PEOPLE OR WHAT RESOURCES HAVE AIDED YOU IN THE PROCESS?

My father-in-law, Mr. William Center, my Uncle Joe Browneyes, my Uncle Floyd Hand, are some of the relatives involved. Not being critical of me because I didn't grow up around Indians, and they take the time to talk to me about any questions about anything and everything. And they worked hard with me to learn the Lakota language, to learn the songs that I've learned. And they've given me a lot of opportunities that should have taken a long time to earn them, but they knew what happened to me as an Indian. They gave me these special privileges without having put in my time, but gave them to me because they saw something special inside me.

ARE THERE PEOPLE WHO HAVE BEEN CRITICAL OF YOU BECAUSE YOU WEREN'T RAISED IN THE LAKOTA COMMUNITY?

Yes.

And what effect has that had on you?

Sometimes it hurts my feelings still even after all these years. I didn't grow up here you know, Native—just grew up here white. It makes me feel bad, because it wasn't my choice to be adopted out. You know, it wasn't my parents' choice for that to happen. And my aunts told me that if my gramps wouldn't have died when they were little, none of this would have happened. I think that the ones that talked down to me because I'm raised by a white family, they're jealous, because I had an opportunity to be something better than being stuck on the reservation.

How has the fact that you're Indian affected both your personal and professional life?

Professionally, here in the Rapid City area, it's very hard to be Indian, and to be in a management position. And an Indian in Rapid City Airport, trying three times as hard as your white counterparts, just because Rapid City has an old school that tells you about Indians being lazy, not willing to pull their weight when it comes to their job. But on the other hand, being a U.S. soldier, they're more than happy to have an Indian within their ranks, because they know the history of the Lakota people.

And how has it affected your life personally?

Personally? Just in these past five or six years, so many gifts have been given to me by the Indian community, the gift of learning their songs, the gift of being a mentor to young boys and young men in the Indian community. Sometimes just being able to just sit down and talk to some of the boys that are having a hard time with their job, trying to talk to them about being good men, being good fathers. Those are gifts that I'd like to pass on to them—those being a father, and being a good man—and have a good impact on me. And I wanted to have that joy passed on to them.

Now, you mentioned that you're married. Can you tell me a little bit about your wife?

My wife's name is Wanda. She's from the Santa Fe community of Pine Ridge. She was born and raised there. And she's a descendant of Chief Thunder of the Pine Ridge area.

And how many children do you have?

Altogether, I have—with our stepchildren—we have seven, plus we adopted a baby last summer.

AND HOW HAVE YOU ADDRESSED THE ISSUE OF CULTURAL IDENTITY WITH YOUR CHILDREN?

We try to make them—not make them, but we show them that there's nothing wrong with being Indian, and tell them you should be proud of who you are. Sort of lately, my daughter has been kind of wondering about her ancestry and her bloodlines, where she comes from, and sometimes, someone—some of the times, they make fun of her for being white-skinned, and having lighter eyes, like the rest of us, our family are all tan and have black hair. I always try to tell her that she's Lakota, and it's nothing to be ashamed of, no matter what somebody says to her. You should be proud of who you are.

AND WHAT PROMPTED YOUR DECISION TO ADOPT AN INDIAN BABY?

The decision to do that came—was in a dream. My grandpa came to me, and he said to remember what happened to me, to not let that happen again to anyone in our family. So I made the choice to adopt an Indian baby. If I hadn't picked up that responsibility, I wouldn't be honoring the values of my society.

WHAT DO YOU THINK YOU'VE LEARNED FROM YOUR EXPERIENCE AS AN ADOPTEE THAT WILL HELP YOU BE A PARENT TO THIS CHILD?

Be close to your family, and some of the things that the Lakota have to offer, better education, and try to accomplish something in your life. And I really want my kids to have a good education, a good life, and they know that being in the white-dominant school, they're going to have a better chance of having an education than they would if they were on the reservation.

WHAT IS YOUR OPINION OF THE INDIAN CHILD WELFARE ACT?

Indian Child Welfare Act? If it is applied the way that it's supposed to, and the states don't undermine it, then it's a good act. But here in the state of South Dakota, there are so many people right now that have cases pending, and it's mostly due—because the state of South Dakota doesn't honor the Indian Child Welfare Act, and put the Indian children into Indian homes. They're being stuck into white families, white homes.

ARE YOU GLAD THAT YOU WERE ADOPTED BY A WHITE FAMILY?

Yes and no. You know, because I had a long haul relearning the things that I needed to learn. I am grateful that they gave me the values of working hard, and for getting an education. I'm grateful for the values my mom and dad had given me—but some of the things that I should have learned as a young man, I'm having to learn as an older man. They are hard and difficult to learn, because sometimes people say, you should already have known that.

But you know, I'm doing the best I can, and a lot of the older men, our headmen, and spiritual leaders, they use me, because they have a hard time talking English. And they use me to talk to white people, because I can understand both languages. And I can understand the white language better than these, the older Indian kids, and they use me to interpret for them.

AND YOU'RE NOT AGAINST WHITE FAMILIES ADOPTING INDIAN CHILDREN?

In general?

YES.

No, I'm not.

AND WHAT ADVICE WOULD YOU OFFER WHITE FAMILIES WHO WOULD WANT TO OR WHO HAVE ADOPTED INDIAN CHILDREN?

Best advice for the ones that have already adopted Indian children is to be open-minded about their culture, because I think that someday in their life, whether sooner or later, it's going to be calling them back to being Indian again. And to help them the best they can, and really, really tell them the values, the value of not being ashamed of being adopted out, as those people that adopted the Indian children did care for them out of their hearts.

But nowadays, the ones that want to? I really couldn't say. Nowadays it seems like the white people are still trying to convert Indian children into what they want them to be, and to not—they're not interested in taking care of that child. They're looking, sort of, to bring some glamorous *Dances with Wolves* image of having something Indian in their household.

WHAT DO YOU THINK YOUR ADOPTED PARENTS COULD HAVE DONE TO GIVE YOU A BETTER SENSE OF YOUR CULTURAL IDENTITY?

I really don't know what else they could have done, because—and I think they did the best they could. It was just—maybe it was just me. I was always looking for things that they couldn't give me. I just think they tried the best they could to do what they had to with the little limited resources they had with them in the Denver area. But it was the path I took because I was wandering for it in my whole life.

THAT WAS THE LAST QUESTION I HAD, JON. IS THERE ANYTHING ELSE YOU THINK I SHOULD HAVE ASKED YOU OR ANY OTHER ISSUES THAT YOU'D LIKE TO ADDRESS?

No, not really. I think the idea of doing that book is good, the thing that you're doing. I hope it helps out a lot of people.

**20**

# TED SMITH*

Ted Smith (Mohawk) spent the first six weeks of his life in foster care until he was adopted by a white couple in 1955. Ted and his adoptive brother grew up in a predominantly white neighborhood in the suburbs. Although he came from a loving home and did not experience any racism growing up, Ted says that he always had "an innate desire to reunite with . . . [his] culture." As a recovering alcoholic, Ted says that looking back he believes that the source of many of his problems may stem from the "alienation" he experienced growing up. He says he was "not able to identify with any specific group" and that "gnawed away at [him] for years." Ted says that once he recognized the source of his discontent, he was able to focus on his sobriety and look for his birth family.

According to Ted, "it took ten years of having doors slammed in [his] face" before he discovered that he could use the Indian Child Welfare Act to unseal his birth records and process his tribal enrollment. Section 1951b of the Indian Child Welfare Act states: "Upon the request of the adopted Indian child over the age of eighteen, the adoptive or foster parents of an Indian child, or an Indian tribe, the Secretary shall disclose such information as may be necessary for the enrollment of an Indian child in the tribe in which the child may be eligible for enrollment or for determining any rights or benefits associated with that membership." After petitioning a

*Identifying information about this participant has been omitted or changed.

judge, Ted's birth records were released to the Department of Indian Affairs who informed him that his birth mother had already enrolled him in the tribe. They did not, however, provide Ted with his birth mother's name so he decided to place an advertisement in the local newspaper, which led to a reunion with his birth mother and "changed [his] life dramatically." Prior to reuniting with his birth family, Ted says that he had never met another Native person and knew nothing about Native culture. Fortunately, he was warmly accepted by his birth family and has since made a conscious effort to learn about his Native American roots.

According to Ted, being "stripped" of your Native identity is the biggest disadvantage of transracial adoption. However, he is hesitant to say that Native children should only be adopted by Native American families, especially because his experience as a transracial adoptee "was extremely positive." He says that "there was a lot of love and a lot of warmth in the non-Native home that [he] was raised in" so he is reluctant to say that non-Native families cannot raise happy, healthy Native children. For adoptive families who have adopted or would like to adopt Native children, he insists that every effort should be made to keep that child connected to the Native community.

WHAT YEAR WERE YOU BORN?

1954.

AND WHERE WERE YOU BORN?

New York State.

DO YOU KNOW HOW OLD YOU WERE WHEN YOU WERE ADOPTED?

Well, I was in a home, children's home until I was six weeks old, and I was picked up by my adoptive parents, and then they had me for, I guess it's like a year, and then the official adoption took place a year after I was born. So it was, like, September of 1955 that I was officially adopted, but I was placed with them at age six weeks.

AND ARE YOU AWARE OF THE CIRCUMSTANCES SURROUNDING YOUR ADOPTION?

Mm-hmm.

CAN YOU TELL ME A LITTLE BIT ABOUT THAT?

Well, it's—obviously, I'm sure there are, you know, many complex stories. I found my birth mother, and I began a relationship with her in 1991. I looked for ten years for her and it was at that time that I learned from her what the circumstances were. She was twenty years old, unmarried, it was just one of those things, and she was from a reserve in Canada, and she had come over to the New York area and, you know, it just happened she was young and she was away from home, so she stayed here and had me here, gave birth, and then she put me up—she knew she was going to put me up for adoption. So she put me up for adoption, and then she returned back to the reserve.

AND DID YOUR ADOPTED PARENTS TELL YOU WHY THEY ADOPTED YOU?

Tell me why they adopted me? Well, they basically wanted children, I mean, and they were unable to have children of their own. That's, you know, why they adopted. I have an adopted brother as well, and they apparently wanted two children, so I was available.

AND DID THEY EVER INDICATE TO YOU WHY THEY ADOPTED AN AMERICAN INDIAN CHILD?

Well, I guess they really didn't—they weren't choosy, they weren't picky, I was available, and you know a child was available, and originally, they had wanted a girl, you know, it was back in the 1950s, get a little boy and a girl, and you know, the white picket fence and that whole thing in the suburbs, and like I said, I was—there I was, so they didn't choose me particularly because I was Native, the only information that they had at the time was that my birth mother was Native, but I don't believe that had any bearing on their decision to adopt.

NOW, YOU MENTIONED YOU HAVE AN ADOPTIVE BROTHER AS WELL. IS HE NATIVE, TOO?

No, he isn't.

CAN YOU TELL ME A LITTLE BIT MORE ABOUT YOUR ADOPTIVE PARENTS, LIKE WHAT THEY DO PROFESSIONALLY AND THAT SORT OF THING?

Well, they were fairly old when they adopted me. My mother passed away back in 1991—yeah, 1991 she passed away. My adoptive father is still alive; he's eighty-seven. My adoptive mother was a stenographer for a large company; she did basically transcription and—she was a typist more or less.

My adoptive father was a blue-collar chemical mixer at a large company. Neither of them had a college education, although my mother did have some business school experience.

HOW WOULD YOU DESCRIBE YOUR RELATIONSHIP WITH THEM?

Very close. Very close. We were a very close family. There were issues, obviously, there were issues of childrearing I think today that they look at with—or my father, maybe, probably—both of them would probably question the level of discipline. I don't think it was done maliciously, I think it was just a kind of a "spare the rod and spoil the child" type thing that they were raised up with. So today, it would be considered physical abuse, but back then, it was just, you know, being a strict and disciplining parent.

WHEN DID YOU FIRST REALIZE THAT YOU WERE ADOPTED?

I always knew. I knew from the earliest days. It was never any secret particularly that I was adopted. It was explained to me—I can remember as early as like age four or five, that's my earliest recollection that I was adopted and that I was somehow, you know, different than the other neighborhood kids. But it was always emphasized and stressed that I was, you know, wanted and loved and it didn't really matter whether I was biologically a product of them or adopted.

AND DO YOU THINK THAT YOUR PARENTS HANDLED THE REVELATION ABOUT YOUR ADOPTION IN A POSITIVE MANNER?

I think so. I think they were honest and they were straightforward, there was no beating around the bush, there was no pretense of trying to hide what were the circumstances around how I came to be with them. So, yeah, I think they were very healthy about it.

AND TO WHOM DID YOU TALK TO ABOUT THE FACT THAT YOU WERE ADOPTED?

To whom I talked to—I really didn't—there was kind of a—you know, with my peer group, there was kind of a dirty little secret type thing. It was something I wasn't particularly comfortable talking about, it was something I didn't really want to get out, although I didn't really make any effort to hide the fact. I mean, I didn't deny it, but then again, I didn't come right out and proudly say I am adopted. I just—basically just—they were my parents, and that's how I looked at it.

NOW, YOU SAID THAT YOUR BROTHER WAS ADOPTED AS WELL. DID YOU TWO TALK ABOUT IT?

Yes, we talked about it. Now, growing up together, we really didn't talk about it too much. I mean, we obviously were aware of it, that each other was adopted. I can recall my adoptive mother telling me of the circumstances behind his coming to be with the family, and his circumstances were a little more tragic, I guess. There was some child abuse involved, and he was adopted and placed with them—placed and adopted by them at a later age. He was something like a year-and-a-half, two years old when they got him.

WAS THE FACT THAT YOU WERE A NATIVE AMERICAN TALKED ABOUT A LOT IN YOUR FAMILY?

It was known—we both—my adoptive brother and I have dark skin, and during the summer, I always get extremely dark, and people would comment about that. And you know—it was not said maliciously to be hurtful or anything, but it was just the two kids are wild Indians and one of them really is an Indian, that sort of thing. So I was aware of the fact that I was Native, but it was never said in a hurtful way, it was just something, a matter-of-fact, I think it was, like, yeah, one of them is Native. But that's about the extent of the Nativeness that I knew about or even understood.

WHAT RACE IS YOUR BROTHER?

He's Caucasian, and his nationality, we believe—or at least from what my adoptive mother told me—I'm not even aware of whether she told him—was that he was Italian, and he certainly has Italian features.

DO YOU THINK IT WAS EASIER GROWING UP WITH A SIBLING WHO WAS ADOPTED AS WELL AND WHO WAS OF A DIFFERENT BACKGROUND?

Absolutely. I can't imagine how difficult it would have been for or is for children who are adopted into a family with, you know, natural born children in it. The two of us both are going to identify with and made us closer—I believe it made us closer in that we both have similar backgrounds that we can identify with.

AND WHERE DID YOU GROW UP?

I grew up in the suburbs. Initially, when I was first placed, my parents were living in the city, and then according to the 1950s suburban idea, you got enough money together so you could buy your house, a plot of land out in the suburbs, and then you moved out for the schools and the safety and to live the American Dream.

WERE THE SCHOOLS YOU ATTENDED MOSTLY WHITE SCHOOLS?

Absolutely. Absolutely. I graduated from a suburban school. My graduating class had—and for this area, a graduating class of 580, which at the time was considered really large, rather—you know, as pretty huge at the time. Out of those 580 high school graduates, later—years and years later, I would find out there was one other Native student. I always thought he was Korean. It never occurred to me that he might be Native. And years later, we would find out that he, too, was adopted, and he too was from my reserve, and I still see him. It would be years later that we made the connection. And I also see him from time to time; he still lives in the area. But yes, by all means, it was—I think out of the 580, I think there were two blacks, two—so it was very, very much, you know, a white school. Kind of the intention, I don't believe, but that's just the way it worked out.

DID YOU ENCOUNTER ANY FORM OF RACISM GROWING UP?

No, I can't say that I did. I really didn't because I wasn't identified as being Native. I mean, there was no proof of that at the time, there was this kind of a, you know, an air of uncertainty, but nothing that could be proven, so it was just—I was looked at as just a dark-skinned white boy.

DO YOU REMEMBER LEARNING ABOUT NATIVE AMERICANS IN SCHOOL?

No, not at all. I knew nothing. I'm Mohawk, and it wouldn't be until I actually found my birth mother and started learning about my culture and ethnicity—I knew nothing about the Iroquois Confederacy, the Haudenosaunee—I mean, that's how naïve I was. I was thirty-seven years old when I finally started discovering my Native roots, and it was just kind of glossed over in public schools here. I really didn't know that much about it. I was aware of culture, but one, I couldn't identify with it, and two, I simply didn't even know any Native people, I never had any contact with Native people. So, you know, I was just kind of disassociated with the entire culture.

ARE YOU AN ENROLLED MEMBER OF A TRIBE?

Yes.

CAN YOU TELL ME A LITTLE BIT ABOUT HOW YOU WENT ABOUT GETTING ENROLLED?

Well, when I discovered my birth mother—when I reunited with my birth mother, I found out that prior to that—it's a complex story. I was the first person in New York State to use the Indian Child Welfare Act to unseal the court records. I hired an attorney to do that, to petition the Family Court to unseal the original birth certificate, which had the birth name—the name of my birth mother on it. That was needed in order for me to make a determination of my tribal identity. And since it was on the birth certificate saying—the only thing it said was that there was—she was Canadian Indian, that led me to believe that, well, okay, I'd better get a hold of Indian and Northern Affairs in Canada, and part of their requirement was they needed the name of the birth mother, obviously. I couldn't get that, my lawyer couldn't get that, nobody could touch that, those were sealed at the time. So I had to petition the court. So I petitioned the court, we went through the whole process, the name was released, but the court only agreed to release her name to Indian Northern Affairs, not to my attorney, and not to me.

So when the name was released to Indian and Northern Affairs, I spoke with a worker up there and I asked her what the procedure was to go through to get enrolled with the tribe, and she said, you already are enrolled, which was news to me. They—you know, they made the association between my birth mother and me and found out that I already was a status Indian, status Mohawk from Canada. So, that's how I found out—came to find out that I had always been enrolled and on the rolls of my reserve.

WHAT PROMPTED YOUR DECISION TO SEARCH FOR YOUR BIRTH FAMILY?

There was something that just—you know, I was always curious about, I always had this syndrome, it's Natives who seem to have this innate desire to reunite with their identity and their culture. And it was something that just burned inside me for years and years. I think, looking back now, how I'm a recovering alcoholic with over twenty-five years' sobriety, and when I went through rehab and detox and did that whole route and finally sobered up, it was just something that, I sat down and said to myself, you know, this is something you got to do. This is just one of those things that, you know, you got to do and maybe, possibly—I'm not saying it is, I'm saying possibly—a source of many of the problems that I was experiencing, feelings of alienation, feelings of being different, of not being able to identify with any specific group. So kind of after I sobered up, that was one of the things that—a goal, if you will, that I'm going to try to take this as far as I can and see how far I can go with this and to find out. And I just kind of kept at it for ten years—it took ten years of having doors slammed in my face and people saying, no, we can't do that and we don't know and—that's kind of how I went about it. It wasn't anything that just—one day, I up and said, hey, I think I'll do this, it's something that just kind of gnawed away at me for years.

WERE YOUR ADOPTIVE PARENTS SUPPORTIVE OF YOUR DECISION TO FIND YOUR BIRTH FAMILY?

Yes, yes, very, very supportive, which was extremely helpful, not only from a psychological point of view, but also they gave me a lot of encouragement because they knew how difficult it was and they knew what I was going through, you know, taking on a legal system and taking on organizations and—actually organizations that didn't even exist that had merged with others groups. So fortunately for me, they were very, very supportive, so I had that on my side.

HAVE YOU CHANGED SINCE FINDING YOUR BIRTH FAMILY?

There's no description for that. There is absolutely no way I can describe the change that that made in my life. It gave me direction, it gave me purpose, it gave me focus, it gave me a point of being able to identify with a group, and it just—it dramatically changed my entire life to the extent that many of the people who knew me prior to me discovering my birth family I've kind of lost touch. I mean, when you're seen as being the white suburban kid who went to college and who is doing the typical suburban routine of job and house, car, and all this other stuff, and then suddenly now you're identifying with an ethnic group that really a majority of Americans have nothing—no concept about. I mean, they're aware that Natives are there, but they don't know what it's about. I lost—I would have to say I lost a number of longtime friends simply—not because they're racist, not because they don't approve; it's just that they don't understand what a dramatic change that meant to me and why I identify as being Native and always have been. It's nothing that they say, Ted, well, he turned Injun. It's not like that at all. I've always been Native—always. And people who know me the best can see that in me. I mean, I've always been Native, and all the traits and the indicators were there, but it's just I never had proof, I never was able to say, yes, you know, here's proof if you need it that I am Native. I knew it all along. They needed proof, and when the proof was shown, they didn't really like it. It's just, you know, we want to think of you as—hell, as the white kid from the suburbs, upwardly mobile, white kid from the suburbs.

AND HOW ARE YOU RECEIVED BY INDIANS ON YOUR RESERVE?

It was amazing, it was—the day that I reunited with my birth mother, that was the first time I had ever been in a Native—a Native's home, it was the first time I ever really talked with Native people. It was just—when I first showed up, you know, everybody was kind of hesitant and uncertain—because they didn't know anything about me, I didn't know anything about them. I knew nothing about Native culture, Native people, nothing, and here I am, meeting the woman who gave birth to me after thirty-seven years. And so they were cautious, I was cautious, and then after we started talking and we sat around—the Indian council in every house, which is the kitchen table, and we sat around and started talking and bit by bit, they started showing up with people, saying I'm your cousin, I'm your uncle, I'm your aunt, blah, blah, blah. And pretty soon, the house was just overflowing with people. It was an enormously and wildly, warmly acceptance into—back, if you will, back into the culture. So it was an amazing experience.

I was accepted very warmly, very well not only by my birth mother, but also by her family and my brothers and sisters. And, you know, to this day, I'm still the guy who made it back, the guy who returned, and it's a bit of an amazing story to not only find, reunite with the birth parent, but to be as warmly accepted as I was because—it was a happy situation, it wasn't digging up the dirty past, it was a happy situation in that everybody was happy. So even today when I go back, there's never a question, it's just, he's Ted, and he's the one with the weird accent, he's from New York, but he's one of us.

DID YOU EXPERIENCE ANY TYPE OF CULTURE SHOCK UPON RETURNING TO THE RESERVE?

Initially?

MM-HMM.

Culture shock—I don't think so. The only thing that really struck me as being different, I guess, or being something I couldn't identify with was the level of—I don't want to say poverty—it was just the standard of living wasn't what I had been used to. And that's not talking down, I mean, by any means, that's just simply—I wasn't accustomed to such—there wasn't an abundance of money, I guess. I don't know how else to put it. There was certainly the love and attention—maybe even more so than I'd ever seen and ever experienced; the warmth, the generosity, the hospitality, the respect was absolutely staggering.

As far as culture shock, it was something new, it was just different, it was part of me, and I was learning about it. I was very much a—you know, like a young Native child being raised again, growing up again on the reserve and in a situation that I really wasn't all that familiar with. So I guess culture shock from the sense that it was different, yes, but in a sense that it was something very difficult, a chore to deal with, no, not really. It was just something like, this is me, this is—yes, I understand and I can identify with these people, so in a way, it was kind of a validation, if you will, of who I was and just the realization that, you know, I'm home, I've returned back to the fold, that sort of thing.

Did the white world you left and the Native world you returned to clash in any way?

All the time. All the time. I live in two worlds. I live in two very different worlds, and I had to function equally well in both, and I managed to work my life into some sort of a situation where I can operate not only both in two different cultural worlds, but in two different political worlds as well. I'm a dual citizen; I found that out when I was reunited with my birth family. I live in the States, but I'm also Canadian, and I've always identified as being Canadian. I had that certain pull toward Canada. So from that sense, I've got to be able to operate in both worlds, and I do. I mean, flip back and forth and there are certain patterns of behavior which are acceptable here in the States that aren't acceptable in Canada, and over the years, I've come to understand that, and I adjust as I cross borders.

So I wouldn't say—the values of the white world, that I was raised with never really seemed to fit, they never really seemed to be—you're told this is what you want to do, you want to go to college, you want to graduate and then get the job at the big company and this area and then you work your way up and then you want to do this—and this is what'll make you happy, this is the way to do it.

And it never really seemed to fit. I went through the motions, I went through and had that, but it never seemed to give me the satisfaction or fulfillment that I needed or I wanted. Yet, the white world is looking and saying, oh, you're doing great, this is exactly what you're supposed to be doing. And all the while, I was saying, yeah, but I'm not happy, and this isn't me. And it wasn't until I really reunited with my culture, my Native culture, or took on my Native identity that I began to see there is another way of seeing things, and that's the way I had been seeing things, was through Native eyes.

And values that had been taught to me all these years and that I'd been raised with—I'm not saying are necessarily wrong, but there was another way of seeing it, and that other way of seeing this was putting the white world over here and the American side could understand, they could identify. How could they? They had no contact with it, I had no contact with the Native culture, how could I identify with something I knew nothing about?

So it was when I reunited with my Native family that I started seeing that, yes, there are different ways of seeing things and doing things and just because they're not often seen in the context that I was raised in does not mean that they were wrong, and it does not mean that they're not right. It may mean for the white world, it's not right, but for me, it fits. And that's really all I need to be concerned about.

YOU MENTIONED THAT YOUR ADOPTIVE PARENTS WERE AWARE OF YOUR NATIVE BACKGROUND. DID THEY EVER DO ANYTHING TO GIVE YOU A SENSE OF YOUR CULTURAL IDENTITY?

I'm not sure. I don't think—it's hard to say—it may just be circumstantial, but the YMCA around here had this program—they may still have it, I don't know—hopefully, they don't—it was called Indian Guides, and it was kind of like a father-son type thing where fathers and their sons would participate and you would have your little tribes, as you were, and you'd make your coffee-can compounds and dress up like Indians, and you know, you'd be given Indian names and stuff like that. And today—boy, I hope that's all gone. That is just—I mean, that's almost an obscenity. I can't believe it would be around—who knows, it may be. But Indian Guides may be—it may have been more of a father-son type thing, getting the fathers and sons—my father and my brother and myself—involved in an activity that we could participate in with other fathers and sons. I doubt—I never asked—I don't know, I doubt that it was ever a factor, that it was an attempt to reunite me with my culture. But other than that, no, there was absolutely no attempt whatsoever to put me in contact with any of my Native culture.

DID YOU READ ANY BOOKS OR WATCH ANY MOVIES OR THAT SORT OF THING ABOUT NATIVE AMERICANS GROWING UP?

Only from the sense of any typical white kid, with the curiosity of cowboys and Indians-type stuff and watching the movies—not specifically that, gee, that's me. A lot of Native adoptees say when they're watching the old 1950s westerns, they always identify with the Indians, they want the Indians to win. I never really had that. It just never occurred to me and I never really identified with—it was a dirty little secret you don't—this isn't something you really want to emphasize, you want to be more like the rest of the kids, you want to fit in with the rest of the kids. So yeah, I had dark skin and I was very dark, but that was about it. I never really had any compulsion, I guess, or motivation to identify or seek out Native identities or role models. It's just, I want to be a white kid, I want to be just like the rest of the kids. It was more—the adoption was the dirty little secret, not the Indian part, and that's something that I kind of—it's not that I pushed it away, it was just kind of like, oh, yeah, there were Indians, there are—this is what happened to them, and that's the end of that. That's about it. I want to be like everybody else.

AND YOU MENTIONED YOU WENT TO COLLEGE. WHERE DID YOU GO?

I went to the State University of New York.

WHAT DID YOU MAJOR IN?

Initially when I went up there, I started out in Computer Science and then I switched majors to Psychology, so I graduated with a B.A. in Psychology with one credit—one course short of a double major in Psychology and Computer Science.

AND WHAT DO YOU DO PROFESSIONALLY TODAY?

I'm disabled today. By trade, I worked in the information technology field, I started out as a computer operator and eventually, when I left a large company—I resigned in disgust because of the corporate world, I just had had it with the nonsense and games and mind-control that they were playing—when I left, I was a database administrator.

DID YOU EVER MARRY?

Yes.

AND WAS YOUR WIFE WHITE OR WAS SHE NATIVE OR—

She was white.

AND DO YOU HAVE CHILDREN?

No.

AND HOW DO YOU IDENTIFY YOURSELF TODAY?

"Identify" as in—

YOUR CULTURAL BACKGROUND, I GUESS.

I identify as Native. Biologically, I'm mixed. I am biracial. I know about my birth father, I never met him—that's something my birth mother did not want to ever tell me about. She passed away in 1999 and one of her sisters, an aunt of mine, knew my birth father, but would never tell me. My birth mother never told the name of my birth father. She would describe him, but I believe there was a great deal—and rightfully so—there was a great deal of animosity. She became pregnant, and then he wanted nothing to do with her, he just, like, see ya, you know, and left. So I can understand—the reasons behind that are maybe somewhat complex, I suspect. I suspect—I don't know—but I suspect, you know, may have been used, one, as a pawn, like, well, you know, I'm going to withhold him from—my birth mother saying I'm going to withhold him from his birth father so he doesn't have that privilege or the right to call him his son. And two, you know, he doesn't need to know about—and that's what she always was saying, you don't need to know about him, he wanted nothing to do with you or me, so you don't need to have anything to do with him. I'm not telling you his name, don't ask.

After she passed away years later, I got the name—his name from my aunt, and I actually spoke with the gentleman, who denied ever knowing. I anonymously called him and—under the pretense of being a writer doing a research project and interviewing him about his stock car profession, and I just kind of dropped hints about the woman, dropped her name, and kind of asked, oh, did you know her and he denied ever knowing anybody. He just simply didn't remember. He's an elderly gentleman. So I left it at that. I left my name and number in case he might get the hint, but he never really called back, he never got in contact with me, so I left it with that. So he was white, but the Native features, physically, psychologically, emotionally, my outlook, everything—the Native gene has just swarmed all over the white gene. I mean, you look at me, and I look Native, I look totally Native. As a matter of fact, I look very much—almost like a twin—I have a cousin who's ten years younger than me, and the two of us could pass as twins. There is a deceased uncle—brother of my mother's—who I saw pictures of, and it was like looking at a picture of me, we look so much alike. So the Nativeness in me, you know, demands and identifies me. It's not something that I choose, but something that I am. That's just the way it is, and I've always been Native. So I'm more Native than I am white, really. I was raised in the white world and that's where I get a lot of the white culture, but you know, the true essence of who I am and my outlook on life is 100 percent Native. I identify as Native very strongly.

How do you think your physical appearance affected the way in which you were perceived by both those in the Native and the non-Native communities?

Well, my mother—my birth mother, once I reunited with her, she point-blank just came right out and said, your nieces and nephews like you so much and they are so at ease with you because you look Indian. I mean it's just—there is no question about it, you look Native. It's not like, you know, you look white at all, it's, you've got all the features of a Native.

You look Native, you act Native, you think Native, you have outlook Native. You are Native, there's no question about that. So my physical appearance is, you know—I fit right in in the Native world. I mean, I go back to my reserve and it's just—you know, I'm back home. Hi, I'm back, here I am. And I just fit in very, very easily; when I meet other Native people, I don't even think about it and they don't think it either.

In the white world, it's strange. The people, strangely enough, that seem to question my ethnicity, it seems to me—I don't want to generalize or just go out and make gross assumptions here—but it seems to me that people who ask about my ethnicity most are black people. They kind of look at me—I know white people are thinking it, but they don't ask it, they just kind of look at me and say, what are you? Are you Puerto Rican, are you Italian, are you Jewish, what are you? I say, no, I'm Native. So in the white world, it's kind of like, he's dark-skinned, but why is he dark-skinned? Is he Italian, is he Mediterranean, what is he, we're not quite sure. So, you know, in the white world, I don't think it's ever been held against me—I can't imagine it was—because, again, in the white world, everybody sees me as a dark-skinned white boy, raised in the suburbs.

HOW DO YOU THINK YOUR PHYSICAL APPEARANCE SHAPED YOUR SENSE OF CULTURAL IDENTITY?

Well, if you look like one, you tend to think of yourself as being accepted as one. You're not fighting to have to prove anything. I know on the reserve—I think Native people—at least from my perspective that I've seen, from the people that I know—are certainly not colorblind. The more Native you look, the more Native you are. It's just kind of superficial—I don't agree with it—but I think the more Native-looking you are, the more you're accepted or the quicker you're accepted, the more easily you're accepted in Native circles. On my reserve, there are people who are more Native than I am who have blue eyes, light skin, light brown hair—they really do not look Native—but they have more Native blood in them than I do, and they told me from the years of talking with them, that they really had a rough time growing up on the reserve because they didn't look Native. So I guess I had that going for me because I looked so Native, when I go back to the reserve and when I'm in Native circles, it's just, like, yeah, you fit in. I mean, it's a leg up, as it were, to fit in and to easily blend in with the rest of the Native people. So that definitely helps. Appearance, you know, as superficial as it may be, you know, it did help.

Do you feel secure or insecure about your Native identity today?

I feel 100 percent rock-solid secure in my Native identity. There is absolutely no question.

And what helped you obtain that security, that sense of security?

Because it was like a validation, a verification of all the years that, you know, there's something wrong with that boy, you know, he always sees things differently, why is he so different. And all the years, if you're not around other Native people and you don't have any validation, you don't have any role models, you don't have somebody saying, no, you're not crazy, you're Native. When I started talking and learning about my birth family and my heritage, people would say, no, you're not crazy. I mean, all the years that you've been told you're crazy and there's something wrong with you because you don't think, look, and act like, you know, a white boy—because you're not. You're Native. I mean, that's why you have this different outlook, that's why you have these feelings, that's why you have these certain senses and why you go through certain changes during the year and have different outlooks, and you see life differently. The reason for that is because you're native and because after finding that out, that validation, that verification after all those years, it was just such—it was a load off my shoulders, it was a sense of relief that after years and years of people saying, you're crazy, there's something wrong with you, and there's nobody to counter that saying, no, you're not, you start to believe it, you start to think, gee, maybe there really is something wrong with me, maybe there really is—it is something about me that doesn't belong here, there's something—I've got to work harder at trying to be more like other people.

And then when I started finding out more about Native people, about my culture, my heritage, then I started saying, wait a minute, no, no. There's nothing wrong with me, I'm Native, and if the rest of you people can't accept that, then I guess we'll just have to kind of part ways here, which, to a large extent, happened. So it was an enormous relief, and it is to this day. Every time I go back, I'm home. This may not necessarily be where I live, but this is where I belong.

What people or resources did you use to learn more about your heritage?

Initially, I started—as I got to know the members of my family—my immediate family, my sisters, one of my brothers-in- law, the traditional chiefs, and my brother, he and my sister live a traditional life, and so I started discovering more about what the traditional side of Native life is like for the

Haudenosaunee and the beliefs and the culture, and it piqued my interest, and I started looking more into the traditional side from sources that are traditional-based, organizations around here that teach the traditional way of life and put out publications. And I started seeking those out and learning about the culture from the Native side instead of looking at it through the side of the white world, who are doing their own interpretation of what it's all about. And then I started realizing and seeing that, hey, this really does make sense. I mean, it makes sense for me. I'm not saying it makes sense for the white people, I'm just saying that for me it really is a way of life that I can identify with and that suits me as more of an appropriate fit than if I go through the rest of my life trying to pretend that I'm something I'm not. I'm not a white guy—I am, in that I was raised in that culture, but I'm not, in the sense that I was not born that. And you have to be true to yourself if you're ever going to be successful in life.

So it was kind of like I wanted to figure out the Native side from the Native perspective, and that's how I started learning, and that's how I started assessing the material and resources that were available to me. So I started learning about the culture that way.

Are there any barriers that have prevented you from fully integrating into the Native community?

Yes. Logistics. I live 160 miles from my reserve in Canada and I live 100 miles exactly from the border of Canada. I live in the States where I don't really—I have more in common with Canada and Canadians and the Canadian First Nations than I do in the States, even though I've always lived here. I just identify more and I have more in common—and my outlook is much more similar to anything over in Canada and on the reserve than here. That's been a source of frustration for me, it really has. I'm no longer in a financial or physical position to be able to do anything about moving over. Someday, I may be, and at that time, hopefully I will leave the country and return to really where I belong. But for now, I'm a Webmaster, I'm really into the Internet, so I keep ties, very close ties, with Canada and with what's going on over in my reserve there. But it still is very, very difficult. I know—many times I've questioned—and many times I ask my birth mother whether she thought it was the right decision to leave me in the States. I kept asking her, Mom, why couldn't you, cross your legs and then cross the border and have me over in Canada, and she'd go, oh, Ted, you know it doesn't make any difference, it's just an imaginary line, there's absolutely no difference. But, I kind of see the difference, and I often wonder whether, one, I think being alive if I had grown up on the reserve, two, whether my career or my life would have been different had I had other opportunities to take part in programs or services for Native people which weren't available to me growing up over here.

WHAT IS YOUR INVOLVEMENT WITH THE NATIVE COMMUNITY TODAY?

My involvement is—it's not as much—on a personal level, I have many, many friends and family who I still see and speak with over on the reserve. The local Native community, once I started—initially, my first contact with the local Native community was after I had gone through rehab and I started seeking out any Native resources and found out there was a Native center in my city, and I went down just to kind of, like, make first contact, as it were. And as I recall, that really was the first contact with any Native people. That was back in 1981. And I just kind of wandered in and started talking to some people and I didn't form any sort of a relationship with that organization—I knew they were there—but it was just kind of—I mean, I'm sure they were looking at me as kind of this wannabe, he doesn't have any proofs, he thinks that he is, we get tons of people coming in thinking they are Native or want to be Native, or they're filled with the Native spirit. And so I think they may have looked at it from that perspective.

After I had proof, which is a horrible, horrible way of saying it, but you need proof, some thing, look, yes, right here, I am Native—then I started becoming more involved with the local Native community, and to this day, I'm fairly well-known around here, although I'm not as active as I really would like to be or should be. I just have a tough time identifying with the United States, particularly at this time. It's not that I have anything against it, I guess, it's just that I just don't identify with it. My focus and the focus of my life is over across the border, and that's where my people are, that's where my history is, that's where my ancestors are, that's where my political views are most common—that's kind of where everything is over in Canada. I'm a member of a heritage organization, United Empire Loyalists of Canada, which are comprised of descendents of Loyalists, people who were loyal to the crown during the American Revolution, and were forced out of the States—to leave the States, get everything up and resettle across the border after the Revolution. One of those ancestors, Joseph Brant—Joseph Thayendanegea Brant, I'm a direct descendant of him, and he was the Mohawk leader who led the people—the Native people, the Iroquois, out of the United States and into the relative safety of Canada. So I identify with that in the context—and through that context, through that organization, I still have contacts with my Native culture over on Six Nations. It ties me in, as it were, along with my family, to my reserve over in Canada.

WHAT DOES IT MEAN TO YOU TO BE NATIVE?

To me, being Native means that you're a different person than from white, you're not simply just a light person, dark-skinned white person, you have a different way of looking at things. It means having a different outlook, having a different—I don't know, it's just connectiveness, there's a certain—it's a very difficult thing to describe, as I'm sure you're aware. My birth mother had four sons and four daughters. I was the first of her eight kids. By the time I met her, one of the sons had been killed in an automobile accident back in the late 1970s, and one brother—the eldest brother—or to that point—the eldest brother of my siblings was in poor physical shape, and I knew him for six weeks before he died in the hospital as I held his hand. And my birth mother would say, I had two real Indians—she would call us Indians—and she said, I have two real Indians: You and your sister.

And the two of us, my sister and I, we could carry on fifteen-minute conversations in what's called the Mohawk grunt. I mean, just kind of guttural tones and gestures, and I—it was just we knew—we weren't clairvoyant, we couldn't read each other's mind, but we knew what each other was saying, and we had senses, we had experiences and feelings that I had always thought was just a sign of madness, I guess, or of being an unbalanced—mentally unbalanced person, but I would find out that there's certain feelings, there's certain senses that are part of the Native experience and aren't to be discounted; they're very important.

So from that aspect, I guess I would have to say that that has been the most, to me, the most poignant part of being Native is those senses and a different outlook and a different perspective. To me, being Native means that we have a connectiveness to the land, to the earth, to the environment in which we live that goes way back. I mean, we're talking thousands and thousands of years. This is where it all began, this is where I'm from. I can't trace my roots back to some feudal kingdom in Great Britain, although I do have British roots in me.

The white side of me, I just—I can't identify with it. I just can't. It's there, but nurture versus nature types—it's how I was raised, but it's not who I was, even though people—a lot of my adopted family—in the white world, the white friends that I grew up, college associates, and work peers, career people who I work with have always discounted that. How can you be Indian if you weren't raised on a reservation. I mean, they just don't get it. They don't get that it's not the environment that you're raised in, it's something that you are. And regardless of who adopts you, that doesn't strip you of being Native, even though that may have been the choice or preference was that okay, you're no longer Native now, and now, you're white; you're just—you just have really dark skin, but you're not a Native because it says so here on the legal paper, adoption paper.

ARE YOU GLAD THAT YOU WERE ADOPTED BY A WHITE FAMILY?

You know, I often say I got the best and the worst of both worlds. I mean, I got the best of one world in that I was—I'm not going to say it was an extravagantly opulent lifestyle; I wasn't spoiled—well, I guess I was spoiled. I never really went without anything as a child, so it wasn't that I was deprived of anything. My parents paid for college education and I had all the material things in life and opportunities to go to schools and all that. And then my birth mother admitted, she said, I wouldn't have been able to give you that, and I realize that, I can see that from my siblings on the reserve; I had a lot of opportunities that they didn't have. So I was very fortunate by that token.

I'm not saying it couldn't have happened had I been raised on the reserve, but it just seems that being adopted by the white people, I got the best of both worlds.

The worst thing that happened to me was that I wasn't raised on the reserve. The best thing that happened to me was that I wasn't raised on the reserve. And I mean it's just—I more than likely—my birth mother, whether my family wants to admit it or not—I've worked with alcoholics and the disease of alcoholism long enough to know he died from alcoholism, she died from the effects of alcoholism, and I was going the same route, I was given one month to live back in 1980 due to severe alcoholism, and I know that had I grown up on the reserve, more than likely, I, too, would have died from alcoholism. I would have been dead. So it was over living—growing up in the white world that there were the safety mechanisms and the safety nets were there to help pull me out or get me to the realization that it's do or die, and I chose to live.

So, there are pluses and minuses. I mean, there are good points, there are bad. The bad points—one of the bad points of being raised in the white world is that I was totally stripped of my cultural identity, I was totally stripped of any natural identity and you got a kid growing up who doesn't know who he is, where he fits in, he's being told he's crazy, and you go through growing up in life from that perspective. I mean, you have nobody you can identify with, you have no role models, you have nothing. I mean, you're just kind of stripped, even though that's what you're seeing, life as. I mean, you're seeing it as a Native. But with no contact with the Native world, you keep that to yourself, you keep it bottled up, you don't verbalize, you don't express yourself, and then that comes out as being, oh, he's truculent, he's antisocial, he's just a loner, he's this, he's that—all pathological—psychologically pathological things that school counselors just couldn't figure out.

So there's pluses and there's minuses. Yes, I'm very fortunate to have grown up in the white world. No, I'm very unfortunate not to have had any contact with the Native world. That's just the way it happened, the roll of the dice.

In general, should non-Natives be allowed to adopt Native children?

You know, there's a whole school of thought on that. I can only answer that from my perspective, and my perspective was overall, I was fortunate. I work with a number of Native adoptees getting together and having a talk, councils. And the horror stories are absolutely gut-wrenching from Native children being raised in non-Native environments. Absolutely some of the most heart-wrenching, pathetic stories you've ever heard in your life. So from their perspectives, no. And I mean, it all depends on the person, it all depends on the family that you're being raised in. For me, it was extremely positive. There was a lot of love and a lot of warmth in the non-Native home that I was raised in and still is; we're a very, very close family. I grew up in a very, very small adoptive family; there was just mother, father, brother, grandparents, one aunt, no uncles, no cousins. It was very, very small, so we were a very small, tight, little family.

Whereas when I went over to the reserve, huge family, absolutely enormous extended family. So, you know, you've got one very small close, tight-knit family, and that worked. I mean, it was never an issue of being forgotten or shuffled to the side or anything, so I guess I would have to say that it really depends; to put down a straight, hard and fast rule and say no, by no means should Native children be allowed to be adopted in non-Native world, I think does a disservice. I mean, there are circumstance—and nobody knows. I mean, who can predict the future, who can say, well, this is going to work, this isn't? A lot depends on the adoptive family, environment in which they were placed.

I think—I believe—and I still do feel very, very strongly that Native children should have access to their culture, they should have some sort of a mentor, some sort of a role model, some sort of contact, some sort of tribal connection in place so that if they choose to talk to another Native or—as a child or as a teen growing up they have that access. I didn't have that, I had nothing, but again, I grew up in the '50s and '60s when there really wasn't that sort of connection to be had. But to blame that on my adoptive parents, right, I can't do that. I mean, it's just—that's just not doing them any justice, and it's just not fair. So it all depends. I mean, it's a big maybe. I can't say yes, I can't say no. In general, though, I would have to say it would be preferable to find a good Native home where Native children could be raised, but that's not always possible, that's not as readily available as in the white world—from my perspective.

WHAT IS YOUR OPINION OF THE INDIAN CHILD WELFARE ACT?

I think—well, as someone who used it for the first time in New York State, it helped me. I have to think that it's helped a lot of other people as well, although many states now are just going one step beyond and saying, well, Native adoptees—adoptees in general, Native and non-Native adoptees deserve to have every right to their biological records as everybody else. I guess I might be considered more of a militant adoptee in that I place the concerns and the focus of the adoptees first, above that of the biological parents, above that of the adoptive parents. We are not just garage sale items that were picked up off the lawn and suddenly you lose your identity, you're ours now. We have as much right to that information as anybody else does; that is about us, that is us. And everybody else has a right to know their biological parents, and I firmly believe that we do, too. I place the onus, the responsibility on the biological parents. If people are going to be having sex, then they're going to have to put up with the responsibility, and sometimes that responsibility is not always pleasant, it's not always the way they want things to work out. That's too bad. I mean, that's just too bad, those are the breaks. You brought a life into the world, now that child has rights as anybody else, the same rights as anybody else, and if that's inconvenient or embarrassing, then maybe the biological parents ought to think twice before they start churning out kids.

DO YOU HAVE ANY QUESTIONS OR ADVICE YOU WOULD LIKE TO OFFER NON-NATIVE FAMILIES WHO WOULD WANT TO OR WHO HAVE ADOPTED NATIVE AMERICAN CHILDREN?

Yes. By all means, make sure if there's any indication whatsoever that the child is Native, there should be every effort made to provide an avenue of contact with having some sort of access and not—I don't mean just saying, yeah, here's the number to call, bud, you're going to have to do it on your own. They should be supportive, and they should be willing to accept that the Native child has every right to his or her Native identity. And they should have a contact with either the local or some sort of a Native organization, Native community so if and when that child needs—feels the need to touch base with a Native person—another Native person, that it's there. I didn't have that. It just wasn't available, it just wasn't there, and I suppose it never occurred to people—I tend to be more of an idealist, of a dreamer, whereas my adoptive family, they were very pragmatic, very down-to-earth. All this hoodoo-voodoo type stuff of the Indian, they didn't understand, and to a large extent, they still don't. They support me totally, and they're very sympathetic to the Native cause, but they don't know—and they couldn't know—they have no way of knowing—what it's like to be Native.

So to expect them to understand these feelings and these outlooks, I don't. They couldn't. That's not being fair to them. But I think there should have been some sort of contact with a local Native community; if they couldn't identify what tribal group, at least say, we have a child here who is Native, we know is Native, and may or may not, at some point wish to pursue that. And that's where I think having contact with a Native mentor or role model would be immensely helpful. So I think for non-Native families, they should make—if it isn't a requirement, they should actively seek out some sort of venue where that could be accomplished.

Is there anything else I should have asked you in this interview?

I don't think so. I could go on for days. I usually do. There is so much behind it that, you know, my circumstance—I know to a lot of people, they look at me and they say, that it's just one of the strangest stories—life stories I've ever heard. But when I'm around other Native adoptees, it's like, yeah. I mean, we all have the same story. Native adoptees have so many similarities, it's eerie. The talking circle that I was at in Ottawa was absolutely amazing, it was just like repeating the same story over and over again, feelings of isolation, feelings of alienation, not fitting in—I mean, it was just repetitious, it was the same feeling over and over again. And to each of us, for each Native adoptee, there is always this tangible, inexplicable pull, there is this draw, there is this pull to reunite with your birth family and the culture. And that's shown time and time again to be more prevalent in Native adoptees than non-Native adoptees.

My birth brother is—you know, my—I'm sorry, my adopted brother, my adopted family saw what I was going through, and my adopted brother is curious about his birth family, but he saw what I went through. It was ten years of hell and red tape—he's not into that. He's very curious, but not to the point where it compels him to go through what he sees what I went through. He doesn't want anything to do with that, I mean, with courts and lawyers and filing petitions and doing all this other stuff, working with government organizations. He's curious, he is also in the final stages of multiple sclerosis, which is a hereditary disease and that may answer—could have answered a lot of questions, but, he's the type that's, well, I'll just keep checking the personals columns in the newspaper and maybe my name and birth date'll turn up—that sort of thing, which is just—I mean, the sod is just so infinitesimal, it's almost to the point of not even being practical. Although it did work for me. I took an ad out on my reserve paper, and that's how I happened to be reunited with my birth family. My birth mother saw it in the reserve paper and that's how we got together. But as far as just scouring the local, you know, city of Rochester paper for the personals, that's just not going to happen.

But, you know, he doesn't have the pull. My adopted brother just does not have that—I guess that innate desire to go through hill and dale. It's just not that important to him; to me, it was.

To me it was something I needed to do; to him, it's not. But he still is very curious. I imagine if somebody would do the work for him, he'd be very, very interested in meeting up with his birth family, but as far as doing it himself, he just does not have that innate compulsion to do so.

Have I answered all your questions? Have I made myself clear? Is there anything that you need clarification on? I'm more than willing to go into further detail or answer any questions, whatever you might have.

NOT SO FAR—I MEAN, I THINK EVERYTHING SOUNDS REALLY, REALLY GOOD. I MIGHT HAVE A FEW FOLLOW-UP QUESTIONS ONCE WE SEE THE ACTUAL TRANSCRIPT, SO WOULD IT BE OKAY IF I CALL YOU BACK?

Just please feel free, and don't be embarrassed or hesitant or anything. I mean, I'm very, very open, I've told this story hundreds of times, it's been in newspapers, it's been on radio, it's been all over. So it's not that it's something—anything I'm embarrassed about, it's something that I want to get out there, I want to let other people know that we Native adoptees are—we're here, and we're not going to be silenced.

And as embarrassing or as difficult as the topic may be, it's something we Native people—Native adoptees need to get out there, need to let people know. So you're doing us a phenomenal service. I mean, this is absolutely wonderful, and I'm more than willing to speak to anybody at any time about this, and I'll give references, I'll do whatever I can because this is something that we really need to do. The time has come.

I run a website, and I've got a number of Native adoptees, links and essays and it's just something that I feel that strongly about because it's altered my life that much and it's been such a positive influence on my life that it's something I want to help other Native people do—Native adoptees do. And if there's any way I can help some Native kid in any way, find—reunite with his—either his birth family or his cultural identity, then I'm all for it. I'm more than willing to help out.

OKAY, GREAT. THANK YOU VERY MUCH.

# IV

# SUMMARY AND CONCLUDING COMMENTS

Of the seven men and thirteen women who participated in this study, six of the men and ten of the women described very close, warm relationships with their adoptive families and feeling very positive about their experiences growing up with non-Native parents and siblings. The four remaining participants, one man and three women, described their relationship with their adoptive parents as negative. For the participants who expressed a negative relationship with their adoptive parents, there is still a sense of bitterness and anger. As adults, all four of them have cut off ties with their adoptive families.

Four female respondents and one male respondent characterized their adoptive parents as racists. Three of the four female respondents not only characterized their adoptive parents as racist, but also accused them of verbally and/or physically abusing them. RoSean Kent believes that one of her foster families "wanted to beat the Indian out." Joyce Gonzales remembers her adoptive mother scrubbing her skin and complaining that she couldn't tell "what was dirt and what was skin." Star Nayea, who also characterized her adoptive family as racist, says that she was physically abused by her adoptive mother. When she was six years old, her adoptive mother threw her out in the snow. Star says she fell into a coma and almost lost both of her legs. Both Joyce Gonzales and Star Nayea believe that their adoptive mothers suffered from mental illness and argue that more effort must be made to place adoptees in a safe environment.

Among the six male and ten female respondents who reported positive or very positive experiences they described their parents as “wonderful,” “warm and loving,” and supportive and helpful when they decided to search for their birth parent. Fourteen of the sixteen respondents who characterized their experiences as positive, also noted that their adoptive parents could not and as a result did not attempt to contribute to their adopted child’s sense of cultural identity. Several respondents believed that their adoptive parents “did the best they could.” Jon Old Horse said, “I think they did the best they could. It was just—maybe it was just me. I was always looking for things that they couldn’t give me.” Denise Engstrom says her parents “did a really nice job of raising [her] . . . but they weren’t familiar with [her tribe] the Tuscarora . . . so they didn’t really talk about it because they didn’t know.” Leslee Caballero says her adoptive parents gave her books to read and admitted they were unfamiliar with Native culture so that “was something that she [would] need to explore when [she got] older.”

Shana Greenberg and Tamara Watchman are the two exceptions in this study. Shana says that her adoptive parents enrolled her in the Indian Education Program at school and attempted to get her involved with the urban Indian community. Similarly, Tamara Watchman’s adoptive mother found her a mentor in the Native community and sent her to a summer camp for Native youth. All of the participants strongly advised adoptive parents to establish a connection within the Native community and urged non-Native families who adopted Native children to do as much as possible to make them aware of their cultural heritage and history. The women also specifically recommended attending powwows, visiting reservations, seeking out other Native children and having books in their home about the history of Native Americans and their treatment by the white American community.

The majority of participants were raised in predominantly white neighborhoods and indicated that they were discriminated against in school by their peers and in some instances, their teachers. Of the twenty participants, twelve females and two males reported racist encounters. The degree of racism they encountered varied from subtle to hostile. According to Leslee Caballero, students and other peers made culturally insensitive remarks in her presence, but says she wouldn’t characterize the remarks as “maliciously racist.” Paul DeMain, on the other hand, recalls much more blatantly racist verbal attacks. He says, being called “a goddamn Indian . . . squaw or something like that became a derogatory thing that [was] directed toward me to hurt me . . . and I just take care of it physically.” Veronica Rose Dahmen and Tamara Watchman indicated that they were discriminated against by teachers. Tamara said her kindergarten teachers told her adoptive mother that she "was dirty and had hygiene problems" and needed to be in special education. In high school, she said she was told that she was not smart enough to go to college. Tamara eventually earned a college degree and now teaches eighth grade.

As adults, all of the participants indicated that they feel secure about their identities as Native Americans, except for Jordan Kennedy who did not discover she was Native American until a year ago when she was twenty-three years old. Although they all feel secure about their Native identities, many of them admit that they still have a lot to learn about their tribal culture, history and traditions. Many have relied upon their birth families to help them with this process.

Eighteen of the twenty respondents actively searched for their birth families. The two respondents who did not search for their birth families were Jordan Kennedy and Tamara Watchman. Less than a year before her interview took place Jordan Kennedy discovered that her birth mother was raped by her birth father and that she was the result of that rape. She decided not to search for her birth mother because she "figured that if [her] biological mother was strong enough and good enough to have [her] even though she was raped," she probably didn't "want [this] brought up again." Tamara Watchman says that she never felt the need to contact her birth parents because she knew that they were extremely young when they had her and that she always felt grateful to them for placing her for adoption. In 1995, however, she reunited with her birth family after accidentally bumping into her cousin as a student at Fort Lewis College in Durango, Colorado. She maintains a close relationship with several members of her birth family today.

Fifteen of the twenty participants reunited with their birth families. Of these fifteen, twelve maintain that they have established positive relationships with their birth families. The remaining three indicated that they have met their birth families, but they decided not to pursue a relationship with them. Several participants indicate that their birth families have played a substantial role in helping them develop and strengthen their cultural identities. In particular, Jon Old Horse and Paul LaRoche both note that they received many gifts from their birth families and other members of the Lakota community, who have taken the time to teach them the Lakota language and traditional songs. Veronica Rose Dahmen says her birth family took her to her first powwow and afterwards "she felt more in tune and more enriched by what [she] saw."

All twenty respondents indicated that they are supporters of the Indian Child Welfare Act and believe that Native children should be raised in

Native households. However, eighteen of the twenty respondents conceded that non-Native families can raise Native children to be happy, healthy, well-adjusted adults. Many of the sixteen respondents who indicated that they were raised in a positive environment by non-Native families seem to struggle with these two conflicting ideas. Rosalyn Hussong maintains that she is "thankful for [the] family [she] grew up," and says, "Am I glad I was adopted? Yes." But notes that she is "really glad that we have ICWA and that we put a stop to what's going on." Shana Greenberg argues that "all things being equal, if you can get a stable Indian family, they should [be allowed] to adopt an Indian kid . . . because it was hard at times growing up and saying, well, this is my white family, even though they were great parents." Similarly, Tamara Watchman believes that regardless of race, "everybody deserves a family." However, she says, "Do I think that [transracial adoption] is the best option? No, I don't because I had a family that was really, really trying to help me, culturally. . . . And, no matter how much they tried to help me and support me, and did help me and support me, it was all about the Native community . . . the Native [community] helped me go through this."

# INDEX

# ABOUT THE AUTHORS

**Rita J. Simon** is University Professor in the School of Public Affairs and the Washington College of Law at American University. She is author or editor of numerous books, including *Women's Roles and Statuses the World Over* (with Stephanie Hepburn, Lexington Books, 2006), and *Adoption across Borders* (with Howard Altstein, Rowman & Littlefield, 2000).

**Sarah Hernandez** is an enrolled member of the Rosebud Sioux Tribe, and currently works at the American Indian College Fund in Denver, Colorado. She earned a master's degree in English from the University of Colorado at Boulder in 2005.